Administrative Reform in Late Eighteenth-Century Britain and its Empire

Studies in the Eighteenth Century

ISSN: 2398-9904

This major series from Boydell & Brewer, published in association with the British Society for Eighteenth-Century Studies, aims to bring into fruitful dialogue the different disciplines involved in all aspects of the study of the long eighteenth century (c.1660–1820). It publishes innovative volumes, singly or co-authored, on any topic in history, science, music, literature, and the visual arts in any area of the world in the long eighteenth century and particularly encourages proposals that explore links among the disciplines, and which aim to develop new cross-disciplinary fields of enquiry.

Series editors: Ros Ballaster, University of Oxford, UK; Helen Berry, University of Exeter, UK; Matthew Grenby, Newcastle University, UK; Mark Knights, University of Warwick, UK

Previously published

Material Enlightenment: Women Writers and the Science of Mind, 1770–1830, Joanna Wharton, 2018

Celebrity Culture and the Myth of Oceania in Britain, 1770–1823, Ruth Scobie, 2019

British Sociability in the Long Eighteenth Century: Challenging the Anglo-French Connection, edited by Valérie Capdeville and Alain Kerhervé, 2019

Things that Didn't Happen: Writing, Politics and the Counterhistorical, 1678–1743, John McTague, 2019

Converting Britannia: Evangelicals and British Public Life, 1770–1840, Gareth Atkins, 2019

British Catholic Merchants in the Commercial Age, 1670–1714, Giada Pizzoni, 2020

Lessons of Travel in Eighteenth-Century France: From Grand Tour to School Trips, Gábor Gelléri, 2020

Political Journalism in London, 1695–1720: Defoe, Swift, Steele and their Contemporaries, Ashley Marshall, 2020

Fictions of Presence: Theatre and Novel in Eighteenth-Century Britain, Ros Ballaster, 2020

Ephemeral Print Culture in Early Modern England, Tim Somers, 2021

The Geographies of Enlightenment Edinburgh, Phil Dodds, 2022

Changing Pedagogies for Children in Eighteenth-Century England, Michèle Cohen, 2023

Transnational Women Writers in the Wilmot Coterie, 1798–1840: Beyond Borders and Boundaries, Alexis Wolf, 2024

Administrative Reform in Late Eighteenth-Century Britain and its Empire

A System of Economy

Sebastian Meurer

THE BOYDELL PRESS

Published in association with

BSECS
British Society for
Eighteenth-Century Studies

First published 2025
The Boydell Press, Woodbridge

ISBN 978 1 83765 098 9

The Boydell Press is an imprint of Boydell & Brewer Ltd
PO Box 9, Woodbridge, Suffolk IP12 3DF, UK
and of Boydell & Brewer Inc.
668 Mt Hope Avenue, Rochester, NY 14620-2731, USA
website: www.boydellandbrewer.com

Our Authorised Representative for product safety in the EU is Easy Access System
Europe - Mustamäe tee 50, 10621 Tallinn, Estonia, *gpsr.requests@easproject.com*

A CIP catalogue record for this book is available
from the British Library

Contents

Acknowledgements

Administrative history does not have a reputation for being a particularly exciting field of research. At times, I irritated my colleagues by chuckling cheerfully while working with administrative sources. It could be amusing to witness historical actors talking past each other. From a historical distance, I could see that they had completely different ideas about administrative issues. But how to determine these different conceptions? Apart from research on corruption and patronage, there was little to be found about administrative ideas in the research literature. There seemed to be even less concern for the notions underlying the actions of the officers themselves. How did these notions relate to the wider field of political, legal, or economic ideas? There is a general question behind this that I have always been fascinated with: how do the ideas of 'great thinkers' impact people's perceptions and everyday actions? This book is an attempt to gain a better understanding of such connections in a concrete case and to show that it can be rewarding to study administrative ideas.

In the many years of researching, writing, and revising, I accumulated many debts. I would like to thank Anne Murphy, who suggested that my book would be a good fit for this series, and the series editors, who took an immediate interest and provided valuable feedback throughout the publishing process. The two anonymous and impressively knowledgeable reviewers played a major role in the final outcome. I am deeply grateful for their suggestions which challenged me to make this a much better book and for providing resources that helped me in this endeavour. I felt very well looked after by Boydell and Brewer and I would like to thank Mari Shullaw, Elizabeth Howard, Elizabeth McDonald, and Christy Beale for guiding me through the review and publication process.

The origins of this book project lie in my doctoral dissertation 'A System of Oeconomy. Approaches to Public Administration in Britain and British India at the Beginning of the Age of Reform', which I completed at the University of Heidelberg in 2014. I sincerely thank my two supervisors, Susan Richter and Thomas Maissen, who supported me with liberality, inspiration, and patience, and have continued to do so ever since. The thesis was written in the context of the Cluster of Excellence 'Asia and Europe in a

Global Context'. At the time, the cluster stood out as a truly international site in a still somewhat self-centred German academic community. Within this cluster, the Junior Research Group A4 'The Fascination of Efficiency', explored the transcultural transfer and adaptation of administrative knowledge. I am thankful for the inspiration, companionship, and support among this group: to Susan as the group's leader and to my colleagues Nicolas Schillinger and Peter Trummer. Among the many other wonderful colleagues, I only mention Laila Abu-Er-Rub, Milinda Banerjee, Barend Noordam, and Elise Wintz, even though many more merit my gratitude.

Heidelberg was a vibrant research environment. Thomas' research colloquium on early modern history was legendary: often late into the evening, sometimes over a glass of wine, always brimming with intense debate and mutual encouragement. Friendships for life were forged in this circle. Some of these friends have also contributed to this book and helped me not to lose heart during the long journey. Pascal Firges was a brilliant advisor when it came to the book proposal. Urte Weeber, Christine Zabel, and especially Lina Weber read and commented on many chapters, sometimes in several versions.

For all the international connections and inspiring community, this work could not have been realised in Heidelberg alone. I have benefited substantially from the German Research Foundation (DFG) that not only funded my livelihood, but also enabled me to undertake extensive research trips. An extended stay in London was also made possible by a scholarship from the German Historical Institute in London. There is something very special about doing research in archives, particularly when abroad. I would like to thank the ever-helpful staff at the Caird Library (Greenwich), the William Clements Library (Ann Arbor), the Postal Museum (London), and, of course, the British Library and The National Archives. I am thankful for the opportunity to meet eminent scholars who were willing to engage with my ideas and provided constructive criticism. In this respect, I am particularly grateful to Jon Wilson, Joanna Innes, and Eckhart Hellmuth. The book has also benefited from discussions at conferences and colloquia in Aarhus, Augsburg, Beijing, Berlin, Bielefeld, Essen, Freiburg, Heidelberg, Koblenz, London, Paris, Rotterdam, and the Villa Vigoni. As invaluable as online resources and videoconferencing have become, they cannot replace the experience of archival work and intense personal discussions.

Much of my work on the book took place during my time in Freiburg, where I was privileged to participate in the truly exceptional Collaborative Research Centre SFB 948 'Heroes – Heroizations – Heroisms'. I would like to mention Ralf von den Hoff, Ulrike Zimmermann, Olmo Gölz, Vera Marstaller, and also Max Jones, who was always more than a guest. It was also a pleasure to work with Jessica Hargreaves, Ellie Norman, and Jordan Reid, the English native-speaking assistants on the editorial team at the SFB. Their work improved the text and made me a better writer.

I am indebted to many other friends who have always supported me and carried me along; I would like to name Christiane Bürger and Oliver Kliesch; Ursula Meinke made me feel at home in London; Pauline Hassan-Suchy, Thomas Hassan, and Teo Hassan welcomed me repeatedly for writing retreats in the Austrian Waldviertel.

Finally, I owe gratitude to my family. To my siblings Arthur and Friederike Meurer I am infinitely grateful that we have grown so close together as adults. My aunt Irene Meichsner followed my academic journey closely and taught me much about how to work with texts. Sadly, my parents, Dorothea Meurer-Meichsner and Dieter Meurer, did not live to accompany me during the research for this book, but they are still with me.

Abbreviations

Add. Mss.	Additional Manuscripts
BL	British Library
CEPA	Commissioners for Examining the Public Accounts
EIC	East India Company
JHC	Journals of the House of Commons
JHL	Journals of the House of Lords
MP	Member of Parliament
NMM	Caird Library, National Maritime Museum, Greenwich
ODNB	Oxford Dictionary of National Biography
OED	Oxford English Dictionary
Parl. Hist.	Cobbett's Parliamentary History of England
Parl. Reg.	Debrett's Parliamentary Register
PRO	Public Records Office
RMA	Royal Mail Archive, London
SSD	Secret and Separate Department of Reform (India Council)
SP	House of Commons Sessional Papers of the Eighteenth Century
TNA	The National Archives, Kew
WCL	William L. Clements Library, Ann Arbor, Michigan

Introduction

In 1780, the British Parliament tasked a group of experts with providing a clearer picture of state finances and uncovering malpractice in the fiscal offices. In the fifteen reports they laid before Parliament until 1787, these Commissioners for Examining the Public Accounts (CEPA) shifted the perception of administrative problems from isolated instances of corruption to a recognition of structural inadequacies. Where others had seen only individual offices and customary practices of accounting, the Commissioners defined offices in reference to a 'system of economy' that fulfilled the duties of state in order to further the public good. The Commissioners opened up a new perspective on the state by describing a system of offices and procedures that could and should be fundamentally reformed to fulfil the duties of state in a better and, ideally, cheaper way.

When reading the reports, the contrast between the Commissioners' analysis of administrative issues and earlier sources compels attention. As a consequence, research literature has presented the Commissioners as heralds of modernity who created the principles of modern bureaucracy *ex nihilo*. A prime example for such an appraisal is John Binney's study of late eighteenth-century British public finance and administration.

> It was the Commissioners themselves who in a few short years ascertained and enunciated those sound principles which determined the direction of a long period of subsequent reform. [...] The period during which they were at work seems to represent the dividing line between the ancient and the modern. Before their work began, the clumsy hand of the Middle Ages is found still heavily [...]; before they had finished their work the enormous task had been commenced of freeing the system of its anachronistic and injurious elements; and the good work continued upon the road they had mapped out until the past had little further power to harm and the accepted standards were the need of the present.[1]

1 John Binney, *British Public Finance and Administration 1774–92* (Oxford, 1958), p. 282.

Indeed, the Commissioners' approach seemed so very familiar to the modern eye, and the unreformed institution that they criticised seemed so strikingly dysfunctional, that similar judgements have often been reiterated, albeit in less theatrical prose. Even John Torrance's differentiated study of 1978 equated the Commissioners' ideas to modern bureaucracy: 'The Commissioners had in fact discovered, and evolved as a secondary goal, what sociologists since Max Weber have called the bureaucratic system of organization.'[2]

Such appraisals of CEPA's role in British administrative history are deeply anachronistic, because the authors set their modern view as a timeless standard. The significance that John Binney and others attested to the Commissioners is firmly rooted in a narrative of progress that teleologically moves towards a modernity marked by efficient bureaucratic organisation. These assessments are symptomatic of some methodological pitfalls haunting administrative history in general. It is quite astonishing how tenaciously the modernisation paradigm has persisted in administrative history, even though the underlying state-building approaches dating back to the modernisation-paradigm of 1950s sociology had otherwise long been rejected.[3] Until well into the 1980s, British administrative history mostly consisted of institutional studies, which tell stories of bureaucratisation within a teleological master narrative of state formation.[4] This process

[2] John Torrance, 'Social Class and Bureaucratic Innovation. The Commissioners for Examining the Public Accounts 1780–1787', *Past and Present*, 78 (1978), 56–81.

[3] On modernisation theory and its significance for state formation narratives see Anthony D. Smith, 'State-Making and Nation-Building', in John A. Hall (ed.), *States in History* (Oxford, 1986), 228–63; Sebastian Meurer, 'Approaches to State-Building in Eighteenth Century British Bengal', in Antje Flüchter and Susan Richter (eds.), *Structures on the Move: Technologies of Governance in Transcultural Encounter* (Heidelberg, 2012), 219–41.

[4] E.g. Elizabeth E. Hoon, *The Organization of the English Customs System 1696–1787* (Newton, 1968); Kenneth L. Ellis, *The Post Office in the Eighteenth Century. A Study in Administrative History* (London, 1969). Henry Roseveare's studies on the Treasury deserve special notice, because he represents the development of that central institution as the long-term motor of the bureaucratisation process. Henry Roseveare, *The Treasury. The Evolution of a British Institution* (London, 1969); id., *The Treasury 1660–1870. The Foundations of Control* (London, 1973). The broader longue-durée studies include Emmeline W. Cohen, *The Growth of the British Civil Service 1780–1939* (London, 1965) and Gerald E. Aylmer, 'Bureaucracy', in Peter Burke (ed.), *The New Cambridge Modern History* (Cambridge, 1979), 164–200. There were also critical voices. For instance, Basil Yamey refuted Max Weber's and especially Werner Sombart's claims on the significance of double entry bookkeeping for modernisation by consistently historicising accounting practices as early as 1949 and repeatedly after. Basil S. Yamey, *Essays on the History of Accounting* (New York, 1978).

of bureaucratisation appears as an administratively endemic, automatic evolution in reaction to increasing complexity and workload in the offices. Many scholars presented the reforms of the 1780s and 1790s as a prelude to the 'revolution in government' that supposedly occurred during the first half of the nineteenth century.[5] The 'Victorian' or 'modern' administration serves as a more or less self-evident frame of reference. What scholars of administration usually meant was the specific organisational form of the civil service, i.e. the supposedly British variant of bureaucracy often attributed to the Northcote–Trevelyan Report of 1854. In his seminal synthesis, Norman Chester (1981) consequently refrained from describing a diachronic evolution, instead juxtaposing two cross-sectional states of the administrative system (c. 1780 and c. 1870). Neither day-to-day politics nor individual reformers have a place in his analysis.[6]

The idea of bureaucratisation is linked to the great narratives of state formation. For historical sociologists, for instance, a large centralised bureaucracy served as a marker of a developed state.[7] In 1990, Peter Jupp reasserted a thesis of an intensified period of government growth in the decades around 1800. According to Jupp, an emerging mercantile elite was instrumental for a process of professionalisation that reflected the expanding scope of governance. Philip Harling and Peter Mandler contradicted Jupp's thesis and emphasised the continuity of the fiscal-military

5 Oliver MacDonagh, 'The Nineteenth-Century Revolution in Government. A Reappraisal', *Historical Journal,* 1:1 (1958), 52–67; Henry Parris, 'The Nineteenth-Century Revolution in Government. A Reappraisal Reappraised', *Historical Journal,* 3:1 (1960), 17–37. This emphasis holds true for older longue durée studies like Henry Parris' history of bureaucracy as well as in the context of Tilly's state-building syntheses. Henry Parris, *Constitutional Bureaucracy. The Development of British Central Administration since the Eighteenth Century* (London, 1969); Wolfram Fischer and Peter Lundgreen, 'The Recruitment and Training of Administrative and Technical Personnel', in Charles Tilly (ed.), *The Formation of National States in Western Europe* (Princeton, London, 1975), 456–561.

6 Norman Chester, *The English Administrative System 1780–1870* (Oxford, 1981).

7 As a matter of fact, the British case never fitted easily into these narratives: Charles Tilly, for example, marvelled at the fact that the UK was so successful in spite of the 'rather low level of stateness' of the pre-Victorian British state. Attempts to determine this *Sonderweg* in the *longue durée* led to the normalisation and anachronistic projection of 'English national culture', which ultimately reflected Whig history: a national spirit of liberty. For Corrigan and Sayer, this weak statehood, expressed for example in the 'Old Corruption'-critiques, was conducive of liberalism and capitalism. Cf. Charles Tilly, 'Reflections on the History of European State-Making', in id. (ed.), *The Formation of National States in Western Europe* (Princeton, 1975), 3–84, esp. pp. 34–5.; Philip Corrigan and Derek Sayer, *The Great Arch. English State Formation as Cultural Revolution* (Oxford, 1985), pp. 87–113.

state instead. In their view, the process of professionalisation should rather be understood as a reaction to government growth and a marker for the landed elite's capacity to react to the pressure. Joanna Innes has pointed out that the plausibility of such clear causal links always rests on underlying narrow definitions of the state. This book corroborates Innes' caveat: at the very least, a close view complicates the assumption of an aggregated state intention or a clear demographic group agency.[8]

Historians of British political history have certainly paid attention to 'economical reform.' After all, from the 1780s onwards, public offices were the subject of heated parliamentary debates. Under the auspices of Whig history, 'economical reform' mostly figured as a brief episode on the road to liberal democracy: radical agitation provided the pressure that prompted willing ministries to conduct sensible reforms.[9] In 2007, Earl Reitan provided a thorough analysis of the politics of economical reform before the Coalition Wars: against the backdrop of ailing public finances, the decrepit situation of the offices provided leverage for both parliamentary and extra-parliamentary opposition groups to demand parliamentary reforms. Reitan stressed the connection between politics, fiscal policy, and administrative reforms and he highlighted the impact of CEPA. However, in his analysis, CEPA's achievement essentially consists of pointing out obvious deficits, the amending of which no one would seriously oppose – a great feat, but not an innovative achievement. In the end, Reitan remained true to the bureaucratisation paradigm: in his view, the description of the deficits resulted in conclusive solutions, which ultimately led to a more efficient state.[10]

Reitan provided an excellent synthesis on the politics of economical reform. However, due to its narrow focus on the political arena, Reitan's history ultimately does justice neither to the intellectual achievement of

[8] Peter J. Jupp, 'The Landed Elite and Political Authority in Britain, ca. 1760–1850', *Journal of British Studies,* 29:1 (1990), 53–79; Philip Harling and Peter Mandler, 'From "Fiscal-Military" State to Laissez-Faire State, 1760–1850', *Journal of British Studies,* 32:1 (1993), 44–70; Joanna Innes, 'Forms of "Government Growth", 1780–1830,' in David Feldman and Jon Lawrence (eds.), *Structures and Transformations in Modern British History* (Cambridge, 2011), 74–99.

[9] E.g. D. L. Keir, 'Economical Reform, 1779–1787,' *Law Quarterly Review,* 50 (1934), 368–85; Binney, *Public Finance*; Herbert Butterfield, *George III, Lord North and the People 1779–80* (London, 1969).

[10] Earl A. Reitan, *Politics, Finance, and the People. Economical Reform in England in the Age of the American Revolution, 1770–92* (New York, 2007). Especially for the politics of economical reform after 1792, John Breihan's unpublished thesis remains a valuable reference. John R. Breihan, 'Economical Reform, 1785–1810,' unpublished PhD thesis (Cambridge, 1977).

CEPA nor to the complexity of the following reform processes. As this book shows, the framing of CEPA's results was anything but self-evident. What is lacking in historical analysis of the reports and subsequent reform processes – and generally in administrative history – is an approach that can highlight and historicise administrative ideas. The present book provides just this: an intellectual-history approach to British administrative history. CEPA did not disseminate self-evident principles of modern administration. Rather, they developed a systematic approach to offices and administrative issues. The first part of this study aims to provide a historicising interpretation of CEPA's remarkable intellectual achievement. It characterises the Commissioners' administrative ideas in contrast to prevailing notions and uncovers conceptual interconnections to previous and contemporary works. The second part of this book explores the significance of (new) administrative ideas in the subsequent reform processes of the 1780s and 1790s and the nature of the transition marked by these reforms. If this transition is not sufficiently explained as a sudden switch to modernity, how can it be more adequately described?

Conceptualising Economical Administration

This book presents the CEPA reports as a major intellectual achievement that marks an important milestone in the history of administration and state formation. From Binney to Reitan, scholars have viewed this achievement in terms of a modern ideal, which they took for granted. For a better understanding of the achievement, the analysis must proceed in a reverse order. We must identify the issues to which the reports responded. It is not enough to relate the reports to older ideas of office, let alone 'administration': presupposing a specified administrative subject area constitutes an anachronistic projection of an idea that was only just beginning to take shape at the time.

The purpose of Chapter 1 is therefore to open up a wider horizon of eighteenth-century ideas on the state, into which the work of CEPA can be situated. In order to mark and contextualise epistemological interconnections, the chapter draws on the 'new history of science', which highlights the conditions of production, social, and cultural contexts rather than presenting an enclosed evolutionary account of scientific discoveries.[11] In

[11] Rachel Laudan, 'The "New" History of Science. Implications for Philosophy of Science', *Proceedings of the Biennual Meeting of the Philosophers of Science Association*, vol. 2 (1992), 476–81.

the eighteenth century, scientific ideas spread beyond the narrow circle of scholars and came to be applied widely. Proponents of the 'new history of science' have even dubbed this process a 'second scientific revolution'. The application of scientific reasoning not only concerned fields like agriculture and engineering, but also society and the state. In the course of the eighteenth century, authors increasingly labelled their arguments as 'philosophical' or 'scientific' in order to claim a rational quality for their ideas. Moreover, these and related terms served to promote a style of debate based on substantiated arguments instead of the prevalent appeals to custom. Throughout Europe, authors contributed to an emerging field of social theory, which, they hoped, would be useful for practical improvements and even to actuate social progress.[12]

One effect of scientific reasoning on political ideas was to expose a number of unresolved issues and areas of tension concealed within the basic constitutional consensus reached during the 'Revolution of 1688'; for instance, tensions between an understanding of the state as an association of persons as opposed to the idea of the state as an institutional structure. Another tension concerned the temporality of the state: between the idea of an ancient constitution as a normative ideal as opposed to a mindset that accepted change as a prerequisite of the historical process – and social progress in the future. These notions were not completely incompatible and they were rarely juxtaposed explicitly, but authors could not help but take a stance on these issues.

From the middle of the eighteenth century, authors such as David Hume, Joseph Priestley, or Helvétius developed utilitarian critiques – in the broadest sense of the term. In Britain, it was particularly in the context of the emerging discipline of political economy that authors engaged in an empirical analysis of social institutions. Eighteenth-century political economy is not sufficiently explained as a precursor of modern economics. The influential Scottish variant was rooted in moral philosophy, but developed into a form of social science based on empiricism and aiming at practical improvements. Moreover, political economists started to reflect on their methods and means of theory formation and thus created a science of the state. They viewed the state as a functional structure of institutions, as a system that could be understood and improved upon.[13]

[12] Johan Heilbron, Lars Magnusson, and Björn Wittrock (eds.), *The Rise of the Social Sciences and the Formation of Modernity: Conceptual Change in Context, 1750–1850* (Dordrecht, 1996).

[13] Cf. e.g. Donald Winch, 'Scottish Political Economy', in Mark Goldie and Robert Wokler (eds.), *The Cambridge History of Eighteenth-Century Political Thought* (Cambridge, 2006), 443–64; Broadie, Alexander (ed.), *Scottish Enlightenment. An*

In addition to such rather abstract contexts, the CEPA reports must be related to their immediate political and social contexts. Perhaps more than contemporaries realised, the Commissioners' reasoning threatened the foundations of Georgian political culture. Chapter 2 focuses on the political debates after the accession of George III. On the one hand, the chapter thereby introduces important contexts and political constellations, starting with the politically unstable 1760s and 1770s and culminating in the Economical Reform Debates of 1779–80, in which the shortcomings of state administration came to the fore. Moreover, the chapter clarifies the semantics of office holding in contemporary political and public discourses. Offices played a fundamental social role in Georgian Britain. Patent offices, in particular, were seen as property titles that conveyed wealth as well as social status. This property theory of office was a social convention rather than an explicit legal norm, but it was rarely challenged. Contemporaries knew the value of attractive offices. In a society that was defined and stratified by property, these offices were coveted commodities. High offices remained the natural reserve of the political elite and some offices, especially at court, were monopolised by the aristocracy. However, most offices were open to both the landed elite and the mercantile middle class.[14]

The central mechanism of the distribution of offices was patronage. Starting with Lewis Namier, scholars of political culture have discarded anachronistic views which depreciated the personal distribution of offices as corruption. Instead, these scholars focused on the social and political functions of patronage and analysed conventions and social practices. Douglas Allen has recently recast the insights of this research in terms of economics. He argues that patronage (along with other ostensibly dysfunctional practices) should be considered a highly functional institution efficiently providing social cohesion for a patrimonial society.[15]

Although the distribution of offices through patronage was an entirely normalised part of eighteenth-century political culture, the practice drew

Anthology (Edinburgh, 1997); Paul Wood (ed.), *The Scottish Enlightenment. Essays in Reinterpretation* (Rochester, 2000).

14 Paul Langford, *Public Life and the Propertied Englishman 1689–1798* (Oxford, 1991); Harry T. Dickinson, *Liberty and Property. Political Ideology in Eighteenth-Century Britain* (London, 1977).

15 J. M. Bourne, *Patronage and Society in Nineteenth-Century England* (London, 1986). For an overview of the wider European research on early-modern patronage see Birgit Emich and others, 'Stand und Perspektiven der Korruptionsforschung. Zugleich eine Antwort auf Heiko Droste', *Zeitschrift für historische Forschung*, 32 (2005), 233–65; Douglas W. Allen, *The Institutional Revolution. Measurement and the Economic Emergence of the Modern World* (Chicago, 2012), pp. 44–79.

criticism. After the accession of George III in 1760, a growing number of voices accused the government and even the Crown of corruption. In the eyes of the critics, there was widespread abuse of patronage that led to personal enrichment at the expense of the general public and undermined parliamentary freedom. Around 1780, critics from different camps joined forces to demand economical reform: opposition Whigs around the Marquess of Rockingham and Edmund Burke, who posed as defenders of parliamentary freedom, but also demanded their own share of patronage and power; urban radicals, who supported the colonies' struggle for freedom and made sharp utilitarian, economic, and legal arguments; and, finally, rural freeholders, who were frustrated with the tax burden and feared the collapse of state finances. The blatant waste, abuse, and profiteering in the state apparatus provided all of these groups with easy targets for accusations of corruption. Since the 1970s, research inspired by the linguistic turn concerned itself with contemporary conceptualisations and valuations of eighteenth-century patronage and showed that such ascriptions were typically negotiated in discourses on corruption.[16]

In *The Waning of 'Old Corruption'* (1996), Philip Harling traced the pertinent British discourse on corruption from the eighteenth to the middle of the nineteenth century and highlighted its sustained political importance and its impact on administrative reforms. Harling did away with the assumption that bureaucratisation was a process detached from short-termed political and social developments. Instead, he argued that the administrative reforms in the late eighteenth and early nineteenth century were the direct result of a political and public discourse on corruption that fundamentally questioned the legitimacy of the political elite's predominance and thereby fuelled administrative reforms.[17]

Most recently, Mark Knights has drawn attention to the persistency and versatility of corruption discourses, which always included ideas of anti-corruption. In *Trust and Distrust* (2021), Knights rejected the idea

[16] See for example Eckhart Hellmuth, 'Why does Corruption Matter? Reforms and Reform Movements in Britain and Germany in the Second Half of the Eighteenth Century', in Timothy C.W. Blanning and Peter Wende (eds.), *Reform in Great Britain and Germany: 1750–1850* (Oxford, 1999), 5–23; Bruce Buchan and Lisa Hill, *An Intellectual History of Political Corruption* (Basingstoke, 2014); Niels Grüne and Simona Slanicka (eds.), *Korruption. Historische Annäherungen an eine Grundfigur politischer Kommunikation* (Göttingen, 2010). There have also been pleas for a general definition and a non-constructivist approach to historical corruption, cf. e.g. Diego Gambetta, 'Corruption. An Analytical Map', in Emmanuel Kreike and William C. Jordan (eds.), *Corrupt Histories* (Rochester, 2004), 3–28.

[17] Philip Harling, *The Waning of 'Old Corruption'. The Politics of Economical Reform in Britain, 1779–1846* (Oxford, 1996).

of a sudden onset of a bureaucratic modernity. Instead, he pointed to the extended history of a long early modernity (he analyses the period from 1600 to 1850). He thus integrated CEPA into the context of a long-running discourse on public accountability. Crucial ideas for the later reformers emerged as early as the seventeenth century, even if they were not fully realised. For Knights, the tension between corruption and anti-corruption was instrumental for defining offices and, ultimately, for establishing standards of good government.[18]

In many regards, this book corroborates Harling's and Knights' arguments. Administrative questions had long been linked to the heated discourse on corruption, and administrative policy-making directly reacted to this discourse. However, this book makes the material point that the public discourse on corruption, whilst an important context, was not tantamount to the administrative discourse that started to emerge with the CEPA reports. In contrast to the political discourse, the CEPA reports do not draw on the language of corruption at all. Instead of staging a polemical corruption tribunal, the Commissioners resorted to a sober exposition of their findings. The very term 'corruption' that was omnipresent in the public discourse rarely appears in the reports and is never at the centre of the Commissioners' argument.

Chapter 3 considers the remarkable reports of the Commissioners for Examining the Public Accounts in detail. It is rarely possible to distinguish between the individual contributions of the commissioners. The reports are therefore analysed as a coherent, albeit sequential, work by a collective author. The chapter argues that the Commissioners delivered far more than the political actors anticipated. Instead of looking for corruption, individual malpractice, or isolated defects, the Commissioners developed a completely new interpretative framework for the public offices. At the heart of this 'system of economy' was the redefinition of office as public trust. Accordingly, offices were determined by the function they performed for the state and, thereby, for the public good. Salaries were to be proportionate to duties, and sinecures were to be abolished altogether. By means of empirical and analytical reasoning, the Commissioners combined subjects that had hitherto not been 'systematically' studied into a coherent subject matter, a system that was characterised by specific principles. By the time

[18] Mark Knights, *Trust and Distrust. Corruption in Office in Britain and its Empire, 1600–1850* (Oxford, 2021). In its comprehensive scope, *Trust and Distrust* is an excellent resource for a nuanced introduction to British administrative history covering a larger timeframe.

they were finished, the chapter argues, the Commissioners' deliberations amounted to a scientific theory of public administration.

The approach of CEPA can be described as a form of historically informed empiricism. The Commissioners carefully surveyed the situation in various offices and compared similar offices in order to identify the best practices. Their analyses repeatedly addressed the consequences of historical change. In their view, many institutions needed reform in order to adapt to the 'present', 'modern', and 'commercial' age. Whilst refraining from political partisanship, the Commissioners clearly positioned themselves against notions of an ideal ancient constitution to return to. Moreover, they consistently examined offices and procedures in terms of public utility. In this regard, their analysis had much in common with the critiques of intellectual radicals. However, in contrast to radical thinkers such as Richard Price or Joseph Priestley, the Commissioners aimed for a strong state. In their reasoning, public institutions existed solely for the benefit of the state and the state solely for the promotion of the public good. The Commissioners thus developed a functional perspective on the state that was not geared towards constitutional theory, but towards the arrangement of institutions. The CEPA reports reveal particularly striking similarities to contemporary (Scottish) political economy, both in terms of language and methods. In fact, 'economy' was the key term that the Commissioners' used to characterise their own approach. The Commissioners employed this term as a signifier for logistics, for the prudent handling of resources – a meaning much more nuanced than the mere cutting of costs that dominated the public discourse. The Commissioners' perspective strikingly resembles the vantage point of the 'statesman or legislator' of Scottish political economy – a projection of an ideal enlightened politician solely acting for the public good.

Practicing Economical Reform

Whilst the first part of this book is primarily concerned with better understanding the development of administrative ideas by the Accounts Commissioners, the second part sets out to determine the significance of changing administrative ideas for ensuing reform efforts in the 1780s and 1790s. The period under consideration coincides with the first part of the so-called Age of Reform. This label of periodisation was originally introduced to characterise the time around the two great reform acts of the nineteenth century, but it now resembles Reinhart Koselleck's *Sattelzeit*, as the period's beginnings are currently placed as early as 1780 or even 1760.[19] Joanna Innes and Arthur Burns made the point that the first decades of the Age of Reform were marked by the aspiration for reform rather than its conclusive practical implementation.[20] Such early aspirations and conceptualisations of public administration are the main concern of this study. In the second part, the spotlight is therefore on the processes of reform, less so on their results.

Apart from being characterised as the Age of Reform, the period under consideration has also been described as an age of crisis, as part of a global crisis marked by the spreading of wars and radical social change, and even revolutions.[21] 'Crisis' is a notoriously difficult concept to pin down because there is no objective benchmark to distinguish periods of crisis from periods of 'normality'.[22] However, 'crisis' can also be understood as a social ascription rooted in the anxiety-ridden belief that the social order is threatened by fundamental problems for which no solutions have yet been found. Such ideas and fears indeed provided crucial momentum to demands of economical reform throughout the period investigated. The wartime context is particularly critical. Only in historical retrospect does the eighteenth century appear as a British success story: in the many wars fought in Europe, America, and South Asia after 1739, Britain prevailed and thus became one of Europe's foremost powers, with a global reach.[23]

[19] For an overview on the Age of Reform as a concept of periodisation and field of research cf. Arthur Burns and Joanna Innes (eds.), *Rethinking the Age of Reform. Britain 1780–1850* (Cambridge, 2003); Timothy C. W. Blanning and Peter Wende (eds.), *Reform in Great Britain and Germany. 1750–1850* (Oxford, 1999); Philip Harling, 'Equipoise Regained? Recent Trends in British Political History, 1790–1867', *The Journal of Modern History*, 75 (2003), 890–918; for the *Sattelzeit*, Reinhart Koselleck, 'Einleitung', in Otto Brunner, Werner Conze, and Reinhart Koselleck (eds.), *Geschichtliche Grundbegriffe: Historisches Lexikon zur politisch-sozialen Sprache Deutschlands*, vol. 1 (Stuttgart, 1972), XIII–XXVII.

[20] Joanna Innes and Arthur Burns, 'Introduction', in id. (eds.), *Age of Reform*, 1–70, p. 1.

[21] James Stafford, *The Case of Ireland. Commerce, Empire and the European Order, 1750–1848* (Cambridge, 2022), pp. 4–8; Christopher A. Bayly, *The Birth of the Modern World 1780–1914. Global Connections and Comparisons* (Malden, 2004), pp. 86–120.

[22] Janet L. Roitman, *Anti-Crisis* (Durham, 2014); J. B. Shank, 'Crisis: A Useful Category of Post-Social Scientific Historical Analysis?', *American Historical Review*, 113:4 (2008), 1090–9.

[23] Hamish M. Scott, 'Britain's Emergence as a European Power, 1688–1815', in Harry T. Dickinson (ed.), *A Companion to Eighteenth-Century Britain* (Malden, 2002), 431–46; id., 'The Fiscal Military State and International Rivalry during the Long Eighteenth Century', in Christopher Storrs (ed.), *The Fiscal Military State in Eighteenth-Century Europe* (Aldershot, Burlington, 2008), 23–54.

For contemporaries of the 1770s up to the 1790s, the situation looked quite different: the American War of Independence turned into a disaster; there were concerns about uprisings in Ireland and even the threat of a French invasion; and in British Bengal, the East India Company (EIC) faced military threats from all directions. The almost constant and global warfare tested the limits of the financial system. Each war resulted in a surge of government spending. A relative decrease in years of peace did nothing to stop this dramatic trend. From 1690 to 1783, government spending increased by 250%. The immense costs could only be covered through a dramatic increase of the national debt. In the War of American Independence, bonds covered 80% of the war expenditure and the costs for servicing these debts rose accordingly. Overall, up to 85% of the budget paid for direct military costs and the servicing of war debts.[24]

In retrospect, the newfound ability to raise unprecedented levels of debt to finance these wars is another British success story. Peter Dickson famously described it as a 'financial revolution': the Bank of England enabled a bond market to emerge, which, in combination with the investors' confidence in the stability of the British system, enabled the British state to borrow enormous amounts of money at reasonable rates.[25] At the time, however, anxieties grew that the state could collapse under the immense national debt. For critics such as David Hume or Richard Price, the question was not whether Britain was headed towards national bankruptcy, but only when this utter collapse of state finances would occur.[26]

In *The Sinews of Power* (1989), John Brewer provided a crucial new stimulus to the institutional history of British administration. He acknowledged Dickson's thesis of a financial revolution, but highlighted the importance of fiscal administration. His concept of the 'fiscal-military state' identifies specific administrative developments after the Revolution of 1688 as necessary preconditions for the British rise to power in the long eighteenth century. Brewer claimed that only administrative innovations, most of all

[24] Julian Hoppit, 'Checking the Leviathan, 1688–1832', in Donald Winch and Patrick K. O'Brien (eds.), *The Political Economy of British Historical Experience, 1688–1914* (Oxford, 2002), 267–94, pp. 279–90; John Brewer, *The Sinews of Power. War, Money and the English State, 1688–1783* (London, 1989), pp. 37–45.

[25] Peter G. M. Dickson, *The Financial Revolution in England. A Study in the Development of Public Credit 1688–1756* (London, 1967); also cf. Douglass Cecil North and Barry R. Weingast, 'Constitutions and Commitment. The Evolution of Institutions Governing Public Choice in Seventeenth-Century England', *Journal of Economic History* 49 (1989), 803–32.

[26] Istvan Hont, 'The Rhapsody of Public Debt. David Hume and Voluntary State Bankruptcy', in id. (ed.), *Jealousy of Trade: International Competition and the Nation State in Historical Perspective* (Cambridge, Mass., 2005), 325–53.

in the Excise, allowed for the stability and low interest rates of the national debt which enabled Britain to finance the almost constant waging of war.[27] Between the Revolution of 1688 and the American War, net tax income more than tripled, with the rate of increase even accelerating afterwards. The bulk of this growth concerned indirect taxes, namely excise and customs duties, whilst the traditional land tax was less affected.[28] Both wartime logistics and tax administration required ever more manpower. Brewer estimates that in 1690, 2,524 full-time employees were concerned with fiscal administration; by 1782/3 this number rose to 8,292. Some departments, such as the Excise, quadrupled in number.[29] The excise needed to be regularly assessed, collected, and monitored at every small producer, e.g., every brewery, candle maker, paper mill in Britain.[30] More than any other department, the Excise rose to the challenge. In a lucid case study, Brewer depicts the Excise as a proto-modern bureaucracy with a centralised structure and clear chains of command. Excise officers received regular salaries, which increased according to rank, and promotions were mostly based on merit. The methodical discharge of duties required hard-working officers with high qualifications in mathematics and accounting.[31]

Brewer's analysis of the British fiscal administration is invaluable to this study, but it requires critical modification. Brewer applauds the Excise as a 'paragon of efficiency'.[32] Whilst he signals its exceptional status, Brewer also claims that 'the Excise best exemplifies new patterns of administrative practice' and constituted 'the model towards which all other branches of the revenue aspired'.[33] Brewer's argument thus implies an ongoing, actively promoted, and coherent process of rational bureaucratisation. However, as Brewer shows himself by comparison to the Customs and the Exchequer, the Excise was the exception and not the rule. Before the 1780s, there was no widespread process of professionalisation in the departments, individual

27 Brewer, *Sinews of Power*. For an appraisal of the concept of the fiscal-military state and its potentials that point far beyond British history, cf. Christopher Storrs (ed.), *The Fiscal Military State in Eighteenth-Century Europe* (Aldershot, 2008). Joanna Innes has analysed the wider social and significance of the fiscal-military state. Joanna Innes, 'The Domestic Face of the Military-Fiscal State. Government and Society in Eighteenth-Century Britain', in Lawrence Stone (ed.), *An Imperial State at War: Britain from 1689 to 1815* (London, 1994), 96–127.

28 Brewer, *Sinews of Power*, pp. 88–101.

29 Ibid., pp. 64–79.

30 A census taken by the Excise in 1759 gives the total number of shops at 166,000, up to 100,000 of which fell under Excise jurisdiction. Ibid., pp. 112–13.

31 Ibid., pp. 101–14.

32 Ibid., p. 114.

33 Ibid., p. 102.

efforts of improvement notwithstanding. Rather, the eighteenth-century administrative structure of the British state comprised an incoherent variety of institutions, most of which stuck to their respective ways of operation. It is therefore difficult to generalise the findings of one branch. John Brewer means to emphasise the effectiveness of the fiscal-military state and focuses on the Excise; in doing so, he overstates the modernity of the British administrative system as a whole.[34]

Chapter 4 analyses administrative reform processes as a triangular nexus between the political arena (consisting of Parliament, Cabinet, and Treasury), reform commissions and committees, and the involved departments. To consider the diverging agency of involved groups is crucial because, whilst there were many unspecific calls for reform, no clear-cut political party or societal group was pushing for systematic reforms. The fact that all ministries in the 1780s and 1790s voiced support for economical reform should not lead us to underestimate the complexity of the reform processes. In fact, few of the Commissioners' reform suggestions were consistently implemented. Lord Shelburne was the only Prime Minister to share CEPA's aspiration for systematic reform, but his ministry did not last long enough to implement many reforms beyond the immediate reach of the Treasury. Generally, knowledge about the details and structure of state administration was very limited, even in the highest ranks of government. Accusations of corruption did not require accurate or detailed information, but reform concepts aiming at practical improvement decidedly did.

For many politicians, economical reform was desirable in principle. In practice, it turned out to be much less politically attractive, because of three interrelated problems. First, reforms soon proved to be complicated affairs. Because they threatened the privileges of politically well-connected personages, reforms provoked massive resistance. Second, due to the discourse on corruption, demands for economical reform were politically entangled with demands for parliamentary reform. The ministry of William Pitt (from 1784) therefore tried to avoid politically volatile debates that might threaten the constitutional order. The third and, arguably, the crucial problem was that the proposed reforms, at best, promised savings in the long term. In the short term, they entailed considerable costs. Due to the American War, as well as the French Revolution and the subsequent Coalition Wars, the Pitt ministry was wary of additional financial, political, and ideological burdens. Initially, a new Commission on Fees (1785–6) was formed to derive concrete reform recommendations from the principles

[34] Cf. Peter Jupp, *The Governing of Britain, 1688–1848. The Executive, Parliament and the People* (London, 2006), pp. 31–2.

developed by CEPA. After this commission became embroiled in a scandal in 1786, it was quickly abolished. While Pitt praised CEPA, he allowed it to expire as well. Pitt made a point of supporting reforms as long as they did not cause a stir, but, at the same time, he tried to keep them under tight control and out of the limelight.[35] Especially after 1786, this political ambivalence resulted in a curious constellation. Economical reform received political support in principle, whilst, in practice, reforms were often undermined or thwarted.

In 1789, the French Revolution changed the rules of the discourse fundamentally. Especially after the publication of Burke's *Reflections on the Revolution in France* (1790), the Revolution was perceived as a domestic ideological threat. In fear of 'English Jacobins' who might try to overthrow the constitution, Pitt's ministry cracked down on radicals indiscriminately. Parliamentary reform was off the agenda and economical reform, which had long been discussed in the same breath, was affected as well. With the onset of the Coalition Wars, the issue initially faded into the background. The switch to a war economy not only triggered a renewed surge of the public debt, war economy also led to widespread profiteering, waste, and an uncontrolled increase in offices.[36]

A major political debate on economical reform did not arise again until 1797. Chapter 6 focuses on the parliamentary Finance Committee of 1797–8. The inquiries of the Finance Committee provide a rich insight into the situation of the departments, almost two decades after the onset of the Economical Reform Debates. Headed by its energetic Chairman Charles Abbot, the Finance Committee decried the fact that that the reform recommendations of the Accounts- and Fees Commissioners had only effected relatively meagre results in the departments. Abbot emphasised the deficits of implementation. The reports of the Finance Committee widened the scope to include departments which had not been considered in terms of administration before, such as the judiciary and the metropolitan police, and even took up Jeremy Bentham's scheme of the Panopticon, a penitentiary on utilitarian principles.

In the almost two decades since the beginning of the Economical Reform Debates, the wider economical discourse had continued to develop and utilitarian ideas gained further acceptance. The reports notably introduced current statistical methods to their inquiry, which made it easy to compare departments in numerical terms. Whilst the implementation of

[35] John R. Breihan, 'William Pitt and the Commission on Fees, 1785–1801,' *Historical Journal*, 27:1 (1984), 59–81; Michael Duffy, *The Younger Pitt* (Harlow, 2000), pp. 74–98.

[36] Philip Harling and Peter Mandler, 'From "Fiscal-Military" State to Laissez-Faire State, 1760–1850,' *Journal of British Studies*, 32:1 (1993), 44–70.

the Accounts- and Fees Commissions' proposals left much to be desired, the reports show that the economical administrative framework was widely accepted. Over a generation of public officers, a recognisable administrative reform language emerged, i.e. a language in the Pocockian sense: a set of statements, assumptions, benchmarks, authorities, and ideals linked to a specific vocabulary. This language was not hermetic, but already solidified in its core in the 1780s. By the end of the 1790s, this language had gained wide acceptance in Britain. Even whilst a war economy provided a boost for patrimonial practices, it became increasingly hard to defend these practices in terms of a patrimonial language.

The Conditions of Empire: Administrative Reforms in British India and Ireland

The peculiarities of the administrative reform process in Britain become much clearer in light of two closely related case studies in the wider empire. Chapter 5 introduces the unique administrative situation of the 'Company-state' in British Bengal, where the EIC had become a territorial power in the 1760s. Ill-prepared, staffed by adventurers, and under constant military pressure, the Company tried but largely failed to rise to the task of administering territorial rule. That the directors of the ailing stock company pressured its local leadership for profitability did not help to stabilise the situation either. Governor General Warren Hastings drew on the language of the ancient constitution to legitimise Company rule by claiming factual sovereignty in succession to an orientalist imagination of an original Mughal constitution. The result was a period of trial and error, which eroded existing Mughal structures without establishing a workable new administration.[37] The anxious atmosphere in Bengal was mirrored by an equally desperate discourse on India in Britain. Company rule in India became the proverbial example for corruption, which even threatened to corrupt the British constitution at home. From 1787 to 1795, the Hastings Impeachment became a point of culmination for this discourse, and it has been consequently in the focus of much research.[38] Edmund Burke famously used the stage for a dramatic discussion of imperial morality,

[37] Robert Travers, *Ideology and Empire in Eighteenth-Century India. The British in Bengal* (Cambridge, 2007).

[38] E.g. Vinod Pavarala, 'Cultures of Corruption and the Corruption of Culture. The East India Company and the Hastings Impeachment', in Emmanuel Kreike and William C. Jordan (eds.), *Corrupt Histories* (Rochester, 2004), 291–336; Jeremy Bernstein, *Dawning of the Raj. The Life and Trials of Warren Hastings* (Chicago, 2000).

but he was not really concerned with administrative problems. Whilst the discussion was a milestone in the discourse on corruption, it had little to do with current administrative ideas.

This study argues that current administrative ideas did, by contrast, play an important role in the administrative reforms in India, which Governor General Charles Cornwallis initiated in 1788. Unlike the ministries in Britain, Cornwallis was in a position to push through a systematic top-down reform of the colonial apparatus of British Bengal within just one year. Cornwallis had been involved with CEPA, when they scrutinised the accounting of the American War. In India, Cornwallis adapted the Commissioners' administrative principles to model his own reform programme. Like reformers in Britain, Cornwallis prioritised 'true economy', i.e. administrative improvement over austerity. The EIC leadership, by contrast, pushed for retrenchment, but was unable to intervene due to the sheer distance. Cornwallis' administrative reforms primarily aimed to discipline the Company's own servants. They started a process that would turn the existing crooked company structures into the highly effective (also elitist and authoritarian) Indian Civil Service, which became a pillar of subsequent imperial rule. In British India, the administrative reformers were also the ruling decision makers. This constellation remained in place in the nineteenth century. Colonial administrators created colonial policy, which the Indian Civil Service enforced. Rationalistic conceptions of administration were thus inscribed into colonial governance in a categorically more pervasive way than economical reform processes were in Britain.[39]

The historiography of British India has long identified a significant break in governance between the tenures of Warren Hastings and Charles Cornwallis.[40] Scholarly interpretations of this rupture in governance vary. One interpretation holds that Hastings laid an institutional groundwork that Cornwallis then perfected, another that Cornwallis successfully transferred the British model to the colonial administration of Bengal.[41] In 2010, Jon

39 Jon E. Wilson, *The Domination of Strangers. Modern Governance in Eastern India, 1780–1835* (Basingstoke, 2008), pp. 182–94. Also cf. Knights, *Trust and Distrust*, pp. 26–46. Knights has also highlighted the link between CEPA and Cornwallis' reforms in British India. Cf. ibid., pp. 216–17.

40 Robert Travers, *Ideology and Empire*. Due to language barriers, Michael Mann's excellent monograph on the formation of the colonial state in Bengal has not been fully appreciated. Michael Mann, *Bengalen im Umbruch. Die Herausbildung des britischen Kolonialstaates 1754–1793* (Stuttgart, 2000).

41 For the former cf. e.g. Lewis S. O'Malley, *The Indian Civil Service 1601–1930* (London, 1965), p. 23; a good example for the latter explanation is Akshoy K. Ghosal, *Civil Service in India under the East India Company. A Study in Administrative Development* (Calcutta, 1944), p. 6.

Wilson showed that this interpretation makes little sense because there was no real British precedent for the rationalistic structures and governance that took hold in Bengal after Cornwallis' reforms. Especially with regard to country administration, Britain and precolonial Bengal had more in common than is usually admitted. Wilson pointedly argues that 'Britain's first modern state emerged in Bengal'.[42] This book suggests a modification of Wilson's thesis. There was no British model administration to be exported to Bengal. Rather, Cornwallis systematically applied administrative ideas recently developed in Britain by CEPA in order to mitigate the crisis in Bengal and to establish control over the colonial establishment.

It must be stressed that the administrative reforms were just one facet of an overall turn towards systematic colonial governmentality, the impact of which is beyond the scope of this study. In the wider perspective, the reforms fit into the rather bleak picture painted by recent empire historiography. Disciplining Company servants may have brought order to Company rule and may even have served to limit malpractice and abuse. Yet, imposing a rigid revenue system on the country that destroyed social structures and enforcing imperial domination with the help of an increasingly elitist and racist civil service brought about catastrophic consequences on the subcontinent.[43]

Chapter 7 focuses on the failed administrative reforms in the course of the union with Ireland in 1801–2, which provide an equally illuminating case of comparison. Whilst the events leading to the passing of the union have been thoroughly studied, there is very little research on this initial attempt at establishing a reformed Irish administration on a British model.[44] James Stafford showed that the Irish situation was intensely debated in the context of contemporary political economy. Economical arguments and the prospect of improvement also played a major role

[42] Wilson, *Domination of Strangers*, p. ix.

[43] Jon E. Wilson, *India Conquered. Britain's Raj and the Chaos of Empire* (London, 2017); William Dalrymple, *The Anarchy. The Relentless Rise of the East India Company* (London, 2020).

[44] Around its bicentennial, the union was intensely studied, cf. e.g. Patrick M. Geoghegan, *The Irish Act of Union. A Study in High Politics, 1798–1801* (Dublin, 1999); Michael Brown, Patrick Geoghegan, and James Kelly, *The Irish Act of Union, 1800. Bicentennial Essays* (Dublin, 2003). Abbot's failed reforms are rather treated as a footnote either to Addington's administration or as a short episode in a less than current administrative history of Ireland. Cf. e.g. R. B. McDowell, *The Irish Administration, 1801–1914* (London, Toronto, 1964), pp. 19–21. Moreover, John Breihan has treated the reforms in his unpublished PhD thesis. John R. Breihan, 'Economical Reform, 1785–1810'. Hoppen's more recent article on British political attitudes towards Ireland has been a valuable addition to the field. K. T. Hoppen, 'An Incorporating Union? British Politicians and Ireland 1800–1830', *EHR*, 123:501 (2008), 328–50.

in the political deliberations in London.[45] To complement the political union with an administrative union based on economical principles was thus a consistent extension of the political agenda. However, subsequent reforms encountered an entirely patrimonial administrative system that had never been involved in the British reform processes of the previous decades. Quite the contrary. In 1798, Pitt had appointed Charles Cornwallis Lord Lieutenant of Ireland and charged him with suppressing an uprising and securing the necessary political majority for the union in the Irish Parliament. Against his own convictions, Cornwallis felt compelled to resort to decidedly patrimonial means to fulfil his task: he abused government patronage and distributed offices on a grand scale in return for votes. This large-scale use of patronage in securing political consent for the union rested on patrimonial usage and strikingly confirmed the property theory for the Irish offices. There is some irony in the point that Cornwallis, who understood and endorsed economical administrative ideas like few others, now concerted an extensive patrimonial effort, which contemporaries and even Cornwallis himself clearly marked as corruption.[46]

In 1801, Prime Minister Henry Addington entrusted Charles Abbot, the former chairman of the parliamentary Finance Committee, with a systematic reform of the Irish administration. Abbot therefore came to Ireland with a similar combination of authority and administrative knowledge as Cornwallis in India. However, the reform efforts clashed with the Protestant elite, on whose support British rule in Ireland relied. Irish personages were anything but prepared to accept or even understand a reform programme based on economical ideas. Consequently, the same type of inquiry, which had long since become a matter of routine in Britain, immediately provoked fierce resistance from the Protestant elite that was primarily concerned with maintaining their power. This elite used their close connections to political circles in London to cause such a stir that Addington and his Cabinet recalled Abbot and even reversed initial regulations; not because they disagreed with Abbot's reforms as such, but because the trouble these reforms caused was politically inconvenient in an already unstable situation.

Viewed in conjunction, these cases cast a revealing spotlight on the workings of the British empire at the end of the eighteenth century. The

45 Stafford, *Case of Ireland*, pp. 139–73.

46 Richard Middleton's recent biography of Cornwallis unfortunately does not really explore the connections between Cornwallis' time in Bengal and his time in Ireland. Richard Middleton, *Cornwallis. Soldier and Statesman in a Revolutionary World* (New Haven, 2022).

eighteenth-century empire was not a centrally and systematically controlled project, though colonial policy did form a pattern marked by control, exploitation, and expansion. British India was intensely discussed in the public discourse, especially in the discourse on corruption. At the same time, the state of knowledge about the actual situation in India long remained poor. The Company directorate, Parliament, and the ministries made far-reaching decisions on the basis of domestic concerns and inadequate assessments of the situation in India, often only reacting to the badly-understood consequences of previous decisions. The long distance forced (but also enabled) the leadership on the spot to take some liberty in adopting these decisions. After Pitt's India Act of 1784 endowed the Governor General with supreme powers, there were no local checks to the vice-regal rule of Cornwallis and Wellesley, whilst central oversight was severely hampered by distance and lack of information.

As the Irish case shows, distance was by no means the only determining factor for the outcome of administrative reforms. Regardless of the question, whether Ireland counted as a colony, the British policy towards Ireland certainly followed an imperial rationale. Far from aiming towards administrative integration, the union was an instrument to continue and strengthen the quasi-colonial domination of Ireland and to address geopolitical concerns. In India, economical reform had contributed to stability; in Ireland, economical reform rather turned out to be a destabilising factor. The Irish case tellingly reveals both connections and disconnections of insular discourses. The elites in Ireland and Great Britain were tightly linked and there was a shared discourse that discussed Ireland in terms of political economy. At the same time, the administrative systems were entirely separate and the British administrative discourse did not register in Ireland at all. Both the Indian case and the Irish case seem to call for methodological caution. Just because India and Ireland were prominently discussed in British public discourses does not mean that there was a comprehensive or continual exchange of information. Conventional ideas of centre and periphery do not do justice to these complexly entangled processes. Rather, much depended on the experience of the individual actors and on their respective (personal) networks. That Cornwallis played an important role in both cases underlines these features of the empire. Cornwallis was sent to Ireland as a troubleshooter, because he had a proven record as a general, but an even stronger track record as the new type of officer who just fit the assignment: a colonial bureaucrat.[47]

[47] Jon E. Wilson, 'The Silence of Empire. Imperialism and India', in David Craig and James Thompson (eds.), *Languages of Politics in Nineteenth-Century Britain* (London, 2013), 218–41.

Deficit descriptions never lead to inevitable solutions that everyone involved immediately comprehended and accepted. When actors – such as Cornwallis and Abbot – boasted pertinent experience and then prioritised administrative reforms, the application of economical reform ideas to specific cases was relatively easy. However, implementing the respective reforms was all the more difficult: not only because these reforms violated tangible interests and privileges, but also because they were almost incomprehensible within a patrimonial frame of reference, as the Irish case very clearly shows. In Great Britain, the economical understanding of administration gradually spread over a generation of public officers: once the economical understanding was widely accepted, it became equally difficult to continue to justify privileges, which, in a patrimonial view, had not required any justification. For the most part, the civil servants of the EIC were just as unfamiliar with the reforms as the actors in Ireland. That Cornwallis was nevertheless able to push through economical administrative reforms in record time was only possible because he had quasi-despotic powers at his disposal while local actors and even the directors were unable to intervene.

Towards an Intellectual History of Public Administration

This book is concerned with administrative thought at the beginning of the Age of Reform. Contrary to the vast literature on political ideas, there are few precedents for an intellectual history of public administration.[48] Therefore, this approach needs some methodological groundwork, starting with the very definition of the subject of such a history. This subject invokes a seemingly universal phenomenon of human civilisation that is usually referred to as either 'bureaucracy' or '(public) administration'.[49] Even though the English term 'bureaucracy' is used more neutrally than its continental counterparts, it generally presupposes a defined structure of offices, vertical hierarchies, and regulated work processes. Moreover, the

48 Leonard Hume conducted a valuable foray in this direction as a prehistory for Bentham's administrative ideas. Hume showed the significance of a wide range of 'economic' ideas, which he took from a plethora of writings from across Europe. Given Bentham's wide intellectual horizon, this makes sense. For an intellectual history that aims to highlight connections to administrative reform practice, this approach is less suited. Leonard J. Hume, *Bentham and Bureaucracy* (Cambridge, 1981), esp. pp. 17–54.

49 Bureaucracy has been taken to represent a (questionable) fundamental structure of Western modernity. See e.g. Alasdair C. MacIntyre, *After Virtue. A Study in Moral Theory* (London et al., 1981); Michael Herzfeld, *The Social Production of Indifference. Exploring the Symbolic Roots of Western Bureaucracy* (New York, 1992).

word carries negative connotations of formalism and inertia, which have been part of its conceptual history since the nineteenth century.[50] Bureaucracy is often associated with Max Weber's ideal type of rational administration. Whilst Weber's take may serve as a useful shorthand for certain types of government, it has instead been employed as an allegedly universal benchmark and the culmination of a teleological history of public organisation.[51] 'Bureaucracy' is therefore not a suitable analytical term to historicise eighteenth-century administrative ideas in a period of transition.

'Public administration' seems more feasible. Whilst public administration is an even more recent concept,[52] it is a compound of words which already bore relevance to the subject in early modern times and continue to do so today. In the eighteenth century, 'administration' was used in a similar manner to 'management of affairs/business' for a variety of pertinent practices and 'public' tied these practices to the state. Jos Raadschelders has recently offered a definition of public administration as a discipline that is also a definition of its subject:

> Public administration is the academic study concerned with the internal structure and functioning of government (i.e., its officials and its organisations) and with government's penetration of society and interaction with its citizens.[53]

This rather open definition results from Raadschelders' advocacy for the opening of a mostly practice-focused discipline to interdisciplinary and, especially, to historical perspectives.[54] Still, the definition still rests on

50 'bureaucracy, n.', *OED*.

51 Max Weber, *Economy and Society. An Outline of Interpretive Sociology*, ed. by Guenther Roth and Claus Wittich (Berkeley, 1968), pp. 956–1005. Tendencies to describe the organisation of government in terms of 'stages of Weberness' are still common. For instance, Marina Ottaway advocated active state-building to facilitate 'a shortcut to the Weberian state.' Marina Ottaway, 'Rebuilding State Institutions in Collapsed States', *Development and Change*, 35:5 (2002), 1001–23, p. 1004.

52 The discipline of Public Administration traces its roots to 1887, when Woodrow Wilson called for a scientific approach to the study of administration. Woodrow Wilson, 'The Study of Administration', *Political Science Quarterly*, 2:2 (1887), 197–222.

53 Jos C. N. Raadschelders, *Public Administration. The Interdisciplinary Study of Government* (New York, 2011), p. v.

54 Since the 1990s, interest in interdisciplinary approaches to public administration has increased. The trilingual Yearbook of European Administrative History, edited by Erk Volkmar Heyen from 1989 to 2008, was an important forum for (inter-)disciplinary reorientation. Cf. e.g. Piero Aimo, 'The History of Public Administration. Some Brief Reflections on an Uncertain Discipline', *Jahrbuch für europäische Verwaltungsgeschichte*, 14 (2002), 317–35. The most recent step is trying to rethink the

Western and, particularly, on modern assumptions, which poses problems for an intellectual history of eighteenth-century public administration. The definition presupposes a modern power state and juxtaposes an active government to a passive society. Erk Volkmar Heyen has pointed to the potential circularity of polity-based definitions of administration. Heyen holds that administration cannot be said to presuppose a polity. Rather, office and polity are two sides of a *longue-durée* institutionalisation process. Heyen argues that 'office' should be considered the core element of administration instead:

> 'Office' (*officium*) can be defined as the relationship between duties (objectives of action) and authorities (means of action) that is normatively contoured in reference to recurring action-compelling situations of a polity, with a claim to the forming of the reality of that polity through the actions of an office-holder.[55]

An office thus originates in the exercise of a certain status in reference to a given polity and is typically characterised by a designation of duties and authorities. This abstract definition allows for the analytical usage of 'administrative' (referring to office) and 'administration' (action by officers, aggregate of actions concerning officers, or interrelationships and organisation of offices) without presupposing specific and potentially anachronistic assumptions. This tentative definition seems to fit well for the administrative horizon of eighteenth-century Britain. For its use in the present book, the only necessary modification is to slightly broaden the characteristics of office (duties and authorities) by the addition of privileges in order to include sinecures. Even as pure *status-cum-privilege*, with no duty or special authority attached, sinecures can fulfil relevant functions for a polity, such as inclusion of political elites or fund-raising through their sale. Following this definition, an intellectual history of public administration deals with historical ideas, arguments, and social attributions of public administration.

---

significance of administrative history that gives up the idea of clear-cut administrative traditions in favour of a more nuanced synthesis of interdisciplinary administrative history. Fritz Sager and Patrick Overeem (eds.), *The European Civil Servant. A Shared Administrative Identity?* (Colchester, 2015).

55 Erk V. Heyen, 'Zum Amtsbegriff als Kernelement des Begriffs der öffentlichen Verwaltung. Überlegungen aus Anlaß eines Leidener Forschungsprojekts', *Jahrbuch für europäische Verwaltungsgeschichte*, 12 (2000), pp. 272–9, quote on p. 272. Translation by SM.

In order to escape the pitfalls of teleology, it is helpful to take seriously individual agency and to relate this agency to its historical contexts. To paraphrase Collingwood, we should not only look for statements, but also search for the problems that the authors addressed by means of these statements.[56] A useful starting point for such an analysis is the methodology of the so-called Cambridge School of intellectual history. Textual sources will be interpreted as speech acts, i.e. as political actions tied to the individual interests of actors, which were influenced by their authors' political, social, biographical, and, especially, by their semantic contexts.[57] In order to aggregate speech acts and identify connections and patterns, John Pocock's concept of 'language' is a useful heuristic device. In this sense, a language is a set of arguments and authorities as well as patterns of speech, vocabularies, topoi, loose associations, and assumptions relating to a fairly clear subject. 'Languages' are suitable for grasping contradictions, malleable standpoints, and changing allegiances. Nevertheless, they are not arbitrary. When one language is dominant for statements on a given range of topics, it very much resembles a Foucaldian 'discourse' that allows some statements whilst precluding others. Moreover, authors consciously or unconsciously transfer elements from different languages and sometimes use them in seemingly contradictory ways.[58]

By taking every text as a political action with potential consequences, the Cambridge School included less well-known authors in their analysis and, thereby, significantly widened the scope of intellectual history. This book widens the scope even further by including quotidian administrative sources. Formal reports differ widely from parliamentary debates, intra-departmental reform concepts, and private correspondence. Some writers may have studied administrative questions, whilst others only reacted unconsciously to changing modes of expression and argumentation. In terms of impact and in terms of conceptual complexity and clarity, there is a huge difference between, for instance, a sophisticated work of David

[56] Robin G. Collingwood, *The Idea of History* (London et al., 1956 [1946]), p. 283. For a similar argument cf. Quentin Skinner, 'Meaning and Understanding in the History of Ideas', *History and Theory*, 8:1 (1969), 3–53.

[57] For a general introduction to the Cambridge School cf. Annabel Brett and James Tully (eds.), *Rethinking the Foundations of Modern Political Thought* (Cambridge, 2006). Both 'founding fathers' of the Cambridge School address these issues in numerous essays, they have each since published as collections: Quentin Skinner, *Visions of Politics*. vol. 1, *Regarding Method* (Cambridge, 2002); John G. R. Pocock, *Political Thought and History. Essays on Theory and Method* (Cambridge, 2010).

[58] John G. R. Pocock, 'The Concept of Language and the metier d'historien. Some Considerations on Practice', in ibid., pp. 87–105.

Hume and a letter written by a clerk to justify his privileges. Nevertheless, both texts were influenced by their semantic contexts and may in turn have influenced these contexts.

Some modifications of the tried-and-tested Cambridge School methodology are necessary. In political debates, authors typically address their subjects openly and try to convince others of their arguments. However, parliamentary speakers frequently debated administrative topics without any specific knowledge of these topics. Statements about offices were, for instance, shaped in political debates on retrenchment and the national debt, or on the alleged corruption of the constitution. In administrative correspondences, distinct sets of administrative assumptions shine out in discussions of concrete measures. Because many pertinent statements did not emerge from an open debate, implicit expressions deserve particular attention. Arguments in which different actors debated a concrete matter based on vastly differing sets of assumptions can produce quite rewarding sources.

In addition to analysing speech acts, this study also draws on conceptual history. In order to analyse the usage of a word, the specific instance must be related to the bandwidth of meaning and ways of employing this word in the same and in different contexts. This includes reference to lexical condensation of prevalent word-usage and reference to conceptual fields. The contradictions between Cambridge-style intellectual history and conceptual history such as Koselleck's *Begriffsgeschichte* are sometimes overstated. On a practical level, some conscious eclecticism in assembling the methodological toolkit can be quite helpful.[59]

In the following chapters, the reports of CEPA are presented as an innovative work of theory. However, unlike partakers of scholarly debates, the Commissioners did not make explicit references to specific works that may have inspired their approach. For the most part, these silent references will not even have addressed administrative matters. Still, the Commissioners' ideas and methods are in need of historicisation and integration in terms of intellectual history. This book places the Commissioners in context of the beginnings of social science and suggests connections and interrelationships with regard to contemporary sources, in particular to political economy and to utilitarian ideas. Ultimately, it must be left to the reader to decide whether they accept that these interpretations are justified.

[59] Timothy D. Goering, 'Concepts, History and the Game of Giving and Asking for Reasons: A Defense of Conceptual History', *Journal of the Philosophy of History*, 7 (2013), 426–52; Hans E. Bödeker, 'Ausprägungen der historischen Semantik in den historischen Kulturwissenschaften', in id. and Mark Bevir (eds.), *Begriffsgeschichte, Diskursgeschichte, Metapherngeschichte* (Göttingen, 2002), 7–27.

Ryan Walter has recently argued that the history of science is particularly prone to certain fundamental fallacies and, consequently, to anachronistic arguments. Most scientific disciplines, as we are familiar with them today, only emerged in the later nineteenth century. Assuming that antecedent discussions followed the same disciplinary logic, Walter warns, will lead to an automatic misclassification of the historical context of argumentation. Moreover, he criticises the characterisation of authors according to 'their model' or 'their method', because these categories, he claims, imply a type of disciplinary debate that would only be established much later. For Walter, neither fallacy can ultimately be avoided as long as one retains anachronistic labels such as 'classical political economy'.[60]

Walter's admonitions are well founded. The quest for the origins of economics and the identification of 'early utilitarianism' has produced many anachronistic interpretations. Nevertheless, with all necessary caution, it is not only unavoidable, but also sensible that our analytical vocabulary goes beyond the language of the sources. The fact that debates on methods were framed differently at the time does not render the study of historical methods impossible. After all, the beginnings of disciplinary cohesion are a rather characteristic element of the second scientific revolution. The Commissioners' conscious use of empirical methods and the identification of a system by its underlying principles builds on epistemological presuppositions, which can be discerned. Even if it may not always be possible to prove references to individual texts or authors conclusively, there are plausible semantic relations.

At least potentially, the methodological approach outlined above may allow us to bridge the gap between theory and practice. The following intellectual history of British public administration in a period of transition therefore aims to highlight the semantic links which connected, for instance, erudite philosophers, contentious politicians, committed reformers, and subaltern accountants. In their respective situations, they all faced institutional change and played their part in shaping this change. Before we can enter the messy arena of everyday politics, consider the efforts of CEPA in developing administrative theory, and trace the complexities of subsequent reforms, we should first establish the broader intellectual horizon. For the eighteenth century saw a profound shift in the way change itself was conceived.

[60] Ryan Walter, *Before Method and Models. The Political Economy of Malthus and Ricardo* (Oxford, 2021), pp. 11–15.

PART I

CONCEPTUALISING ECONOMICAL ADMINISTRATION

1
Science and the State

The eighteenth century can be characterised by its increasing emphasis on reason, methodical analysis, and empiricism. Discussions on the significance of 'the Enlightenment' aside, there was a trend towards a critical scrutiny of all spheres of activity. Savants sought to understand the world and the human condition hoping to improve them, and the ideas of these thinkers increasingly affected reform practices.[1] In the seventeenth century, scientific knowledge revolutionised natural philosophy with its mathematical and experimental methods. However, the 'scientific revolution' remained mostly confined to a small elite of experimental philosophers within the Republic of Letters. The process of consolidation and dissemination of scientific knowledge happened mostly in the eighteenth century and the effects of this process were, arguably, just as revolutionary.[2] Scientific knowledge entered public knowledge because it was more widely applied than before. In this process, the division of scholarship into natural and moral philosophy and the cogency of related vocabularies lost their appeal. Instead, intellectual practices slowly began to emerge as distinct disciplines. This epistemic transformation did not happen overnight, but through a slow process: especially in the second half of the eighteenth century, scholars increasingly employed historical and empirical methods to identify the fundamental principles of complex phenomena and analyse them as 'systems'. Designations as 'science' or 'scientific' implied the questioning of self-evident, customary notions and reflected the growing self-confidence in such approaches.[3]

1 Clare Jackson, 'Progress and Optimism', in Martin Fitzpatrick (ed.), *The Enlightenment World* (London, 2004), 177–93.

2 Laurence Brockliss, 'Science, the Universities, and Other Public Spaces. Teaching Science in Europe and the Americas', in Roy Porter (ed.), *Eighteenth-Century Science* (Cambridge, 2016), 44–86, pp. 80–1; Margaret C. Jacob, *The Cultural Meaning of the Scientific Revolution* (New York, 1993), pp. 3–9.

3 Roy Porter, 'Introduction', in Roy Porter (ed.), *Eighteenth-Century Science* (Cambridge, 2016), 1–20; Björn Wittrock, Johan Heilbron, and Lars Magnusson, 'The Rise of the Social Sciences and the Formation of Modernity', in Johan Heilbron, Lars

In the eighteenth century, expectations of progress challenged the former certainty of a static world order. While questions about the nature of progress were primarily the domain of a rather abstract philosophy of history,[4] such questions came to resonate in discussions of concrete institutions.[5] Throughout the eighteenth century, successive areas of public life were discussed in terms of 'improvement', 'reformation', and, finally, 'reform'. This means that 'the idea that institutions or practices or people can be recast or made better'[6] became a central issue not only for thinkers, but also for informed citizens, who began forming societies for various moral, municipal, or political purposes.[7]

In constitutional and legal theory, emerging scientific perspectives revealed a tension that was not easily dissolved. For instance, the personal and institutional understandings of the state remained unreconciled to the end of the eighteenth century, and empiricist arguments on the significance of institutions did not at first devaluate the normative force of the constitutional origin story. In the second half of the century, the emerging discipline of political economy generated a functional perspective on the state. Political economists empirically developed theories in order to suggest practical improvements to the state's institutions and policies. The modern history of economics has mostly reduced classical political economy to its contributions to the realm of finance. However, it is this development of an empirical analysis of the state in practical terms that represents a crucial achievement of political economy; a development that provided crucial methodological foundations for the administrative reform ideas of the 1780s and 1790s.

Magnusson, and Björn Wittrock (eds.), *The Rise of the Social Sciences and the Formation of Modernity: Conceptual Change in Context, 1750–1850* (Dordrecht, 1996), 1–34; Clifford Siskin, 'The Problem of Periodization: Enlightenment, Romanticism and the Fate of System', in James Chandler (ed.), *The Cambridge History of English Romantic Literature* (Cambridge et al., 2009), 101–26.

4 Robert Nisbet, *History of the Idea of Progress* (London, 1980).

5 Sebastian Meurer, 'The Dawning of the Age of Reform. Epistemic and Semantic Shifts in Georgian Britain', in Susan Richter, Thomas Maissen, and Manuela Albertone (eds.), *Languages of Reform in the Eighteenth Century: When Europe Lost its Fear of Change* (New York, 2020), 62–84.

6 Joanna Innes, '"Reform" in English Public Life. The Fortunes of a Word', in Arthur Burns and Joanna Innes (eds.), *Rethinking the Age of Reform: Britain 1780–1850* (Cambridge, 2003), 71–97, p. 72.

7 Joanna Innes, 'State, Church and Voluntarism in European Welfare, 1690–1850', in Hugh Cunningham and Joanna Innes (eds.), *Charity, Philanthropy, and Reform: From the 1690s to 1850* (Basingstoke, 1998), 15–65.

Constitutional and Legal Theory

The British experience changed rapidly after the Revolution of 1688 and the Revolution Settlement, and so did the practice of government. Eighteenth-century theory of the state, however, was constrained by a number of assumptions developed in the previous century. It is worth pointing out these assumptions here, as they affected the conceptualisation of subsequent reforms of the state and public administration. On the one hand, the state was thought of in personal terms – as a hierarchically structured composite of persons, held together by voluntaristic power relationships that originated with the will of the sovereign. On the other hand, the state was also understood as a system of functionally differentiated institutions that simultaneously complemented and controlled each other. These two views were not mutually exclusive, but over the course of the eighteenth century, they increasingly formed a field of tension.

In order to gauge these aspects of eighteenth-century constitutional thought, it is helpful to go back to Thomas Hobbes (1588–1679). Even in the eighteenth century, very few writers openly agreed with Hobbes. Nevertheless, his philosophically rigid conception of the sovereign state endured and became a blueprint for political thinkers of diverse political persuasions.[8] In a Hobbesian state of nature, independent and ultimately asocial humans are engaged in the 'war of all against all', fuelled by individual appetites and aversions. To enable social order and peace under those conditions, the state must enforce social control. At the same time, the Hobbesian state is composed of individuals who surrender their natural liberty and will. As epitomised in the famous frontispiece and opening chapter of the *Leviathan*,[9] the state incorporates these individuals in a mechanistic unity of absolute sovereignty, second only to God. According to Hobbes, the state monopolises force and asserts social order through the law, which manifests its will and needs no further legitimation. The institutional dimension of the state is made up of public officials who are endowed with delegated authority and bound by law-like will and salaried contract, and are, in every way, subordinate to the sovereign.[10] In Hobbes' famous introduction, he characterised the state as an artificial man, a consciously created *automaton*,

8 Mark Goldie, 'The Reception of Hobbes', in J. H. Burns and Mark Goldie (eds.), *The Cambridge History of Political Thought, 1450–1700* (Cambridge, 1991), 589–615.

9 Thomas Hobbes, *Leviathan. Or the Matter, Forme and Power of a Commonwealth Ecclesiasticall and Civil* (Oxford, 1946 [1651]).

10 Ibid., pp. 208–9; Leonard J. Hume, *Bentham and Bureaucracy* (Cambridge, 1981), pp. 17–20.

> in which *sovereignty* is an artificial *soul*, as giving life and motion to the whole body; the *magistrates*, and other *officers* of judicature and execution, artificial *joints*; reward and punishment, by which fastened to the seat of the sovereignty every joint and member is moved to perform his duty, are the *nerves*, [...] *salus populi*, the *people's safety*, its *business*.[11]

This metaphor of the *automaton* – the machine – increasingly gained currency with political theorists towards the end of the seventeenth century and, with it, the notion of the system.[12] When Hobbes' contemporary James Harrington (1611–77) wrote *A System of Politics*[13] in the late 1650s, its title was unusual. By the time of its publication in 1700, however, 'system' was widely used. After the first scientific revolution, 'system' was rarely used to refer to the whole of creation anymore, but rather to describe more specific groups of items or ideas thought to constitute a coherent nexus. The increased usage of 'system' points to a paradigmatic change in political theory that occurred around the turn of the century: the rise of a new, systematic science of politics marked by the understanding of the state as a machine.[14] The comparison of constitutions to mechanical systems implied the depersonalisation of political arrangements as functional principles, and causal connections replaced moral categories. Generally, thinking in terms of systems gained acceptance without causing contestation. In a collection of sermons published in 1726, the theologian Joseph Butler (1692–1752) claimed that 'the body is a system or constitution: so is a tree: so is every machine.'[15] In his *Dissertation Upon Parties* of 1735, Henry St. John, first Viscount Bolingbroke (1678–1751) defined the constitution as 'a noble and wise system, the essential parts of which are so proportioned, and so intimately connected, that a change in one begets a change in the whole.'[16] The mechanical imagery

11 Hobbes, *Leviathan*, p. 5.

12 David Wootton, 'Introduction, Understanding the Constitution,' in David Wootton (ed.), *The Essential Federalist and Anti-Federalist Papers* (Indianapolis, 2003), pp. xxix–xxxi.

13 James Harrington, 'A System of Politics,' in John G. A. Pocock (ed.), *The Political Works of James Harrington* (Cambridge, 1977), 833–54.

14 David Wootton, 'Liberty, Metaphor, and Mechanism. "Checks and Balances" and the Origins of Modern Constitutionalism,' in David Womersley (ed.), *Liberty and American Experience in the Eighteenth Century* (Indianapolis, 2006), 209–74; Barbara Stollberg-Rilinger, *Der Staat als Maschine. Zur politischen Metaphorik des absoluten Fürstenstaats* (Berlin, 1986).

15 Joseph Butler, Fifteen Sermons Preached at the Rolls Chapel, London 1726, quoted in 'system, n.,' *OED*.

16 Bolingbroke, Henry St. John Viscount, *A Dissertation Upon Parties* (London, 1735).

and the systemic language remained closely connected, but they did not always coincide. The mechanical imagery emphasised the causal mode of interaction between defined parts, while systemic reasoning looked for the effects caused by the complex interplay of multitudinous factors. Starting from the 1720s, a language of self-organisation of complex systems started to emerge, which made it easier to describe and scrutinise such effects of complexity, even without a full comprehension of all factors.[17]

By the middle of the eighteenth century, it seemed increasingly feasible to approach politics and the constitutional system scientifically, as David Hume (1711–76) claimed in *That Politics may be Reduced to a Science* of 1741. The text stressed the effects of the overall constitutional systems as opposed to the merely incidental virtue of the men who executed them.[18] In Hume's reasoning, a system of laws can and must control the weaknesses of individual humans:

> Legislators, therefore, ought not to trust the future government of a state entirely to chance, but ought to provide a system of laws to regulate the administration of public affairs to the latest posterity. Effects will always correspond to causes; and wise regulations in any commonwealth are the most valuable legacy that can be left to future ages.[19]

Thus, it is possible to establish laws that can – by the logic of cause and effect – lead to desired results. In his view, institutions can persevere, and the system they form can be improved rationally by means of law-giving.

The emphasis on the rationally recognisable and adjustable causal relations adds to the constitutional tension between person and institution. Moreover, the idea of rational improvement is at odds with the customary legitimation of the state: it clashes with the widespread normative idea of the ancient constitution of liberties and laws. In the constitutional disputes of the seventeenth century, parliamentary common lawyers had used the 'ancient constitution' to argue against the royalist idea of a divine right of kings. According to their reasoning, the origins of the British constitution and its ideal form lay in the immemorial past; the constitution had endured continuously and without fundamental alterations to the present. In addition to the normatively charged origin, ancient constitutionalists argued

17 Jonathan Sheehan and Dror Wahrman, *Invisible Hands. Self-Organization and the Eighteenth Century* (Chicago, 2015), pp. ix–xviii, 3–10.

18 David Hume, 'That Politics may be Reduced to a Science', in Eugene F. Miller (ed.), *Essays, Moral, Political, and Literary* (Indianapolis, 1987), 14–31, pp. 14–22.

19 Ibid., p. 24.

that the common law embodied the condensed experience of the centuries. If anything were at fault in the present, it could only be a consequence of a deviation from the hypothetical original model. In this mode of reasoning, change for the better could only be conceptualised as the correction of a defect and the return to an earlier ideal.[20] This idea persisted in the eighteenth century because the Revolution Settlement had obsessively rejected the idea that 1688 constituted a break in constitutional history. Even though the embedded historical narrative was being increasingly challenged by philosophical history,[21] ancient constitution arguments remained influential throughout the eighteenth century. More often than not, the mere age of an institution was considered sufficient to legitimise its current form. Even in the last quarter of the eighteenth century, it remained hard to frame arguments for institutional change other than by claiming a return to an ideal origin.[22]

Hume agreed that the system should not be changed arbitrarily. However, contrary to many others, Hume did not apply the ancient constitution as a normatively rendered model. Rather, Hume stressed the importance of customs, manners, and habits – which today might be called the path dependency of the system.[23] Institutions could be altered, but failing to be considerate of habits and customs would delegitimise any modification:

> For instance; a government is establish'd for many centuries on a certain system of laws, forms, and methods of succession. The legislative power, establish'd by this long succession, changes all of a sudden the whole system of government, and introduces a new constitution in its stead. I believe few of the subjects will think themselves bound to

[20] For the idea and structure of the notion of the ancient constitution cf. especially John G. A. Pocock, *The Ancient Constitution and the Feudal Law. A Study of English Historical Thought in the 17. Century*, reissued (Cambridge, 1987 [1957]); Colin Kidd, *British Identities Before Nationalism. Ethnicity and Nationhood in the Atlantic World, 1600–1800* (Cambridge, 1999).

[21] Karen O'Brien, *Narratives of Enlightenment. Cosmopolitan History from Voltaire to Gibbon* (Cambridge, 1997).

[22] Susan Richter, Sebastian Meurer et al., 'Introduction: Languages of Reform and the European Enlightenment', in Susan Richter, Thomas Maissen, and Manuela Albertone (eds.), *Languages of Reform in the Eighteenth Century: When Europe Lost its Fear of Change* (New York, 2020), 1–26; Pocock, John G. A., 'Modes of Political and Historical Time in Early-Eighteenth-Century England', in id., *Virtue, Commerce, and History: Essays on Political Thought and History, Chiefly in the Eighteenth Century* (Cambridge, 2002), 91–102.

[23] Alain Marciano, 'Benevolence, Sympathy, and Hume's Model of Government. How Different is New Political Economy from Classical Political Economy?', in Steven G. Medema and Peter J. Boettke (eds.), *The Role of Government in the History of Economic Thought* (Durham, 2005), 43–70.

> comply with this alteration, unless it have an evident tendency to the public good: But will think themselves still at liberty to return to the antient government.[24]

In Hume's writings, the state emerges as a law-based system of corresponding institutions and customs. Legislators could change parts of this system as long as they remained within the framework and paid attention to the effects of their alteration for the whole system.

In the mid-eighteenth century, law pervaded almost all social strata as the foremost normative source and arbiter of social conflicts. In light of the enormous increase in parliamentary output and the perceived lack of a system, many contemporaries – legal professionals and the laity alike – felt that English law was in urgent need of improvement.[25] The most prominent exponent of this position was William Blackstone (1723–80), who became the first Vinerian Professor of English Law in 1759. Blackstone's appointment to the chair was the realisation of his desire to establish English law as an academic science:[26]

> that a science, which distinguishes the criterions of right and wrong; which teaches to establish the one, and prevent, punish, or redress the other; which employs in its theory the noblest faculties of the soul, and exerts in its practice the cardinal virtues of the heart; a science, which is universal in its use and extent, accommodated to each individual, yet comprehending the whole community; that a science like this should have ever been deemed unnecessary to be studied in an university, is matter of astonishment and concern.[27]

In typical Enlightenment diction, Blackstone denounced his unnamed critics as 'wedded to monastic prejudice', while praising the 'more open and generous way of thinking [that] begins now universally to prevail'.[28] In

[24] David Hume, *A Treatise on Human Nature* (Oxford, 1896 [1739]), p. 561.

[25] Julian Hoppit, *Britain's Political Economies. Parliament and Economic Life, 1660–1800* (Cambridge, 2017), pp. 38–65; David Lieberman, *The Province of Legislation Determined. Legal Theory in Eighteenth-Century Britain* (Cambridge, 1989), pp. 13–28.

[26] Wilfrid Prest, 'Blackstone, Sir William (1723–1780)', *ODNB*. Throughout the early modern period, university jurists had been concerned with (Roman) civil and with canon law, while English common law was exclusively taught at the Inns of Court. Jayne E. Archer, Elizabeth Goldring, and Sarah Knight (eds.), *The Intellectual and Cultural World of the Early Modern Inns of Court* (Manchester, 2011).

[27] William Blackstone, *Commentaries on the Laws of England*, vol. 1 (Oxford, 1765), p. 27.

[28] Ibid., pp. 26–7.

his seminal *Commentaries on the Laws of England* (1765–9), Blackstone organised the common law by means of rational principles to create a comprehensible system.[29] Blackstone understood this operation as the act of uncovering the inherent system of the common law, not as a construction of systematics for a contingent body of precedents and statutes.[30] Still, even in his panegyric of the law, it is evident that, as it stood, the system of laws did not quite match his ideal:

> We have taken occasion to admire at every turn the noble monuments of antient simplicity, and the more curious refinements of modern art. Nor have its faults been concealed from view; for faults it has, lest we should be tempted to think it of more than human structure: defects, chiefly arising from the decays of time, or the rage of unskilful improvements in later ages.[31]

Overall, Blackstone adhered to the ancient constitution tradition, projecting the ideal state of the legal system and the constitution into the past, so that defects appear as the result of history or incompetent legislation, which had largely failed to account for changing contexts. This criticism reveals Blackstone's frustration with the growing body of inconsistent statute law. In his praise of simplicity as an ideal for the structure of laws, Blackstone conformed to many contemporary European legal thinkers, such as Montesquieu (1689–1755).[32] Unlike his continental counterparts, Blackstone had to accommodate the primacy of the non-systematic common law tradition against the Roman civil law. Even while he insisted on the systematic character allegedly inherent to the laws, he could not solve the practical problems of mediating countless individual laws within the context of different complementary, and sometimes conflicting, legal systems.[33] His systematic approach strained the ancient constitution paradigm.

The tension between the Enlightenment's need for a consistent legal and constitutional system and the reality of historically contingent statutes and precedents is at the core of Blackstone's project. In order to deal with this tension, he supplied a historical exposition of the constitution and legal

[29] Lieberman, *Province of Legislation*, p. 32.

[30] William Blackstone, *Commentaries*, vol. 4 (Oxford, 1769), p. 436.

[31] Ibid.

[32] Montesquieu, Charles Louis de Secondat de, 'De l'esprit des lois', in Roger Caillois (ed.), *Montesquieu. Oeuvres complètes* (Paris, 1951), vol. 2, 973–1574.

[33] Michael Lobban, *The Common Law and English Jurisprudence* (Oxford, 1993), pp. 17–46.

system that significantly modified the bedrock of the ancient constitution.[34] Blackstone's history of the law constitutes a curious combination of ancient constitution thinking and Enlightenment confidence in progress, evident in the title of the chapter in question: 'Of the Rise, Progress, and Gradual Improvements, of the Laws of England'.[35] To accommodate his conviction of the systematic character of the law, Blackstone projected desirable qualities such as unity, clarity, and simplicity onto its very foundations. However, he refrained from ascribing them to the immemorial core of the law, which still played a big role in legal reasoning, including his own. Rather, he attributed them to the reign of the medieval King Alfred (848/9–899) and depicted King Alfred's England as a modern state:

> WHEN [...] king Alfred succeeded to the monarchy of England [...] his mighty genius prompted him to undertake a most great and necessary work [...] No less than to new-model the constitution; to rebuild it on a plan that should endure for ages; and, out of its old discordant materials, which were heaped upon each other in a vast and rude irregularity, to form one uniform and well connected whole. This he effected, by reducing the whole kingdom under one regular and gradual subordination of government [...]; all under the influence and administration of one supreme magistrate, the king; in whom, as in a general reservoir, all the executive authority of the law was lodged, and from whom justice was dispersed to every part of the nation by distinct, yet communicating, ducts and channels: which wise institution has been preserved for near a thousand years unchanged, from Alfred's to the present time.[36]

Blackstone's ideal constitution is a regular, uniform, centralised whole; its institutions are connected in clear-cut, legal ways. His utopian projection of a general top-down reconstitution substantiates his efforts for legal improvement based on positive law-giving, without quite sacrificing the scaffolding of the ancient constitution.

Blackstone aimed at scientific improvements of the legal system without calling into question conventional constitutional assumptions. He based his exposition of the present-day constitution on Hobbes' concept of sovereignty. For Hobbes, the will of the sovereign equalled law. Blackstone twisted the argument by reducing sovereignty to legislation – the source from which all other forms of legitimate power and authority were derived.

34 Lieberman, *Province of Legislation*, pp. 36–67.

35 Blackstone, *Commentaries*, vol. 4, pp. 400–36.

36 Ibid., pp. 403–4.

The state was held together by power connections, all of which expressed 'one uniform will'.[37] The source of this clear and unchallenged will was the social contract, in which everyone submits his will to create an unconfined sovereign centre. Blackstone's identification of sovereignty with legislative power lifts Parliament to a paramount position within the state. Formally, the seat of sovereignty in the British mixed constitution was neither Parliament nor King, but 'King in Parliament'; Blackstone was therefore at pains to highlight the checks and balances of the mixed constitution. Informed by a Whig conviction that the ideal mixture of the classical ancient types of constitution had been (re)asserted in the Revolution of 1688, Blackstone's description of the status quo turns into a panegyric:

> And herein indeed consists the true excellence of the English government, that all the parts of it form a mutual check upon each other. In the legislature, the people are a check upon the nobility, and the nobility a check upon the people; by the mutual privilege of rejecting what the other has resolved: while the king is a check upon both, which preserves the executive power from encroachments.[38]

The state envisioned here is, at least in its foundations, an ideally constructed machine, tasked with upholding liberty and the public good:

> Like three distinct powers in mechanics, they jointly impel the machine of government in a direction different from what either, acting by themselves, would have done; but at the same time in a direction partaking of each, and formed out of all; a direction which constitutes the true line of the liberty and happiness of the community.[39]

Blackstone provided a systematic view of the constitution, which conciliated Hobbes' voluntaristic concept of sovereign power and the rule of law. His panegyric accentuates the particularly English excellence of the mixed constitution and resonates with ancient constitutionalist convictions. The *Commentaries* were well received and widely read: eight editions were published within ten years, and many more followed throughout the eighteenth and nineteenth centuries. While the finer points of Blackstone's take on the systematisation of the laws were discussed only in legal circles, and his efforts to change legal practice arguably failed,[40] his characterisation of

[37] Ibid., p. 52.
[38] Ibid.
[39] Ibid., p. 151.
[40] Lobban, *Common Law*, pp. 1–16.

the British constitution and the legal system became a standard view that was widely known and that provided a common ground across party lines. The *Commentaries* quickly became a key work for the general education of gentlemen and remained so until at least the mid-nineteenth century.[41]

Utilitarian Ideas

Taking care of the public good was an attribute of good rulership and had thus been an aspiration of the Stuart monarchy. In the turmoil of the mid-seventeenth century, however, local initiatives, rather than the monarchy, had increasingly taken up projects of reformation and improvement concerning poor relief, health policies, and public order. After 1688, furthering of the public good was considered an essential purpose of the state as such, even though concrete measures were still mostly managed locally.[42] Whilst criticising the monarch for his rule could still be dangerous, the more abstract state and its institutions could be discussed freely. With the rise of empirical science, thinkers increasingly enquired whether an institution in question made a useful contribution to the public good. 'Utility' became a central term that was widely applied, at least in the rather vague sense of 'the rational adjustment of means to ends in society', as Leonard Hume has put it.[43]

The emphasis on this seemingly simple relation was underpinned by profound discussions of the conception of man under the auspices of utility. Moral philosophers set out to differentiate anthropological qualities from historically or regionally contingent qualities, and they attempted to derive morality itself from human nature, thus challenging its religious foundations. These authors took up Epicurus' idea that justice was valuable – but only because it was useful for the happiness of the people, not as a value in itself. As early as 1726, Francis Hutcheson (1694–1746) postulated a 'moral sense' and determined the consequences of action for others, the 'greatest happiness of the greatest number', as a central ethical guideline. Starting from the 1750s, authors such as David Hume and Adam Smith (1723–90) in Scotland, Joseph Priestley in England, as well as Cesare Beccaria (1738–94) and Helvétius (1715–71) on the continent, took up this thread. Utility thus advanced to a central philosophical concept.[44]

41 Lieberman, *Province of Legislation*, pp. 31–2.
42 Slack, *Reformation to Improvement*, pp. 53–166.
43 Hume, *Bentham and Bureaucracy*, p. 32.
44 Frederick Rosen, *Classical Utilitarianism from Hume to Mill* (London, 2003); Matthias Hoesch, 'Das Nutzenprinzip als neues Paradigma. Zur "Verfestigung" des

For the purposes of this chapter, it is not so much the details of this controversial discussion on anthropology and ethics that is important, but rather the consequences that authors drew with regard to public institutions and the state. Generally, 'utility' highlighted the relation of means and ends, of resources and purposes. In a utilitarian perspective, any institution was open to criticism. In contrast to the statically conceived ancient constitution ideal, this perspective hinted at change: invigorated by the idea of progress, utility opened up a morally based imperative for improvement, a duty to reform. The radical Presbyterian and natural philosopher Joseph Priestley (1733–1804) assembled the pieces in his *Essay on the First Principles of Government* (1768).[45] For Priestley, the public good constituted the one and only benchmark for any social institution:

> This one general idea, properly pursued, throws the greatest light upon the whole system of policy, morals, and, I may add, theology too. [...] Virtue and right conduct consist in those affections and actions which terminate in the public good; justice and veracity for instance having nothing intrinsically excellent in them, separate from their relation to the happiness of mankind; and the whole system of right to power, property, and everything else in society, must be regulated by the same consideration: the decisive question, when any of these subjects are examined, being, What is it that the good of the community requires?[46]

For Priestley, the claim that the mere age of an institution signified an intrinsic value and an argument for the preservation of this institution was utterly absurd. 'To say that these forms of government have been long established, and that these oppressions have been long suffered, without any complaint, is to supply the strongest argument for their abolition.'[47] In the course of history, circumstances changed, and legal regulations needed to change with them. Belief in social progress was a cornerstone of Priestley's thought, and social progress necessarily meant that even laws which had been just and prudent when they were first introduced deteriorated over time. This deterioration applied equally to small-scale laws and to the

---

Utilitarismus zwischen Hume und Bentham', in Christel Gärtner and others (eds.), *Normative Krisen: Verflüssigung und Verfestigung von Normen und normativen Diskursen* (Tübingen, 2019), 137–60.

45 Robert E. Schofield, *The Enlightenment of Joseph Priestley. A Study of his Life and Work from 1733 to 1773* (University Park, 1997), pp. 202–26.

46 Joseph Priestley, 'Essay on the First Principles of Government', in J. T. Rutt (ed.), *Theological and Miscellaneous Works of Joseph Priestley* (New York, 1972), 1–144, p. 13.

47 Ibid., p. 19.

constitution as a whole. Not only could the constitution be changed, in Priestley's view it had to change or become oppressive.[48]

Priestley's political ideas were rather moderate. Above all, he was concerned with the establishment of unreserved religious freedom. He was generally content with the constitution and argued for its gradual reform rather than sudden change.[49] In his view, this gradual improvement of the state would follow from a science of the state. Priestley was not so much concerned with founding an academic discipline, but rather with an incrementally deeper understanding of public affairs. Still, the term is no empty metaphor, as Priestley very consciously drew on a Newtonian understanding of science:

> All civil societies, and the whole science of civil government on which they are founded are yet in their infancy. Like other arts and sciences, this is gradually improving; but it improves more slowly, because opportunities for making experiments are fewer. [...] Taking it for granted, therefore, that our constitution and laws have not escaped the imperfections which we see to be incident to every thing human; by all means, let the closest attention be given to them, let their excellencies and defects be thoroughly laid open, and let improvements of every kind be made.[50]

Historical change necessitated the changing of laws. Conversely, Priestley saw the state as an instrument that could empower progress. The state was to secure the liberty of its citizens and thus enable human ingenuity to flourish. Progress sprang from the irresistible urge towards knowledge and improvement that was rooted in human nature. To Priestley, it was 'the glory of human nature, that the operations of reason, though variable, and by no means infallible, are capable of infinite improvement.'[51] Science was at the heart of progress: as knowledge advanced, every generation would surpass the preceding ones. Priestley himself was an enormously productive polymath, whose writings covered various areas of natural philosophy, linguistics, history, pedagogics, and theology. For him, social progress was the realisation of providence: God had deliberately set up the world in such a way that man could make an effort to improve their conditions.[52]

48 Ibid., pp. 19, 122.

49 Roy Porter, *The Creation of the Modern World. The Untold Story of the British Enlightenment* (London, 2000), p. 413; Margaret Canovan, 'The Un-Benthamite Utilitarianism of Joseph Priestley', *Journal of the History of Ideas*, 45:3 (1984), 435–50.

50 Priestley, 'Principles', p. 122.

51 Ibid., 47.

52 Martin Fitzpatrick, 'Joseph Priestley, Political Philosopher', in Isabel Rivers and David L. Wykes (eds.), *Joseph Priestley. Scientist, Philosopher, and Theologian* (Oxford,

Priestley's friend and associate Richard Price (1723–91) read from the same page. In his 1759 sermon *Britain's Happiness and the Proper Improvement of it,* he exulted at the progress of knowledge that resulted from the state of liberty in Britain:

> The researches of learned men among us have been pushed further than ever they were in any nation. An absolute and unbounded scope is given to enquiries of all kinds; and the consequence of this has been, that the greatest improvements have been made in all the sciences, and that we are now become the Fountain-head of knowledge and the Instructors of the world.[53]

Price called upon his audience to be all the more motivated to continue working for improvement out of appreciation for this privileged situation. Whilst Priestley assumed infinite progress, Price's optimism was rooted in his millenarian hope that progress could soon bring a 'general amendment in human affairs' – progress in knowledge, rational religion, and free government would sound the bell for the return of the Messiah.[54] After the American Revolution, Price's confidence would give way to a rather fierce radical criticism, even though he never abandoned his optimistic belief in progress.[55]

Where Priestley and Price sketched the rough outlines of a philosophy of state oriented towards the public good and progress, Jeremy Bentham (1748–1832) unfolded a systematic critique of conventional constitutional ideas. As a young student, Bentham had attended Blackstone's lectures in Oxford. Inspired by Priestley's *Essay on the First Principles of Government,* Bentham started working on a systematic refutation with the working title 'A Comment on the Commentaries' in 1774.[56] In 1776, he anonymously published a part of it, the *Fragment on Government,* which exclusively treats the introduction of Blackstone's *Commentaries* to disprove it paragraph by paragraph. Bentham meticulously exposed a lack of conceptual clarity

2008), 113–43.

53 Richard Price, 'Britain's Happiness, and the Proper Improvement of it', in David O. Thomas (ed.), *Richard Price: Political Writings,* (Cambridge, 1991 [1759]), 1–13, p. 5.

54 Jack Fruchtman, 'The Apocalyptic Politics of Richard Price and Joseph Priestley. A Study in Late Eighteenth-Century English Republican Millennialism', *Transactions of the American Philosophical Society,* 73:4 (1983), 1–125.

55 See chapter 2.

56 Bart Schultz, *The Happiness Philosophers. The Lives and Works of the Great Utilitarians* (Princeton, 2017), pp. 66–78; J. H. Burns and H. L. A. Hart, 'Introduction', in id. (eds.), *A Comment on the Commentaries and a Fragment on Government* (1977), xix–li, pp. xix–xxviii.

and accused Blackstone of obscuring deep inconsistencies in his argumentation. Worse still, Bentham depicted Blackstone as a fabulist, trading in fictions in order to vindicate the status quo. For instance, Bentham refused the idea of a philosophical state of nature and the original contract as one such unfounded fiction.

There was no space for an ancient constitution origin in Bentham's reasoning. In fact, he even stripped the constitutional system that legitimised legislation of its own foundation. The *Fragment* was a theoretical critique and not a revolutionary pamphlet. Although it dismantled Blackstone's reasoning and, potentially, the validity of the whole legal system, the *Fragment* hinted at a solution. It was here that Bentham introduced the principle of utility – 'the greatest happiness of the greatest number that is the measure of right and wrong'[57] – as a conceptual silver bullet to solve all the problems he pointed to. While Bentham acknowledged that the principle of utility had been employed before – for example, by Hutcheson, Hume, or Priestley –, he lamented with how 'little method and precision [...] the consequences of this fundamental axiom [... have] been as yet developed.'[58] Improvement of the legal system, according to Bentham, needed a systematic critique of the whole code, absolute conceptual clarity, and a science of legislation strictly based on the principle of utility.[59]

When the *Fragment* appeared, commentators speculated about the identity of its anonymous author. As it became clear that the *Fragment* was the work of a yet nondescript young writer, the attention ebbed away. Later on, Bentham and other self-styled utilitarians exerted a massive influence on ideas of the functional state and administrative reform in particular – especially from the 1830s onwards. In the 1770s, Bentham's early writings were located on the extreme fringes of the discourse. They show just how radical a scientific perspective on the state could be conceived at the time. However, Bentham's initial impact was very limited. The *Fragment* certainly did not shake the constitutional consensus or Blackstone's reputation as its foremost interpreter.

57 Jeremy Bentham, 'A Fragment on Government', in James H. Burns and H. L. A. Hart (eds.), *A Comment on the Commentaries and a Fragment on Government* (London, 1977), 393–501, p. 393.

58 Ibid.

59 Ibid., pp. 415–16.

Scottish Political Economy

Long before Jeremy Bentham and other utilitarians defined utility as the all-important benchmark for their theories, other authors searched for useful and immediately applicable solutions in a variety of contexts. In the second half of the eighteenth century, the discipline most directly concerned with questions of practical improvement for the public good was the nascent political economy. Political economy focused on public resources and the regulations of social interaction and was therefore concerned with many particular topics that had hitherto been addressed in practical terms only. Its key question became how to regulate the life, trade, and interaction of citizens and external agents in order to maximise the public good. While legal discussions of legislation asked for formal clarity, and sometimes for effectiveness of laws, political economy strived for practical utility.[60]

Phenomena that we now classify as 'economic', such as currency, taxation, trade, and industry, loomed large for eighteenth-century political economy, but only as particular issues among others within a much wider subject area. This subject area encompassed all interactions among people and the consequences of these interactions, as well as the public policies that could improve these interactions for the public good.[61] In this larger sense, political economy also cut across the field that was summarised as 'police', as political economy concerned itself with municipal concepts of ordered communal life and the institutions devised to grapple with its challenges: hospitals, poor houses, crime fighting, and the handling of convicts.[62]

From the sixteenth century onwards, the term 'oeconomy' became widely used in English, and has since denoted a variety of meanings.[63] Starting in the seventeenth century, one of the most common usages of the term signified frugality. Oeconomy referred to the stewardship of resources, especially in the context of the household – *oikos* – consisting of a family and its servants and estates. Oeconomy was closely connected with the realm of agriculture and pointed towards the 'activity of preserving and sustaining, rather than getting and spending'.[64] In the seventeenth century, the household in question was increasingly associated with all of creation, i.e. with nature, for which God acted as the ideal manager. As a consequence,

60 Hume, *Bentham and Bureaucracy*, p. 32.

61 Margaret Schabas, *The Natural Origins of Economics* (Chicago, 2005), pp. 1–5.

62 Hume, *Bentham and Bureaucracy*, pp. 32–5.

63 For a thorough conceptual history of economy cf. Keith Tribe, *The Economy of the Word. Language, History, and Economics* (Oxford, 2015).

64 Ibid., p. 28; Schabas, *Natural Origins*, pp. 1–21.

oeconomy became a key term for natural philosophy and natural history in the first half of the eighteenth century, with characteristic coinages of terms such as 'animal oeconomy', 'body oeconomy', or the 'oeconomy of love'.[65] From the middle of the eighteenth century, 'oeconomy' or, increasingly, 'economy' became a key term for enlightened discourses in reference to many spheres of human activity, particularly on society and the state. Even while the meaning of (o)economy was still broad, its increased usage mirrored a heightening of focus on questions of resources and the means of their organisation that was so profound that it warrants the designation as an 'economic turn'.[66]

Many important impulses for the methodological advancement of political economy originated with Scottish thinkers. Scottish universities emancipated themselves from ecclesiastical dominance and became centres of innovative erudition, unrivalled by their English counterparts. Moreover, questions of disparate economic and societal development appeared particularly urgent in a country in which the cities contrasted sharply with rural areas, where wheeled carriages were still considered rare technical wonders. The goal of practical improvements led Scottish savants from moral philosophy to a distinct form of empirical political economy that Enlightenment thinkers across Europe recognised and often admired. Scottish writings also had an inestimable advantage for reception in England: they were available in English, allowing for a much wider audience than even books in French could muster.[67]

Eighteenth-century political economy emerged from natural philosophy and moral philosophy and initially retained a wide scope. A key figure in this history was David Hume, who contributed strongly to the development of political economy by subjecting social phenomena to rigid philosophical analysis. Hume's works cover a wide range of subjects. He wrote on epistemology, moral philosophy, history, political theory, as well as economics. For Hume, many of these fields were just different aspects of an all-encompassing science of man, which addressed the natural realm as well as the

65 'economy, n', *OED*.

66 Steven L. Kaplan and Sophus A. Reinert, 'The Economic Turn in Enlightenment Europe', in Sophus A. Reinert and Steven L. Kaplan (eds.), *The Economic Turn: Recasting Political Economy in Enlightenment Europe* (London, 2019), 1–33.

67 John Robertson, 'The Scottish Contribution to the Enlightenment', in Paul Wood (ed.), *The Scottish Enlightenment. Essays in Reinterpretation* (Rochester, 2000), 37–62; Hugh Trevor-Roper, 'The Scottish Enlightenment', *Blackwood's Magazine*, 322 (1977), 371–88.

moral realm.[68] Hume presupposed a fundamentally constant human nature that was, however, subject to historically changeable circumstances. Building on the work of Isaac Newton (1642–1727), whom he regularly cited, Hume maintained that it was possible to understand the natural and moral principles that drive human nature and, from that, deduce explanations of human behaviour. Human nature was undeniably a very complex natural phenomenon, and this complexity made its explanation a demanding task; to Hume, such difficulties did not make it less promising to study human nature than to study the weather, which also, at first, seemed too complex to predict.[69] Moreover, Hume's science of man pursued utilitarian goals. He aimed at utility, at improving the happiness of society.[70]

In his influential essays, Hume applied Newtonian science to the moral realm. His *Essays, Moral and Political,* published across 1741 and 1742, contained the aforementioned methodological key article *That Politics may be reduced to Science,* and treated constitutional questions along with moral themes such as avarice and love. A decade later, in his *Political Discourses* of 1752, Hume broadened the scope of his science of man even further. In its first essay, *Of Commerce,* he propounded his methodological creed and anticipated the objection that a scientific approach was not suited to economical topics:

> I thought this introduction necessary before the following discourses on commerce, money, interest, balance of trade, &c. where, perhaps, there will occur some principles which are uncommon, and which may seem too refined and subtile [sic] for such vulgar subjects. If false, let them be rejected: But no one ought to entertain a prejudice against them, merely because they are out of the common road.[71]

Just as he had opened up constitutional and political subjects to Newtonian reasoning in *That Politics may be reduced to Science,* here he explicitly included economical subjects in his science of man. Hume was conscious of breaking new ground and he justified this step by expounding the different properties of 'particular deliberations' and 'general reasoning'. Analysing social phenomena by means of particular deliberations might well fail in

68 This is not to say that Hume's work formed a perfect unity or followed a prearranged masterplan. For a critical discussion of this question, cf. James A. Harris, *Hume. An Intellectual Biography* (Cambridge, 2015), pp. 2–14.

69 Schabas, *Natural Origins*, pp. 58–78.

70 Rosen, *Classical Utilitarianism*, pp. 29–57.

71 David Hume, 'Of Commerce', in Eugene F. Miller (ed.), *Essays, Moral, Political, and Literary* (Indianapolis, 1987), 253–67, p. 255.

the face of the complexity of human interaction, but Hume branded those who confined themselves to particular deliberations as 'shallow' thinkers, unable to discern the general principles occurring in different particulars.[72] The derivation of general principles and the development of sound theorems required subtlety and exact reasoning:[73]

> the difference between a common man and a man of genius is chiefly seen in the shallowness or depth of the principles upon which they proceed. [...] [H]owever intricate they may seem, it is certain, that general principles, if just and sound, must always prevail in the general course of things, though they may fail in particular cases; and it is the chief business of philosophers to regard the general course of things. I may add, that it is also the chief business of politicians; especially in the domestic government of the state, where the public good, which is, or ought to be their object, depends on the concurrence of a multitude of causes.[74]

Hume implied that general reasoning leading to scientific principles, even in the field of economic activity, had a great potential for practical governance. Hume thus drew the boundaries for a science of government and rendered a synthesis of its many related phenomena feasible. After the publication of the *Political Discourses*, Hume focused on writing his seminal *History of England*; but he left the economical synthesis to others.[75]

By 1780, two seminal works had been published in English which delivered on Hume's aspiration: James Steuart's *Inquiry into the Principles of Political Oeconomy* (1767) and Adam Smith's *Wealth of Nations* (1776). Steuart's pioneering *Political Oeconomy* was well received and widely available, and it remained an essential textbook until the end of the century, despite the fact Adam Smith's *Wealth of Nations*, published a decade later, refuted many of Steuart's ideas without ever mentioning him.[76] For the most part, later historians of the two works concentrated on their role in a prehistory of classical economics. Nineteenth-century economics heroised Smith as its founding figure and discounted Steuart as the last

[72] Ibid., pp. 253–4.
[73] Ibid., p. 254.
[74] Ibid.
[75] Harris, *Intellectual Biography*, pp. 269–82, 302–4.
[76] Gary M. Anderson and Robert D. Tollison, 'Sir James Steuart as the Apotheosis of Mercantilism and His Relation to Adam Smith', *Southern Economic Journal*, 51:2 (1984), 456–68, pp. 464–7.

'mercantilist'.[77] Steuart was the intellectual opponent Smith actively tried to prevail over, but once we draw back this epistemological curtain, it becomes clear that the two works have more in common than not.[78] Both Steuart and Smith presented political economy as a science that concerns the resources of the state from the perspective of the (hypothetical) 'statesman or legislator'. Both developed principles on a wide empirical basis and urged politicians to make use of them in practical policies. Smith's work is arguably more elegant. Its organisation is rigidly systematic; it not only aims at clarity, but also readability. In contrast, Steuart's style is more unwieldy and he discloses a caution that borders on insecurity, while meticulously developing his principles.[79] Steuart provided a fresh perspective on the functioning state, creatively processing continental influences; and whilst the cautious approach may have hampered casual reading, it delivered a very accessible methodology.

Steuart composed the first two volumes of his *Political Oeconomy* whilst staying in Tübingen. Due to a Grand Tour and, later on, prolonged exile as a Jacobite, he spent many years on the continent, during which he learnt several languages, met contemporary savants, and acquainted himself with *Staatswissenschaften* and other strands of continental thinking.[80] His approach to political economy drew on these experiences and shows a rather Aristotelian perspective on the state, which was more common in mainland Europe than in Britain:

77 Cf. Donald Winch, 'Scottish Political Economy', in Mark Goldie and Robert Wokler (eds.), *The Cambridge History of Eighteenth-Century Political Thought* (Cambridge, 2006), pp. 443–9; Knud Haakonssen, *The Science of a Legislator. The Natural Jurisprudence of David Hume and Adam Smith* (Cambridge, 1981); John G. A. Pocock, 'Political Thought in the English-Speaking Atlantic, 1760–1790. Part 2: Empire, Revolution and the End of Early Modernity', in id., *The Varieties of British Political Thought, 1500–1800* (Cambridge, 1993), 283–317, pp. 291–4.

78 Cf. Anderson and Tollison, 'Apotheosis of Mercantilism'; Salim Rashid, 'Smith, Steuart, and Mercantilism: Comment', *Southern Economic Journal,* 52:3 (1986), 843–52.

79 Noboru Kobayashi, 'On the Method of Sir James Steuart's Principles of Political Economy', in Ramón Tortajada (ed.), *The Economics of James Steuart* (London, 1999), 102–20, pp. 103–4; T. W. Hutchison, *Before Adam Smith. The Emergence of Political Economy, 1662–1776* (Oxford, 1988), p. 337.

80 Keith Tribe, 'Cameralism and the Sciences of the State', in Mark Goldie and Robert Wokler (eds.), *The Cambridge History of Eighteenth-Century Political Thought* (Cambridge, 2006), 525–46, pp. 545–6; Andrew S. Skinner, 'Introduction. Sir James Steuart and the Jacobite Connection', in Ramón Tortajada (ed.), *The Economics of James Steuart* (London et al., 1999), 1–23.

> Oeconomy in general is the art of providing for all the wants of a family, with prudence and frugality. [...] What oeconomy is in a family, political oeconomy is in a state: with these essential differences however, that in a state there are no servants, all are children. [...] The principal object of this science is to secure a certain fund of subsistence for all the inhabitants, to obviate every circumstance which may render it precarious.[81]

Steuart elaborated on the transfer of the private household to the public household (in other words, the state), and focused on the 'statesman or legislator' as *pater familias*. In this sense, political economy had been discussed in continental Europe for a long time. In the German territories, an extensive body of economical writings, the *Hausväterliteratur*, systematically developed this neo-Aristotelian transfer of the household to the state from the early eighteenth century onwards, within the increasingly institutionalised setting of cameralism.[82] In German writings, the loanword 'Oeconomie' indubitably designated a practical science; 'Oeconomie' was distinguished from the German word 'Wirtschaft' that was used for practical husbandry.[83] The vast body of continental literature had little impact in Britain, not least due to language barriers.[84] However, the publication of Steuart's *Principles* in 1767 led to a surge in interest in continental political economy. A number of translations of continental works were translated into English around 1770.[85]

81 James Steuart, *An Inquiry into the Principles of Political Oeconomy*, ed. by Andrew S. Skinner (Edinburgh, London, 1966 [1767]), vol. 1, pp. 15–17.

82 Keith Tribe, 'Cameralism and the Science of Government', *Journal of Modern History*, 56:2 (1984), 263–84.

83 Tribe, *Economy of the Word*, pp. 32–5.

84 Tribe, 'Cameralism', pp. 545–6.

85 Cesare Beccaria's economical treatise of 1768 appeared the following year in translation as *A Discourse on Public Oeconomy and Commerce*, published in London. Jacob Friedrich Bielfeld's works may have been more accessible, as Bielfeld mostly wrote in French. His pertinent *Institutions Politiques*, although not translated, must have been known to a considerable English speaking readership around 1770; a London edition of his letters and a translation of his *Érudition universelle*, both published in Dublin, praised Bielfeld as the author of 'the political institutes': Jacob F. Bielfeld, *Letters of Baron Bielfeld. Secretary of Legation to the King of Prussia [...] &c. Author of the Political Institutes* (London, 1770); Jacob F. Bielfeld, *The Elements of Universal Erudition [...] By Baron Bielfeld, Secretary of Legation to the King of Prussia [...], Author of the Political Institutes, &c.* (Dublin, 1771). The latter work also touches on economical topics. Both works, though by different publishers, share the same translator, W. Hooper.

Steuart delineated the scope and subject matter of political economy in a deliberately methodical way, with a pronounced awareness of the tension between theory and practice. His emphasis on methodological reflection shows a deep distrust of enclosed philosophical systems, which, he felt, were prone to oversimplification. The tension between this perceived danger and the need to develop sound and usable principles pervades the whole work, from the very first sentence of the preface: 'It is with the greatest diffidence that I present to the public this attempt towards reducing to principles, and forming into a regular science, the complicated interests of domestic policy.'[86] Essentially, Steuart shared Hume's conviction that it was possible, desirable, and promising to approach policy matters scientifically. A scientific approach regarded the objects of domestic policy as a system, identified the system's central principles, and determined their connections. Yet, in order to produce results that could inform practical policy issues, Steuart highlighted the necessity of the utmost caution in the establishment of principles, and encouraged restraint in philosophical reasoning. Reflection, to him, built on observation; experience and reason needed to converge:

> [This inquiry] goes little farther than to collect and arrange some elements relating to the most interesting branches of modern policy, such as population, agriculture, trade, industry, money, coin, interest, circulation, banks, exchange, public credit, and taxes. The principles deduced from all these topics, appear tolerably consistent; and the whole is a train of reasoning, through which I have adhered to the connection of subjects as faithfully as I could: but the nature of the work being a deduction of principles, not a collection of institutions, I seized the opportunities which my reasoning threw in my way, to connect every principle, as I went along, with every part of the inquiry to which it could refer.[87]

Steuart's method is historical, in the sense that it considers economic phenomena as rooted in a spatially and temporally changeable socio-historical reality; historicity and empiricism are just two sides of the same coin.[88] Steuart observed that the 'modern' – an adjective he frequently used – circumstances were fundamentally different and much more complex than those of former times. Like many political thinkers, he likened

[86] Steuart, *Political Oeconomy*, p. 3.

[87] Ibid., pp. 6–7.

[88] Robert Urquhart, 'Steuarts Method. Aristotelian Political Economy', in Ramón Tortajada (ed.), *The Economics of James Steuart* (London, 1999), 121–36, pp. 124–8.

modern governments to machines. His point was, however, that governments had become such complex machines that they were in constant need of supervision to avoid breaking down:

> It is of governments as of machines, the more they are simple, the more they are solid and lasting; the more they are artfully composed, the more they become useful; but the more apt to be out of order. The Lacedaemonian form may be compared to the wedge, the most solid and compact of all the mechanical powers. Those of modern states to watches, which are continually going wrong; sometimes the spring is found too weak, at other times too strong for the machine; and when the wheels are not made according to a determinate portion [...] they do not tally well with one another; then the machine stops, and if it be forced, some part gives way; and the workman's hand becomes necessary to set it right.[89]

The very complexity that characterises modern governments and makes them 'useful' also makes them vulnerable to defects. Reversely, not only did Steuart deem it possible to intervene in the workings of the system of government, he deemed it imperative.

Steuart encouraged the maintenance and active improvement of the state and government. However, his methodological restraint kept him from choosing the method of improvement that, to many of his contemporaries, followed logically from such an assessment: if complexity was the cause of the problems, was the consequent solution not to be found in simplification? Étienne Bonnot de Condillac (1714–80) argued in his influential *Traité des Systèmes* (1749) that 'a system is more perfect as the principles are fewer in number: it is even to be hoped that they could be reduced to one'.[90] Steuart conceded that complexity could be problematic. However, in his empirical view, an adequate system of governmental practice needed to reflect the inherent complexity of modern reality, because abstract hypothetical theories often missed their mark:

> Let theorists, therefore, beware of trusting to their science when in matters of administration, they either advise those who are disposed blindly to follow them, or when they undertake to meddle in it themselves. An old practitioner feels difficulties which he cannot reduce to

[89] Steuart, *Political Oeconomy*, vol. 1, p. 217.

[90] Quoted in Richard Olson, 'The Human Sciences', in Roy Porter (ed.), *Eighteenth-Century Science* (Cambridge, 2016), 436–62, p. 439; cf. ibid., pp. 437–40.

> principles, nor render intelligible to every body; and the theorist who boldly undertakes to remedy every evil, and who foresees none on the opposite side, will most probably miscarry, and then give a very rational account for his ill success. A good theorist, therefore, may be excellent in deliberation, but without a long and confirmed practice, he will ever make a blundering statesman in practice.[91]

Here, too, Steuart's approach reveals its Aristotelian core. Steuart aimed at *phronesis*: the explicitly practical form of deliberation that suits politics and ethics.[92] Throughout his work, Steuart takes the perspective of the 'statesman or legislator'. This omnipresent figure stands in for the unspecified seat of sovereignty in a state: 'The statesman [...] is a general term to signify the legislature and supreme power of government.'[93] At the same time, this figure also idealises the kind of policy maker Steuart aspires to address: not a philosopher-king, but an enlightened statesman with extensive practical experience, who disinterestedly aims for the public good.

Steuart based his work on his personal experience of the regional varieties of state policies that he observed during his travels. He stressed the need to always consider particular contexts, as well as the 'circumstances and spirit of the nations'.[94] What seems like a severe limitation on the utility of political economy turns out to be the springboard for its potential impact. The statesman informed by political economy was not just able to maintain and slightly modify historically determined institutions. Rather, if he were aware of both the principles and the specific contexts, he would be able to remodel the institutions and guide the opinions of the subjects:

> The great art therefore of political oeconomy is, first to adapt the different operations of it to the spirit, manners, habits, and customs of the people; and afterwards to model these circumstances so, as to be able to introduce a set of new and more useful institutions. [...] It is the business of a statesman to judge of the expediency of different schemes of oeconomy, and by degrees to model the minds of his subjects so as to induce them, from the allurement of private interest, to concur in the execution of his plan.[95]

91 Steuart, *An Inquiry into the Principles of Political Oeconomy*, p. 73. The section containing the quote is not reproduced in Skinner's edition of Steuart's work.

92 Urquhart, 'Steuart's Method', pp. 123–4.

93 Steuart, *Political Oeconomy*, p. 16. Cf. Kobayashi, 'Method'.

94 Steuart, *Political Oeconomy*, pp. 5–6.

95 Ibid., pp. 16–17.

As Steuart envisioned it, political economy provided the scientific groundwork for rational policy makers. He explicitly conceptualised theory as a means to improve practice by expediently adjusting policies to the intricacies of social reality.

More explicitly than his predecessors, Steuart designed a perspective that focused on the functioning state.[96] Like no other author of his time, he offered a methodological toolkit for a consciously rational approach to institutional practice that was not confined to a narrow field of financial and economic policy. Adam Smith also subscribed to this functional and systematic view on the state. However, Smith's essayistic masterpiece emphasises the need to consider the pressing questions of economic policy more than it encourages methodological deliberations. While the *Wealth of Nations* caused a stir, the initial debates it fuelled mostly revolved around the benefits and disadvantages of free trade.[97] The administrative reformers of the early 1780s could find more hands-on tools in Steuart's *Principles*.

96 Cf. Urquhart, 'Steuart's Method', pp. 126–31.

97 Richard F. Teichgraeber III, '"Less Abused than I had Reason to Expect". The Reception of The Wealth of Nations in Britain, 1776–90', *Historical Journal*, 30:2 (1987), 337–66.

2
Corruption, Crown Influence, and Reform

The initial impetus for administrative reforms arose in the winter of 1779/80 from a sense of general crisis. The almost constant warfare of the eighteenth century had caused the tax burden and national debt to skyrocket, and the American War of Independence further added to that strain. Fighting a war on the other side of the world was an unprecedented logistical and financial challenge for the already struggling fiscal-military state. As a civil war, it was also an unprecedented ideological challenge for the government and the Crown. The resisters' arguments resonated with the public in England and added momentum to opposition interests in Parliament. The arguments resonated even more with radicals outside of Parliament who, since the 1760s, had increasingly organised themselves into political societies and associations. That the public offices were becoming a political issue was due to the dire financial and logistical situation and it followed from ideological polarisation. The topic was brought up by the extra-parliamentary Yorkshire Association Movement, which hoped to use the administrative deficits as a lever to pressure for tax cuts and parliamentary reform. The opposition in Parliament took the issue up and launched a fierce attack against the ailing ministry of Lord North.

Public offices added focus to a discourse on corruption that had been a constant feature of the political debate since George III ascended to the throne in 1760. Debates revolved around the 'corrupt influence of the Crown', i.e. the idea that the country was in the clutches of a corrupt power elite that was shamelessly enriching itself at the expense of the general public. This, critics argued, was driving the country to ruin and deliberately undermining the liberal constitution – under the leadership of a King who was suspected of despotic ambitions. The perception of crisis added to the plausibility of such arguments, and the government came close to dissolution. By instating the Commissioners for Examining the Public Accounts in the spring of 1780, the ministry held out the prospect of reforms in order to gain some breathing space. It succeeded in temporarily diverting attention from the even more dangerous issue of parliamentary reform.

Corruption is an ambiguous concept that has been around since antiquity, with ever-changing emphases. Two interconnected meanings of corruption can be discerned. The first meaning focuses on individual corruption: bribery, embezzlement, any abuse of a public position – be it a mandate or an office – for personal enrichment. In the early modern period, this personal corruption was understood as a deficit of (political) virtue. The yardstick had not primarily been the execution of offices, whose duties were seldom clearly defined. The central bone of contention was rather the exercise of patronage: the allocation and distribution of offices, pensions, titles, and contracts. Patronage was a central structural mechanism of premodern statehood. It allowed the integration of political elites and the reward for political loyalty through status and, above all, economic security. Recent historical research on corruption has shown that corruption should be understood primarily as an ascription. In social life, many competing norms had to be fulfilled; a balancing act that could never succeed entirely. Patronage created networks based on personal loyalties and dependencies. Since individual advantages and personal connections were thus always in evidence, the exercise of patronage was invariably susceptible to accusations of corruption. There was simply no clear standard for the regularity of appointments. Whether someone was considered corrupt was often a question of the degree of enrichment, the publicity of their actions, and their general reputation.[1]

The second meaning of corruption refers to collective or constitutional degeneration. In this sense, corruption is closely linked to the idea of the constitutional cycle that originated in antiquity. According to this notion, a monarchy would inexorably deteriorate into despotism sooner or later. The underlying constitutional theory gained urgency in the discussions concerning the 'mixed' English constitution in the aftermath of the Revolution of 1688. According to arguments made by opposition groups, the balance of the mixed constitution was threatened by growing corruption and had to be guarded vigorously. This concern about corruption as

1 Bruce Buchan and Lisa Hill, *An Intellectual History of Political Corruption* (Basingstoke, 2014); Ronald Kroeze, André Vitória, and Guy Geltner, 'Introduction. Debating Corruption and Anticorruption in History', in id. (eds.), *Anticorruption in History: From Antiquity to the Modern Era* (Oxford, 2018), 1–17; Hillard von Thiessen, 'Normenkonkurrenz. Handlungsspielräume, Rollen, normativer Wandel und normative Kontinuität vom späten Mittelalter bis zum Übergang zur Moderne', in Arne Karsten and Hillard von Thiessen (eds.), *Normenkonkurrenz in historischer Perspektive* (Berlin, 2015), 241–86.

constitutional degeneration fed into the discussion of administrative practice in the 1780s.[2]

Patronage, the Civil List, and the 'Corrupt Influence of the Crown'

Public offices were conceptualised as externalised executive functions of the monarch. Formally, all executive power resided with the monarch. As it was impossible for the monarch to perform all their functions in person, they conferred duties and privileges to trusted officials as royal grants. William Blackstone still held up this principle, even though it had little to do with the complex administrative structures of the eighteenth-century state:

> THE king is likewise the fountain of honour, of office, and of privilege: and this in a different sense from that wherein he is stiled the fountain of justice; for here he is really the parent of them. [...] [A]nd the law supposes, that no one can be so good a judge of their several merits and services, as the king himself who employs them. It has therefore intrusted with him the sole power of conferring dignities and honours, in confidence that he will bestow them upon none, but such as deserve them.[3]

After the Revolution Settlement, the monarch's power of personally disposing offices steadily declined. Parliament secured financial supremacy and control over the greater part of the public budget, while the King was left with the Civil List, by far the smaller part of national finances, over which he could exert direct control. The Civil List comprised the Privy Purse and Household expenses, but also the civil government and pension list. The exact amount of the Civil List was negotiated and granted for the lifetime of an individual monarch, who would then dispose of it without further parliamentary interference. This meant that the monarch could, at least in principle, hand out places, sinecures, or pensions at his will.[4]

2 Buchan and Hill, *Political Corruption*, pp. 1–8, 125–54; Eckhart Hellmuth, 'Why does Corruption Matter? Reforms and Reform Movements in Britain and Germany in the Second Half of the Eighteenth Century', in Timothy C. W. Blanning and Peter Wende (eds.), *Reform in Great Britain and Germany: 1750–1850* (Oxford, 1999).

3 William Blackstone, *Commentaries on the Laws of England*, vol. 1 (Oxford, 1765), pp. 261–2.

4 Earl A. Reitan, 'From Revenue to Civil List, 1689–1702. The Revolution Settlement and the "Mixed and Balanced" Constitution', *The Historical Journal*, 13:4 (1970), 571–88; id., 'The Civil List in Eighteenth-Century British Politics. Parliamentary

In the delicate balance of the mixed constitution, this setup was to guarantee the independence of the Crown. In his essay *Of the Independency of Parliament* (1742), David Hume refined this argument. According to him, Crown patronage not only kept the Crown independent; it also served as an effective counterweight to the overwhelming power of Parliament. Hume argued that the power left to the Crown mainly consisted in its executive function, and the exercise of this power required considerable amounts of money. If left unchecked, Parliament would use its financial supremacy as a lever to gradually dominate the executive, thereby unhinging the balance of the constitution:[5]

> the interest of the body is here restrained by that of the individuals, [...] the House of Commons stretches not its power, because such an usurpation would be contrary to the interest of the majority of its members. The crown has so many offices at its disposal, that, when assisted by the honest and disinterested part of the house, it will always command the resolutions of the whole, so far, at least, as to preserve the ancient constitution from danger. We may, therefore, give to this influence what name we please, we may call it by the invidious appellations of corruption and dependence; but some degree and some kind of it are inseparable from the very nature of the constitution, and necessary to the preservation of our mixed government.[6]

Because MPs could hope to profit individually from Crown patronage, Hume argued, they had generally more to gain by constructively supporting the Crown than by trying to undermine its independence. The lure of office subtly stabilised the constitution, as it helped to keep personal ambitions within constructive boundaries.[7]

The establishment of the Civil List constituted a compromise within the post-revolution struggles and was well integrated into constitutional law. Still, the Civil List became a bone of contention whenever it amassed debts that had to be settled by Parliament. This happened five times over

---

Supremacy versus the Independence of the Crown', *Historical Journal*, 9 (1966), 318–37.

5 Hume, David, 'On the Independency of Parliament', in Eugene F. Miller (ed.), *Essays, Moral, Political, and Literary* (Indianapolis, 1987), 42–6, pp. 44–5.

6 Ibid., p. 45.

7 For a systematic description of the various ways patronage was employed see Bourne, *Patronage and Society in Nineteenth-Century England* (London, 1986), pp. 3–47; the classical account on patronage as foundation of the Georgian system is Namier, *The Structure of Politics at the Accession of George III* (London, 1963 [1929]).

the first half of the eighteenth century. Each time, Parliament grudgingly settled the debts.[8] During the reign of George III, however, the Civil List became a highly controversial issue. Contrary to his predecessors, George had accepted a Civil List defined by a fixed sum and not by revenue titles. Because of significant inflation, the Civil List effectively shrank in value and consequently went into arrears over and over again.[9]

After the almost constant quarrels of the seventeenth century, the first half of the eighteenth century had been marked by relative internal stability. Starting in the late 1750s, but especially after the succession of George III (1738–1820) in 1760, the political climate changed. The 1760s were characterised by distrust, quarrelling, and the hardening of positions. In the venomous political atmosphere, the perceived overspending raised questions about the nature and the role of the Crown.[10] The young George III was determined to exercise his constitutional role in a more active manner than his predecessors. To George's resentment, Thomas Pelham-Holles, Duke of Newcastle (1693–1768), won the first general election after George's accession. George all but forced Newcastle out of office in 1762 and scandalised many MPs by installing a Scotsman, his mentor John Stuart, Earl of Bute (1713–92), in his stead. In the so-called 'massacre of the Pelhamite innocents', Bute dismissed many of Newcastle's followers from office and replaced them with 'king's friends', as they were commonly called. This large-scale exercise of the Crown's constitutional right to dispose of state offices caused political upheaval and served as a rallying point for opposition groups which were starting to take on characteristics of modern parties.[11] In the view advocated most forcefully by the Whigs who gathered around Charles Watson-Wentworth, the 2nd Marquess of Rockingham (1730–82),[12] the Crown had abused its patronage powers. In

8 The Civil List debts of Anne, George I and George II needed settling in 1713, 1720, 1721, 1724, and 1747, each time on the scale of roughly £500,000. Robert Bucholz, 'Introduction', in J. C. Sainty and R. O. Bucholz (eds.), *Officials of the Royal Household 1660–1837*, part I, *Department of the Lord Chancellor and Associated Offices* (London, 1997), pp. lxvi–lxx.

9 Earl A. Reitan, 'The Civil List in Eighteenth-Century British Politics. Parliamentary Supremacy versus the Independence of the Crown', *Historical Journal*, 9 (1966), 318–37.

10 John Brewer, *Party Ideology and Popular Politics at the Accession of George III* (Cambridge, 1976), pp. 3–25.

11 Frank O'Gorman, 'The Myth of Lord Bute's Secret Influence', in Karl W. Schweizer (ed.), *Lord Bute: Essays in Re-Interpretation* (Leicester, 1988), 57–81; Brewer, *Party Ideology*, pp. 77–94.

12 S. M. Farrell, 'Wentworth, Charles Watson, second marquess of Rockingham (1730–1782)', *ODNB*.

a direct reversal of Hume's position cited above, Rockingham argued that through this abuse, it was the Crown that threatened the balance of the constitution. While he did not question the prerogative as such, Rockingham argued 'that the spirit of the constitution required, that the Crown should be directed to the exercise of this public duty by public motives, and not by private liking and friendship.'[13] The Crown was bound to the public good and should choose its servants accordingly: a directive that the 'massacre' had, in his view, openly defied. The opposition started branding this alleged abuse of patronage as the 'corrupt influence of the Crown.'

Due to the development of government practice in the first half of the eighteenth century, the term 'Crown' had become ambiguous. In the Revolution Settlement, it had been taken for granted that 'Crown' pointed to the constitutional role of the monarch as the head of the executive. It was the King's government that Parliament aimed to restrict. With the rising importance of cabinet government, the King shared this role with increasingly self-determined ministers, who in turn relied on the administrative structure of their ministries. Ever since, 'Crown' could be used to address either the constitutional role of the monarch, the monarch themselves, or the current ministry. In contrast to the King's sacrosanct person, the constitutional role of the executive could be discussed freely, allowing for stinging criticism.[14] The King could thus be attacked indirectly, even though the old legal maxim still held that 'the King can do no wrong.' Any mistake or misdeed of the Crown was by definition the fault of the King's ministers and their ill advice. This maxim was decisive for opposition politics. Ministers were not only accountable to the King, but also to Parliament, which claimed the duty of scrutinising the government. The idea of a favourite influencing the King without parliamentary check therefore exasperated opposition politicians.[15]

In connection to his critique, Rockingham formulated criteria that the King should heed when choosing officers:

> great talents, great and eminent services to the nation, confidence amongst the nobility, and influence amongst the landed and mercantile interests, were the directions, which the crown ought to observe in the exercise of its right in nominating officers of state.[16]

13 *The Annual Register, or a View of the History, Politicks, and Literature, for the Year 1763* (London, 1764), p. 41.

14 Cf. Peter Jupp, *The Governing of Britain, 1688–1848. The Executive, Parliament and the People* (London, 2006), pp. 3–32.

15 Brewer, *Party Ideology*, pp. 112–36.

16 *Annual Register*, p. 41.

Rockingham's idea of an ideal officer focused on the officer's role within the elites. The ideal officer was someone well-connected and trustworthy, who sported a certain independent power base in the political environment that was built on personal ties. A good officer was a man of proven abilities in a very general sense. This idea of merit also underlies Hume's concept. Public service should merit reward, such as the allocation of a profitable office. This implicit assumption explains the opposition's outcry at the 'massacre': loyal men had been deprived of their merited rewards.

Neither the end of Bute's ministry in 1763 nor Rockingham's own short ministry of 1765–6 could pacify the Whigs' contention that the Crown's influence was corrupting the constitutional balance. What there was of Whig party cohesion was built on this contention that took on characteristics of a conspiracy theory.[17] In 1770, the philosopher and politician Edmund Burke (1729–97), the strategic mind of the Rockingham Whigs, spelled out the notion in his *Thoughts on the Present Discontents* that became a sort of Whig manifesto: 'The power of the Crown, almost dead and rotten as Prerogative, has grown up anew, with much more strength, and far less odium, under the name of Influence.'[18] The Crown, Burke claimed, was using the patronage opportunities of the Civil List to install dependent placemen who would purposefully undermine parliamentary independence, and this threatened the fragile balance of the constitution and could potentially lead to despotism.[19]

Radical Critiques

During the contentions of the 1760s, active out-of-door politics began to take shape. The group of politically informed and involved citizens became much more socially diverse than the previous radical fringe.[20] This development is closely connected to the career and affairs of the radical John Wilkes (1727–97), the *enfant terrible* of British politics in the

17 Ian R. Christie, 'Myth and Reality in Late-Eighteenth-Century British Politics', in id., *Myth and Reality in Late-Eighteenth-Century British Politics and Other Papers* (London, 1970), 27–54.

18 Edmund Burke, 'Thoughts on the Present Discontents', in Paul Langford (ed.), *Party, Parliament, and the American Crisis,* The Writings and Speeches of Edmund Burke, 2 (Oxford, 1981), 241–323.

19 Richard Bourke, *Empire and Revolution. The Political Life of Edmund Burke* (Princeton, 2015), pp. 257–67; Brewer, *Party Ideology*, pp. 240–64.

20 John A. Phillips, 'The Structure of Electoral Politics in Unreformed England', *Journal of British Studies,* 19:1 (1979), 76–100.

1760s and 1770s. Notoriously ugly and an awkward public speaker, Wilkes excelled as a polemical writer.[21] In 1762, after Bute had taken office, Wilkes made full use of this gift in his weekly *North Briton*, excoriating the unpopular Prime Minister and the young monarch.[22] In the famous *North Briton no. 45*, published shortly after Bute's resignation, Wilkes went so far as to call the former premier 'a single, insolent, incapable, despotic minister'. Taking up the issue of ministerial responsibility, he ended on an explicit discussion of the King's executive role:

> The *King of England* is only the first magistrate of this country; but is invested by the law with the whole executive power. He is, however, responsible to his people for the due execution of the royal functions [...] The *prerogative* of the crown is to exert the constitutional powers entrusted to it in a way not of blind favour or partiality, but of wisdom and judgement. [...] The people too have their *prerogative* [...] Freedom is *the English Subject's* Prerogative.[23]

Wilkes' direct attack on the King rests on a confident and rather concrete interpretation of the public good as the decisive yardstick for rulership. He thereby reduced the King to a functionary and claimed a collective prerogative of the people. This was more than the political elite could stomach: Parliament declared the *North Briton* seditious libel and the ministry went after Wilkes.[24]

As it turned out, persecution only served to invigorate Wilkes and his rapidly growing group of followers. In countering the attacks, they managed to change the rules of the game. In a combination of bold polemic and legal action, they succeeded in turning each attack on Wilkes into a grave constitutional issue. For instance, arrest by means of general warrants was abolished as a direct result of legal action following the attempted arrest of Wilkes. To avoid persecution, Wilkes fled to France in 1764. After running up debts, he returned to England four years later and successfully ran for a parliamentary seat in Middlesex. The election was annulled three times, because Wilkes was an outlaw, but he also won the following by-elections three times. The ensuing controversy toppled the Grafton ministry.[25] These

21 Peter D. G. Thomas, *John Wilkes, a Friend to Liberty* (New York, 1996), pp. 13–26.

22 Arthur H. Cash, *John Wilkes. The Scandalous Father of Civil Liberty* (New Haven, 2006), pp. 65–95.

23 John Wilkes, 'The North Briton No. 45, Saturday, April 23, 1763', *The Works of the Celebrated John Wilkes*, vol. 2 (London, [1765]), 227–41, pp. 239–40.

24 Cash, *John Wilkes*, pp. 96–120.

25 Ibid., pp. 165–236.

sketched episodes revealed the potential power of extra-parliamentary politics. For a few years, Wilkes served as a strong symbol for various groups of radicals. The Wilkite craze established new forms of private political organisation, which would play an important role in the political struggles to come. The first of many political societies, the *Society of Gentlemen Supporters of the Bill of Rights*, was founded in 1769 to support Wilkes by covering his debts and supporting his claim to the Middlesex seat.[26]

Wilkite lawyers insisted on the necessity of due process according to the law, in order to prevent favouritism and partial justice. Good governance was to be governance by consent, as the final goal of government was always the public good. Therefore, officers had to account to the public for their actions. These were not revolutionary claims. In relentlessly exposing individual infringements in the press and often taking action against them in court, Wilkites raised public awareness of the regular violations of these standards. They also built on the annoyance that many men of business felt towards Excise and Customs officers who frequently transgressed their already strong legal powers.[27] Together, the many trials and pieces of polemical writing conveyed a plausible picture of ubiquitous corruption and the infringement of liberty rights to the advantage of a small elite which deeply concerned politically-informed citizens, among them many moderates, who did not generally share radical goals or convictions.[28]

Radical writing flourished in the 1770s. With the situation in the American colonies heating up, and finally turning into war in 1775, there was more than enough fuel for conflict.[29] Radicals on both sides of the Atlantic were in close contact and exchanged ideas. The main grievances of the American colonists, such as questions of representation and taxation, also applied to Great Britain. The American radicals' language of reason and natural rights particularly appealed to well-educated urban middle-class circles. Once again, coffee houses and informal clubs were abuzz with philosophical and political debates. The so-called 'Honest Whigs', an informal club

[26] Thomas, *Friend to Liberty*, pp. 109–24; cf. Peter Clark, *British Clubs and Societies, 1580–1800. The Origins of an Associational World* (Oxford, 2000), pp. 94–140.

[27] John Brewer, 'The Wilkites and the Law, 1763–74. A Study of Radical Notions of Governance', in id. and John A Styles (eds.), *An Ungovernable people: The English and their Law in the Seventeenth and Eighteenth Centuries* (London, 1980), 129–71, pp. 130–8.

[28] Ian R. Christie, *Wilkes, Wyvill and Reform. The Parliamentary Reform Movement in British Politics 1760–1785* (New York, 1962), pp. 25–67; Kathleen Wilson, *The Sense of the People. Politics, Culture and Imperialism in England, 1715–1785* (Cambridge, 1995), pp. 206–36.

[29] John Sainsbury, *Disaffected Patriots. London Supporters of Revolutionary America, 1769–1782* (Kingston, 1987).

who met every second Thursday in a London coffee house, became particularly committed to radical causes. The group included luminaries such as Richard Price, Joseph Priestley, the famous republican historian Catherine Macauley (1778–1841), as well as Benjamin Franklin (1706–90), who regularly attended the meetings while he acted as a colonial agent in London. As was the case in other philosophical societies in London, dissenters educated at Scottish universities or dissenting academies formed the largest group among the members. Barred from Oxford and Cambridge, dissenting scientists were eager to find alternative places of scientific exchange. The Honest Whigs started out as a philosophical discussion club and they remained dedicated to science as long as they existed. However, contrary to other philosophical societies, they also engaged in political discussions. Some of the most influential radical writings of the 1770s emerged from this group, notably James Burgh's *Political Disquisitions* (1774/5) and Richard Price's *Observations on the Nature of Civil Liberty* (1776).[30]

Since 1750, the Scottish schoolmaster James Burgh (1714–75) had operated a successful academy in Newington Green, a London neighbourhood dominated by dissenters. Burgh had made a name for himself as a publicist writing on education, self-management, public morals, and politics. His political writing combined a moralist attitude with polemic flair. His *magnum opus*, the *Political Disquisitions*, was an extensive compilation of radical arguments, rather than a philosophically refined system. Burgh reproduced many republican and Country positions; however, he no longer invoked an ancient constitution, but embraced commercial modernity, even as he continued to bemoan the decay of liberties and to deplore licentiousness and corruption. Instead of the independent gentleman of the Country persuasion, Burgh's social ideal was that of the productive citizen or merchant. In addition to the long-established criticism of the electoral system and the demand for shorter parliaments, Burgh complained about the lack of social representation in the House of Commons. Repeatedly, his radical rhetoric invoked class antagonism as he juxtaposed a productive, and therefore virtuous, bourgeoisie and an exploitative landed elite corrupted by luxury.[31] The *Political Disquisitions* mark a shift in the radical criticism of the parliamentary system. To Burgh, Parliament no longer

30 Verner W. Crane, 'The Club of Honest Whigs. Friends of Science and Liberty', *William and Mary Quarterly*, 23:2 (1966), 210–33; Jerome R. Reich, *British Friends of the American Revolution* (Armonk, 1998), pp. 40–9.

31 Isaac Kramnick, 'Republicanism Revisited. The Case of James Burgh', Proceedings of the American Antiquarian Society, 102:1 (1992), 81–98; Martha Zembrowski, 'The Corruption of Politics and the Dignity of Human Nature. The Critical and Constructive Radicalism of James Burgh', *Enlightenment and Dissent*, 10 (1991), 78–103.

appeared as the guardian of liberty threatened by the corrupt influence of the Crown. Rather, in Burgh's eyes, Parliament was itself part of the 'juntocracy'[32]: a willing tool of the landed interest in the hands of greedy idlers, who enriched themselves at the taxpayers' expense.

This shift in perspective also informed Burgh's discussion of placemen. Large parts of the second volume deal with places and pensions in detail – both in a domestic and a colonial context. Burgh took up the argument that placemen undermined Parliament because they lacked independence, but turned the point into a polemical sting: 'Why do we suffer men to sit in the house of commons who do receive alms, that is, *pensions*, and are upon the parish, that is, the nation?'[33] Burgh argued that the political elites had the means to remedy the problems, but were in fact unwilling to apply themselves to the task, because they profited from the *status quo*.

> To make straight what is crooked, [...] is matter of labour, as well as of genius, and ministers love ease better than toil, and the card-table and bottle of *Burgundy* better than reading and thinking. Then they cry out, You must not expect that statesmen should make themselves gally-slaves. Thus even laziness is dragged in as an apology for corruption. And then they pay on and drudge on in the beaten track, and all is well so long as they can hold their places; for their pockets are growing fuller and fuller every day.[34]

To Burgh, pensions and salaried places were fundamentally problematic, not only because of their alleged abuse by the Crown, but because they undermined public confidence in the state and a patriotic sense of duty.

> The salaries annexed to those places, the holders of which do *real* service to their country, naturally lead people to a very wrong way of thinking, *viz.* That we are not obliged to serve our country, unless we be *paid* for our service; whereas, the truth is, that serving our country to the utmost of our power, is [...] our indispensable duty, *previously* to any *emolument* we may expect on that account.[35]

If patriotism and public duty did not suffice to motivate the nobility and gentry for public service, Burgh polemically remarked, the bourgeoisie would be more than willing to step in. As a tongue-in-cheek proposal,

32 James Burgh, *Political Disquisitions. Or an Enquiry into Public Errors, Defects, and Abuses* (London, 1774–5), vol. 1, p. 50.

33 Ibid., vol. 2, p. 60.

34 Ibid., p. 162.

35 Ibid., p. 92.

he suggested putting the high offices out to tender and awarding them to the lowest bidder. After all, the high offices were 'places which any man of common sense and common honesty can fill; the public business being all a mere routine.'[36] This argument constituted a moral critique of the political elite and, *ex negativo*, formulated an ideal of civic virtue: Burgh's ideal statesman acted out of a sense of duty and patriotism, not from a desire for profit.

Burgh formulated a wide array of demands: annual parliaments, true representation, disbanding the standing army in peacetime, the abolition of pensions and sinecures, etc., and he called for a renewal of political virtue and productivity. After 1769, Burgh repeatedly brought up the formation of associations, i.e. bottom-up organisations, which would initiate both a moral and a political renewal, be it as a 'Grand Association' of peers or as an extra-parliamentary opposition of all taxpayers.

A neighbour of Burgh, Richard Price had accepted the pastorate of the Presbyterian chapel at Newington Green in 1758, and they became close friends. Against a backdrop of economic crisis, the Wilkes affairs and the American crisis, Price decided to engage in politics. His *Observations on the Nature of Civil Liberty*, published in the spring of 1776, shared many of Burgh's arguments and, in many cases, brought them together more clearly. The *Observations* show a curious tension between Price's belief in progress and lamentations of decline and impending doom. On the one hand, Price continued to emphasise that Great Britain was a free country that allowed science to flourish. To him, the American Revolution confirmed his millenarian belief in progress. On the other hand, Price expressed the sad conviction that the foundations of Britain's prosperity and liberty were eroding at a threatening pace. He even likened Britain to the Roman Empire falling apart in consequence of its outer expansion and its inner decadence – a popular theme at the time; the first volume of Edward Gibbon's *Decline and Fall of the Roman Empire* appeared in the same year.[37]

Price was especially concerned about state finances, a field in which he boasted exceptional expertise. His *Observations on Reversionary Payments* (1771) had provided the mathematical basis for economically sound life-insurance policies. In the same year, he published his *Appeal to the Public on the Subject of the National Debt*, in which he called for responsible financial

36 Ibid., p. 97.

37 David O. Thomas, *The Honest Mind. The Thought and Work of Richard Price* (Oxford, 1977), pp. 127–150; Henri Laboucheix, *Richard Price as Moral Philosopher and Political Theorist* (Oxford, 1982), pp. 23–7. For Gibbon: Karen O'Brien, *Narratives of Enlightenment. Cosmopolitan History from Voltaire to Gibbon* (Cambridge, 1997), pp. 167–203.

administration and a sinking fund in order to secure public credit.[38] Price took up this theme again in his *Observations on the Nature of Civil Liberty* and invoked the spectre of an imminent collapse of the currency and subsequent national bankruptcy.[39] Against this background, the war in America was not only morally and politically wrong; it was also doomed to failure. In his famous *Common Sense*, published shortly before Price's *Observations*, the former Excise-man Thomas Paine (1737–1809) had made the same point by means of a simple calculation:

> Britain is oppressed with a debt of upwards of one hundred and forty millions sterling, [... and] as a compensation for her debt, she has a large navy; America is without a debt, and without a navy; yet for the twentieth part of the English national debt, could have a navy as large again.[40]

Price evidently thought along the same lines. For him, the enormous national debt posed an existential threat to stability. Moreover, he identified the national debt as the main cause of the increasing tax burden: 'Was there no public debt, there would be no occasion for half the present taxes.'[41]

In the eyes of Price and his fellow radicals, the British state – Crown, government, and Parliament alike – was failing to address the crisis and, thus, their obligation towards the public good. This perception led Price towards a fundamental constitutional critique based on universalistic and utilitarian arguments. From an enlightened point of view, he claimed, it was simply absurd to assume that God would have the bulk of human beings at the mercy of the will of a small circle in order to deal with them as they pleased. Instead, Price assumed an ultimately Lockian social contract and raised demands for popular sovereignty, universal suffrage, and true representation: 'Government is an institution for the benefit of the people governed, which they have the power to model as they please.'[42] Political authority was but a delegated public trust. The people, not Parliament or King in Parliament, were the sovereign:

38 Thomas, *Honest Mind*, pp. 234–59.

39 Richard Price, 'Observations on the Nature of Civil Liberty, the Principles of Government, and the Justice and Policy of the War with America', in David O. Thomas (ed.), *Richard Price. Political Writings* (Cambridge, 1991), 20–75, p. 60.

40 Thomas Paine, 'Common Sense', in Moncure D. Conway (ed.), *The Writings of Thomas Paine: 1774–1779* (New York, 1967), 69–120, p. 102.

41 Price, 'Obervations', p. 60.

42 Ibid., p. 27.

> They [Parliament] possess no power beyond the limits of the trust for the execution of which they were formed. If they contradict this trust, they betray their constituents and dissolve themselves. All delegated power must be subordinate and limited.[43]

This principle of subordination and limitation equally applied to individual officers and public institutions, which always needed to prove their usefulness. Otherwise, they could be dissolved at any time. Price called for a lean state, which should provide security whilst serving improvement and, ultimately, progress. In combination with his criticism of national debt, Price summed up his radical programme in a concise formula: 'In every free state every man is his own Legislator. All taxes are free-gifts for public services.'[44]

The Yorkshire Association Movement

Much to the chagrin of both radicals and Rockingham Whigs, the instalment of Frederick, Lord North (1732–92) as Prime Minister in 1770 had stabilised the highly volatile political situation to a certain degree. The preceding decade had seen six ministries come and go; Lord North would stay in office until 1782. He was not a visionary politician, but he managed to maintain a good working relationship with George III, whilst remaining respected and personally well liked in the House of Commons.[45] This is not to say that the 1770s were a politically quiet decade. There was certainly no dearth of discontent and criticism. Opposition Whigs and radicals alike hounded North's ministry. The aggravation of the American conflict fuelled contention, but the outbreak of the civil war also prompted a patriotic surge that bolstered the government and pushed the radicals to the political margins. Towards the end of the decade the course of the war in the colonies seriously weakened the ministry. The national debt and taxation continued to surge and the hardships became more and more palpable.[46] After the Battle of Saratoga in 1777, alarming news from the war came in regular intervals, especially after the entry of France into the war in 1778 and Spain in June 1779. In that summer, the government struggled to weather the storm of converging crises. A Franco-Spanish invasion fleet came within

43 Ibid., p. 28.

44 Ibid., p. 23.

45 Peter Whiteley, *Lord North. The Prime Minister who Lost America* (London, 1996).

46 Colin Bonwick, *English Radicals and the American Revolution* (Chapel Hill, 1977), pp. 114–49.

sight of Plymouth, whilst in Ireland it seemed as if armed companies, raised against the threat of invasion, would turn against the English government. The ministry came close to dissolution. The opposition within and outside of Parliament were finally ready to attempt another attack.[47]

The chain of events that made the public offices the rallying point of the opposition did not start in Parliament, but in the northern English county of Yorkshire. Here, the politically independent Reverend Christopher Wyvill (1740–1822) directed an extra-parliamentary political movement. Wyvill had been educated in Cambridge and thereafter secured a lucrative position as rector in the Essex parish of Black Notley, but soon left its execution to a proxy. An heir to considerable estates in Yorkshire, it was as a landed gentleman that he became politically active in 1779. Confident, recognisably incorruptible, and enormously productive, Wyvill inspired the support of many among the country gentry. He aimed for a gradual change of the constitutional reality, the cleansing of morals, and a return to the alleged core values of the ancient constitution. These were mostly moderate Country persuasion positions. However, in order to accumulate support, he also drew heavily on the ideas of London radicals, especially on Burgh's *Political Disquisitions.* Wyvill and his close collaborators sent out hundreds of circular letters in order to attract a sizeable number of Yorkshire freeholders to a general meeting. Their goal was to mount a petition, or rather a wave of synchronised petitions from counties throughout England and Wales, in order to convey the impression of general public concern. The result surpassed all expectations. Newspapers both in Yorkshire and in London took up the issue and contrasted reports of ministerial extravagance with the general waning of both trade and landed interest. As a result, more than 600 people attended the general meeting on 30 December 1779 and sanctioned Wyvill's petition text.[48]

The petition opened by pointing out a critical economic situation in Britain. Due to years of war, the national debt and the tax burden had increased considerably, whilst trade, industry, and land rent declined. This description leads up to the petition's main criticism:

[47] Herbert Butterfield, *George III, Lord North and the People 1779–80*, 2nd edn. (London, 1969), pp. 26–177; Frank O'Gorman, *The Long Eighteenth Century. British Political and Social History 1688–1832* (London, 1997), pp. 195–200.

[48] Harry T. Dickinson, 'Wyvill, Christopher (1738–1822)', *ODNB*; Herbert Butterfield, 'The Yorkshire Association and the Crisis of 1779–80', *Transactions of the Royal Historical Society, Fourth Series,* 29 (1947), 69–91, pp. 76–8. Christopher Wyvill, *Political Papers. Chiefly Respecting the Attempt of the County of York,* vol. 1 (York, 1794), p. 4; for the debate see Wyvill, *Political Papers*, pp. 9–40; in newspaper renderings of the proceedings, e.g. the *Gentleman's Magazine*, even that one dissenting vote was omitted. 'Historical Chronicle', *Gentleman's Magazine* (January 1780), p. 42.

> Alarmed at the diminished resources and growing burthens of this country, and convinced that rigid frugality is now indispensably necessary in every department of the State, your petitioners observe, with grief, that, notwithstanding the calamitous and impoverished condition of the nation, much public money has been improvidently squandered, and that many individuals enjoy sinecure places, efficient places with exorbitant emoluments, and pensions unmerited by public service, to a large and still increasing amount.[49]

The deficiencies of the state apparatus – sinecures, disproportionate incomes, and unmerited pensions – served as concrete indicators of the alleged waste. In targeting public offices and officers, the text painted the picture of a state that was corrupted to the core, a state that served as a self-service outlet for its servants.[50] For Wyvill, the corruption of the political elite was evident in the opulence of politicians and led to enormous waste and speculation of public funds: the enrichment of the few on the backs of the many freeholders was weakening the nation.

The petition tied its criticism to the Whig theme of the corrupt influence of the Crown. The King and the government enriched themselves and, worse still, actively subverted the constitutional freedom, '[w]hence the crown has acquired a great and unconstitutional influence, which, if not check'd, may soon prove fatal to the liberties of this country.'[51] Initially, Wyvill had been reluctant to allow party politicians to influence his movement because they belonged to the very elite he sought to criticise. Only after intense discussion with his inner circle did Wyvill add the above sentence at the last minute. Taking up the parliamentary opposition's theme of Crown corruption potentially increased the petition's impact, but also jeopardised the movement's independence.[52]

The petition also called on Parliament to exercise its responsibility for national finances. The petition claimed that, as long as the stated malpractice continued, any raising of taxes 'will be injurious to the rights and property of the people, and derogatory from the honour and dignity of Parliament.'[53] By setting 'the rights and properties of the people' in parallel to 'the honour and dignity of Parliament' the petition issued a challenge to the House of Commons: was Parliament still representing the people or had it

49 Wyvill, *Political Papers*, p. 8.

50 Philip Harling, *The Waning of 'Old Corruption.' The Politics of Economical Reform in Britain, 1779–1846* (Oxford, 1996), pp. 32–6; Hellmuth, 'Why does Corruption Matter?,' pp. 20–1.

51 Wyvill, *Political Papers*, p. 8.

52 Butterfield, 'The Yorkshire Association and the Crisis of 1779–80,' p. 78.

53 Wyvill, *Political Papers*, p. 8.

become an instrument of oppression? The petition concluded on a rather bold demand:

> Your petitioners therefore appealing to the Justice of this Honourable House, do most earnestly request that, before any new burthens are laid upon this Country, effectual measures may be taken by this House, to inquire into and correct the gross abuses in the expenditure of public money; to reduce all exorbitant emoluments; to rescind and abolish all sinecure places and unmerited pensions; and to appropriate the produce of necessities of the State, in such a manner as to the wisdom of Parliament shall seem meet.[54]

Through the petition administrative deficiencies obtained unprecedented importance. The deficiencies became tangible symbols for the perceived crisis of the constitution and society at large. The demand for amendment introduced the situation of the offices as a testable marker for the ministry's willingness for reform. For the next decades, administrative reform would be an issue closely tied to the fiscal situation of the nation, as well as to parliamentary reform as a means to address the crisis of representation.

The political goals of Wyvill and his close circle went far beyond administrative reform or tax cuts. After resolving the petition, Wyvill had the general meeting sanction the establishment of a so-called committee

> to carry on the necessary correspondence for effectually promoting the object of the petition, and to prepare a Plan of an Association on legal and constitutional grounds to support that laudable reform, and such other measures as may conduce to restore the Freedom of Parliament.[55]

With his plan, Wyvill took up James Burgh's idea of an extra-parliamentary association. This association was to consist of deputies from institutionalised freeholder assemblies in the counties. Endowed with 'true' representative legitimacy, the association was to pressure for extensive parliamentary reform, or even to ultimately substitute the House of Commons.[56]

In comparison, the promotion of 'laudable reform' was a rather vague and, arguably, a secondary goal. As it turned out, it would become the legacy

54 Ibid., pp. 8–9.

55 Ibid., pp. 4–5.

56 Butterfield, *Yorkshire Association*, pp. 74–5, 83–4.

of the Yorkshire Association Movement. The petition certainly marks an important moment for the conceptual history of 'reform'. Throughout the eighteenth century, the word most often used to mark active amelioration was 'improvement'. It originally referred to the gradual amelioration of land and kept its positive connotations even as its use widened.[57] 'Improvement' excluded 'innovation', which had negative connotations, as it implied a breach of custom. 'Reformation', too, implied a better past. Its use generally implied that betterment lay in the return to a supposed original moral purity, a notion that was closely connected to the Reformation of the Church. 'Reformation' pointed to the perceived corruption of the morals of the people, and also of government and the governing elites. This changed rather abruptly in the Economical Reform Debates. 'Reformation', or, increasingly, 'reform', soon predominantly meant intentional, future-orientated, and institutional change for the better. In the 1780s, calls for reform often concerned matters of state, most of all parliamentary reform and economical reform, comprising the reform of public finances and public offices. Soon, many other public institutions were discussed in terms of reform, for instance prisons, the police, and the Army.[58]

The petition had struck the right chords. For a while, Wyvill managed to rally both country gentlemen and urban radicals to his cause, including the strong Wilkite base. In the following months, dozens of similar committees sprang up throughout England and Wales, leading to a surge in petitions on a hitherto unprecedented scale. Between February and April 1780, the House of Commons received no less than forty-one petitions, aggregating roughly 60,000 signatures. At first, the movement also made progress with regard to the goal of parliamentary reform. The committees set a date for the constitutive meeting of the national association (11 March) and even reached a basic consensus on their goals: shorter parliaments, more equal representation, and a test of disposition for MPs. As that date drew nearer, however, the movement began to lose its cohesion. One reason for its waning was that the parliamentary opposition took up the movement's

57 Slack, *From Reformation to Improvement*, pp. 77–84; Joanna Innes, '"Reform" in English Public Life. The Fortunes of a Word', in Arthur Burns and Joanna Innes (eds.), *Rethinking the Age of Reform: Britain 1780–1850* (Cambridge, 2003), 71–97; Paul Langford, *Public Life and the Propertied Englishman*, pp. 156–66.

58 Innes, 'Reform', pp. 83–7; id., 'Politics and Morals. The Reformation of Manners Movement in Later Eighteenth-Century England', in Eckhart Hellmuth (ed.), *The Transformation of Political Culture: England and Germany in the Late Eighteenth Century* (Oxford, 1990), 57–118.

momentum and bent it to suit their own goals, but managed to marginalise the aspect of parliamentary reform that hardly suited their interest.[59]

The Economical Reform Debates

The events in Yorkshire in late November 1779 were followed with a keen interest in London from the outset. Early in December, before the general meeting was even advertised, the opposition took up the public concern about administrative deficits and waste of public money. Opposition politicians both supported the movement in their constituencies and tried to influence its direction. Wyvill was reluctant to cooperate too closely, but the parliamentary opposition cultivated close ties to the involved Wilkite circles who had no such qualms. The Rockingham Whigs saw the movement as something to be used for their own ends, but at the same time, to be contained. The Marquess of Rockingham personally attended the Yorkshire general meeting on 30 December and instantly forwarded the text of the petition to London, where Lady Rockingham[60] (1735–1804) distributed it in opposition circles. Wyvill politely thanked the attending MPs, but barred them from direct influence. In many other constituencies, Rockinghamites took central positions, or even initiated the county meetings themselves.[61]

Just as it did beyond Parliament, the movement also led to a closing of ranks within Parliament. The leading voice in the House of Commons was once again Edmund Burke. In the House of Lords, this role fell to William Petty-Fitzmaurice, 2nd Earl of Shelburne (1737–1805), who headed the second largest opposition group. Shelburne and his followers generally supported the Rockinghamites during the debates, even though the two of them had not been on friendly terms personally. Shelburne was close to both the city radicals and some Yorkshire reformers, who accepted him whilst they excluded Rockingham. He corresponded with leading radical

59 Harry T. Dickinson, 'Radicals and Reformers in the Age of Wilkes and Wyvill', in Jeremy Black (ed.), *British Politics and Society from Walpole to Pitt 1742–1789* (Basingstoke, 1990), 123–46; Christie, *Wilkes*, p. 90.

60 Mary Watson-Wentworth, Marchioness of Rockingham, was a political activist in her own right, especially in extra-parliamentary circles and within the inner circle of the Rockingham Whigs. S. M. Farrell, 'Wentworth, Mary Watson, marchioness of Rockingham (bap. 1735, d. 1804)', *ODNB*.

61 Christie, *Wilkes*, pp. 75–7; N. C. Phillips, 'Edmund Burke and the County Movement, 1779–1780', *EHR*, 76 (1961), 254–78, pp. 267–8; Bourke, *Empire and Revolution*, pp. 421–4.

thinkers in Britain and Enlightenment thinkers throughout Europe. With his considerable practical experience of government and economy that he had garnered as First Lord of Trade and Southern Secretary during the Grenville and Pitt ministries in the 1760s, he was one of the few politicians boasting pertinent expertise for the reform issues at hand.[62]

On 15 December 1779, Burke announced a plan 'for public economy and reduction of influence'[63] to be delivered after the Christmas recess. On the same day, Shelburne moved for commitment to a policy of savings and proposed a joint committee of both Houses to enquire into the public expenditure. Several opposition motions followed throughout the winter, pressuring the ministry. The ensuing debate on economical reform turned into one of the fiercest parliamentary battles during the reign of George III. After the winter recess, a constant influx of almost identically worded petitions fuelled the debate.[64] With the ministry still disorganised, many independent members were swayed, allowing for opposition motions to pass. For instance, George Savile (1726–84), the MP most closely linked to the Yorkshire Association Movement, successfully disclosed lists of positions and pensions on 21 February.[65] Despite their differences, the joint opposition presented a united front for the key issue of the corrupt influence of the Crown and reproduced the accusations of the 1760s and 1770s. However, Burke and Shelburne emphasised different aspects of the issue.

Burke gave his seminal address on economical reform on 11 February 1780. The address provided the debates their name and, in many ways, set their tone. Burke proposed 'a plan of reform in the constitution of several parts of the public oeconomy.'[66] His rhetorical strategy was to claim advocacy for the will of the people, while, in reality, he was narrowing the topic down to the key issues of his party. In a rather lofty opening, he claimed

[62] John Norris, *Shelburne and Reform* (London, 1963), pp. 125–9; John Cannon, 'Petty, William, second earl of Shelburne and first marquess of Lansdowne (1737–1805)', *ODNB*.

[63] Edmund Burke, 'Speech on Public Expenses, 15 December 1779', in W. M. Elofson and A. Woods (eds.), *Party, Parliament, and the American War*, The Writings and Speeches of Edmund Burke, 3 (Oxford, 1996), 466–76, p. 474.

[64] Ian R. Christie, 'Economical Reform and "The Influence of the Crown", 1780', in id., *Myth and Reality in Late-Eighteenth-Century British Politics and Other Papers* (London, 1970), 296–310.

[65] John Cannon, 'Savile, Sir George, eighth baronet (1726–1784)', *ODNB*; Parl. Hist., 21, February 1780 to March 1781 (London, 1814), col. 83–104.

[66] Edmund Burke, 'Speech on Economical Reform, 11 February 1780', in W. M. Elofson and A. Woods (eds.), *Party, Parliament, and the American War*, The Writings and Speeches of Edmund Burke (Oxford, 1996), 481–551, p. 483.

to act 'in conformity to the unanimous wishes of the whole nation.'[67] Burke built up a rather enclosed chain of reasoning: the petitions proved a justified demand of the people; Parliament in general and the Rockingham Whigs in particular were the people's legitimate advocates against the potential despotism of ministry and Crown. Burke's own proposals fulfilled the people's just demands. He was 'follow[ing] the sense of the people, [...] pursuing their interest according to [his] own ideas.'[68] The advocacy for the people against the spectre of despotism was a recurring theme in the Rockingham Whig rhetorical canon. Already in the *Present Discontents,* Burke had introduced popular protest as a marker for ministerial misconduct or constitutional aberrations and claimed that the House of Commons was 'the express image of the feelings of the nation.'[69]

Burke's main line of attack directly built on the programme he had set down in 1770. As then, he targeted the Crown, both ministry and King, by calling for the regulation of the Civil List.[70] On 7 December, Richmond had introduced the theme of Civil List regulation in a relatively conciliatory manner. '[R]igid and exact oeconomy' was imperative, and that meant 'a reduction of the civil list expenditure [...] by reforming all useless expences.' Such a reduction, Richmond held, 'would be an example well worthy of his Majesty's paternal affection for his people.'[71] Burke attacked the Civil List far more aggressively. He promised a plan that would reduce expenses, ensure the provident administration of public money, and check incurring debt. Yet, he made it very clear that these were not his main goals.

> But what, I confess, was uppermost with me, what I bent the whole force of my mind to, was the reduction of that corrupt influence, which is itself the perennial spring of all prodigality, and of all disorder; which loads us, more than millions of debt; which takes away vigour from our arms, wisdom from our councils, and every shadow of authority and credit from the most venerable parts of our constitution.[72]

In particular, Burke singled out the King's Household as a 'Gothic establishment,' built upon 'feudal principles' and 'adverse to the living oeconomy of the age.'[73] It was in dire need of reform. Using the example of the Royal

67 Ibid.

68 Ibid., pp. 492–3.

69 Burke, 'Present Discontents,' pp. 255, 292; cf. Bourke, *Empire and Revolution,* pp. 381–5.

70 For the 1770 rendering of the Civil List theme see Burke, 'Present Discontents,' pp. 262–3, 288, 304–8.

71 Parl. Hist, 20, December 1778 to February 1780 (London, 1814), col. 1257–8.

72 Burke, 'Economical Reform,' p. 483.

73 Ibid., pp. 508–10.

Household, Burke elaborated on the method of reform. 'If therefore we aim at regulating the household, the question will be, whether we ought to oeconomize by *detail*, or by *principle*?'[74] This rhetorical question started one of the most polemical parts of the speech. Burke pointed to recent reform attempts of the royal kitchen by Lord Talbot (1710–82) and attributed the failure of the reform to the selfish resistance of high-ranking sinecurists who defied public needs for their personal advantage:

> His whole scheme of oeconomy was dashed to pieces; his department became more expensive than ever;—the civil list debt accumulated—Why? It was truly from a cause, which, though perfectly adequate to the effect, one would not have instantly guessed;—It was *because the turnspit in the king's kitchen was a member of parliament.*[75]

Burke deploys this last sentence as a polemical catchphrase, repeating it several times using the image of the ridiculed parliamentarian-turnspit to condense his depiction of an entirely outdated and absurd system.

Accordingly, Burke drew the conclusion that the only effective way to reform would be to employ 'principles of radical oeconomy'. Such reforms should be enforced on a high level of political authority and draw on the knowledge of experts.[76] Burke suggested abolishing all the offices of the royal kitchen and entrusting the cooking to short-term contractors instead.[77] The key to a successful reform, he claimed, was 'simplification'. Having come to this conclusion discussing the rather marginal royal kitchen, Burke applied the idea to a number of institutions within and beyond the Civil List: the Wardrobe, Jewel Office, the Board of Works, the Mint, the Ordnance, and even the Artillery.[78] He also formulated the principle of central fiscal control by the Treasury – a principle that would prove to be hard to establish.[79]

74 Ibid., p. 511.

75 Ibid., p. 512.

76 Ibid., p. 513.

77 Even though Burke was no friend of James Burgh's ideas, his polemics seem to echo the similarly stinging Court criticism in Burgh's *Political Disquisitons*: 'Cannot our good king have a poached egg for his supper, unless he keeps a purveyor of eggs, and his clerks, and his clerk's deputy-clerks, at the expence of 500 £ a year? While the nation is sinking in a bottomless ocean of debt?' Burgh, *Political Disquisitions*, vol. 2, p. 129. Burgh, too, had suggested putting out Court offices for tender. However, Burgh introduced the idea rather to ridicule the great offices of state rather than to make a serious proposal. Cf. ibid., p. 97.

78 Burke, 'Economical Reform', pp. 513–19.

79 Henry Roseveare, *The Treasury 1660–1870. The Foundations of Control* (London, New York, 1973), pp. 118–82.

In addition to the curtailments proposed in the 'plan of reduction', Burke developed a 'plan of arrangement' for the disbursement of emoluments, in order to prevent the accumulation of Civil List debts. He suggested dividing the Civil List into nine classes according to functions, from the most to the least important, and, inversely, by rank and power. Judges were placed in the first class, whilst the First Lord of the Treasury (the Prime Minister) and the Chancellor of the Exchequer were placed in the ninth class. Payment was to follow this order strictly and only up to the budget voted for in Parliament. Burke argued that this arrangement would encourage the high officers to prevent undue enrichment and the bloating of offices in the lower orders, because their own payment would depend on it.[80]

Burke marked this systematisation, this 'system of economy', as the centrepiece of his plan. This hypothetic system, Burke claimed, would strengthen central functions of the state. It would provide the government with information on the workings and expenditure in the departments and lead to timely accounts without straining the office-holders or infringing on their private (property) rights. Most of all, '[i]t extinguishes secret corruption almost to the possibility of its existence.'[81] Burke's plan mainly advanced the party's agenda and it would prove hard to put into practice. However, for the moment, it set a high benchmark for reform measures.

Shelburne shared many of the Rockinghamites' assumptions, but his speeches typically pointed out deficits more clearly and in a more differentiated manner. In his initial speech on 15 December 1779, for instance, he too castigated the overall economic situation, but specifically pointed towards the vast deficits caused by the Army extraordinaries in the American War, which were an expenditure beyond parliamentary grant, but which the current system could not prevent.[82] In the previous year, Shelburne's friend Colonel Isaac Barré (1726–1802) had argued along similar lines and proposed a 'Committee to enquire into the Public Expenditure' in the Commons.[83] Now, Shelburne forcefully announced his intention to introduce a similar committee. The announcement itself contains a dense summary of the deficits as Shelburne perceived them, as well as a prospective course of action:

80 Burke, 'Economical Reform', pp. 541–5.

81 Ibid., p. 546.

82 Parl. Hist., 20, col. 1291.

83 Parl. Hist. 19, col. 972–80.

> That a committee be appointed, consisting of members of both Houses, possessing neither emolument nor pension, to examine without delay into the public expenditure, and the mode of accounting for the same; more particularly into the mode of making all contracts: and at the same time to take into consideration what savings can be made consistent with public dignity, justice, and gratitude, by an abolition of old or new created offices, or reversion of offices, the duties of which have either ceased, or shall on enquiry prove inadequate to the fees, or other emoluments arising therefrom; or by the reduction of such salaries, or other allowances and profits as may appear to be unreasonable.[84]

Both practices of accounting and contracting were closely connected to the war in North America. The logistics and expenditure necessary to keep forces on the other side of the world in operation dwarfed even the scale of the Seven Years' War. Key officials handled immense sums more or less unchecked, and the enormous contracts obscurely assigned to private enterprises practically invited embezzlement on a large scale. Shelburne opened up a whole range of possible measures for retrenchment, from abolishing or merging offices to the reduction of emoluments. Shelburne, too, was conscious of the offices' property character, but he emphasised the want of detailed information that would allow their assessment on a case-by-case basis.

The main point of the proposed committee was to improve the state of administrative information. When introducing the motion on 8 February 1780, Shelburne claimed that, even with his own considerable expertise, it was impossible to reconstruct the state of finances in the Exchequer, 'because every thing was buried in chaos and endless obscurity'. The first goal of the proposed committee should therefore be to trace any movement of public money, and put the making of accounts 'upon a more clear and simple footing'. Secondly, they were to open up all contracts to competitive bidding. Thirdly, they must abolish all high salaried sinecure places and, fourthly, all offices 'that answered no other end but that of increasing the undue and unconstitutional influence of the Crown.'[85]

The influence of the Crown thus played an important role in Shelburne's reasoning, but it was not the deciding point in the matter. Shelburne carefully introduced the distinction between an originally intended constitutional influence and the unconstitutional influence that, he claimed, it had become. The constitutional influence was the rightful prerogative of

84 Ibid., col. 1293.
85 Ibid., col. 1331.

the monarch to grant promotion based on merit providing an incentive to secure the independence of the Crown. In contrast, the unconstitutional influence favoured 'the unworthy, the servile, and the grovelling', and undermined the independence of Parliament.[86]

Shelburne's more balanced stance did not mean that his and his followers' speeches lacked polemics. Nor did the joint opposition onslaught on the ministry in the Lords fall short of its counterpart in the Commons. The attacks on the ministry, which included charges of 'undue', 'secret', or 'corrupt influence', put the ministry in a defensive position. North's followers invoked the dignity of the monarch and flatly denied the existence of any undue influence. Yet, the opposition increased the polemic pressure insinuating 'a system of corruption, public venality, and despotism, as never before took place in any limited government'.[87]

The contest reached its climax on 6 April, when the Commons concerned themselves with the petitions. The session was dominated by John Dunning (1731–83), a respected lawyer and adherent to Shelburne who had become deeply involved with the Association Movement.[88] Dunning managed to pass a number of motions, the most famous of which is by now almost invariably referred to as 'Dunning's motion': 'It is the opinion of this committee [of the whole house], that it is necessary to declare, that the influence of the crown has increased, is increasing, and ought to be diminished.'[89] With a lead of eighteen votes, the House of Commons thereby endorsed what had been the opposition's core credo for the last decade. Using the momentum, Dunning successfully asserted parliamentary fiscal oversight of the Civil List.

The euphoria of what seemed like a total opposition victory did not last long. Dunning's motion marks the high point of opposition success. Even though the central claims of the opposition had passed, they had not yet been converted into practical measures. The tide was turning.[90] Government supporters at first struggled to invalidate the crisis assessment and the opposition reproaches. Only gradually did North's supporters find a stance. They did not deny the crisis or the necessity of reform in general. Instead, North's tactic was to agree to the general idea, whilst opposing all concrete proposals. North's followers also challenged the opposition's claim of speaking for the people and accused them of exerting influence over the Association Movement. Namely, Burke felt the need to swear upon his honour that he had 'neither interfered directly or indirectly in the

[86] Ibid., col. 1319–20.
[87] Rockingham during the debate on the Shelburne Notion. Ibid., col. 1346.
[88] John Cannon, 'Dunning, John, first Baron Ashburton (1731–1783)', *ODNB*.
[89] Parl. Hist. 21, col. 347.
[90] Bourke, *Empire and Revolution*, pp. 428–30.

county association of York'[91] – a blunt lie that was, however, not exposed in his lifetime.

When North finally found his stance, it seemed to follow on from Shelburne's proposal of an accounts committee. The ministry faction had first blocked Shelburne's proposal in the Lords for formal reasons, stating that it would meddle with the Commons' financial sovereignty.[92] A week later, Barré announced that he would move for a parliamentary committee of accounts in the Commons again. North criticised the idea of a parliamentary committee but hinted at his general willingness to cooperate in order to attain some transparency over accounts and the departments of state. In light of the shared assessment of crisis, it was hard to argue against attempting to get a better grasp of the disclosed problems. Many independents agreed.[93]

Before Barré could introduce his motion, North had finally caught up with the developments and anticipated Barré's move. On 2 March 1780, North announced that he intended to propose a bill to appoint a commission of accounts himself.[94] This was a shrewd move. Whilst he showed that he took the opposition's concern seriously, North introduced an instrument that better suited his own ends. Contrary to Shelburne's and Barré's proposals, he aimed at a commission – not a committee – of accounts. A committee of MPs would have kept the matter under parliamentary control. From the 1640s to the 1710s, Parliament had repeatedly established committees of public accounts to investigate corruption and exercise parliamentary financial control. However, these parliamentary committees were politicised and, in some cases, suspected of being corrupt themselves.[95] North, in contrast, proposed an external expert commission of salaried specialists. He argued that past committees had failed because of their relative lack of authority. The new commissioners would receive extensive competencies in order to check accounts and to develop remedies against the identified deficits.[96]

North caught the opposition off guard. Barré rather sulkily defended the idea of a committee, but to no avail. North officially introduced the motion on 13 March. On 1 May, a bill for the appointment of CEPA followed. The opposition protested every step, but could not do more than criticise the selection of individual commissioners. North had taken back the lead on the issue, and the newly appointed commissioners set themselves to work.[97]

91 Parl. Hist., 20, col. 1382.
92 Ibid., col. 1332–64.
93 Parl. Hist., 21, col. 75–7; Norris, *Shelburne and Reform*, pp. 117–20.
94 Parl. Hist., 21, col. 145–6.
95 For an overview on these committees, cf. Knights, *Trust and Distrust*, pp. 203–10.
96 Ibid., col. 145–9.
97 Ibid., col. 552–70.

3
A System of Economy

From 1780 to 1787, the Commissioners for Examining the Public Accounts produced fifteen reports, filling more than 1,200 large-format pages in the Journals of the House of Commons. The results of the Commissioners' work went well beyond the intended remit of their assignment. Instead of the expected description of particular abuses and accounting deficits, the Commissioners delivered a systematic survey of British public offices. In this survey, public administration appeared as a coherent subject for the first time.

The appointment of the Commissioners was a result of the financial and political crisis, which was exacerbated by the alarming course of the American Revolutionary War. The Economical Reform Debates had exposed serious administrative deficits and a lack of overview of the state's financial administration that was disturbing to an already shaken ministry. In their reports, the Commissioners reacted to this sense of crisis. In their eyes, piecemeal corrections or the exposure of corrupt individuals was not enough. A general reform was needed to resolve the crisis. To work out lasting solutions, the Commissioners made good use of the powers they had received. They examined books and systematically interviewed office-holders under oath. By comparing equivalent departments, they identified best practices. In their inquiries, the Commissioners brought to bear their diverse expertise, which shaped their joint approach and allowed for a perspective that was very different from the perspectives dominating the parliamentary discussion. It is likely that the members with a background in military administration were crucial for the Commissioners' familiarity with the administrative structures. Their expertise was essential for the Commissioners' examination of the logistics of war, especially the in-depth examination of the American War finances. The bankers brought strong mathematical skills to the table, which manifested themselves, for example, in the use of model calculations. Their knowledge of the practicality of cashless financial flows also meant that they were able to rebut spurious arguments made by officers in defence of deficient practices. Building on the expertise of their members from the legal profession, the

Commissioners developed a new definition of office as a public trust and did not shy away from calling into question the property theory of office.

More crucial than the Commissioners' experience in individual areas was their consistent application of a scientific approach. The Commissioners viewed their subject matter as a system, and aimed to derive the principles of this system through methodical empirical surveys. From the fundamental considerations and principles derived from their surveys, the Commissioners developed a 'system of economy'. In the Commissioners' eyes, the offices and processes it comprised could and ought to be understood in conjunction with one another. Understanding the system's principles facilitated the improvement of the system and enabled the Commissioners to propose reforms to solve the state crisis.

This scientific approach cannot easily be explained by the backgrounds of the Commissioners alone. However, it makes sense when read against the backdrop of contemporary discourses, particularly with regard to utilitarian ideas and Scottish political economy. In fact, the methodological and terminological similarities strongly indicate that the Commissioners deliberately drew on Scottish political economy. Just like the Scottish political economists, the Commissioners understood the state as a system of functional institutions, which they then situated in a historically changing social context. By drawing on the methodology of Scottish political economy, the Commissioners developed the foundations of an overall theory of public administration.

An Appointment of Experts

The nomination of candidates was prepared by Charles Jenkinson (1729–1808), the grey eminence among Lord North's inner circle, who was closely advised by the Chief Justice William Murray, Earl of Mansfield (1705–93). Jenkinson's letters to North show a careful consideration of candidates.[1] It was to be expected that the nominated candidates would be closely examined by the opposition. Therefore, the candidates needed to be demonstrably competent and above political suspicion. As Jenkinson quoted Mansfield, 'the Bill either meant to do some real good, or to have the appearance of it.'[2]

1 See the letters of Charles Jenkinson to Lord North of 25 March, 6 May, and 8 May 1780, in BL, Add. Mss. 38307, fols. 153^{r}, 173^{r}, 173^{v}; Reitan, Earl A. *Politics, Finance, and the People. Economical Reform in England in the Age of the American Revolution, 1770–92* (New York, 2007), pp. 63–7.

2 Charles Jenkinson to Lord North, 6 May 1780, in BL, Add. Mss. 38307, fol. 173^{r}. Jenkinson here recounts Lord Mansfield in a private conversation.

When Lord North first presented the ministry's selection of candidates on 1 May 1780 to Parliament for confirmation, he explained that he had deliberately chosen candidates from three different backgrounds, namely the Army, the legal profession, and the mercantile domain, who were 'likely to be the best judges of buying and selling either by contract or otherwise'.[3] North's first choice for a chairman was Thomas Bowlby (1721–95), the Comptroller of Army Accounts, but opposition had vetoed his nomination, because he was both an active officer and an MP.[4] In his stead, North designated Sir Guy Carleton (1724–1808), who had served as a Captain General and Governor-in-Chief of Quebec. He was the most prominent member of the group, but he did not put much effort into the commission's work. In 1782, Carleton returned to North America as commander in chief to organise an orderly retreat of the British forces.[5] The other military man in the commission, James Tierney (died 1782), had been in the Army Pay Office, although no details are documented.[6] The leading voice of the Commissioners and, from 1782, their chairman was Thomas Anguish (1724–85), an equity lawyer and Accountant General at the Court of Chancery.[7] Arthur Piggott (1749–1819) had served as Attorney General in Grenada.[8] Three members represented private business. Both Samuel Beachcroft (died 1796) and Richard Neave (1731–1814) served as directors of the Bank of England and members of the Bank's treasury committee.[9] Beachcroft had been the Bank's governor from 1775 to 1777. Neave made his fortune trading with America and the West Indies, where he owned plantations and slaves. In 1783, Neave, too, was appointed governor of the Bank of England and continued to act as a Commissioner during his term. George Drummond (1758–89), the third member of this group, was a senior partner at Drummond's Bank, a well-established London-based

3 Parl. Hist., 21, col. 553–4.

4 Mary M. Drummond, 'Bowlby, Thomas', in Lewis Namier and John Brooke (eds.), *The House of Commons 1754–1790*, vol. 2 (London, 1964), 108–9.

5 James Sturgis, 'Carleton, Guy, first Baron Dorchester (1724–1808)', *ODNB*.

6 The Lords of the Treasury took note of his death on 6 August 1782. See Treasury minutes, July to August 1782, in WCL, Shelburne Papers, vol. 162.

7 W. S. Holdsworth, *A History of English Law*, vol. 1 (London, 1903), p. 446.

8 R. A. Melikan, 'Pigott, Sir Arthur Leary (1749–1819)', *ODNB*; *The Annual Biography and Obituary. For the year 1822* (London, 1822), pp. 441–3.

9 *The New Annual Register. Or General Repository of History, Politics, and Literature for the Year 1796* (London, 1797), p. 75; Amanda Phillips, 'Neave, Caroline Hannah (1781–1863)', *ODNB*; and: http://thepeerage.com/p6034.htm#i60340 (accessed 20 March 2022).

private bank that was popular among Army agents.[10] When Tierney died in 1783, Anguish nominated William Roe (1748–1826) as Tierney's successor. Roe had recently made a name for himself as a political commentator and quickly became one of the most active Commissioners. Roe's diary, though not very detailed, is a valuable source.[11]

Historians have based different assessments on the Commissioners' backgrounds. John Torrance pointed to a keen rationalism that he ascribed to the influence of equity law. He characterised CEPA as exponents of a 'new, self-conscious national class consciousness' of the rising upper middle class, which placed great emphasis on economy.[12] For Philip Harling, the Commissioners were 'well-connected government insiders', whose ideas represented an intra-governmental discourse shifting towards an ideal of public service.[13] The scarcity of sources pertaining to the Commissioners does not justify such far-reaching interpretations. Their biographies do not sufficiently explain the genesis of the Commissioners' ideas. With the exception of Guy Carleton, the Commissioners were not very prominent, but they were respected and politically independent. Their combined backgrounds mark them as well-educated and experienced professionals, who were able to contribute extensive legal, mercantile, and administrative experience, and had a wide range of contemporary theoretical reasoning at their disposal.

The act instituting CEPA passed on 5 July 1780, shortly before the summer recess.[14] The act defined the Commissioners' initial tasks and competencies. Its full title reads:

> An Act for appointing and enabling Commissioners to examine, take, and state, the publick Accounts of the Kingdom; and to report what Balances are in the Hands of Accountants, which may be applied to the publick Service; and what Defects there are in the present Mode of receiving, collecting, issuing, and accounting for, publick Money; and

10 Anne Murphy, *Virtuous Bankers. A Day in the Life of the Eighteenth-Century Bank of England* (Princeton, 2023), pp. 10–11; Hector Bolitho and Derek Peel, *The Drummonds of Charing Cross* (London, 1967).

11 William Roe, *The Private Memorandums of William Roe of Withdean in the County of Sussex 1775–1809* (Brighton, 1928), i, pp. 4–5; John Binney, *British Public Finance and Administration 1774–92* (Oxford, 1958), pp. 11–12.

12 Torrance, 'Social Class and Bureaucratic Innovation', quote on p. 78.

13 Philip Harling, *The Waning of 'Old Corruption'. The Politics of Economical Reform in Britain, 1779–1846* (Oxford, 1996), pp. 59, 61.

14 JHL 36, 25 November 1779 to 16 October 1783, col. 173.

> in what more expeditious and effectual, and less expensive, Manner, the said Services can in future be regulated and carried on, for the Benefit of the Publick.[15]

The act established public money and its management as the defining points of reference, setting the scope of the inquiry.[16] The Commissioners were expected to provide a clearer picture of public finances and accounting practices. The act acknowledges the poor state of information on public affairs. There was no comprehensive national budget. Rather, whilst Parliament voted on and allocated national finances, their appropriation allotted to a multitude of particular accounts, which were never up to date and were incomprehensible in their entirety.[17] The act expressed the expectation that 'His Majesty, and the People of this Kingdom, may be satisfied and truly informed,' whether or not public money was being 'faithfully issued out, disposed, ordered, and expended.'[18]

The scope of the mandated enquiry is remarkable. It covered the fiscal administration, i.e. Treasury and Exchequer, but also the Army and the Navy, as well as various revenue departments. The act conceptualised public administration in personal terms, as groups of interconnected office-holders, rather than as a structure of offices, institutions or branches. The Ordnance, for example, appeared as '[t]he Master General, Lieutenant General, Surveyor General, and Officers compounding the Board of Ordnance, and all other the Officers dependent upon or under Controul of the said Master General, Lieutenant General, Surveyor General, and Officers compounding the Board of Ordnance.'[19] Other groups were characterised by how they handled public money: 'all Governors, Commissaries, or other Persons having the Power of granting Warrants, or of issuing, disbursing, or expending Money belonging to the Public, or of drawing Bills, or making Contracts, or purchasing Provisions or Stores, or other Necessaries.'[20] No previous enquiry into public finance had come close to such a comprehensive reach. With the noteworthy exception of those at the Royal Household and the judiciary, all officers in 'publick service' could potentially come under investigation.

15 20 Geo III 54.

16 The terms 'public money' and 'public accounts' were widely used since the 1640s. Cf. Mark Knights, *Trust and Distrust. Corruption in Office in Britain and its Empire, 1600–1850* (Oxford, 2021), p. 188.

17 Henry Roseveare, *The Treasury 1660–1870. The Foundations of Control* (London, New York, 1973), pp. 91–3; Binney, *Public Finance*, pp. 244–55.

18 20 Geo III, c. 54, s. 1

19 Ibid., s. 3.

20 Ibid.

The act of appointment mirrored the parliamentary discourse on administrative questions, in which individual corruption loomed large. Officers figure as 'accountants', those who handed in accounts to the Exchequer because they held public money.[21] These accountants' misconduct could seriously burden the financial integrity of their departments. The act explicitly tasked the Commissioners with examining 'any corrupt and fraudulent Practices, or other Misconduct, committed by any Person or Persons concerned in the Management of any [...] Monies.'[22] In addition, the act commanded the Commissioners to identify any defects in the mode of the financial management and actively suggest how to improve procedures – to look for a 'more expeditious and effectual, and less expensive, Manner the said services can in future be regulated and carried on.'[23] Ideally, administration was to become more effective and, at the same time, cheaper; neither of the two conflicting goals was given precedence. This mandate to develop and suggest reform proposals was unusual. Hitherto, the established function of statutory commissions had been confined to the investigation into a limited subject matter.[24]

Since the scope of the Commissioners' inquiries was comprehensive, the act defined a starting point, namely the issue of money in the hands of accountants. This phrase referred to the established practice of officers withdrawing money from the Exchequer early, to only pass it on months later. Officers would use their private bank accounts for the transactions and kept the interest. At times, substantial losses occurred because officers lost public money in private high-risk investments. The political advantages of setting this issue are apparent. It was a well-known problem with a huge potential for retrenchment, but it had not figured in the parliamentary debates yet. Improving on this issue would neither affront the opposition, nor could the opposition claim potential successes for itself.[25]

The act gave the Commissioners extraordinary powers. To start with, the act authorised the Commissioners to request any accounts and any documentation concerning public money. In addition, the act bestowed the Commissioners with the authority to summon officers for interviews and to administer an oath to ensure the respondents would answer truthfully, an authority that had only rarely been granted to a commission.[26] However, it was the combination of powers that truly stood out. No auditing

21 Binney, *Public Finance*, p. 11, n. 3.
22 20 Geo III, c. 54, s. 4.
23 20 Geo III, c. 54.
24 Torrance, 'Social Class and Bureaucratic Innovation', p. 56.
25 Earl A. Reitan, *Politics, Finance, and the People. Economical Reform in England in the Age of the American Revolution, 1770–92* (New York, 2007), pp. 25–6.
26 Ibid.; BL, Add. Mss. 38307, fol. 153^{r}.

institution in the British state could draw on a similar set of powers. In turn, the Commissioners were banned from holding public office whilst their inquiry lasted, and they were themselves bound by an oath to 'faithfully, impartially and truly execute the several Powers'[27] granted by the act.

The Commissioners at Work

The Commissioners did not waste any time setting themselves up. They established an office in Surrey Street on the Strand and got to work. As their first secretary, they employed William Molleson (c. 1732–1804), a North American loyalist merchant, who had supported North during the war.[28] For the *First Report*, the Commissioners concentrated on the Tax Office, whose receivers general obtained the revenue from the collectors, passed them on to the Exchequer, and prepared the districts' overall accounts. The Tax Office was, most likely, a deliberate choice. Responsible for the land tax and related property taxes, the Tax Office was the oldest of the revenue departments. The act had emphasised the need for quick results and the ancient Tax Office could be expected to yield ample deficits.

Following the act's direction, the Commissioners started with the issue of money in the hands of accountants. They distinguished three classes of accountants by their function in the financial system.[29] The first class consisted of the revenue officials who collected (tax) money and passed it on to the Exchequer. To establish how much public money was currently being held in private hands, the Commissioners requested the accounts of the previous two decades from all fifty-one receivers general, their deputies, as well as the accounts of the central Tax Office in London. The Commissioners presented the returns in a table that specified not only the amount of money held in the hands of each officer, but also the date of submission. The total sum of public money in private hands amounted to a dazzling figure of over £650,000.[30]

[27] 20 Geo III, c. 54, s. 7.

[28] In 1785, Molleson became Comptroller of Army Accounts and joined the newly established auditors for the public accounts. The Commissioners employed the well-known archivist Thomas Astle (1735–1803) as his successor. Binney, *British Public Finance*, p. 12; Nigel Ramsay, 'Astle, Thomas (1735–1803)', *ODNB*.

[29] Namely, those receiving (tax-)money to be paid to the Exchequer, those who received money from the Exchequer, and a third type, 'sub-accontants', who received public money from those in the second class. CEPA, 'First Report, 27 November 1780', *JHC 38: 31 October 1780 to 10 October 1782*, 74–85, p. 74.

[30] Ibid., p. 76. The practice of taking profit from public money had often been criticised, but it was not considered illegal. Cf. Knights, *Trust and Distrust*, pp. 194–7.

The Commissioners summoned George Rose (1744–1818), Secretary of the Tax Office, as well as several receivers general to testify under oath about the reasons for the keeping of outstanding money. The testimonies were included in the report as an appendix. The form of these testimonies hints at structured interviews, even though the questions were omitted in the published report. Apparently, the questions first covered the respective officials, how long they had been in office, which duties their office entailed and how they were paid, before moving on to the manner of the collaboration with collectors, the mode of financial transactions and accounts, and, finally, to the central question of public money in their private accounts. Law required the receivers to submit revenues to the Exchequer within forty days at the latest. In practice, they held money for up to two years. The interviewed accountants consistently provided two arguments for this practice. Firstly, they pointed out the difficulties involved in the cashless remittance of money from remote places to the Exchequer in London via bills from local banks. Secondly, the officers confidently stated that they considered the generated interest as a legitimate, customary part of their emoluments of office and argued that their payment by two-penny poundage, i.e. about 0.8% of the money they accounted for, was far too low by itself to sustain their living standards.[31]

In order to validate these arguments, the Commissioners interviewed receivers from another branch of the revenue, the Excise, which was known for its strict internal control. Indeed, the situation at the Excise proved to be strikingly different. No money at all was held by Excise officials for longer than sixty days, even in the remotest districts. Written instructions and a system of supervision enforced compliance. Officials were required to provide a security of £5,000, earned a relatively low annual salary of £120 plus expenses, and took an oath to never accept any sort of fee. Furthermore, the Excise officers indicated that the cash-free remittance of money rarely caused any difficulties. In stark contrast to over £100,000 of default in the Tax Office, the Excise reported only a single case of a collector who had gone bankrupt before the issued bills became payable, which amounted to a mere £3,600.[32]

As a result of this comparison, the Commissioners rejected the Tax officials' arguments. Making use of a model calculation, the Commissioners computed the public losses incurred by the practice in exact terms. By

[31] CEPA, 'First Report', pp. 77–81.

[32] CEPA, 'First Report', pp. 75–85. Cf. John Brewer, *The Sinews of Power. War, Money and the English State, 1688–1783* (London, 1989), pp. 101–14.

establishing an average amount[33] of money held by the receivers general of the Tax Office and attaining an interest rate of 4%, they calculated a yearly loss of £13,362 in interest, in addition to the more than £113,000 of arrears and defaults accumulated during the preceding two decades.[34] Based on these findings, the Commissioners determined that the practice of holding on to public money created a counterproductive incentive that threatened the revenue:

> The revenue should come from the Pocket of the Subject directly into the Exchequer; but to permit Receivers to retain it in their Hands, expressly for their own Advantage, is to furnish them with the strongest Motive for withholding it. A private Interest is created, in direct Opposition to that of the Public; Government is compelled to have Recourse to expensive Loans; and the Revenue itself is finally endangered.[35]

The private interest of the receivers general directly translated into public losses, because it added to the national debt – a strong argument in a perceived debt crisis.

The *First Report* already shows a deliberately methodical approach. The Commissioners purposefully collected data from a large number of accounts and presented it in tables. Tables were a common tool in political arithmetic. The use of hypothetical model calculations, by contrast, shows the Commissioners at the height of the 'quantifying spirit' of the late eighteenth century. In his *Observations on Reversionary Payments* (1771), Richard Price had made extensive use of model calculations to relate the rates of life insurance annuities to mortality tables. The book was well received and arguably established the practical potential of demographic data in the public discourse. In the following year, Price applied similar methods to the national debt and used model calculations to argue for a sinking fund. Using model calculations in the context of government data was thus a creative strategy in line with recent scientific advances taken up at insurance companies and the Bank of England, but not yet by the Treasury.[36]

[33] The Commissioners calculated the average using a reference date after the July quarterly returns; the calculated amount of £346,362 therefore fell far short of the current amount of over £650,000, which the Commissioners had calculated from the individual accounts. The model calculation was thus relatively cautious.

[34] Ibid., pp. 75–7.

[35] Ibid., p. 76.

[36] David O. Thomas, *The Honest Mind. The Thought and Work of Richard Price* (Oxford, 1977), pp. 234–59; Julian Hoppit, 'Political Arithmetic in Eighteenth-Century Britain', *Economic History Review*, 49 (1996), 516–40, pp. 533–4; Johan Heilbron, 'Introductory

In the *First Report*, state finances and administration appeared as a complex system, in which even seemingly remote phenomena were interrelated and ought to be viewed in context of the whole. The Commissioners identified best practice models by means of qualitative comparisons. Quantification added to the cogency of their arguments as well, by highlighting the necessity and potential impact of regulation in exact terms. Finally, the closing argument shows the Commissioners' use of psychological arguments: they made the point that the system's framework influenced the officers' actions.

After their *First Report*, the Commissioners developed their approach as they worked. Having established their line of action in their initial report, they proceeded quickly to the remaining types of accountants prone to holding public money. By August 1781, they had released four more reports. The *Second Report* covered all the remaining revenue departments, namely Customs, Salt, Hackney Coaches, Hawkers and Peddlars, Stamps, and the Post Office, as well as the offices concerned with a variety of miniscule, often church-related taxes. Having formulated general rules on the issue of money in hands, the application of these rules came relatively easily.

The *Third, Fourth,* and *Fifth Reports* considered the second class of accountants, which referred to those receiving money from the Exchequer. This consideration led the Commissioners to the big spenders of public money: the Navy and the Army. Here, matters were more complicated than in the revenue departments. Responsibility for the appropriate use of public money lay with the departments' heads of finances, the Treasurer of the Navy and the Paymaster of the Army. These officers were personally liable for their accounts and their responsibility did not end with their discharge, or even with their death. As long as the accounts for their years in office remained open, they, or the executors of their heritage, kept the money as well as the liability, sometimes for decades. The Commissioners' approach came into conflict with the established personal logic of offices in this issue. It had been easy enough to disprove the argument that interests from public money constituted a rightful part of the emolument. With the personal liability of the treasurers and paymasters, the Commissioners unearthed a structural problem. In the Commissioners' view, this problem required equally structural measures. Firstly, public money should, in future, be exclusively kept in public bank accounts.[37] Secondly, the respon-

Essay', in Tore Frängsmyr, Johan Heilbron, and Robin Rider (eds.), *The Quantifying Spirit in the Eighteenth Century* (Berkeley, Los Angeles, Oxford, 1990), 1–23.

37 CEPA, 'Third Report, 7 March 1781', *JHC* 38, 247–70, p. 249.

sibility of open accounts should pass to the successors in office as quickly as possible.[38] The solution for the question of money in hands resulted in a much stricter separation of person and office.

In tracing the flows of public money, the Commissioners revealed the interaction of different institutions: from the revenue departments to the Exchequer, and, especially in the other direction, from the granting of a budget in Parliament via the Exchequer to the great military spenders. These findings led the Commissioners to their subsequent choice of subjects. The following five reports dealt with the military departments in connection to the Exchequer. In the *Sixth Report,* the Commissioners formulated key themes relating to the understanding of office. With reference to the Exchequer pay office, the Commissioners came to demand the abolition of all sinecures and a regularisation of emolument: salaries should replace all forms of fee-based remuneration. The Commissioners then turned to the overall process of the military (Navy and Army) accounts. The *Seventh Report* traced the Army extraordinaries[39] since 1776, which effectively covered the accounting of the American War of Independence. The Commissioners published the report in June 1782, a year before the war was officially ended in the Peace of Paris. The *Eighth* and *Ninth Reports* treated the passing of military accounts at the Exchequer, whilst the *Tenth Report* went into details regarding Army sub-accounts, such as those for widows' pensions.

In the *Eleventh Report,* the Commissioners addressed another extensive topic: the management of national debt and the lottery. For the first time, the Commissioners were able to calculate the overall amount of the national debt and its annual costs in full and to the penny. Never before had the managerial costs, which included the salaries, fees, and gratuities arising from debt, been calculated.[40] After an in-depth analysis of the procedures at the Ordnance, i.e. military logistics and artillery, in their *Twelfth Report* of June 1784, the Commissioners finally homed in on the Exchequer office of the Auditors of the Imprest, the central auditing office that they had repeatedly come across before.

The Commissioners dedicated the three remaining reports to the Customs Office. They treated the passing of Customs accounts in the Exchequer in the *Thirteenth Report,* before turning to Customs internals for the port of London in the *Fourteenth,* and the out ports in the *Fifteenth.*

38 CEPA, 'Fifth Report, 10 August 1781,' *JHC 38*, 572–92, p. 577.

39 'Extraordinaries' meant the money spent in addition to the budget sanctioned by Parliament. Especially in times of war, these comprised by far the greatest part of the overall expenditure.

40 CEPA, 'Eleventh Report, 5 December 1783,' *JHC 39*, 771–823, p. 781.

However, this description does not do justice to this set of reports. These three reports constitute an exemplary in-depth survey of one of the largest departments of state. In these reports, the Commissioners minutely applied, refined, and clarified the principles that they had developed during the preceding four and a half years and developed fundamental reform proposals for the whole administrative structure. The three reports took two years to assemble and their combined volume almost matches that of all of the previous reports together.[41]

Over the course of the Commissioners' inquiries, their objectives changed considerably. In the beginning, they assertively followed the directives of the acts of appointment. As the reports advanced, the inner logic of the inquiry gradually replaced the reference to these acts; their findings lead the Commissioners to new questions. In the later reports, the Commissioners only invoked the legislature to add emphasis to their own arguments. In the detailed study of the Customs, the Commissioners refined their theory and they finally claimed that their principles provided a systematic template for future inquiries.

In carrying out their examinations, the Commissioners trod carefully. The political atmosphere remained highly charged and many officers felt threatened by the inquiries. Although hostile reactions are not reported, as the testimonies taken under oath were hardly the place to voice discontent, the Commissioners reflected on widespread resistance in their *Fourth Report*:

> We are well aware of the Difficulties that must for ever attend the introducing Novelty of Form into ancient Offices, framed by the Wisdom of our Ancestors, and established by the Experience of Ages; they are considered as incapable of Improvement; the Officers educated in, and accustomed to the Forms in Use, are insensible of their Defects, or, if they feel them, have no Leisure, often no Ability, seldom any Inclination, to correct them; alarmed at the Idea of Innovation, they resist the Proposal of a Regulation, because it is a Change, though from a perplexed and intricate, to a more simple and intelligible System.[42]

Behind the remarkably polite prose, the Commissioners' assessment of typical counter-arguments against reform is visible enough. Resisters emphasised customary usage and invoked an office's ancient constitution to preserve the status quo and defend the perceived property rights to their

41 Whilst the first five reports each had between ten and twenty pages in the JHC, the 'Fifteenth Report' alone filled 257 pages.

42 CEPA, 'Fifth Report', p. 577.

offices. Such arguments had been valid for a long time and they still made sense in the general discourse. But these arguments no longer made sense to the Commissioners. The longer the Commissioners worked, the more dysfunctional and even absurd their findings appeared to them. This assessment of the Commissioners' feelings is based on the increasingly dry humour that at times surfaces in the otherwise sober and formal reports. In the passage above, the Commissioners were subtly mocking the way the argument of custom and the ancient constitution was invoked.[43] In the *Ninth Report*, the humour is conspicuous. After having meticulously exposed widespread embezzlement in the military administration, the Commissioners described their stance on a relatively minor point as follows:

> We do not mean to convey the most distant Idea, that we have the least Reason to imagine any undue Advantage has been taken of this Mode of Clothing the Army by any Person whatsoever; but we are well grounded in suggesting a Reform, where an Usage is open to Abuse.[44]

The irony here – implying the opposite of the literal meaning – conveys the idea of a practice that was rife with corruption and abuse, whilst avoiding individual finger pointing. Writing the passage may also have served as an outlet for feelings of frustration and incredulity. This sense of frustration stems from the utter incompatibility of the inner logic of established practice with the scientific scrutiny of the Commissioners. The frustration was caused by the confrontation of two incongruous modes of reasoning applied to administrative offices and practices.

Reconceptualising Office

The notion of office was a centrepiece of the Commissioners' administrative doctrines. It was generally assumed that offices were property titles; but what that meant in concrete legal terms was not clear. The Commissioners defined offices as public trusts instead, and as obligations to perform useful duties for the state and public. The need for this redefinition arose from the Commissioners' engagement with the inconsistent remuneration of offices. The Commissioners quickly identified a plethora of fees and gratuities as a burden to the state. To address this issue, the Commissioners found it

[43] Ibid.

[44] CEPA, 'Ninth Report, 31 March 1783', *JHC* 39, 325–44, p. 332.

necessary to determine what an office was and to what extent it was legally possible to change existing offices.

Remuneration of offices followed no clear pattern and bore no relation to the usefulness of the offices or the effort they required. The value of many profitable offices lay in the gratuities and fees an office-holder could expect to receive. This was especially true for the more ancient departments, such as the Exchequer, which the Commissioners covered in their *Sixth Report.* In the year 1780, fees incurred in processing military accounts at the Exchequer amounted to a staggering sum of £39,000 for Army accounts alone. To the Commissioners, these overblown fees constituted a 'pressing and increasing Evil'.[45] There seemed to be much room for improvement on the military side of accounting, but the situation at the Exchequer almost defied description. A telling example is the Clerk of the Pells, whose sole task was to forward accounts within the Exchequer and register this action. For this function, generally executed by a deputy, the Clerk of the Pells received thirteen different allowances and a number of additional fees, amounting to annual emoluments of more than £9,000. Granted for life, the Clerk of the Pells was one of the most profitable sinecures available. From a viewpoint of utility, it served no function at all.[46] Many salaries had been fixed when the offices were established centuries earlier and had never been adjusted. Some of the more profitable offices only paid a salary of £5 but hundreds in fees and gratuities.[47]

The Commissioners drew far-reaching conclusions from the case of the Exchequer. Fees of any kind, they argued, hurt the public and were liable to abuse. They demanded

> that in the Place of all these Salaries, Fees, and Gratuities, there should be substituted and annexed to each of these Offices, of whatever Rank or Denomination, One certain Salary, paid to the Officer by the Public Quarterly, and free of all Deductions; this Salary should be an ample Compensation for the Service required; and the Quantum estimated by the various Qualifications and Circumstances necessary for the Execution, and which together form the Title to Reward.[48]

[45] CEPA, 'Sixth Report, 9 February 1782', *JHC 38*, 702–78, p. 702.

[46] Ibid., p. 707; CEPA, 'Eighth Report, 12 December 1782', *JHC 39*, 45–80, p. 45; Knights, *Trust and Distrust*, pp. 189–90.

[47] CEPA, 'Sixth Report', p. 709. In the office of the Treasurer of the Navy, for instance, the basic salaries had been fixed in 1699 and had remained unchanged in spite of inflation. Ibid., p. 703.

[48] CEPA, 'Sixth Report', p. 714.

This statement goes far beyond pointing out singular potentials for cuts or loopholes of abuse. The Commissioners connected the salaries to the services that an office fulfilled and the specific qualifications[49] the office required. These criteria only played a subsidiary role in the prevalent practice of patronage.

Issues of remuneration cut to the core of the question of what an office actually was. These issues led the Commissioners to general deliberations on the nature of office-holding and to a redefinition of office:

> The Principle which gives Existence to, and governs every Public Office, is the Benefit of the State. Government requires that various Branches of Business should be transacted, and Persons must be found to transact them. The Acceptance of a public Office implies an Engagement to do the Business, and a Right to Compensation: The Officer has Powers delegated to him necessary for the Execution; but he has no other Right to any specific Quantity of Business; that Quantity must fluctuate according to Circumstances, or may be regulated by the Convenience of the State: [...] the Officer cannot oppose to the Regulation, the Diminution or Annihilation of his Profits; because not the Emolument of the Officer, but the Advantage of the Public, was the Object of the Institution: To suppose in him a Right to make such an Objection, would be to suppose the Office created for his Benefit; that is, to suppose it to originate in a Violation of Public Trust, an Abuse of Power, and an Offence against the State.[50]

The passage is a direct inversion of the conventional constitution of office as stated by William Blackstone. Blackstone envisioned the King as the 'fountain of honour, of office and of privilege'.[51] The King's foremost constitutional role was to act as the executive. Formally, all positions were merely delegated parts of the monarch's prerogative. The King was 'not only the chief, but properly the sole, magistrate of this nation; all others acting by commission from, and in due subordination to him.'[52] This principle resonated in Blackstone's deliberations on the nature of office:

[49] Whilst the Commissioners occasionally touched on qualification, they did not explore the point in any detail. It would only rise to the centre of the administrative debate in the early nineteenth century.

[50] CEPA, 'Eleventh Report', p. 779.

[51] William Blackstone, *Commentaries on the Laws of England*, vol. 1 (Oxford, 1765), p. 261.

[52] Ibid., p. 243.

> honours and offices are in their nature convertible and synonymous. All offices under the crown carry in the eye of the law an honour along with them; because they imply a superiority of parts and abilities, being supposed to be always filled with those that are most able to execute them. And, on the other hand, all honours in their original had duties or offices annexed to them: an earl, comes, was the conservator or governor of a county; and a knight, miles, was bound to attend the king in his wars.[53]

To Blackstone, an office was simply one of the various forms that a personal grant by the Crown could assume. An office was granted as a freehold, and like all such grants, it typically entailed privileges and duties. However, these duties were by no means the foundation of the office. Blackstone's patrimonial approach relied on a conception of a state that was constituted by personal legal ties proceeding from the monarch. By contrast, the Commissioners' notion of the state was thoroughly abstract. They depicted the state as an institutional structure, tied by constitutional law. The state's only right to exist was for the good of the community. By means of this abstraction, the Commissioners identified the benefit of the state with the public good to a degree that they could not be discerned anymore: what was good for the state was, by definition, also good for the public. In this view, an individualistic conception of office appears as directly antagonistic to the public good.

For Blackstone, an office was defined by the original, personal Crown grant. If the grant came with a duty and that duty was still necessary, the office-holder needed to ensure that the duty was fulfilled, but not necessarily in person – in the same way that no one would expect an earl to see to all affairs of their county personally. The Commissioners inversed the relation between duty and privilege. To them, an office was defined by its duties, i.e. its function. Whilst the execution of an office entitled the officer to compensation, this compensation was not the office's function. This differentiation aimed at the many beneficiaries of profitable offices, whose defensive argumentations relied on the older principle. Many officers received fees or poundages dependent on every transaction or on the amount of money accounted for. When the office was defined by its function, any practice aimed at maximising personal emolument was malpractice or, worse, a violation of public trust.

[53] Ibid., p. 262.

The notion that an office was a 'public trust' encapsulates the Commissioners' conviction that an office was defined by its duties, which in turn depended on the current necessities of the state. It was the antithesis to the argument that offices were personal property titles. The Commissioners thus brought a concept to bear that had been instrumental in political debates since the previous century, mostly concerning the role of the monarch.[54] 'Public trust' was regularly used in the seventeenth century to emphasise the King's duty and responsibilities towards 'the people' or 'the public.' John Locke (1632–1704) argued that the prerogative of summoning and dismissing Parliament did not constitute a superior authority of King over Parliament, because, like all prerogatives, it was only a trust placed in him by the people. The breach of this trust, Locke had argued, would put the King in a state of war with the people, which in turn justified their resistance. Similarly, the concept was employed in the constitutional debates of 1688 to argue that the King's breach of trust constituted an abdication, even though he had not formally resigned.[55] The notion that all political power was a trust became commonplace from the seventeenth century. Even Charles I (1600–49) accepted the concept, but he interpreted it as a mere rephrasing of the basic idea that power comes with responsibility, and he insisted that his rule was a trust conveyed to him not from the people, but from God, for the people.[56]

In the course of the eighteenth century, usage of 'trust' in public contexts increased. It was used to emphasise that offices came with responsibilities to the public. The concept was commonly applied to MPs to stress their role as representatives with delegated authority from the people. It was also applied to officers of chartered companies, who were often suspected of undue profiteering. Mark Knights convincingly argued that this increasing usage was part of a trend towards a more legalistic and impersonal understanding of office.[57] Joseph Priestley's remarks on offices in his *First Principles of Government* certainly pointed in this direction:

> if any man hold what is called a high rank, or enjoy privileges and prerogatives in a state, it is because the good of the state requires that

[54] Knights, *Trust and Distrust*, pp. 109–25.

[55] John W. Gough, 'Political Trusteeship,' in id. (ed.), *John Locke's Political Philosophy: Eight Studies* (Oxford, 1973), 154–92, p. 163. Peter Laslett (ed.), *John Locke: Two Treatises of Government. A Critical Edition with an Introduction and Apparatus Criticus* (Cambridge, 1960), pp. 387–90.

[56] Frederic W. Maitland, 'Introduction,' in Frederic W. Maitland (ed.), *Otto Gierke: Political Theories of the Middle Age* (Cambridge, 1913), vii–lxxx; 'Trust and Corporation,' in H. D. Hazeltine, G. Lapsley, and P. H. Winfield (eds.), *Frederic W. Maitland: Selected Essays* (Cambridge, 1936), 141–222; Slack, *Reformation to Improvement*, pp. 53–76; Gough, 'Political Trusteeship,' pp. 167–9.

[57] Knights, *Trust and Distrust*, pp. 125–34.

> he should hold that rank, or enjoy those privileges; and such persons, whether they be called kings, senators or nobles [... are] the *servants of the public*, and accountable to the people for the discharge of their respective offices.
>
> If such magistrates abuse their trust, in the people, therefore lies the right of *disposing*, and consequently of punishing them.[58]

However, in the following deliberations, Priestley lamented that, except in free states, it was impractical for the people to take this power 'into their own hands'. Priestley envisioned a government that was the people's instrument, and his deliberations on office aimed at controlling this state through the people.

More recently, Richard Price had employed the concept of the public trust for his fundamental critique of the state in his *Observations on the Nature of Civil Liberty*: 'Government, as has been before observed, is, in the very nature of it, a trust, and all its powers a delegation for gaining particular ends.'[59] In his *Additional Observations* (1777), he applied the concept more specifically to office-holders, whom he sharply criticised: 'Civil governors consider not themselves as servants but as masters. Their stations they think they hold in their own right.'[60] The opposite, he maintained, was true. Price's determination of office resembled that of the Commissioners:

> The authority of magistrates is the authority of the state, and their salaries are wages paid by the state for executing its will and doing its business. They do not govern the state. It is the state governs them and had they just ideas of their own stations they would consider themselves as no less properly servants of the public than the labourers who work upon its roads or the soldiers who fight its battles. A king, in particular, is only the first executive officer, the creature of the law, and as much accountable and subject to the law as the meanest peasant.[61]

Price especially emphasised the accountability that came with the delegation of authority that was always bound to a useful purpose for the public good. This line of thought resulted in a more abstract notion of state administration. However, Price made his argument mainly in order to criticise

58 Priestley, 'Principles of Government', p. 18.

59 Price, 'Observations', p. 28.

60 Richard Price, 'Additional Observations on the Nature and Value of Civil Liberty, and the War with America', in David O. Thomas (ed.), *Richard Price: Political Writings* (Cambridge, 1991), 76–100, p. 89.

61 Ibid., p. 88.

an allegedly corrupted state. He took aim at MPs and the high officers of state, who allegedly abused their power instead of serving the public. In his view, the state itself should be strictly controlled and severely limited. Even though the focus shifted, 'trust' still tended to juxtapose 'the state' and 'the people'. Whilst by the seventeenth-century reasoning, 'trust' served as a check against executive despotism, the eighteenth-century usage mirrored misgivings about Parliament and the political elite that fuelled a radical critique of the state.

In principle, the Commissioners conceptualised 'public trust' in a very similar way as Price: the delegation of authority and conferment of appropriate rewards for the execution of specific, useful duties. However, they linked this idea to their strong understanding of the state. By identifying the state with the public interest, the Commissioners legitimised the state to act against the private interest of individual office-holders. In doing so, the Commissioners were not primarily concerned with the political personage who also held office, but with the office-holder as a public functionary. The duty and responsibility towards the public constituted an office and always took precedence over private interest. It was the state that allocated an individual officer's duties and controlled his conduct.

Public trust drew on a moral category. It assumed a shared sense of royal and civic duty that politically justified norms. As such, it was a political and not primarily a legal concept. However, the matter is more complicated, as public trust could also be a legal metaphor, analogy, or the application of the legally binding equity instrument of the 'trust'. Based on the Court of Chancery's exertion of the royal right to grant pardons, equity was by origin and definition no formal legal system. Nevertheless, it supposedly moderated and complemented the common law by means of simple doctrines of evident validity. By the end of the eighteenth century, equity had become formalised to such a degree that its distinction to law was mostly customary.[62] The development of 'trust' is a good example of this process. Originally, 'trust' settled the use of property on behalf of another person or purpose; for example, if an heir were underage at the time of the bequest. From a morally binding agreement used in the late middle ages to circumvent the seigneurial share in inheritances, 'trust' developed into the predominant legal form for all sorts of consortia and societies. Rather than an individual, any purpose that was 'charitable', i.e. beneficial to the public or a group of people, could become the formal beneficiary for whom or for which the

[62] John Baker, *An Introduction to English Legal History*, 3rd edn. (London, 1990), pp. 126–8.

trustee(s) managed the property.[63] In terms of equity, too, trust therefore constituted concrete legal obligations towards an abstract public benefit.

Thomas Anguish, the chairman of the Commissioners from 1782 to 1785, served as accountant general and master at the Court of Chancery. He was nominated by Chief Justice Mansfield and participated in appropriate legal discussions. The Commissioners consistently used 'public trust' after 1781.[64] The precedent set in 1783 at King's Bench in the trial of the Crown vs. Bembridge seemed to validate their interpretation. Charles Bembridge, an accountant in the Army Pay Office, was convicted for the embezzlement of £48,000. On the grounds of the judgement, Chief Justice Mansfield argued that

> [Bembridge] was a trustee of the public and the Paymaster, for making every charge and every allowance he knew of [...]. If the defendant knew of the omission [...] and if he concealed it, his motive must have been corrupt. That he did know was fully proved and he was guilty, therefore, not of an omission or neglect but of a gross deceit. [...] The law does not consist of particular cases but of general principles, which are illustrated and explained by these cases. [A] man accepting an office of trust, concerning the public, especially if attended with profit, is answerable criminally to the King for misbehaviour in his office.[65]

Whilst the judgement has an important place in the history of anticorruption, it did not immediately change administrative litigation.[66] The case was itself entangled with the ongoing political struggles on economical reform and served as an example for the resolute conviction of a corrupt officer.[67] Crown vs. Bembridge showed that a case could be made against the prevailing assumption that offices were unrestricted property titles. However, given the sanctity of property rights in public discourse, generalising from this case was politically tricky, to say the least. All told, the legal status of office was not entirely clear.

63 Maitland, 'Trust and Corporation', p. 185 and passim. The interpretation of this purpose became so loose that even at the height of religious persecution, religious dissenters could rely on the Court of Chancery to protect their property.

64 CEPA, 'Fifth Report', p. 577.

65 Thomas Sergeant and John C. Lowber (eds.), *Reports of Cases Argued and Determined in the English Courts of Common Law*, vol. 26 (Philadelphia, 1853), pp. 220–1.

66 Mark Knights, 'Anticorruption in Seventeenth- and Eighteenth-Century Britain', in Ronald Kroeze, André Vitória, and Guy Geltner (eds.), *Anticorruption in History: From Antiquity to the Modern Era* (Oxford, 2018), 181–95, p. 189.

67 Knights, *Trust and Distrust*, pp. 55–7.

The Commissioners engaged in this difficult discussion in their *Fourteenth Report* to argue for the abolition of all sinecures, even though they knew their argument could impact the economic interests of influential office-holders:

> We are aware of the Consequence some of these Officers derive from the Power by which they are granted, and the Extent of the Interest. A Freehold, held under the Grant of the Crown, is a solemn Right, to be treated with Respect, Delicacy, and Caution: but if the Subject of that Grant be a Public Office, and a Stipend be annexed to it, payable out of the Revenue of the Public; if rendering a Service useful to the State, as the Consideration for the Stipend, be of the Essence of such an Office [...] where the Utility of the Service is either wanting at the Time of the Grant, or in Process of Time ceases to exist, the Grant either had not at first, or has lost, the Quality essential to its Support; and no Power of the Grantor, no Condition of the Grantee, or Duration of the Interest, can supply the Defect: It cannot be supported in the Shape of an Office; for it has not the Character that distinguishes an Office from an Annuity or a Pension.[68]

For the Commissioners, there could be no office that did not fulfil a useful public function. The Commissioners' concession that offices were freeholds to be respected rings hollow. In their argumentation, the property rights to offices appear massively restricted, almost void. However, the legal cogency of the Commissioners' argument was certainly disputable. The Commissioners claimed that the duty originally assigned to an office in its patent was its essential trait. As the Commissioners had defined an office as a public trust of executing a useful duty for the state, the ceasing of that utility would automatically revoke the grant. The argument depended on an ex-post redefinition of office that did not fit the customary practice. In a legal logic based on precedent, the abundance of sinecures, which had been passed on innumerous times, testified to an established practice. The Commissioners responded to this point with a curious mixture of precedent-based, and legal-positivistic arguments. On the one hand, they supplied the precedent of a fourteenth-century statute that supported their reasoning in a specific case: 'The Wisdom of our Ancestors declared the Freehold to be void in its Creation; and the Office, turned into a Sinecure, to be forfeited.' On the other hand, immediately following this, the Commissioners highlighted the necessities of the present to undermine the normative force of older principles:

[68] CEPA, 'Fourteenth Report, 27 January 1786,' *JHC 41*, 9–151, p. 23.

> The present Age has the strong Pleas of Necessity and Justice, to demand, that such Portions of their Revenue as have been applied to the Support of such Offices, should be hereafter dedicated to the Service of the Public.[69]

The Commissioners made a fundamental historical argument here: changes over time had consequences for the necessities of state, and offices therefore needed to change with the times. The argument also drew on the sheer persuasiveness of the general sense of crisis. The shaken state could not afford to squander its money. Still, if offices were freeholds, their abolition equated to expropriation of the office-holder, who may have received a sinecure as a reward for public service. One solution for this dilemma was to substitute sinecures with pensions. Rewarding merit had to be possible and if reward was a customary function of offices, patentees who lost their offices could be entitled to compensation, 'equal both in Value and Duration to the full Emoluments of their Offices.' This may have been a tacit admission or a fall-back position to offer a compromise. After all, the Commissioners' main concern was the comprehensive abolition of sinecures:

> But we are of Opinion, that the Mode of Reward, by either creating or continuing, for that Purpose, a useless Office, is calculated to mislead the Public; who conceive, that by a continual Exertion of the Labour and abilities of the Officer in their Service, they are receiving back an Equivalent for the Emoluments they allow him. It tends to entail a perpetual Incumbrance upon the Revenue; for a Subject will be for ever found to deserve it.[70]

Even if it were deemed necessary to compensate the same amount as a sinecure or useless office cost, the Commissioners argued, its abolition would still be desirable. The very existence of sinecures undermined the legitimacy of the state. Moreover, their costs would not cease with the demise of an individual officer. By the logic of patronage, sinecures would always be reassigned for the purpose of reward, without any appropriate scaling.

The irregular nature of offices created problems for the state. Problems that, in the eyes of the Commissioners, could only be amended by a systematic reform based on overarching principles:

69 Ibid.

70 CEPA, 'Fourteenth Report,' p. 23.

> The Regulations in the Management of the Revenue [...] rest upon these Principles:- First, No Office should be holden but by legal Tenure;- Secondly, Every Office should have an useful Duty annexed to it;- Thirdly, Every Officer should execute, himself, the Duty of the Office;- Fourthly, Offices where the Duty is of the same Kind, should be consolidated.[71]

These principles not only strove to regulate each single office but also the overall structure of public offices. Every office was supposed to perform a useful duty and no duty should be performed by more offices than necessary. This last point was born from the intention to save money. On top of that, the Commissioners had come across instances of a single duty being assigned to too many different officers, and this led to dysfunctional results. Namely, in the delicate field of audit, the Commissioners argued that charging too many officers with the appliance of checks would tempt them to disregard their individual responsibility. Such redundant offices needed consolidating. To regulate, to consolidate and, where needed, to abolish offices became a basic operation of reform.

A Simple, Regular, and Accordant System

From the very beginning, the Commissioners approached their task in a consciously methodical manner. They deliberately picked who to interview, they had a plan to both verify and appraise their findings by means of comparisons, and they had an eye for the presentation of their results by arrangement, proof, and model calculations. However, it was only in the course of their work that their approach matured into something different: a general system for the revenue offices based on empiricism and abstract reasoning – a scientific theory for public administration.

In their final report, the Commissioners supplied a retrospective characterisation of their work:

> Our Aim has been to establish, upon good Foundation, the main and predominant Parts of the System; trusting, that if they be well arranged, and soundly constituted, it will not be a Matter of Difficulty, or beyond the ordinary Powers of the Office itself, to regulate, conformably, those which stand in a subordinate Place.

[71] Ibid., p. 18.

> In prosecuting our Work thus directed, there are Two Ends which we regard as supreme, and to the Accomplishment of which we have unremittingly bent our Attention.
>
> 1st. The Reduction of the Expence to the Public for the Management of this Revenue.
>
> 2nd. The Introduction of a more simple, regular, and accordant System into the Internal Frame of the Office.[72]

The Commissioners named the reduction of expense first, but the justification strongly emphasised their second objective: the introduction of a regular system. Their self-set task was now to redefine the foundations of public administration in order to rebuild the structure of offices on clear principles. By providing the key elements of a well-grounded system, they argued, the departments would be enabled to carry out reforms accordingly.

The Commissioners' frequent and deliberate use of 'system' points towards their scientific methodology. It had never before been considered that the public offices should form a systemic whole. The Commissioners characterised this system by determining its constituting principles. In analysing the fundamental administrative problems, the Commissioners subsequently followed a systemic logic that was typical for contemporary scientific perspectives on the state. By this logic, most deficits of the administrative system stemmed from its unnecessary complexity. To simplify the system meant to improve the system. In the fifteen reports, 'simplicity' is one of the Commissioners' key concepts, invariably carrying positive connotations. The Commissioners used it both to characterise their methodological endeavour and to substantiate individual measures. In their *Fourth Report*, for instance, the Commissioners deplored the prevalent resistance to change, 'though from a perplexed and intricate, to a more simple and intelligible System.'[73] The passage relates their abstract deliberations to workaday practice: simplicity meant intelligibility. Accountants would make fewer mistakes in their calculations and take less time to accomplish them. A Customs officer's work would be enormously facilitated by a consolidation of duties. Simplification would have even more impact when applied to the interaction of different branches of the system. Simplification of office structures could be achieved through unification, and unity thus became another guiding principle. 'Simplicity and Unity, [are] Qualities essential to the apt and expedient Conduct of Business,'[74]

[72] CEPA, 'Fifteenth Report, 1 March 1787,' *JHC* 42, 7–264, p. 24.

[73] CEPA, 'Fifth Report,' p. 577.

[74] CEPA, 'Fifteenth Report,' p. 33.

the Commissioners claimed in their *Fifteenth Report*. It was through the achievement of uniformity that equivalent phenomena, be it of practices or institutions, could be simplified because they corresponded to the same general principles.[75]

From the notion of uniformity, the Commissioners developed the claim that their recommendations could be applied throughout the administrative system. The Commissioners developed their principles during the process of their empirical survey. In many cases, they only framed their findings in general form towards the end of their operation. Yet, although the results were formulated by referencing concrete findings in particular offices, they could and were supposed to be transferred to equivalent cases:

> Uniformity in the Course and Modes of transacting the Business of the Public ought to be introduced and pursued, as far as is practicable, in similar Offices: It causes the Intercourse between Offices connected to be carried on with greater Ease and Expedition, and facilitates the Means of acquiring official Knowledge to those Persons who pass through the different Departments of the State to the high Stations of Administration; and thus, when a Regulation is clearly of general Utility, it should be extended to every Office, the Constitution and Objects of which will admit of the Application.[76]

The matters under consideration appeared as an enclosed subject matter, the principles of which could be understood, improved upon, and transferred within the system. For the first time, a topic resembling public administration was opened up to scientific scrutiny. The Commissioners set great store by the identification of general principles, which they developed by empirically analysing and comparing particular departments. They presented these principles as a coherent system. The Commissioners' claim that the principles could be transferred with ease turns their findings into a general theory. These methodological operations show a consciously applied epistemology. By transferring Newtonian reasoning to the analysis of human (inter)action, David Hume created the science of man. In consecutive steps, he first applied his science to political subject matters, and then to economical. The Commissioners' accomplishment constitutes an equivalent epistemological operation: they used empirical theory to combine various subjects into a coherent subject matter – a system, the specific principles of which could be conceived and formulated.

[75] CEPA, 'Fourteenth Report', p. 21.

[76] CEPA, 'Twelfth Report, 11 June 1784', *JHC 40*, 111–93, p. 120.

The Commissioners discovered a system of accounts and offices. They aimed to turn it into a 'system of economy', which was rationally structured to fulfil its functions more effectively and at a lower cost. The Commissioners operated against the background of an all-pervading sense of crisis and the fear of national bankruptcy. Two years into their work, the Commissioners presented their results as a key to solving the crisis.

> To reduce an enormous Public Debt, indispensably requires a System of general Oeconomy; an Oeconomy co-extensive with the Receipt and Expenditure of the Public Revenue, and that pervades every Branch of both; [...] Powerful and effectual may be the Operation of a Principle universally diffused, and steadily adhered to; and upon such an Operation only depends the Character of national Justice, the Support of national Credit, and the Preservation of the Public Welfare.[77]

This is a powerful formulation of the Commissioners' systemic thinking. By means of the right principles, a system could be transformed, and such a transformation of the public revenue would have wide-reaching effects. A systematic and comprehensive reform of the offices would relieve the nation.

Given CEPA's origin in the Economical Reform Debates, it is hardly surprising that economy itself features prominently in the reports. In fact, the Commissioners presented economy as the conclusive principle at the heart of their endeavour. However, the political debates also show that it was by no means clear what exactly economy meant, even if the reduction of expense featured prominently. The Commissioners offered a definition of 'economy' in their *Sixth Report*:

> By strict Oeconomy, we apprehend, is not meant such as either derogates from the Honour and Dignity of the Crown, or abridges the Servant of the Public of the due Reward of his Industry and Abilities; we mean an Oeconomy that steers between extreme Parsimony on the one Hand, and Profusion on the other; that is consistent with Justice as well as Prudence; that gives to all their full Due, and to none more; that supports every useful and necessary Establishment, but cuts off and reduces every superfluous and redundant Expense. Such Regulations built upon the Principle of Oeconomy thus defined, have for their Objects, the Offices, the Officers and their Emoluments.[78]

[77] CEPA, 'Eighth Report', p. 57.
[78] CEPA, 'Sixth Report', p. 711.

The Commissioners' definition of 'economy' stresses moderation, the careful consideration of the given functions, necessities, and legitimate interests. In its rather Aristotelian framing and its insistence on proportion and methodological caution, the passage is reminiscent of Steuart's reasoning.[79] A system built on a 'principle of economy' and framed in such a way was not reducible to purely financial concerns. The Commissioners used 'economy' as a signifier for logistics, and for the prudent handling of resources. Its meaning was much more nuanced than in the public discourse, where retrenchment predominated. This broad meaning similarly characterised contemporary political economy. Political economy was concerned with the analysis of national and international systems of resources, the development of the best means of furthering wealth through the institutions, and the manners and customs of a nation. This set of objectives links writers such as Beccaria, Price, Steuart, and Smith, even though they differed in their answers.

It is instructive to relate the concept of a 'system of economy' to contemporary discourse. 'System of economy' was used in two meanings: either to imply unity for a conglomerate related to national resources, or to refer to a strict resource-oriented theory. Adam Smith identified two systems of (political) economy 'with regard to enriching the people' in the *Wealth of Nations*: the commercial system and the agricultural system.[80] By studying such systems, their inherent principles could be understood, and this understanding allowed one to draw consequences. The *Wealth of Nations* was not, however, a system of economy in the second sense, because Smith came to the conclusion that nature should be allowed to run its course, rather than controlled by economic policies. Trying to remodel the systems on artificial principles would only hinder their natural economy.[81] When Edmund Burke called for a 'system of economy' in his economical reform speech, he used the concept in the second meaning. Burke called for a reform by principle and suggested that the Civil List expenditure should be reduced. The plan of disbursing salaries in an inversed order of rank was a rationally keen construct that Burke designed as a check against Crown influence and the accumulation of Civil List debts. The Commissioners' use of 'system of economy' oscillates between the two meanings. The Commissioners used the concept to characterise the administrative system as

[79] Tribe, *Economy of the Word*, pp. 53–4.

[80] Adam Smith, *An Inquiry into the Nature and Causes of the Wealth of Nations* (Oxford, 1976 [1776]), vol. 1, p. 428 [book IV: 'Of Systems of Political Economy'].

[81] Tribe, *Economy of the Word*, pp. 55–9.

a resource-oriented complex that needed to be studied, and they used the results of their studies to prescribe principles for the reform and remodelling of this system.

The Commissioners' system of economy was essentially related to the state and, in their eyes, needed to be regulated by the state. Their concept has been called 'statist', and for good reason.[82] In their view, institutions existed solely for the benefit of the state, whilst the state existed only for the public good. The state, rather than the individual, should decide how public welfare was best promoted. The reports do not contain a complete theory of the state. They do not address the sovereignty of rulers or the election of representatives, nor the process of political decision-making. However, the reports exhibit a clear-cut perspective on the state that was geared towards the functional arrangement of institutions. Structurally, the Commissioners' approach is very similar to political economy. Both analysed the state with regard to its empirical context and to its interactions with society. The question of sovereignty or the original source of authority was irrelevant to the concerns of the Commissioners. Hierarchy and authority, on the other hand, were of practical importance.

Authority and controlling power were in fact key elements of the Commissioners' system of economy. There were few well-defined hierarchies in the British office structure. Interaction between offices was sometimes set by individual provisions in patents, but mostly determined by customary usage. One exception was the Ordnance, where the Master General and the Ordnance Board were 'intrusted with the superintending Power and Controul over the Whole.'[83] The powers of the Master General and the individual board members were clearly defined.[84] This way, officers with the necessary knowledge of their department could, at least in principle, adjust the structure of their department according to its tasks. Moreover, the Board had access to all papers and authority over the personnel, allowing them to audit accounts on a reasonable basis of facts. The Commissioners urged for the superintending power to be expanded to the whole system, and explicitly considered it as a component of the system of economy:

> This Regulation is a Part of the System of Oeconomy that ought to be extended to every Revenue Department, whether of Receipt or Expenditure. [...] Were the same Steps taken in other Offices, the same

82 Torrance, 'Social Class and Bureaucratic Innovation', p. 70.
83 CEPA, 'Twelfth Report', p. 121.
84 Ibid., pp. 113–15.

> End would be attained: There is hardly any Office but possesses the like Powers, lodged either with the supreme Officer or a Board; and, should any Defect or Obstruction check the Exercise of the Power, the Legislature can lend their Aid.[85]

The Commissioners regularly used 'revenue' as a general term to encompass income and expenditure. As there was no established general term like 'the administration' or 'the bureaucracy', they used 'revenue' to point to the public office structure. Under this guise, public administration took shape as a cohesive subject matter. All departments receiving or spending public money responded to the same principles and were to be reformed by the introduction of a system of economy – a rational, scientific mode of administration.

Towards Reform

The appointment of CEPA was a consequence of the Economical Reform Debates, and they had been explicitly charged with the task of developing suggestions for improvement. It was in the context of these debates that 'reform' acquired its new meaning of intentional, future-oriented (institutional) change. The Commissioners consistently employed the term in its new meaning. At no point did they suggest that a defect could be solved by restoring an original state, which was the older and still prevalent meaning. Rather, in the Commissioners' usage, 'reform' is closely related to improvement. The reports convey a strong belief in progress. To the Commissioners, the ancient offices, in particular, were in urgent need of reform; a view that directly opposed customary argumentations.

The Commissioners did not merely express a preference for the new over the old. Rather, they drew on an empirical interpretation of history. To them, institutions were rooted in their social context, and this context changed throughout history. The Commissioners often determined the origins of a given practice to argue that the historical change of its context necessitated reform. The *Sixth Report*, for instance, contains a historical overview of the original context of poundage fees. When financial transactions still involved the physical delivery of money, 'the Poundage was a Mode of Reward that bore a Proportion to the Labour.' After all, various sorts of coins needed to be examined, counted, and transported. 'But in these Times, when all Money Transactions are carried on [...] by the

[85] Ibid., p. 121.

Substitution of Paper, by Cash Notes, Drafts, or Bills to any Amount [...], an increase in the Magnitude of the Sums, though to a vast Amount, is the Addition of a few Figures, or of a few Entries, only.'[86] In their original context, poundage fees relating to the overall amount of handled money may have made sense, but this context had thoroughly changed.

> Since then, on the one Hand, Improvements of the Age have taken away the Foundation upon which this Species of Reward was built, it is but reasonable the Superstructure should fall with it; and, on the other Hand the Exigencies of the Age having converted what was designed to be the Reward of Industry, into the Means of rendering some Offices lucrative to Excess, and of supporting others that are useless to the Public.[87]

The described defects did not arise from the deterioration of formerly well-established structures. Rather, the problems arose because the institutional superstructure had failed to change in relation to its historical context. Reform was intended to make up for this failure by means of deliberate and rational adjustment. The Commissioners took up this point again, more generally, in the cautious argumentation for Exchequer reform. The statement shows the customary foil against which they argued.

> An Office of the highest Antiquity, that has subsisted for Ages under its present Form; that has the Receipt and Custody of the Public Treasure, upon the due Administration of which depends the national Credit and Safety of the Realm; an Office of such a Description is entitled to the utmost Respect, and Alterations in its Establishment should be well weighed, and proposed with caution and Diffidence: But, as Change in the Manners, Customs, and, above all, in the Finances of this Nation, since the Origin of this Office, together with peculiar Circumstances of the Times, may render Regulations necessary, we have judged it a Part of our Duty to examine into the Receipt of the Exchequer, with a View to an oeconomical Reform.[88]

The passage helps to show how the Commissioners' argumentation related to contemporary ideas. For instance, Joseph Priestley emphasised that governments needed to revise their rules and set new precedents 'in the changing course of human affairs.' And he polemicised against the defence of obsolete institutions by means of precedent: 'that these oppressions have

86 CEPA, 'Sixth Report,' p. 712.

87 Ibid., p. 713.

88 Ibid., p. 711.

been long suffered, without any complaint, is to supply the strongest argument for their abolition.'[89] In the Commissioners' argument, the 'change in the finances' necessitated regulations, but the change in 'manners' and 'customs' directly points to the theoretical foundations of the argument. 'Manners' and 'customs' were key terms of a contemporary conception of history typical for the Scottish Enlightenment. It was in history that the progress of human societies was thought to unfold.[90] Whilst overall conjectural designs, such as stadial history, seem at first to be detached from the practical concerns of the Commissioners, they rest on the same assumptions. The Scottish Enlightenment understanding of history directly translated to its empiricism. History could serve as an equivalent to experimentation in a cautious search for universal human traits as well as the ever-changing 'manners' and 'customs'. Careful empirical studies were equally important for political or economic subjects, especially with a view to reform. In the preface to his *Principles of Political Oeconomy*, James Steuart emphasised the necessity 'to adapt the different operations of it to the spirit, manners, habits, and customs of the people'[91] when trying to improve institutions. The empirical contexts changed over time; the present 'manners' were fundamentally different from those of the past. Steuart argued 'from the plain principles of common sense, that our present situation is the unavoidable consequence of the spirit and manners of the present times.'[92] Bygone eras were essentially equivalent to foreign countries; only the deeper understanding of the specific circumstances allowed for an adequate understanding of human action and its careful (re)shaping.[93]

The Commissioners' argumentation echoed this conception of historical empiricism. After understanding the original circumstances and determining in what way they had changed, a particular measure or a particular department could be reformed. Unlike William Blackstone, who had projected a timeless ideal for the use of the present into the history

89 Priestley, 'Principles', p. 19.

90 Robertson, 'Scottish Contribution', pp. 49–51; David Spadafora, *The Idea of Progress in Eighteenth-Century Britain* (New Haven, 1990), pp. 253–320.

91 Steuart, *Political Oeconomy*, vol. 1, p. 16.

92 Ibid., p. 12.

93 For the development of this equation in Hume's work see Paul Cheney, 'Constitution and Economy in David Hume's Enlightenment', in Carl Wennerlind and Margaret Schabas (eds.), *David Hume's Political Economy* (London, 2008), 223–42, pp. 227–31; Moritz Baumstark, 'David Hume. The Making of a Philosophical Historian. A Reconsideration', PhD thesis (Edinburgh, 2007), pp. 104–15; Melvin Richter, 'The Comparative Study of Regimes and Societies', in Mark Goldie and Robert Wokler (eds.), *The Cambridge History of Eighteenth-Century Political Thought* (Cambridge, 2006), 147–71, pp. 161–5.

of King Alfred's rule, the Commissioners argued as James Steuart did, by means of historical empiricism. The Commissioners' reasoning was clearly designed to contradict resistance to reform that invoked the 'wisdom of the ancestors'. The Commissioners set their historical empiricism against the normative ancient constitution and aimed for institutions to mirror the improvements of the age.

Whenever the Commissioners argued for reform, their perspective matched the perspective of the 'statesman or legislator' of political economy. They based their suggestions on empirical findings, which they synthesised methodically. The Commissioners aimed at the development of differentiated reform measures, which they laid before Parliament and the ministry. For Scottish political economy, the figure of the 'statesman or legislator' epitomised power as a precondition for effecting reforms and the orientation towards the public good. Steuart presented the figure as the educated and disinterested politician, whose policies were based on appropriate information and careful deliberation, and who might heed Steuart's informed advice. Adam Smith took up this figure in his definition of political economy as 'science of the statesman or legislator'. The Commissioners similarly conceptualised theory as a means to improve practice, knowing that theory had to be consciously adapted to the complexity of social reality.

Once the 'system of economy' had taken shape, the Commissioners related their findings to the current crisis and strongly argued for the implementation of their reform proposals. Starting with the *Eleventh Report* that treated the management of the national debt, the Commissioners often concluded their reports with moral appeals. The Commissioners claimed that the crisis could be managed, but also insisted that this management called for a huge material and moral effort from both citizens and the state. In the crisis, economical reform became a moral imperative. The Commissioners depicted the taxpayers as stakeholders, who would gladly fulfil their civic obligation.[94] The Commissioners thus subscribed to a patriotic view of the crisis.[95] The commitment, however, needed to be mutual. It was the statesman's duty to reduce expenditure and to set the example of wise and economical conduct. As a result of the crisis, improving institutions for the public was no longer just the stateman's business, but his duty and

94 CEPA, 'Eleventh Report', p. 783.

95 Cf. Linda Colley, 'The Apotheosis of George III. Loyalty, Royalty and the British Nation 1760–1820', *Past and Present*, 102 (1984), 94–129.

moral obligation. In the closing statement of the *Fourteenth Report*, the Commissioners juxtaposed the duties of the government and its subjects:

> where the Subject is grievously oppressed by the Burthen of an enormous Debt, the Reduction of which is essential to the Justice, the Credit, and Security of the State, [...] a Duty presses, both upon the Government and Subject, of no common Obligation. The one is bound, in the Administration of the Revenue, to cut off every unnecessary and redundant Expence; to suppress every useless and superfluous Office; to correct every Abuse in the Public Receipt and Expenditure; and religiously to apply to the Service of the State the Produce of every Branch of the Revenue. The Subject is bound, chearfully and liberally, every one in Proportion to the Extent of his Abilities, to contribute, without Evasion, his Share to the Support, Defence, and Security of the State, and to the Relief of the Necessities of his Country.[96]

Whilst noting the mutuality of the necessary effort, the Commissioners emphasised the role of government. In fact, they took up parts of the assessment of the Yorkshire Petition and depicted the subjects as being oppressed by over-taxation and debt. The Commissioners even presented the administrative deficits in a notably government-critical stance and a similar moralistic Country rhetoric. However, whilst the Commissioners took up the appeal and the sentiment of crisis, they never insinuated intentionality or corruption. Rather, they presented their reform suggestions as instruments for resolving the crisis and urged the state to act decisively by putting these instruments into practice.

As the Commissioners' ideas advanced, the practicality of reforms – as opposed to the description of better practices – came into view. The Commissioners proposed to implement reforms by means of 'regulations', a word that had also denominated the intentional reshaping of administrative practice in the act of appointment.[97] The Commissioners used 'regulation' frequently in their reports and took its meaning for granted. 'Regulations' needed to be 'practicable and useful'.[98] A regulation was to bring about changes for a specific purpose, for example, the change of salaries in the Army: 'The Object of our Regulations is the Mode of Payment only, and the rendering that Mode more simple and intelligible, more uniform and equal'.[99] The regulation in question did not address the specific amount of payment. Rather, the proposed regulation aimed to simplify the variety of duties and deductions to

96 CEPA, 'Fourteenth Report', p. 23.
97 20 Geo III, c. 54.
98 CEPA, 'Twelfth Report', p. 118.
99 CEPA, 'Ninth Report', p. 331.

the salary. The passage is informative about questions of practical implementation: 'In the Regulation of an Office, it is prudent to keep as near as possible to the Forms in Use: The less they are departed from, the less averse will the Officers be to admit the Improvement.'[100] The sentence points to substantial resistance to reform, which appears as an empirical fact. The statesman could influence the level of resistance by keeping close to established forms, by taking into account the minds of the officers; a point both David Hume and James Steuart made when they discussed institutional change.

The Commissioners addressed the practical challenges for reforms and even reflected on reform as a process. Often, reforms aimed to simplify overly complex situations and this complexity foreseeably created difficulties for the implementation.

> In a Revenue that embraces such a Variety, it is hardly possible to introduce, at once, Regulation coextensive with the Objects. It must be a Work of Time. A practicable System must be formed upon Principle, and carried by Steps and Degrees into Execution.[101]

This passage condenses the Commissioners' three-step approach to reform. The first step was to gather detailed empirical information; second, this information would be used to develop principles; third, these principles would tailor the system to the needs of individual departments. If a reform addressed complex issues, this called for careful step-by-step implementation. Still, as the Commissioners emphasised, the reform would be consistent because it followed from scientifically clear principles.

On 16 January 1787, after finishing their *Fifteenth Report,* William Roe and Arthur Piggott presented to Prime Minister William Pitt a number of observations the Commissioners had resolved the day before:

> it is the opinion of this Board, that the Principles upon which they have grounded the said Recommendations in regard to the Customs, are adapted to other Offices of a like nature, and that as far as such Offices labour under similar defects, or stand in need of similar regulations the beneficial ends of Reform may be accomplished by the application of the said principles.[102]

100 Ibid.

101 CEPA, 'Thirteenth Report, 21 March 1785,' *JHC 40*, p. 668.

102 CEPA: Minutes of 15 January 1787, TNA, PRO 30/8/282, fol. 147^{V}. The minutes covering CEPA's last session seem to be the only internal documents of the Commissioners still existing. They may only have survived because they were accidentally included in collection of papers of the similar sounding Commissioners for Auditing the Public Accounts. See also Roe, *Private Memorandums*, pp. 15–16.

In other words, the Commissioners reemphasised their point that the principles developed under the scrutiny of the Customs Office over three reports were meant to serve as a blueprint for a reform of the entire revenue:

> having maturely considered the nature and extent of the Subjects investigated and the Reports made by this Board, and the aptitude and facility with which the Principles and Suggestions contained in those Reports may be applied to other Subjects, that the main purpose of their Institution are answered.[103]

The Commissioners thus laid claim to having successfully developed the principles for a general reform of the revenue departments, a scientific method of administrative reform. Although they offered to conduct further inquiries if required, they advised their own discontinuation:

> it is the Opinion of this Board that their own Institution is in its nature temporary [...] that the support of the said Institution is attended with considerable expence to the Public. That it is the Opinion of this Board, that in conformity with the System by which they have governed their Inquiries, and formed their Judgments upon Offices and Subjects coming under their Investigation, they are in Duty bound to deem the continuance of their Institution inexpedient and unsalutary if not essential to the attainment of Public Benefit.[104]

With this extraordinary statement, the Commissioners added considerable weight to the result of their work. Of course, this line of action was not what suddenly ended the commission. The previous year, its continuation had already been uncertain. The Commissioners may not have expected to be continued in the first place. It was a strong statement notwithstanding, and it was well received.[105] By voluntarily making their offices available, they personally demonstrated their fundamental argument: offices did not exist for the benefit of the individual holding the position but for the utility of their duties. Only the expectation of public benefit could justify their costs. When their function was no longer needed, offices needed to be abolished. The Commissioners' final statement forcefully pointed out the essence of their 'system of economy'.

[103] CEPA: Minutes of 15 January 1787, TNA, PRO 30/8/282, fol. 148^{v}.

[104] Ibid., fol. $148^{r/v}$.

[105] The Commissioners were granted the considerable premium of £7,500 each and took until June to dissolve their office. Finally, William Roe, who headed the commission after the death of Thomas Anguish late in 1785, was appointed a Commissioner of the Customs in 1788. Roe, *Private Memorandums*, pp. 12–19.

PART II

PRACTICING ECONOMICAL REFORM

4

Great Britain I: Initiating Reform

After the Economical Reform Debates of 1779/80, administrative reform became a major political issue. The potential consequences of this reform impulse were at first unclear. When debating reforms, Parliament and the political public mostly concentrated on general issues such as the military and political crisis, national debt, and corruption. With the reports of CEPA, public administration also became a specific subject. Even though few appreciated the minutiae of state administration, administrative reform was in demand. The prospect of reform aroused great expectations, but also great fears.

Prior to the end of the eighteenth century, five ministries dealt with the call for reform: the ministries of North (1770–82), Rockingham (1782), Shelburne (1782–3), Portland ('Fox–North,' 1783) and, finally, Pitt the Younger (1783–1801). Of these five ministries, the Shelburne ministry and the Pitt ministry provided crucial stimuli for administrative reform. Shelburne announced a 'general and grand reform' and took this promise seriously. His ministry sent out a wave of information requests to the departments in order to amend the lack of knowledge about the administrative system. At the same time, Shelburne commissioned a number of agents to prepare reform recommendations for various departments. Although a reform of the Treasury was the only one to be completed, the impetus of the ministry's information gathering effort and reform activity extended far beyond the Treasury. During the Shelburne ministry, administrative reform began to take concrete shape. Pitt also had the reputation of a reformer. After his initial efforts, however, Pitt shifted the issue out of the political limelight, as it proved to be an issue which was vulnerable to attacks from the opposition. A decisive action taken by the Pitt ministry was the establishment of the Commissioners on Fees, whom the ministry charged with developing concrete reform recommendations based on the findings of CEPA and, above all, with introducing regular salaries.

Reforms were not promoted by a homogeneous group of government insiders. Rather, a heterogeneous group of actors engaged with the reform impulse from their individual positions. Alongside the Undersecretaries,

Shelburne welcomed a diverse range of individuals to help instigate the reforms, from politicians and experienced administrators to businessmen. In some cases, individual actors in the departments took the initiative. For instance, Navy Comptroller Charles Middleton attempted to utilise the impulse for reform to push his own reform agenda against the will of his superiors. In the Navy and in many other departments the prospect of reform sparked internal disputes, as it forced actors to position themselves. Pro-reform officers turned to economical arguments, whilst officers who resisted change were under increasing pressure to find arguments in defence of the status quo. Even the clerks had agency. They defended their privileges or seized the opportunity to improve their economic situation. Across the board, actors mostly positioned themselves according to personal motives and concrete interests rather than along party lines.

This diverse constellation of actors was reflected in the initially open and at times confused discourse that unfolded. Against the background of crisis, 'economical reform' entailed a normative claim, even though it was far from clear what this reform would entail in concrete terms. The parliamentary debate only provided vague directions for making administration cheaper and better, and for curtailing the influence of the Crown. It soon became apparent that as long as there was no political will to challenge the property theory of office, an improvement in structures would not enable savings but would, in fact, initially involve substantial costs. It also turned out that it was not so much the influence of the Crown as the influence of individual interests that stood in the way of reforms. The reform concepts developed during the Shelburne ministry show a wide range of ideas for improvement. A recurring theme in the description of defects pointed to the problems caused by sinecures and fee-based remuneration. As a consequence, administrative reforms primarily aimed to introduce regular salaries and a clearer structure of functional offices without fundamentally questioning the property claim of the old offices. It was generally assumed that an office-holder, whose position or fees were regulated, had a right to compensation. The Pitt ministry did not question this approach. The Fees Commission in turn confronted the departments with the economical principles of their predecessors. Whilst it was still possible to dismiss this thrust towards economical administration in the early 1780s on tacit patrimonial assumptions, resistance progressively shifted towards justifying exceptions, delaying reforms, or maximising salaries. Arguments based on custom retained some weight, but increasingly lost their persuasive power compared to economical arguments. The implementation of economical ideas always depended on specific power structures, but the fundamental principles of economical reform were questioned less and less.

Politics of Economical Reform

During the crisis of 1779/80, Lord North's ministry had wavered and nearly fallen apart. In the summer of 1780, the ministry profited from better news from the American War and a temporary relaxation of the situation in Ireland. The Gordon Riots of 1780, though a crisis in their own right, worked in favour of government authority, as the riots produced a public desire for stability. This new-found stability did not last long. On 17 October 1781, General Charles Cornwallis (1738–1805) surrendered at Yorktown. In Parliament and even within the ministry the conviction grew that the war with the former colonies in America could not be won. North's ministry was held responsible for the defeat, but its hands were tied by King George's categorical refusal to seek peace. When the King finally relented, North had lost his majority in Parliament. After twelve years as Prime Minister, North resigned on 20 March 1782.[1]

Consequently, the former opposition raised a claim to the ministry, but this opposition was itself divided. George III offered the ministry to Shelburne, who declined the offer after a realistic assessment of his own insufficient parliamentary influence, but agreed to help form a joint Whig government. Until his death on 1 July, Rockingham managed to hold his second ministry together through his personal presence, but the ministry never overcame the diverging interests between the different groups. Rockingham presided over the ministry, but he never gained the trust of George III. The King preferred to communicate through Shelburne, who became his only confidant in the ministry.[2]

During the three months it lasted, the Rockingham ministry introduced a number of statutes on economical reform issues, largely following the logic of 'corrupt influence':[3] Crewe's Act and Clerke's Act prevented revenue officers and contractors from occupying parliamentary seats in order to restrict the number of placemen.[4] The focus on influence also informed the Civil Establishment Act, the somewhat watered down version of Burke's original plan to control the Civil List.[5] The ministry's working relationship with CEPA was rather cool and the ministry discussed replacing the Commissioners by a parliamentary committee dedicated to the issue

1 Ian R. Christie, *The End of North's Ministry 1780–1782* (London, 1958).

2 John Norris, *Shelburne and Reform* (London, New York, 1963), pp. 145–50.

3 Ibid., pp. 151–8.

4 22 Geo III, c. 41 and 22 Geo III, c. 45. See Betty Kemp, 'Crewe's Act, 1782', *English Historical Review*, 68 (1953), 258–63; Christie, *Wilkes, Wyvill and Reform*, pp. 152–3. In fact, there had been fewer placemen in 1780 than twenty years before.

5 22 Geo III, c. 82.

of influence.[6] Edmund Burke took up a number of CEPA's issues when he prepared the ministry's final piece of legislation that regulated the office of the Paymaster of the Forces.[7] No longer was the Army budget to be handled through the Paymaster's personal bank account, but through an office account that would be passed on to his successor once he left office. Above all, the act addressed the question of fees, which were soaring during wartime. Whilst fees would still be collected, they were fed into a joint fund to be used for salaries and the support of invalid officers, widows, and orphaned children. Burke's solution promised to be cost-neutral and much easier to implement than the outright abolition of fees.[8] Much depended on the way in which these statutes would be implemented and the ministry persisted just long enough to reveal the profound disagreement of its members on this question. Rockingham, weakened by illness and burdened by the divisions within his ministry, was hardly inclined or able to focus on his position as the First Lord of the Treasury to promote details of administrative reform. The development of a reform policy for the Treasury was a task he left to his successor.[9]

Shelburne used his position as the King's man to build up his own power base. On Rockingham's death, he accepted the King's renewed offer of the premiership on an improved, though far from stable, footing. Charles James Fox (1749–1806), who rallied the former Rockingham group, tried to prevent Shelburne from building a ministry by resigning and publicly attacking him, but Fox's strategy backfired and lead to a schism in his own party. Those who resigned along with Fox were easily replaced. Among others, Shelburne brought in Henry Dundas (1742–1811) as Treasurer of the Navy, and Parliament's prodigy, the barely twenty-three year-old William Pitt (1759–1806), as Chancellor of the Exchequer.[10]

Contrary to Rockingham or North, Shelburne was politically tied to administrative reform. Shelburne's advance towards a committee of inquiry in February 1780 had been well received, especially among the corresponding committees of the Yorkshire Association.[11] In his first speech after taking office, Shelburne made administrative reform a centrepiece of the

6 Norris, *Shelburne and Reform*, pp. 158–61, 202.

7 22 Geo III, c. 81, amended 23 Geo III, c. 50.

8 23 Geo III, c. 50.

9 Norris, *Shelburne and Reform*, pp. 158–70.

10 John Cannon, 'Lord Shelburne's Ministry, 1782–3. "A Very Good List"', in Nigel Aston and Clarissa C. Orr (eds.), *An Enlightenment Statesman in Whig Britain: Lord Shelburne in Context, 1737–1805* (Woodbridge, 2011), 161–75.

11 Eight similar letters of appreciation can be found in WCL, Shelburne Papers, vol. 168, box I, n. pag.

ministry's agenda, announcing his ambition to 'introduce a general system of economy, [...] into every office whatever'. He aimed at nothing less than 'a general and grand reform'.[12]

Shelburne's grandiose promise of reform resonated with public sentiments. For instance, one Edward Gordon wrote to Shelburne on the topic of the Scottish revenue establishment. In order 'not only to admire, but to contribute [...] to reformation & oeconomy', Gordon presented a number of proposals. In particular, he recommended lowering salaries:

> A common Officer of Excise is not to expect to have a salary to support the station of a gentleman, as many of them affect. [...] Being enabled to keep company, they frequent it. By frequenting Company they neglect their duty. [...] I know of few officers of excise, who are not egregious drinkers. Drink destroys the best principles. A Drunken man is open to bribery. [Decreasing the salary] will be the best means to make him temperate, and temperance will enable him to do his duty.[13]

Gordon's understanding of reform aimed at Puritan notions of morality rather than institutional concerns and it framed 'reform' as a return to moral purity. Gordon's letter in no way represents a general consensus. It rather illustrates the initial indetermination of the discourse. Economical reform won decisive battles in Parliament and public opinion. The issue of reform raised hopes, precisely because it consisted of a number of untested notions, which left room for people to project their own expectations onto it.

Shelburne's 'General and Grand Reform'

In the Economical Reform Debates, Shelburne had pointed out that even the government lacked the necessary information to deal effectively with the obvious problems of corruption, inefficiency, and waste. Upon taking office at the Treasury, Shelburne personally took it upon himself to remedy this lack of information and to deliver on his promise of reform. He engaged in the regulation of the Treasury as well as the control of the Civil List, and mandated agents to develop reform proposals for a variety of offices.

12 Parl. Hist., 23: May 1782 to December 1783 (London, 1814), col. 139–40; John Ehrman, *The Younger Pitt*, vol. 1: *The Years of Acclaim* (London, 1969), pp. 89–91.

13 Edward Gordon to Shelburne, 9 November 1782, in WCL, Shelburne Papers, vol. 115, pp. 75–86, here 75, 80.

Shelburne was eager to engage systematically with reform and was intellectually well prepared to grapple with its intricacies. During his days at Christ Church he had embraced Blackstone's reading of the constitution and its foundation in property and liberty. Afterwards, Shelburne broadened his intellectual horizon by actively seeking out economical, utilitarian, and politically radical thinkers. From the 1760s on, he engaged with the Scottish philosophers and considered himself a disciple of Adam Smith. Following Smith, Shelburne condemned the close 'mercantile' connection between politicians and merchants as corrupt and became a propagator of free trade.[14] A supporter of Wilkes, Shelburne was a founding member of the Society for the Bill of Rights and he tried to bring together free trade, country interest, and city radicalism. From the early 1770s on, Shelburne regularly conversed with Richard Price on the topics of national finances and free trade. They agreed that the tax system should be consolidated and unnecessary trade barriers should be removed. In both cases, they agreed simplification would increase efficacy and create a much-needed surplus for the state finances.[15] Joseph Priestley, who served as a salaried companion to Shelburne from 1773 until the mid-1780s, was an even greater influence. Whilst Price provided a methodical, arithmetic perspective on finances, Priestley introduced Shelburne to a utilitarian foundation of politics that was at odds with customary arguments. Jeremy Bentham, who further developed and radicalised utilitarian ideas, benefited from Shelburne's patronage after 1781. Shelburne's intellectual contacts were not confined to these British thinkers whom he invited to his estate in Bowood. Unlike most contemporary British politicians, Shelburne was involved in the international Republic of Letters and engaged with intellectual pioneers on the continent. He met Cesare Beccaria in Italy and attended salons in Paris, where he was introduced to Turgot (1727–81) and the leading French *philosophes* and formed a particular friendship with the political economist André Morellet (1727–1819).[16] Systematic reform thinking came naturally to Shelburne. He embraced the image of himself as the 'statesman or legislator' of political economy.

In addition to his intellectual background, Shelburne could also draw on extensive knowledge of the practicalities of British public administration

[14] Richard Whatmore, *Terrorists, Anarchists, and Republicans. The Genevans and the Irish in Time of Revolution* (Princeton, 2019), pp. 222–30.

[15] Ibid., pp. 230–3; Norris, *Shelburne and Reform*, pp. 55–68, 82–7.

[16] Edmond Dziembowski, 'Lord Shelburne's Constitutional Views in 1782–3', in Nigel Aston and Clarissa C. Orr (eds.), *An Enlightenment Statesman in Whig Britain: Lord Shelburne in Context, 1737–1805* (Woodbridge, 2011), 215–32; Robin Eagles, '"Opening the Door to Truth and Liberty", Bowood's French Connection', in ibid., 197–214.

from his tenure as Southern Secretary in the Chatham ministry (1766–8). Moreover, Shelburne had acquired the papers of James West (1703–72), the long-serving Exchequer and Treasury Secretary of the Newcastle ministry, which helped Shelburne to understand the details of accounting procedures at the financial centre of the state.[17]

Shelburne's ideas had much in common with the ideas of CEPA. He shared their systemic perspective and the utilitarian appreciation of the public interest. However, like Rockingham, Shelburne initially distrusted the Accounts Commissioners. Had they not been North's instrument to thwart his very own design of the February motion? John Norris holds that Shelburne shunned the Commissioners, whom he saw as competitors for the recognition of the development of the pioneering reforms.[18] Still, on many issues, Shelburne followed their recommendations closely and arrived at similar conclusions. Contrary to the Rockingham Whigs, Shelburne strove for administrative economy, whilst combating the 'influence' waned to a side issue. Relations between Shelburne and CEPA improved to the point where Shelburne asked them to comment on a draft of a reform concept for the Treasury and the Exchequer.[19]

Shelburne concerned himself intensely with the Commissioners' seminal *Sixth Report* on fees and gratuities that had been presented to Parliament in February 1782. 'The commissioners give very proper advice about Fees, & their proposal ab[ou]t Poundage merits serious examination', he commented in his personal notes, '[t]he great objection to fees is that they fall ultimately on the Public with double weight'.[20] Shelburne had formed similar conclusions during his tenure as Southern Secretary in 1767/8, when he had been engaged in a major reorganisation of his office. At the time, he had qualified his former adherence to the property theory of office and rejected a petition of the established clerks for a reintroduction of their franking fees. Instead, he had tried to adjust the clerks' salaries and even offered to forgo a substantial sum of his own fees to pay for it, but failed to convince the Treasury.[21] Now, he aimed to convert all fees and gratuities to regular and sufficient salaries whilst adjusting the office structure to better fit their purposes.

17 Norris, *Shelburne and Reform*, pp. 25–9, 99–100.

18 Ibid., p. 200.

19 Ibid., pp. 206–7; Inspection into Certain Offices in the Exchequer; with Remarks on the Regulations Proposed Therein by the Commissioners of Accounts, n.d., in WCL, Shelburne Papers, vol. 166.

20 Shelburne's notes on the report on fees, civil list, WCL, Shelburne Papers, vol. 168, box 3, fols. 11–24, quote on 14^{r}, col. 3.

21 Norris, *Shelburne and Reform*, pp. 27–30.

The preparation of reforms primarily fell to the Treasury Undersecretary George Rose.[22] Rose had acquired a reputation as an able administrator in the important post of Secretary to the Tax Office, where he had been concerned with an internal reform in 1778. Although he would later state that he had always disliked Shelburne, Rose became a key figure for the development of reform policy in the ministry and remained so for the next quarter of a century.[23] Rose handled the correspondence with the departments, keeping track of and advising on various reform cases.[24] From August to November 1782, Rose wrote to a wide variety of offices requesting financial accounts, detailed lists of personnel, and evidence of all forms of emolument received within the previous years.[25] Some offices answered within days, others took several weeks; the Excise took almost three months to respond. In most departments, the state of information was not much better than that of the Treasury. The heading of a table received from the Navy Victualling Office, for instance, candidly promised accounts, 'as near as the respective Parties can make it up from recollection, and the instruments in Office.'[26] In addition to problems of sloppy book-keeping, the compilation of accounts was hindered by reluctance on the part of some of the office-holders. At the Customs Board, William Musgrave (1735–1800) complained that

> [t]he late inquiries of the Commissioners of Accounts have made the Officers very shye of any Question relative to their Emoluments, wherefore I have been under the necessity of giving this Account according to my own Idea suggested from the transactions of business [...] what difference may appear between this acco[un]t and that to be delivered by the Commissioners, I shall be glad to know, as thereby I may be able to get nearer to the truth.[27]

22 Cf. Treasury minute of 15 July 1782, WCL, Shelburne Papers, vol. 162, part 1.

23 Joanna Innes, 'The British Way of Bildung. The Formation of George Rose, Secretary to the Treasury and Vicepresident of the Board of Trade 1782–1812,' in Anke Fischer-Kattner et al. (eds.), *Schleifspuren: Lesarten des 18. Jahrhunderts* (München, 2011), 204–15.

24 Cf. e.g. a letter from Rose to John Morin concerning the Civil List reform, 25 March 1783, Shelburne Papers, vol. 168, box 3.

25 See the listing in WCL, Shelburne Papers, vol. 129, p. 1.

26 Victualling Office, 11 November 1782, Shelburne Papers, vol. 129, p. 11.

27 William Musgrave, The supposed emoluments of the different Offices exclusive of their Salaries, n.d. [before November 1782], in WCL, Shelburne Papers, vol. 114, p. 273.

The inquiries of the Treasury and CEPA had an effect on the offices by themselves and this effect increased through the public attention on economy and reform.

Together with Rose, Shelburne implemented the introduction of salaries for staff in their immediate reach, namely at the Treasury. They took up Burke's fees-fund solution and fully converted emoluments to regular salaries, which even resulted in a moderate entrenchment. The reform put an end to the execution of office by deputy and, taking up a line of action discussed years before under North,[28] it introduced promotion grounded in merit. The reform also targeted the institutional structure of the office. The Treasury was reorganised into six division, each comprising senior and junior staff and concentrating on an individual field of business.[29] Whilst central creeds of economical office reform could be tackled with relative ease at the Treasury over which Shelburne presided, their application to the other departments proved more difficult.

The most politically pressing reform issue for the ministry was the implementation of Burke's Civil Establishment Act, the single most important legislative consequence of the Economical Reform Debates up to that point. Whilst Burke's act specifically abolished a number of positions, it left most of the details of implementation to the Treasury; a task Shelburne's ministry now had to tackle.[30] Shelburne assigned his trusted second Treasury Undersecretary, Thomas Orde (1746–1807), the task. The bill was a result of fierce debates in Parliament and was shaped by more abstract political beliefs and assumptions, but its implementation needed to address practical realities. Engaging with it personally, Shelburne's judgement on the bill was damning. To Lord Grafton he wrote:

> It is impossible to describe to you, how provokingly my time is taken up with the nonsense of Mr. Burke's bill. It was both framed and carried through without the least regard for *facts*: and penned so that every line required the opinion of the Attorney General.[31]

[28] Treasury minute of 22 February 1776, TNA, T 29/45.

[29] Treasury minute of 30 November 1782, TNA, T 29/52. Cf. Roseveare, *Treasury*, pp. 122–4; Norris, *Shelburne and Reform*, pp. 199–204.

[30] 22 Geo III, c. 82, s. 4.

[31] William R. Anson, *Autobiography and Political Correspondence of Augustus Henry Third Duke of Grafton* (London, 1898), p. 338.

The bill was so ambiguous both in wording and substance that the Attorney General was consulted several times for its interpretation.[32] The main problem was hard to face for former oppositionists. Even with harsh cuts and reformed structures, the fixed amount of the Civil List was simply too low for its purpose and the portion that was used for direct political influence was surprisingly low. Only a trifling £1,140 out of £45,000 qualified as direct political interest.[33] Shelburne and Orde wrestled with the task of reducing the overall amount of the pension list, in many cases simply by turning them into regular pensions paid at the Exchequer. Notwithstanding these regulations, the Civil List remained underfunded. Under these circumstances, neither Shelburne nor any of his successors even tried implementing Burke's scheme of classed payments.[34]

Reforming Perspectives

Whilst Shelburne personally oversaw the development of all plans, he also integrated reform-oriented officers outside of the ministry, if their agenda corresponded to his plans. The variety of agents that Shelburne enlisted mirrors the wide scope of his reform agenda. The group comprised government insiders and outsiders, long-serving administrators, and private businessmen, but only a few active politicians. These agents were keen to question the status quo, to measure it by the yardstick of economy, and to suggest measures for improvement.

Shelburne tasked Thomas Gilbert (bapt. 1720–98) with the reform of the Royal Household. Gilbert had been involved in a minor Household reform that resulted in some savings in 1778 and he was one of the most outspoken opponents of Burke's attempt at an operative Household reform by Parliament. Gilbert strove to simplify structures and to reduce waste and corruption. One paymaster's office and one defined mode of accounting should replace the wide variety of means and offices handling financial transactions, while new managing offices – a Superintendent of the Household, a Paymaster of the Civil List, and an Inspector of Works – would supervise all operations of the Household. These officers would be appointed by the Lord Steward and the Lord Chamberlain, but they would also be responsible to the Treasury.[35]

32 Norris, *Shelburne and Reform*, pp. 176–9.

33 For details, cf. ibid., pp. 186–95.

34 Ibid., pp. 195–8; for a differentiation of the classed-payment scheme cf. Reitan, 'Civil List', pp. 331–5.

35 Norris, *Shelburne and Reform*, pp. 179–85; Richard S. Tompson, 'Gilbert, Thomas (bapt. 1720, d. 1798)', *ODNB*.

The idea of the permanent involvement of the Treasury in the operation of the Household encountered the fierce resistance of the Lord Chamberlain George Montagu, fourth Duke of Manchester (1737–88).[36] Manchester had complied with Gilbert's request to access the accounts only after much protest. Opposing Gilbert's plan, Manchester argued that creating new offices would 'cause more expence and confusion in the management of the Majesty's Household than [...] at present.'[37] Despite these appeals to economy and clarity, Manchester was primarily concerned with defending the authority and patronage of his own office: 'The Lord Chamberlain is by Law, the Superintendent of all the King's Household, the appointing of another Superintendent, wou'd [sic] be infringing the rights of his office.' He insisted that the Treasury's financial oversight did not justify any operational interference.[38] This argument at first seems like a patrimonial appeal to the rights of office, however, the authority that Manchester claimed was not ancient at all, but rather a side effect of Burke's bill. The Attorney General had decided that the bill implied operational functions for the great offices of the Household, offices that had been largely ceremonial sinecures for more than a century. Manchester threatened to 'make my sentiments public, if the scheme shou'd be carry'd on',[39] which could only mean joining ranks again with Fox's opposition Whigs, but his threat turned out to be toothless. With the backing of the King, Shelburne went even further than Gilbert had proposed. In the end, the plan stipulated the creation of a single office of Superintendent of the Household and Paymaster of the Civil List that was appointed by and responsible to the Treasury alone.[40] For most of his political career, Shelburne had promoted parliamentary scrutiny of the Civil List as a means towards curbing oligarchism and corruption. Executive control of a reformed institutional system suited his goals even better.[41]

At the Customs Office, Shelburne could rely on a particularly experienced reformer, whose appeals for reform had previously fallen on deaf ears. William Musgrave had served as a Commissioner of Customs since 1763. Even as early as the 1770s, Musgrave had actively sought to enhance internal transparency and improve procedures. For instance, he published a comprehensive collection of statutes relating to the Customs in 1780 and established a continuing index to the proceedings of the Customs Board.[42]

36 John Cannon, 'Montagu, George, fourth duke of Manchester (1737–1788)', *ODNB*.

37 WCL, Shelburne Papers, vol. 125, p. 381.

38 Ibid., p. 383.

39 Ibid.

40 Norris, *Shelburne and Reform*, pp. 182–3.

41 Whatmore, *Terrorists*, pp. 231–2; Dziembowski, 'Constitutional Views'.

42 William Musgrave (ed.), *A collection of all the statutes now in force, relating to the revenue and officers of the Customs in Great Britain and the Plantations*, 2 vols.

Musgrave showed that the problems of an overly complicated structure of duties as well as the corruption of officers had already been discussed around the turn of the preceding century. This discussion had even resulted in statutes and orders banning the sale of offices, enforcing the personal discharge in residence, and explicitly limiting the freehold-character of letters patent.[43] However, few of these regulations had been implemented and none of them had proved effective in the long run. Rather, the number of sinecures had increased further. Customs officers had simply ignored regulations of fee-rates and the catalogue of customs duties had become ever more complicated.[44] In 1777, Musgrave had developed plans to consolidate the branches, to revise the outdated and complicated catalogue of duties, and to simplify their collection.[45]

Whilst little had come from his earlier proposals, Musgrave eagerly supplied Shelburne with a new plan, this time aimed at the suppression of useless offices and the abolition of fees.[46] The plan consisted of four comprehensive objectives. First, office in Customs should only be held by appointment of the Customs Board; all other grants were to be annulled. In future, appointments would be only during pleasure (i.e. terminable) and offices were always to be conducted in person. Secondly, sixty-four 'obsolete and useless Employments' were to be abolished and another seventy-two converted into efficient offices. Thirdly, he proposed the abolishment of all fees and, fourthly, he called for promotion on strictly meritocratic grounds only.[47] Musgrave's plan was entirely focused on the regulation of business and the establishment of effective structures and authority. Musgrave even proposed compensating for the loss of emoluments by the ceasing of offices or fees in full. Savings appeared as a beneficial side effect. Most of all, the plan constituted a sweeping blow against all patrimonial clauses

(London, 1780); C. J. Wright, 'Musgrave, Sir William, sixth baronet (1735–1800)', *ODNB*.

[43] The precedents limiting the letters patent for example stretch from the fourteenth (Richard II) to the sixteenth century (Edward VI): 7 Rich II, c. 5; 14 Rich II, c. 10; 31 Hen VI, c. 5; 1 Hen VI, c. 5. WCL, Shelburne Papers, vol. 114, pp. 285–8, also various precedents are mentioned or copied, pp. 220–48.

[44] WCL, Shelburne Papers, vol. 114, pp. 286–8.

[45] Plan for consolidating the different branches of the Treasury in one aggregate, 9 April 1777, WCL, Shelburne Papers, vol. 114, pp. 53–70. Cf. 'Sketch of an Act for consolidating the various Branches of the Revenue of the Customs, with two Schedules, and Remarks upon the whole Annexed', 4 pp, in WCL, Shelburne Papers, vol. 135, part 2; 'Of the manner of Exporting Goods from the Port of London under the care and Inspection of the Officers of the Customs, 1777', 14 pp., n. pag. WCL, Shelburne Papers, vol. 135, part 2.

[46] A Plan for vacating certain unwarrantable Grants, and for abolishing various obsolete and useless Offices in the Customs, n.d. [November 1782], WCL, Shelburne Papers, vol. 114, pp. 285–320.

[47] WCL, Shelburne Papers, vol. 114, pp. 289–90.

and particular rights as well as self-interested patronage. Musgrave did not shy away from openly contesting the theory of office as property. He cited a broad base of legal precedents from the reigns of Richard II to Elizabeth I, which limited an officer's claim to their legal titles.[48] In 1774, Attorney General Edward Thurlow (1731–1806) had confirmed that the patent offices in question were not forms of freehold property, but that they depended on the exercise of duties deemed necessary by the Customs Board. Shelburne apparently agreed and tasked the current Attorney General Lloyd Kenyon (1732–1802) with moving against Manchester, who, in addition to his position as Lord Chamberlain, long held a sinecure at the Customs.[49]

In December 1782, along with yet another list of sinecures and useless offices, Musgrave wrote to Shelburne, stressing the expected benefits of his reform for 'the satisfaction of the merchants, the improvement of trade & the consequent Increased safety of the Revenue'. He then drew Shelburne's attention to another benefit: 'at the same Time it will strengthen and enlarge the proper Influence that Government ought always to have.'[50] In Musgrave's reasoning, influence appeared as a purpose and the best means to proceed against what the opposition had blamed it for: corruption, ineffectiveness, and waste. Musgrave was preaching to the converted. Notwithstanding his proximity to radical ideas, Shelburne's wider reform agenda aimed to decisively strengthen the power of the executive.[51]

Shelburne commissioned Francis Russell (1740–95), Surveyor General of the Duchy of Lancaster, to inquire into the mode of collection of small revenues by Sheriffs. Russell's report was the first study on the work of the Sheriffs since 1683.[52] The Sheriffs constituted a decidedly patrimonial, and arguably archaic, institution of local government. Russell advised a general overhaul of the system, including a division of the Sheriffs' judicial and revenue-related functions and the discontinuation of the ineffective (and expensive) mode of pseudo-accounting that reviewed the Sheriffs' personal integrity instead of their accounts.[53] In his report, Russell masterfully employed a vocabulary of economical reform:

48 Ibid., p. 285.

49 Norris, *Shelburne and Reform*, p. 212.

50 WCL, Shelburne Papers, vol. 114, pp. 330–1.

51 Dziembowski, 'Constitutional Views'.

52 Matthew Hale, *A Short Treatise Touching Sheriffs Accompts* (1683).

53 For details of the Shrievalty see Alfred H. Smith, *County and Court. Government and Politics in Norfolk, 1558–1603* (Oxford, 1974), pp. 139–54; Arthur L. Cross (ed.), *Eighteenth Century Documents Relating to the Royal Forests, the Sheriffs and Smuggling* (New York, 1928), pp. 15–20; for details of Russel's plan see Norris, *Shelburne and Reform*, pp. 216–19.

> Amongst other Benefits which will obviously result from a Reform of this kind, the Introduction of Simplicity, perspicuity, Dispatch and Oeconomy in the Place of the Present, intricate, Obscure, dilatory and expensive Mode of Accounting, and the Retrenchment of a few thousands per Annum on the one hand, and a sure addition of at least a few thousands more to the Public Revenue, in the Actual furtherance of Justice on the other, are of themselves objects well worthy Public Attention.[54]

Russell's plan called for the abolition of a number of useless offices and some fees. However, given that his plan retained both the execution by deputy and poundage-based emoluments, the condensed jargon-like employment of economical reform language primarily appears as a rhetorical strategy designed to win over Shelburne.[55]

Shelburne also included businessmen in his group of agents. The agents' economically informed outsider perspective yielded particularly radical opinions. For instance, Shelburne put the industrialist Samuel Garbett (1717–1803) in charge of the inquiry into the Royal Mint. Whilst Garbett identified a number of sinecures in his report, he also insisted that the true problem was the lack of internal checks. Garbett implied that this lack of checks had allowed the Master of the Mint, Lord Cadogan (1728–1807), to reap enormous private profits and he insinuated that the Bank of England was complicit.[56] John Call (1732–1801), a typical nabob, and Arthur Holdsworth (1757–87), who belonged to a prominent family of overseas traders, inquired into the revenue collection of the Crown lands in England and Wales.[57] Call and Holdsworth blatantly stated that economical reform measures like the abolition of useless offices and the regulation of fees would save a mere £1,000 and could therefore hardly 'be held out to the

54 Francis Russell, 'Report concerning the Revenues of the Crown in the Collection of Sheriffs in England and Wales, and the Manner of their Accounting in the Exchequer with Plans for the Increase of those Revenues, and Retrenchment of the present Expences of accounting for them, February 15th 1783', in Cross, *Sheriffs*, 165–233, pp. 167–8; WCL, Shelburne Papers, vol. 135.

55 Ibid., p. 193.

56 Julian Hoppit, 'Economical Reform and the Mint, 1780–1816', *British Numismatic Journal*, 84 (2014), 177–90, pp. 177–81.

57 'Report on the present state and an Opinion on the future Disposition of the Crown Lands in Wales addressed to the Lords of the Treasury, 10 April, 1783', in WCL, Shelburne Papers, vol. 122; Ray Freeman, 'The Holdsworth and Newman Families in Dartmouth', Dartmouth History Research Group (n.d.), https://www.dartmouth-history.org.uk/dhrg-books/the-holdsworth-newman-families.

Public as a striking reform'.[58] Instead, they recommended to sell the lands in question entirely. Even after paying pensions and other charges, they argued, the interest of the capital raised in such a way would produce an annual surplus. To Call and Holdsworth, as well as to Garbett, the decision between customary and profitable establishments was clear.

Administrative Contestations in the Navy

The ministry's preparations of reform created ripples that reached far beyond Shelburne's group of reformers. Some officers feared for their perquisites, whilst others saw individual opportunities. In many cases, this dynamic created contestations throughout the ranks of the departments, from the board members down to the clerks. The most prominent case for such contestation created by the prospect of reform was the civil administration of the Navy. This administration was no trifling affair. The Navy dockyards, for instance, constituted by far the largest industrial branch in Britain. A single ship of the line, with its complement of often more than 500 people, can be compared to a large factory by contemporary standards. Building, repairing, and victualling the largest fleet in Europe was an enormous logistical task that was vital for the constantly warring state. However, the logistical structures which kept the Navy and dockyards going had changed little since the previous century.[59]

The Comptroller of the Navy, the Scotsman Sir Charles Middleton (1726–1813) presented himself as an especially zealous reformer. Middleton actively tried to enlist Shelburne's help to implement his own vision of the Navy Board, which entailed the reorganisation of the civil administration of the Navy and a shift of authority affecting the whole Navy. Middleton had been appointed in August 1778 by the First Lord of the Admiralty John Montagu, Lord Sandwich (1718–92) and quickly acquired a reputation as a capable and productive officer. A devout Evangelical, Middleton set great store by morally upright conduct, and did not shy away from conflicts. His

58 'Report on the Present State and an Opinion on the Future Disposition of the Crown Lands in Wales addressed to the Lords of the Treasury, 10 April, 1783', in WCL, Shelburne Papers, vol. 122, p. 1.

59 Roger Morriss, *The Royal Dockyards during the Revolutionary and Napoleonic Wars* (Leicester, 1983); John R. Breihan, 'The Addington Party and the Navy in British Politics 1801–1806', in Craig L. Symonds (ed.), *New Aspects of Naval History* (Annapolis, 1981), 163–89, pp. 165–6.

stern, direct, even confrontational character made him enemies within the Navy Board.[60]

Middleton started corresponding directly with Shelburne soon after the latter had entered office in July 1782. On 9 September, he sent Shelburne a comprehensive concept for administrative reform of the civil departments of the Navy.[61] Middleton praised Shelburne's plans for reform and presented his own reform ideas in a letter containing no less than twenty-seven heads, covering a broad range of topics from sinecures, useless offices, fees, and the effect of the constant Navy debts on contracting prices, to the dire consequences of the shipwrights' customary privilege of taking timber chips for firewood. However, he mostly focused on patronage and organisational questions, especially concerning his own position.[62]

In Middleton's presentation, the Comptroller was the second most important post in the Navy. Middleton suggested that the First Lord of the Admiralty should focus on the military direction of the Navy, whilst the Comptroller directed the whole of the civil branch, i.e. all logistics, shipbuilding, and the maintenance of the fleet.[63] Though only the First Lord held Cabinet rank, the Comptroller should be included in the strategic decision-making. Middleton therefore called for a seat on the Admiralty Board.[64] Middleton's interpretation of his position stemmed from his erstwhile cooperation with Lord Sandwich, but he had no formal claim to this central position. Full authority and the patronage of senior positions belonged to the Board of Admiralty, whilst the subordinated Navy, Victualling, and Sick and Hurt Boards oversaw large departments without disciplinary power. All these boards were strictly collegial, so that decision-making always necessitated the reconciliation of their members.[65] With Sandwich's backing, Middleton implemented various regulations to improve Navy administration and also initiated technological innovation, such as the introduction of copper sheathing which increased the ships' speed and

60 Roger Morriss, 'Middleton, Charles, first Baron Barham (1726–1813)', *ODNB*; J. H. Broomfield, 'Lord Sandwich at the Admiralty Board. Politics and the British Navy, 1771–1778', *Mariner's Mirror*, 51 (1965), 7–18.

61 Middleton to Shelburne, 9 September 1782, in WCL, Shelburne Papers, vol. 151, no. 40.

62 Middleton to Shelburne, 15 July 1782, in WCL, Shelburne Papers vol. 151, no. 15; Middleton to Shelburne, 9 September 1782, in WCL, Shelburne Papers, vol. 151, no. 40.

63 Ibid., no. 40, § 19.

64 Ibid., no. 40, § 8.

65 Roger Morriss, *Naval Power and British Culture, 1760–1850. Public Trust and Government Ideology* (Aldershot, 2004), pp. 28–34; Breihan, 'Commission on Fees', pp. 66–7.

delayed their decay.[66] The good cooperation, however, ended abruptly after the Fall of the North ministry in 1782 with the inauguration of a new First Lord of the Admiralty. Viscount Keppel (1725–86) was a political enemy of Sandwich and he opposed the former First Lord's protégé.[67]

In his reform concept, Middleton recommended replacing the prevailing structure of collegial boards with clear leadership positions throughout the Navy: 'Every Office should have a Head distinguishing his responsibility and a salary adequate to his Rank and extraordinary trouble. When there is no Head, nothing to be found but Irregularity, delay, & contradiction.' For Middleton, 'economy' followed from the concerted conduct of good men in positions of leadership: 'the sums that might be saved, by oeconomical Men at the Heads of these Boards acting on a plan of consistency would appear incredible.'[68] Middleton personally lay claim to recent improvements and simultaneously drew on customary rhetoric to insist that his own course realised the original constitution of the Navy Board:

> the Navy Board is now put on a plan of attaining Efficiency, Order & Oeconomy; that strength comprehended in its first Institution, has seldom been carried into practice. [...] [now] it becomes necessary to settle it on a footing, that would enable it to go on, without depending entirely on the casual application of one man.[69]

In order to continue his course, Middleton asked for unabridged authority second only to the First Lord, including full control of patronage in the civil departments of the Navy. To Middleton, patronage was in essence the disciplinary power necessary to appoint and to control subordinate officers in order to improve Navy logistics. That patronage was used for political purposes or in consideration of personal interest filled him with horror. He had nothing but disdain for Admiral Keppel's patronage practice:

> it appears, that when this patronage loses sight of skill, industry, merit & vigor in its appointments to become a political Engine in pursuing the news of a party, the whole natural strength and active force of the Kingdom with respect to its insular situation must be diverted from its proper purpose, to the great hurt & ruin of the state.

[66] John E. Talbott, *The Pen and Ink Sailor. Charles Middleton and the King's Navy, 1778–1813* (London, 1998), pp. 45–60; Roger J. B. Knight, 'Sandwich, Middleton and Dockyard Appointments', *Mariner's Mirror*, 57 (1971), 175–192.

[67] Breihan, 'Commission on Fees,' pp. 66–7; Broomfield, 'Lord Sandwich.'

[68] Middleton to Shelburne, 9 September 1782, in WCL, Shelburne Papers, vol. 151, no. 40, § 6.

[69] Ibid., no. 40, § 19.

> The present state of the Fleet, its want of discipline, the little subordination existing amongst the Officers, the service of particular ships, made to submit to the parliamentary attendance of Commanders, the shamefull corruption that meets the Eye in the several departments of the Dock Yards, are all melancholly proofs of the prostitution of it.[70]

This passage constitutes a rather insolent attack on Middleton's principal, a minister of Cabinet, addressed to the Prime Minister. The general critique of the established patronage practice demonised politics as an arena of corruption, not dissimilar to the points raised by Christopher Wyvill. Middleton insinuated that politicians were sacrificing the public good and were even endangering the nation's integrity for their personal profit. The moral imagery is particularly vivid: the political abuse of patronage turned the Navy into a brothel. Shelburne did not take offence at Middleton's blunt tone. The summary of Middleton's letter in Shelburne's personal papers is full of praise.[71]

Besides the questions of authority and patronage, Middleton's reform concept suggested the abolishment of all poundages as well as the pooling of fees into a fees-fund that was to be used to defray salaries.[72] However, when Rose's official request to detail the establishment and the fees of the clerks reached the Navy office, Middleton tried to shift focus to other issues. Despite having reasserted that he thought 'the more extensive the Reformation, the more agreeable to him', he was 'sorry that Fees of Office sho[ul]d have been taken up so early.'[73] Middleton argued that little would be gained by curbing the emoluments of a few clerks, whilst keeping sinecures and maladjusted structures of authority.[74] For the ministry, the reform of emoluments and the suppression of excessive fees was the most pressing matter. Within the Navy administration, the prospect of such a reform triggered an internal conflict of interest. This conflict allows a rare glimpse on the perspective and agency of clerks – subaltern officers who would be directly affected by a reform.

70 Ibid.

71 Naval 1782, abstract of contents, in WCL, Shelburne Papers, vol. 151.

72 Middleton to Shelburne, 9 September 1782, in WCL, Shelburne Papers, vol. 151, no. 40, § 7.

73 Middleton wrote two letters on the subject of the clerks to Shelburne on 26 September 1782, in WCL, Shelburne Papers, vol. 151, nos. 41, 42. Quotes are taken from the abstracts. Also see the official answer to Rose's request: Navy Office. Allowances made to the Clerks of the Pay and Navy Office, in Addition to their salaries, 27 September 1782, ibid., no. 85.

74 Middleton to Shelburne, 26 September 1782, WCL, Shelburne Papers, vol. 151, no. 41.

Middleton put forward that he had almost lost one of his best head clerks due to the implicit accusation of profiteering that Rose's request insinuated. He forwarded and endorsed a letter, in which this head clerk, Thomas Davies, justified the immense increase of his emoluments in the course of the war.[75] Davies argued that

> Every Emolument arising to me is entirely a Free-gift, No Fees or Gratuities being ever demanded or ask'd for – some give at one take, some at another, [...] and against many Nothing: The Quantum is never questioned by me, excepting in my refusal in very numerous instancy to receive more than Custom had establishe'd or to receive any when judg'd it could not be fairly afforded or was not honorably offer'd.[76]

Davies did not explicitly raise a property claim to the emoluments of his office, nor did he enter into a general discussion on gratuities. Customs, in his eyes, safely marked the line between established practice and corruption. In addition, Davies pointed to the immense increase in workload that had triggered his gains in the first place. 'Public Business [has] become so multiplied in the Branches, so extensive & enormous in my point of view that I often feel myself very nearly borne down by it, a situation to which in my mind no advantages whatever can be adequate.' The annual number of bills he had registered in 1781, he stated, was five times that which had been usual before the start of the war. Having dutifully shouldered the immense increase of workload during wartime, Davies was wounded at the very implication of misconduct.[77]

Davies and other clerks close to Middleton had much to lose by a reform of salaries.[78] Others had equally as much to gain. As Middleton did not take up their case, these clerks went over their superior's head to make themselves heard. In anonymous letters to the ministry, they used their detailed internal knowledge to reveal just how numerous, complex, and voluminous the customary perquisites, gifts, and premiums at the Navy offices really were.[79]

75 Middleton wrote two letters on the subject of the clerks to Shelburne on 26 September 1782, in WCL, Shelburne Papers, vol. 151, no. 42.

76 Mr. Davies to Middleton, 5 October 1782, in WCL, Shelburne Papers, vol. 151, no. 43.

77 Ibid.

78 Cf. e.g. the letters from Richard Gregson to Shelburne of 22 and 27 September as well as 17 December, in WCL, Shelburne Papers, vol. 151, nos. 76, 78, and 87. Cf. Morriss, *Naval Power*, pp. 128–32.

79 Norris, *Shelburne and Reform*, pp. 208–10.

The anonymous officer who styled himself 'Candour and Propriety', for instance, wrote several times to expose the extent of wartime fees and to call for reform. The total earnings of certain clerks surpassed the salaries of the Navy Commissioners.[80] In place of these unequable fees, the regular salaries of the clerks should increase. Such a regulation would restore the hierarchy and lead to enormous savings.[81] Against the contention that the abolition of fees would only profit the contractors, 'Candour and Propriety' argued that the public would benefit because contractors would adjust their prices if the fees were dropped. The increased workload could easily be covered by a regular increase of salary during wartime. The author's arguments and language were on the whole sober, calculating, and rational. In fact, 'Candour and Propriety' explicitly endorsed CEPA's scientific approach:

> The Scientific Information will convey sufficient Groundwork for your Lordships Improvement. Peruse the Reports of the Commissioners of Accounts, and your Lordship will perceive these sentiments are built on that Great and just Rational Basis: and what is very strenuously recommended for an Immediate Remedy; to correct the prevailing Mock-transacting the Public Accounts: receiving such immense Fees as are now paid.[82]

Other letter writers argued in similar tones, taking on arguments and parts of the language of administrative reform imbued with moral associations.[83]

The conflict of interest in the Navy offices mirrored the fundamental arguments regarding administration and its reform. Whilst the first-quoted clerks argued along patrimonial lines – emphasising customary practice and their own just reward – the anonymous letter writers took up the language and arguments of economical administrative reform to promote the abolition of fees, hoping that a general reform would even out the field and leave them with a higher salary. On the insistence of the ministry, Middleton eventually developed a concept for the pooling of fees in spite of his

[80] 'Candour and Propriety' to Shelburne on 9 October 1782, 30 December 1782, and 27 January 1783, Shelburne Papers, in WCL, vol. 151, nos. 88, 90, 93.

[81] 'Candour and Propriety' to Shelburne, 30 December 1782, in WCL, Shelburne Papers, vol. 151, no. 90.

[82] 'Candour and Propriety' to Shelburne, 9 October 1782, in WCL, Shelburne Papers, vol. 151, no. 88.

[83] E.g. 'Friend to Merit & the Public' to Shelburne, 29 January 1783, in WCL, Shelburne Papers, vol. 151, no. 92. 'Rewarder of Merit' even offered a full table specifying suitable salaries for officers at the Navy Office. 'Rewarder of Merit' to William Pitt, 17 January 1783, in WCL, Shelburne Papers, vol. 151, no. 91.

misgivings.[84] At the same time, he kept trying to persuade Shelburne of his larger concerns throughout the winter of 1782/3.

The Shelburne ministry did not last long enough to implement either the fees reform or attempt further reforms. Shelburne had never commanded a comfortable majority in Parliament and he never stabilised his position. This was partly due to his character and leadership style. Neither jovial like North nor fierce like Fox, he had never been a charismatic leader.[85] In Parliament, Fox and his followers framed Shelburne as an insolent politician, who allowed corrupt influence to endure and picked on the powerless lower office-holders.[86] The conflicts over reforms contributed to the instability of the ministry, but its fall was mostly tied to the results of the negotiations of the American peace treaty.[87] For many MPs, the results of the peace negotiations were hard to stomach: recognition of full sovereignty, large territorial concessions, and no security for loyalists. Shelburne and his followers may have been too confident that North would finally come to their aid. Instead, North did what had seemed unthinkable. He formed a coalition with Fox under the nominal leadership of William Cavendish-Bentinck, third duke of Portland (1738–1809). Shelburne yielded office on 2 April 1783.[88]

In a bitter attempt to justify his actions, Shelburne later claimed that 'no one man in Administration or Opposition was in earnest in the support of any reform.' Moreover, he bemoaned a square refusal of any reform on the side of the officers. The established officers, he claimed, were thoroughly corrupt and 'conscious of abuses which if reformed, however liberally, would not only change their whole existence, but in the course of the examination might prove their criminality'; the new ones, 'now they were in, could not brook the idea of foregoing the fortunes which their predecessors had made.'[89] Shelburne's assessment failed to take into account the enormity of the task he had set himself. Shelburne tried to change the administrative structure and culture overnight. It is hardly surprising that he encountered resistance and failed to implement changes across the board within nine

84 'Navy, Victualling and Sick & Hurt Offices. A Plan to prevent the taking of Fees, Gratuities, or Emoluments', n.d., in WCL, Shelburne Papers, vol. 151, no. 94.

85 John Cannon, *The Fox-North Coalition. Crisis of the Constitution, 1782–4* (Cambridge, 1969), pp. 36–7.

86 Norris, *Shelburne and Reform*, pp. 176, 184–5.

87 Ibid., pp. 240–70.

88 Ibid.; for details of the new ministry's formation cf. Cannon, *Fox-North Coalition*, pp. 38–81.

89 E. G. P. F. Fitzmaurice and W. P. M. Lansdowne, *Life of William, Earl of Shelburne, Afterwards First Marquess of Landsdowne* (1876), pp. 328–37.

months. Rather, it is striking that the short period of reform activity did, in fact, unsettle established practices.

The ensuing Fox–North coalition did not regard economical reform as a key issue. Fox argued that most of Rockingham's reform demands had already been fulfilled and agreed not to press for any further action in that field. The new ministry ignored the forays undertaken during Shelburne's ministry and actively rolled back Gilbert's Household reform. However, the Fox–North coalition was formed against the will of the King and it did not last long. The ministry stumbled during its attempts to reorder the East India Company (EIC) and government intervention in colonial India. Fox's India bill gave the impression that the ministry would only try to secure India patronage for their own camp. In the end, the bill failed due to the personal intervention of George III, who seized his chance to undo a ministry he despised and put word out that he would consider every supporter of the bill his personal enemy. Consequently, the bill failed in the Lords and George III tasked the twenty-four-year-old William Pitt with forming a new ministry on 19 December 1783.[90]

William Pitt and Reform

Whilst the Fox–North coalition had once again confirmed public perceptions of ministerial extravagance, undue enrichment, and greed, Pitt came to epitomise a new type of politician: the independent, personally disinterested manager and reformer, who ostensibly only strove for the public good.[91] Pitt himself actively maintained this image. When the Shelburne ministry faltered, Pitt repositioned himself in a two-hour speech on patriotism and public duty. Invoking the legacy of his father, the 'great commoner', he asserted:

> My earliest impressions were in favour of the noblest and most disinterested modes of serving the public. […] On those principles alone I came into parliament, and into place […]. [H]owever I may stand chargeable with weakness of understanding, or error of judgment, nothing can be imputed to my official capacity which bears the most distant connection with an interested, a corrupt, or a dishonest intention.[92]

90 Cannon, *Fox-North Coalition*, pp. 49, 124–44; Norris, *Shelburne and Reform*, p. 185; Ehrman, *Years of Acclaim*, pp. 123–7.

91 Harling, *Waning of 'Old Corruption'*, pp. 38–9.

92 Speech on 23 February 1783, W. S. Hathaway (ed.), *The Speeches of William Pitt*, vol. 1 (London, 1806), pp. 50–64, quotes on pp. 62–3.

Where other politicians would have earned ridicule for showmanship, Pitt earned only praise. He was perceived as youthful and idealistic, but also credited as being consistent in his high ideals.[93] After all, Pitt's actions seemed to live up to his words. Even during his rapid rise to success, Pitt had never fully attached himself to any political party. On the onset of the Rockingham ministry, he announced that he was not interested in any subordinate position. Trusting Pitt's talent, Shelburne placed him at the head of the Exchequer. When Shelburne was shunned after his fall, no blame fell on Pitt, who had supposedly been too inexperienced to resist Shelburne.[94]

Pitt was not only perceived as incorrupt. He was seen as a reformer. As Chancellor of the Exchequer, he had been involved in the preparation of reform bills and actively (though unsuccessfully) propagated two reform bills from the opposition bench during the Fox–North ministry, the Custom House Reform Bill and the Bill for Preventing Abuses.[95] At the start of his tenure, Pitt also continued to show interest in parliamentary reform and even corresponded with Christopher Wyvill on moderate measures.[96] Public demonisation of the Fox–North coalition and high praise for Pitt resulted in a very favourable outcome in the parliamentary elections of 1784. In his first years in office, Pitt indeed set a number of reform measures in motion. Yet he soon learned the pitfalls of reform and he never again raised economical reform of the offices to the priority it had enjoyed in Shelburne's era.

On 17 February 1785 Pitt addressed the Commons and applauded CEPA. He stressed that

> It was impossible for him, or for parliament, to speak in adequate commendation of the labours of these gentlemen; they had given lights to parliament on subjects hitherto involved in the most inscrutable obscurity, which if pursued by the legislature with equal energy and wisdom, would be productive of the most valuable benefits.[97]

The assertive backing of the Prime Minister must have been valuable to the Commissioners. Economical reform of the offices continued to be sanctioned government policy. Pitt went on to review the twelve completed reports and to summarise their results. Against the backdrop of the

93 Michael Duffy, *Younger Pitt*, pp. 11–12.

94 Harling, *Waning of 'Old Corruption'*, p. 47.

95 House of Commons Sessional Papers of the Eighteenth Century 1715–1800, vol. 35, *Bills 1782–1783 and 1783–1784*; Ehrman, *Years of Acclaim*, pp. 91–3; Parl. Reg., 11, 1783, p. 263.

96 Ibid., p. 14.

97 Parl. Hist., 25, February 1785 to May 1786 (London, 1815), col. 299.

conceptual depth and breadth that the Commissioners had achieved by this point, Pitt's conspectus was remarkably bland. The summary merely provided a vague view on the objects that the Commissioners had scrutinised, enabling Pitt to maximise achievements instead of focusing on systematic deficiencies.[98] After expanding on the introduction of institutional bank accounts in a number of offices, Pitt tackled one deficit that the Commissioners had criticised: the mostly useless, but highly expensive, Exchequer auditing by the Auditors of the Imprest. Pitt moved a bill that replaced the Auditors of the Imprest with a central salaried Commission for Auditing the Public Accounts and provided this commission with a clear business routine. The shunned Auditors received pensions of £7,000 each in compensations, which, though enormous, were still far lower than their former peacetime earnings.[99]

In the following years, the ministry's economic policy focused on the consolidation of state finances leading to the introduction of the sinking fund in 1786. Administrative reforms of the Pitt ministry were single case solutions, not general measures. There was a broad agreement across party lines that most sinecures and useless offices should, in principle, be abolished. However, due to the property theory, the elimination of these offices threatened to cause large expenses for compensations or to cause extensive legal controversies. The Pitt ministry suppressed a number of sinecures when they became vacant, but also reassigned sinecures for political reasons. Pitt denied a number of lucrative spoils for himself, but finally accepted the Warden of the Cinque Ports at King George's insistence.[100] The ministry made no move to implement the systematic reform recommendations of CEPA. A general reform of the Customs, for instance, would have entailed the potentially expensive abolition of 180 offices; a huge effort that Pitt was not prepared to invest.[101] Nor did the Pitt ministry attempt to even gradually change the Civil List offices. After securing two parliamentary bailouts to the tune of £60,000 (1784) and £210,000 (1786), Pitt simply left the Civil List alone, even though it continued to accumulate massive debts. When Pitt left office, the Civil List was almost an entire year

98 Ibid.

99 Among the first members of the new commission, Pitt appointed William Musgrave, who had advised Shelburne on the reform of the Customs, as well as William Molleson, the former Secretary to CEPA. Ehrman, *Years of Acclaim*, pp. 175–6; Binney, *British Public Finance*, p. 13; CEPA to William Pitt, 18 March 1786, in TNA, PRO 30/8/282, part 2, p. 143.

100 Ehrman, *Years of Acclaim*, pp. 189–90. His predecessor as Lord Warden of the Cinque Ports had been Lord North, who died in 1792.

101 Duffy, *Younger Pitt*, pp. 85–6.

in arrears, necessitating a massive grant of £990,000, which led to another round of inquiries in 1802 and 1804.[102]

William Pitt the Younger is often remembered as a reformer. This assessment matches widespread contemporary perceptions, at least during Pitt's first years in office. However, the lackadaisical efforts of the Pitt ministry with regard to economical reform seem to contradict this assessment. As Michael Duffy has pointed out, there are indications that Pitt did not see any need for a grand reform. Pitt regularly praised the British constitution and primarily displayed a conservative idea of reform. In his eyes, defects should be addressed without essentially changing the status quo. For example, when introducing his parliamentary reform motion in 1783, he stressed that he did not mean 'to innovate, but rather to renew and invigorate the spirit of the constitution, without deviating materially from its present form.'[103] He was comfortable with complicated contexts and saw no need for systematisation. Government, he felt, should follow experience and sound judgement, not general principles or theories.[104] Whilst he applauded the Commissioners of Accounts for their efforts at bringing light to the administrative system, Pitt never adopted their principles. Even as late as 1797, Pitt still endorsed the patrimonial creed that 'sinecure offices are given in the nature of a freehold tenure.'[105] Where Shelburne's official line had been geared towards 'a general and grand reform', Pitt reconfigured the subject and limited its scope to the identification and elimination of discrete defects in revenue collection, expenditure accounting, and auditing.

The Commission on Fees

The one general issue that Pitt could not ignore was the regulation of salaries. The Fox–North ministry had discontinued the efforts of the Shelburne ministry to gain an overview over the departments and Pitt did not make the matter a priority either. In 1785, Pitt created a new commission to prepare concrete regulations instead. The new Fees Commissioners received the same authorities as CEPA but reported to the Privy Council, not to Parliament.[106]

102 Ibid., pp. lxxix–lxxxi.

103 Speech on parliamentary reform, 7 May 1783, in Hathaway (ed.), *Speeches of William Pitt*, pp. 72–81, quote on p. 75.

104 Duffy, *Younger Pitt*, pp. 84–5, 88–9.

105 Parl. Hist. 33, March 1797 to November 1798 (London, 1818), col. 87.

106 For their instructions cf. Order directing the Comm[issione]rs appointed by an Act passed this Session to enquire into the Fees, Gratuities etc., 26 August 1785, PRO 30/8/231, pp. 135–7.

The Fees Commission consisted of only three members.[107] The most prominent among them, Francis Baring (1740–1810), was a successful city merchant and banker, who had made a fortune during the American War and almost continuously served as a director of the EIC from 1779 to his death. Baring had served as financial advisor to Shelburne and entered Parliament in 1784.[108] The other two members, John Dick (1721–1804) and William Molleson, held offices as Comptrollers of Army Accounts and belonged to the newly formed Auditors of the Public Accounts. Molleson had also served as a secretary to CEPA. None of the three boasted a particularly impressive public record and, as John Breihan laconically asserts, '[b]y the late 1780s, Baring was becoming deaf, whilst Dick was nearly blind – serious disadvantages for official investigators.'[109]

The act of appointment was much shorter than the one that had instituted CEPA in 1780. It ordered the new commission

> to inquire into the Fees, Gratuities, Perquisites, and Emoluments, which are or have been lately received in the several Publick Offices therein mentioned; to examine into any Abuses which may exist in the same; and to report such observations as shall occur to them, for the better conducting and managing the Business transacted in the said Offices.[110]

The Act made no mention of CEPA, but it shows the effects of their work. Whilst the act still referenced departments by their principals, it also addressed 'any Clerk or Officer within any of the before mentioned Offices or Departments respectively.' The act charged the Fees Commissioners with the task of identifying malpractice and, implicitly, to apply the lessons of their predecessors. Their main objective was to develop concrete proposals for the regulation of salaries, 'for the Correction of Abuses which may have arisen, and to effect such Savings as may be made.' The act also encouraged the Fees Commissioners to offer observations for 'improvement' and 'the better conducting and managing the Business,' but it avoided the politically more volatile term 'reform.'[111]

[107] Breihan, 'Commission on Fees,' pp. 62–3.

[108] John Orbell, 'Lord Shelburne, Finance, and Sir Francis Baring,' in Nigel Aston and Clarissa C. Orr (eds.), *An Enlightenment Statesman in Whig Britain: Lord Shelburne in Context, 1737–1805*, Studies in Early Modern Cultural, Political and Social History (Woodbridge, 2011), 97–113.

[109] Breihan, 'Commission on Fees,' 1785–1801, p. 63.

[110] 25 Geo III, c. 19.

[111] Ibid., pp. 501–2.

For the most part, the Fees Commission's ten reports confined themselves to the application of the principles of CEPA on the offices of the Secretaries of State, the Treasury, the Post Office, and various administrative branches of the Navy.[112] Each report first provided an establishment of the surveyed office that specified the officers with their emoluments and nominal working hours. The Fees Commissioners determined which offices were 'efficient', i.e. vested with duties and conducted personally by the office-holder. The reports considered all positions, from board members via the clerks to lower attendants like door-keepers and messengers, and offered observations for 'future regulation', 'correction', and 'improvement' – the reports rarely spoke of 'reform'.[113] The Fees Commissioners had an eye for financial detail and relentlessly disclosed unnecessary expenses or seemingly trifling gratuities like stationary, Christmas gifts, or the occasional bottle of liquor, which collectively could amount to considerable costs.[114]

By applying the principles of CEPA, the Fees Commissioners could recommend uniform procedures from the outset. In fact, uniformity was one of their main creeds and at times appeared as an end in itself. Whilst 'establishing an exact uniformity through the whole system'[115] of vouchers and accounts throughout the Navy victualling system directly addressed confusion and abuses in accounting, this can hardly be said about the introduction of uniform working hours from ten to four, even where flexible schedules had never led to problems: 'The attendance given at this, and every other public office should, we conceive, be regulated and enforced upon the principles stated in our Fifth Report; it being of great importance that an uniformity of practice do prevail in this respect.'[116]

The regulation of establishments and salaries followed a standardised procedure. The Fees Commissioners estimated the number of necessary offices by workload and often recommended the consolidation or abolition of offices, though they sporadically also suggested an addition.[117] Regular

[112] *Reports of the Commissioners Appointed to Inquire into the Fees Gratuities Perquisites and Emoluments which Are or Have Been Lately Received in the Several Public Offices* (London, 1793).

[113] Ibid., passim.

[114] Fees Commissioners, 'Sixth Report, Dock Yards', *Fees Reports* (London, 1793), 105–56, pp. 155–6.

[115] Fees Commissioners, 'Eighth Report, Victualling Office', Fees Reports (London, 1793), 169–227, p. 215.

[116] Ibid., p. 225. They even included high offices such as the Treasurer of the Navy. Fees Commissioners, 'Fourth Report, Treasurer of the Navy', *Fees Reports* (London, 1793), 55–67, p. 63.

[117] As an example, see the consolidation of the office of the Paymaster of Marine Forces at the Admiralty: Fees Commissioners, 'Third Report, Admiralty', *Fees Reports* (London, 1793), pp. 37–54.

salaries should invariably replace individually received fees, gratuities, and other forms of remuneration. Comprehensive tables specified propositions of regular, moderately raised salaries. Moreover, the Fees Commissioners castigated abusive pension schemes, for example, pensions for officers who only switched positions, or deductions from current salaries for payments to former office-holders. The Fees Commissioners proposed a uniform pension for those retiring for reasons of age or infirmity only, at 50% of the former salary.[118]

Like all contemporary reformers, the Fees Commissioners faced a problem of representation in a political discourse that emphasised retrenchment. Whilst they were able to calculate the additional costs of their schemes in exact terms, they could only hold out a vague promise of future savings:

> It appears therefore that, after paying to every officer a full compensation for the duty required of him, the annual difference of expence will be only 5000 £, an inconsiderable sum compared with the advantages which will be obtained, particularly that of removing the contract between the public officer and the contractor; but this sum too will be compensated by the fees received for the use of the public.[119]

To finance the increased expenses, the Commissioners proposed a single poundage of 1% on all bills to feed a fees-fund, which defrayed the salaries. The fees-fund solution necessitated no radical change of financial structures, but it did not continually secure the funding of salaries either. It is remarkable in this regard that the Fees Commissioners expressly reflected the substantial fluctuation of funds between times of peace, when the poundage would be insufficient, and times of war, during which the poundage would soar. The calculations rested on the expectation of continued warfare. The solutions show a rationalised hardwiring of the fiscal-military state.[120]

Systematic economy, the Fees Commissioners argued, went far beyond the mere reduction of costs. To explicate this creed, the Fees Commissioners provided an almost verbatim quote of the CEPA-definition of 'strict oeconomy, which neither derogates from the honour and dignity of the crown, nor abridges the servant of the public of the due reward of his industry and

118 Fees Commissioners, 'First Report, Secretaries of State', *Fees Reports* (London, 1793), 1–20, p. 20.

119 Fees Commissioners, 'Fifth Report, Commissioners of the Navy', *Fees Reports* (London, 1793), 68–104, p. 102.

120 Ibid.

abilities.'[121] The system should encourage 'faithful and economical' conduct that avoided unnecessary expense, and it needed to preclude embezzlement and abuse wherever possible. Simply cutting back necessary costs, especially salaries, would eventually backfire:

> the payment of every public officer, and the accounts of each establishment relative thereto, will be simplified; the loss which is sustained at present, from the circuitous manner in which those taxes are paid, collected, and re-imbursed, will be avoided, and a considerable fund will accrue therefrom; whilst the arrangement we propose is in every respect, and will upon every occasion, prove to be founded upon the principle of real and substantial oeconomy.[122]

For the Fees Commissioners, economical reform – 'real and substantial economy' – aimed at a profound improvement of the administrative system by means of the consistent implementation of economical principles; failure to assume this systemic perspective equated to false or insubstantial economy.

The empirical development and systematic implementation of principles was just as much the centrepiece of the Fees Commissioners administrative thinking as it had been the centrepiece of CEPA's. Whilst explicit empiricist reasoning did not take up much room in the reports, it is clear that the Fees Commissioners adopted CEPA's empirical ideas. Three reports contain historical sketches of institutions 'to illustrate the observations.'[123] The Fees Commissioners considered it possible and necessary to react to changed circumstances by modifying the given institutions. They also reproduced their predecessors' guarded empiricist rhetoric to anticipate ancient-constitution objections:

> We are moreover averse to innovation upon general principles, from a conviction that the abandoning of an ancient system, and the adoption of a new one, can only be justified when the preference in favour of the latter is sufficiently evident, or correctly ascertained.[124]

[121] Fees Commissioners, 'Ninth Report, Naval and Victualling Departments at Foreign Ports', *Fees Reports* (London, 1793), 228–48, p. 248.

[122] Fees Commissioners, 'Eighth Report', p. 227.

[123] Fees Commissioners, 'Fifth Report', p. 89; cf. Fees Commissioners, 'Seventh Report, Sick and Hurt Office', *Fees Reports* (London, 1793), 157–68, pp. 162–3; Victualling, see id.: 'Seventh Report. Sick and Hurt Office', pp. 142-3; Fees Commissioners, 'Eighth Report', pp. 169–70.

[124] Fees Commissioners, 'Eighth Report', p. 211.

The passage should not be understood as a vindication of customary practice. Rather, it constituted the rhetorical assurance that the suggestions followed from a sound empirical basis. The dissociation from 'innovation upon general principles' refuted possible reproaches of unrealistic and untested theorising. Notwithstanding the reassurance of reluctant innovation, the reports left little doubt that the Fees Commissioners associated 'ancient' institutions with deficiencies, which necessitated future-oriented reform. For example, the Commissioners singled out the Victualling Office at Deptford 'from the circumstance of being the extension of an ancient system [... that] will require material alterations for its better government in future.'[125]

In contrast to the pioneering work of their predecessors, the results of the Fees Commission failed to impress either contemporaries or historians.[126] Generally, the Fees Commissioners are credited for only one original idea. They suggested a Permanent Undersecretary at the Treasury and the Secretaries' Offices, who would stay in office even after a change of ministry. In hindsight, this idea seemingly anticipated later notions of separated political and administrative spheres.[127] However, in the Fees Commissioners' framing, the idea was rather geared towards continuity, qualification, and commitment to business, which 'seems of a nature too important to admit sudden or frequent changes in office, and too laborious to allow of other avocations.'[128] Overall, the Fees Commissioners fulfilled their task. They prepared detailed reform plans for departments, not only applying the solutions of CEPA, but also bringing to bear their predecessors' methods and epistemological conception. The Fees Commissioners' work formed an expedient preparatory step for the kind of general reform that CEPA recommended, notwithstanding the ex-post fact that no such reform followed. The results would only be implemented slowly and fragmentarily. Originally, the Fees Commissioners had been charged with examining a far wider range of offices, including the Army, all revenue and tax offices, and the royal woods and forests.[129] However, the Fees Commissioners' efforts were cut short because they became entangled in a political scandal.

125 Ibid., p. 197.

126 For historians' assessments cf. e.g. Breihan, 'Commission on Fees'; Binney, *British Public Finance*, pp. 16–17.

127 E.g. John Torrance, 'Sir George Harrison and the Growth of Bureaucracy in the Early Nineteenth Century', *EHR*, 83:326 (1968), 52–88, pp. 53–4.

128 Fees Commissioners, 'Second Report, Treasury', *Fees Reports* (London, 1793), 22–36, p. 30.

129 25 Geo III, c. 19, s. 1. For the Crown lands and for Customs, distinct commissions were instituted in 1787 and 1789. Breihan, 'Commission on Fees', p. 63.

At first, Pitt's strategy to keep administrative issues from causing a stir in Parliament was successful. The Fees Commissioners delivered their reports to the Privy Council and the Treasury, where initially nothing was done with them. The interlude of calm ended in May 1787 when the young Charles Grey (1764–1845) attacked Pitt on a range of corrupt practices at the Post Office, mainly the sale of offices and massive private profiteering by packet-boat contracts. On their own, these practices were no scandal, but Grey alleged that the Prime Minister had dismissed one of the joint Postmasters General, Grey's uncle Lord Tankerville (1743–1822), to stop him from intervening. Grey could be sure of opposition support, because Pitt had appointed Charles Jenkinson, a red rag to the opposition, as Tankerville's successor. The Foxite Richard Brinsley Sheridan (1751–1816) duly framed the matter as 'corrupt use of the influence of the Crown' and contended 'that Mr. Pitt had always promised and professed purity, but had acted with as much self-attention, and as much neglect for reform, as any minister whatever.'[130] Pitt and his followers spurned any critique and invoked the ministry's initial reform results and the appointment of the Fees Commissioners, whose agenda also included the Post Office. Abuses at the Post Office certainly needed to be addressed, the ministry argued, but not by Parliament. The opposition assailed the Fees Commissioners and demanded to see their results. Francis Baring pointed to the complexity of their current inquiry, holding 'that he could sooner make an entire report, like those of the commissioners of accounts, than write a single line of the [current] report.'[131] The opposition ridiculed Baring and held him up as an example for incompetence and the ministry's lack of reform effort.

Tankerville's own narrative is worth noting, as he vehemently positioned himself in favour of economical reform, but, in doing so, used arguments which remained deeply rooted in a patrimonial understanding of office. Tankerville called for an inquiry of the Post Office by CEPA and accused Pitt of abusing influence in dismissing him:

> It has been generally understood in this Country, that Persons entitled by their Rank to fill Departments of high Confidence and Importance in the State would condescend to accept such Offices, subject to the degrading Contingency of being discarded, without Ceremony or Qualification, at the arbitrary Pleasure of any Man, or for the Purposes of every occasional Arrangement. A Pretension of this Sort may have existed in the Minds of Ministers, but the Principle has never been avowed.[132]

[130] Parl. Hist., 26: 1788 (London, 1816), col. 1178–9.

[131] Ibid., col. 1190.

[132] Narrative of Lord Tankerville, *JHC 42*: 23 January 1787 to 16 October 1787, col. 805.

According to Tankerville, the traditional elites were both privileged and obliged to fulfil the high offices of state, whilst the ministry's leadership claim was pretentious at best. For Tankerville, Pitt had not only reduced his own credibility as a reformer, but also actively promoted abuse. Tankerville's stance culminated in the classical, patrimonial Whig point: the abuse of influence by the ministry amounted to corruption, which thereby spread throughout the departments of state.[133]

Whilst Grey and the opposition carried the debate, the immediate consequences of this victory were small. Pitt ordered the Fees Commission to prepone the examination of the Post Office and asserted executive control over matters of reform to prevent prolonged parliamentary involvement. In their first nine reports, the Fees Commissioners had followed in the tracks of CEPA by concentrating on a systematic examination of the offices. In the *Tenth Report* on the Post Office, the Commissioners now felt the pressure to get to the bottom of all abuses. In terms of political finesse, taking this approach was not particularly astute. By confirming allegations of abuse without actively refuting the opposition's interpretation of Pitt's personal conduct, the Fees Commissioners got on the wrong side of the Prime Minister. When the newly appointed joint Postmaster General Lord Walsingham (1748–1818) challenged the factual validity of some of the Commissioners' statements, Pitt reacted swiftly and discontinued the Fees Commission, whose members received neither an address of thanks nor even reimbursement of their expenses.[134]

For the next decade, until Pitt was forced to approve of the Finance Committee in 1797, no more general inquiry into administrative matters would be launched. Following a query from the house of Lords, the fees reports were disclosed to Parliament in 1793, but did not cause a notable stir. The same year, the reports were published in a small edition with little circulation.[135]

Implementing the Fees Reports

In October 1789, two years after the discontinuation of the Fees Commissioners, the Privy Council instituted a special committee to address the

[133] Ibid., col. 805–7.

[134] Fees Commissioners, 'Tenth Report, Post Office,' *Fees Reports* (London, 1793), 249–312; Breihan, 'Commission on Fees,' p. 72; Ellis, *Post Office*, pp. 112–15.

[135] In 1805, George Canning (1770–1827) asked Pitt for a copy, because they were 'not to be found at any Bookseller in town.' Canning to Pitt, 23 March 1805, TNA, PRO 30/8/120, 207^{r}.

reports. However, it set no schedule for future committee meetings and in fact the committee did not meet until 1792.[136] At the time of its first meeting, the committee consisted of Pitt, Jenkinson, and Dundas. They simply passed the reports on to the departments in question for comment. The reports on the Treasury itself and on the Post Office were thus referred to Pitt's Treasury, the Secretaries of State – among them Dundas as Home Secretary – received theirs, whilst the remaining reports went to the Lords of the Admiralty. The special committee gave the departmental heads free rein and set no deadline for their answers.[137]

The first answers followed a year later, when the Lords of the Treasury submitted their considerations on 25 May 1793.[138] Shelburne's Treasury reform of 1782 had already centred on remuneration by salary and personal exercise of office. The Fees Commissioners accordingly had had relatively little to complain about. The reforms 'appear to have been wise, judicious, and effectual, and at the same time that they have diminished the abuses, have very much added to the accuracy and dispatch in conducting the business of this important public office.'[139] Still, in the eyes of the Fees Commissioners, there was room for improvement, 'to complete other parts of the system, which seem as yet imperfect.'[140] The Treasury Board's answer was signed by William Pitt together with Edward James Eliot (1758–97) and Richard Hopkins (1728?–99), two trusted yet inconspicuous senior politicians. They took up a number of smaller suggestions on technicalities and often generally agreed but proved less enthusiastic about the systematic implementation of principles. The answer shows the reluctance of the Pitt ministry to touch existing privileges or offices. The few remaining sinecures would be abolished only after the death of their current office holders and also retain their remuneration scheme, by which the operative deputy was partly paid by the nominal office-holder. Similarly, the Treasury Board agreed that no pensions should be paid to people who had only shifted office, but would not take away pensions already granted in that line.[141] The Treasury Board outright denied to introduce an oath of

[136] Draft minute of the Privy Council, 20 October 1789, TNA, PC 4/5.

[137] Miscellaneous council papers, TNA, PC 1/19/27, n. pag.

[138] Report of the Commissioners of the Treasury to the Committee of the Lords of His Majesty's most hon[ourab]le Privy Council on Regulations recommended by the Commissioners of Enquiry to be adopted in the Office of His Majesty's Treasury, 25 May 1793, in TNA, PC 1/20/31, n. pag.

[139] Fees Commissioners, 'Second Report', pp. 29–30.

[140] Ibid.

[141] Report of the Lords of the Committee of Council upon the Second Report of the Commissioners, 18 June 1793, TNA, PC 1/20/31, n. pag.

fidelity, one of the favourite measures of the Fees Commissioners for the prevention of abuses, and they refused to abolish New Year's gifts. In both cases, the Lords of the Treasury simply replied that 'no inconveniences' followed from the current practice. Reform, according to their reasoning, was not the introduction of a new system, but the suppression of individual defects or abuses. Where they saw no problem in the current practice, they saw no need for intervention.[142]

Together with their reply on their own department, the Lords of the Treasury handed in their answer to the report on the Post Office.[143] The Treasury did not engage in detail with the recommendations of the scandal-ridden *Tenth Report*, instead only endorsing the observations of the two joint Postmasters Lord Walsingham and Lord Chesterfield (1755–1815).[144] The leading voice was Thomas de Grey, second Baron Walsingham, whose intervention on factual mistakes in the *Tenth Report* had led to the discontinuation of the Fees Commission.

The Postmasters' observations engaged more with the details of the Fees Commissioners' arguments than with their general reasoning. In addition to the proposed new establishment of the Post Office, the observations broke down the recommendations into a table of almost 100 single points, with a short statement annexed to each of them. Backing these statements, the observations included fifty appendices: copies of letters, minutes, and individual accounts. The observations constitute an almost total rejection of the Fees Commissioners' proposals.[145]

The Fees Commissioners had proposed that the Accountant General of the Post Office be endowed with more competencies in order to strengthen the internal audit of the Post Office. This, it was hoped, would be a central measure in helping to check embezzlements there.[146] The Postmasters General objected to this measure, as it would – necessarily – restrict their own central authority. They argued that 'if their Officers are to be exempted from Obedience to them perpetual confusion must ensue.'[147] The Postmasters did accept the introduction of a fees-fund. The regularised salaries were, however, markedly higher than the Fees Commissioners had proposed and the

142 Ibid.

143 Report of Treasury Commissioners on the Office of H[is] M[ajesty]'s Post Master General, 25 May 1793, in TNA, PC 1/20/31, n. pag.

144 Observations of the Postmaster General on the report of the Commissioners' Enquiry, 1793, RMA, POST 59/178.

145 Ibid., fols. 1–14.

146 Breihan, 'Commission on Fees,' p. 73.

147 Observations of the Postmaster General on the report of the Commissioners' Enquiry, 1793, RMA, POST 59/178, fol. $7^{v/r}$, fol. $8^{v/r}$.

observations retained a long list of exceptions. This list included the 'Fees on registering Packets of Value in the Foreign Office', which had proven to be especially open to abuse, as clerks had turned a blind eye to smuggling in exchange for voluntary fees. The Postmasters General argued that 'These Fees are optional, if they went to the Public the Merchants would not pay for them, therefore the clerks would lose a profit which the Merchants now pay willingly & which the Public would not then get.'[148] Private persons would voluntarily pay individual officers, but certainly not into the cash box of an institution.

Another notable exception was the franking privilege of the Clerks of the Roads. The remuneration scheme of these clerks depended on their privilege of privately trading newspapers outside of London. Up to 1764, trading newspapers had even been their monopoly (shared with the clerks at the Secretaries' of State offices). Even without a monopoly, the clerks enjoyed many advantages in the trade because they were a central part of the postal distribution system.[149]

The objection was based on two remarkable letters written by the clerks in question. The clerks complained that they had never been recompensed for the loss of their monopoly and other privileges in 1764.[150] However, this conventional patrimonial argument did not constitute the clerks' main pattern of argumentation. Rather, the clerks relied on economic reasoning and even Smithian points of market economy to make their point. Against the Fees Commissioners' proposal to form a newspaper office financed by a franking tax via a fees-fund, the Clerks of the Roads argued that this price increase would result in a decline of demand and, consequently, of revenue.[151] The clerks proposed keeping their privilege and offered to lower their charge for distribution. The lower prices, they explained, would create a market scenario in which all stakeholders – the public, the revenue, and the clerks – profited:

> By preserving the privilege of franking to the Clerks of the Roads a competition will be occasioned between them & the other Dealers, the Public will be supplied on more moderate terms, and an increase of consumption will be promoted but should this competition be destroyed by the abolition of the privilege of the Clerks of the Roads,

148 Ibid., fol. $9^{v/r}$.

149 Ellis, Post Office, pp. 47–59.

150 Observations of the Postmaster General on the report of the Commissioners' Enquiry, 1793, Appendix Ae, The clerks of the roads to the Postmasters General, n.d., in RMA, POST 59/178, p. 87.

151 Ibid., p. 84.

> the principal Dealers purchasing the business carried on by less extensive circulation might thereby occasion a monopoly and then fix the price as it might suit their private interest and diminish the Number of Newspapers circulated thereby greatly injuring the Revenue.[152]

The argument is questionable in terms of market economy. The clerks depicted their private competitors as a collective monopolist, whilst the privileged clerks appear as the element of competition. But more than this curious reversion of terms, it is the clerks' application of rather sophisticated economical reasoning in defence of a customary privilege that stands out. Whilst the clerks clearly did not take recourse to arguments of administrative economy, they made an economic argument. In spite of their vastly different understanding of terms, the Clerks of the Roads did thereby base their argument on the proposed benefit to the state, which they offered to maximise by use of economic theory.[153] In the table, the Postmasters General emphasised the privilege's origin in statute as well as the missing compensation and finally referred to the clerks own objections without reproducing the clerks' argument.[154]

The Postmasters General answered in considerable detail to the recommendations, but they rarely engaged with the Fees Commissioners' larger arguments. They treated the recommendations as mere proposals with no normative weight. The Lords of the Treasury, in this case William Pitt, Richard Hopkins, and Lord Camden (1759–1840) passed the observations on to the Privy Council committee on 27 May 1793, which read them on 18 June and gave its approval, which in turn was confirmed by the King and Privy Council on 21 June.[155]

Two years later, and only after some urging by Pitt, the Secretaries of State submitted their answer in 1795. In their letter, the Duke of Portland, William Wyndham Grenville (1759–1834), and Henry Dundas, all members of Cabinet, expressed their general refusal of the Fees Commissioners' recommendations. The Secretaries could not quite ignore the government policy of introducing salaries, but they defended the option of fee-based emoluments:

152 Observations of the Postmaster General on the report of the Commissioners' Enquiry, 1793, Appendix Af, The Clerks of the Roads to the Postmasters General, n.d., in RMA, POST 59/178, pp. 83–4, quote on pp. 92–3.

153 Ibid., pp. 89–93.

154 Observations of the Postmaster General on the report of the Commissioners' Enquiry, 1793, in RMA, POST 59/178, fol. 8$^{v/r}$.

155 Report of Treasury Commissioners on the Office of H[is] M[ajesty]'s Post Master General, 27 May 1793, in TNA, PC 1/20/31, n. pag.; Minutes of the Privy Council of 18 and 21 June 1793, TNA, PC 2/138, pp. 330, 346.

> With regard to the general Question of Fees and Gratuities, those which are now received in our respective Offices are, as we conceive, in their extent so moderate, and have so long been authorized by Order of Council, or by Custom, that we see no ground for their abolition.[156]

The Secretaries reluctantly agreed to introduce a fees-funds, which, they argued, would prevent any individual acceptance of advantages in the future. At the same time, they subverted this ban on individual fees and gratuities by proposing to reward a meritorious clerk by a poundage on the volume of collected money.[157]

The Fees Commissioners had proposed to consolidate some functions in order to reduce the number of clerks and messengers and to abolish the remaining sinecures.[158] The Secretaries, in contrast, defended the necessity of places by reference to the war situation and they questioned the Fees Commissioners' competence in an openly confrontational tone that is rarely found in similar internal documents. For example, the Secretaries stated that '[t]he reasoning of the Commissioners on the nature of the Duty of the Chamber Keepers does not appear to be well founded' and declared that the Commissioners 'do not appear to have understood' the accounting process of messenger bills.[159] The defence even included unambiguous sinecures, even though they conceded that the offices in question fulfilled no noteworthy duties.

> The Nomination to these Offices however [...] affords almost the only means which the Secretaries of State have of rewarding Officers for diligence and long Services; and it is on this footing that we are disposed to recommend their continuance.[160]

This justification refers to the typically patrimonial aspect of gratification. The Secretaries clearly did not agree to the principle of a clear differentiation of pensions or annuities from offices. Though not high in number, these places directly concerned the Secretaries' patronage capital. The Secretaries addressed patronage as a specific means to reward meritorious service. A strict salary scheme, they argued, lacked incentives for exceptional effort or ability.

156 Portland to Dundas, 26 February 1795, in TNA, PC 1/24/43, n. pag.
157 Ibid., PC 1/24/43, n. pag.
158 Fees Commissioners, 'First Report', pp. 15–17.
159 Portland to Dundas, 26 February 1795, in TNA, PC 1/24/43, n. pag.
160 Ibid., n. pag.

Pensions were the most common instruments of reward. The Secretaries ostensibly agreed to the Fees Commissioners' proposals but refused the suggested regularisation at 50% of a former salary. Instead, the amount 'ought to be decided on a consideration of the merit and services of such Officer, and not by any fixed rate'. Nor did the Secretaries see the need to strictly limit pensions to retirement for reasons of age or infirmity, because 'cases may sometimes happen (tho' perhaps seldom) when a strict adhesion to the Regulation may be found inconvenient, and that it will not be adviseable [sic] to establish it as a fixed principle.'[161] The explicit argument could be summarised as flexibility – why restrain the Secretaries' discretionary power? To the Secretaries there was simply no point to what they saw as unnecessary constraints. The Secretaries' defence of their authority makes sense in a Blackstonian understanding of the state: the King externalised executive functions to the Secretaries, who, in turn, externalised these functions to subordinate officers. In a strictly patrimonial understanding, the allocation of a pension was always an act of grace, even if every officer could expect to receive it. Keywords like 'economy', 'uniformity', or even 'reform' were not used in the documents at all, 'system' only in the most general sense. All issues with regard to the offices appeared as discrete cases personally dependent on the Secretaries.[162]

The Secretaries' concept was read and approved first by the committee of the Privy Council and, on its recommendation, accepted by the Privy Council in the presence of the King on 27 February 1795 with minor changes. The Secretaries had refrained from setting their own salaries and only suggested that the current wartime surplus to their fees-income be taken into account. The Privy Council set the salaries at £6,000, a hefty £1,500 above the Fees Commissioners' suggestion.[163] Apparently, the implementation of the Fees Commissioners' reform ideas that went beyond the introduction of salaries had little weight in the Privy Council. The formal separation of institutions involved in the decision-making – the Secretaries, the Privy Council, and its committee – was a farce. The Secretaries' letter to the Lord President of the Privy Council dates to 23 February. On that day, the three Secretaries sat together with Pitt, Charles Jenkinson, and the Lord President to discuss a minor point concerning embargos, which was the only official matter at the Privy Council that day.[164] The letter was officially read on 26 February, when almost the same group was attending to

[161] Ibid., n. pag.

[162] Ibid., n. pag.

[163] Privy Council Committee Minute of 27 February 1795, in TNA, PC 4/5, n. pag.; Order of Council of 27 February 1795, in TNA, PC 2/142, pp. 168–70.

[164] Council minute of 23 February 1795, in TNA, PC 4/5.

council business.[165] Whilst the Secretaries were not part of the committee, Henry Dundas had been part of it before and again appears as one of eight members, who resolved the committee's decision paper.[166] There was no critical appraisal of the Secretaries' concept by an independent institution. Rather, a small group of Pitt's inner circle informally came to an agreement and then recorded it formally. The ministry's inner circle mostly remained attached to a patrimonial understanding of office and did not attribute much significance to administrative reform.

The Fees Commissioners and Navy Reform

Of the ten reports the Fees Commission had finished before it was discontinued, seven dealt with different departments of the civil administration of the Navy. As soon as the Fees Commissioners started working on these reports, they became involved in the ongoing internal contestations within the Navy. More specifically, Charles Middleton attempted to win the Fees Commission over for his ongoing efforts to reform Navy administration from the inside.

As soon as Pitt assumed office, Middleton resumed his efforts to carry on his reform agenda. He now went behind the back of Lord Howe (1726–99) as First Lord of the Admiralty, who disapproved of Middleton's plans as strongly as his predecessor.[167] Middleton happily provided the Fees Commissioners with information and added his own matured plans in December 1786. The Fees Commissioners gratefully accepted the Comptroller's input and closely cooperated with Middleton on their reports.[168]

Middleton did not materially change his former concept, but he revised some points and notably improved on the presentation.[169] He equally refined the language of his *Observations on the Navy Board.* Now, he made excessive use of keywords such as 'simplicity', 'method', 'principle', and 'economy', though he used 'arrangement' or 'machine' rather than 'system' when he referred to the Navy departments and generally emphasised morally upstanding and purposeful conduct over institutional structures. Whilst he

165 Instead of Henry Dundas, Lord Auckland is noted as present. Council minute of 26 February 1795. TNA, PC 1/24/43.

166 Privy council minute of 27 February 1795, in PC 2/142, p. 166.

167 Ehrman, *Years of Acclaim*, pp. 314–15.

168 Baring, Dick, and Molleson to Middleton, 11 December 1786, in John K. Laughton (ed.), *Letters and Papers of Charles, Lord Barham Admiral of the Red Squadron, 1758–1813*, vol. 2 (London, 1910), p. 250.

169 Talbott, *Pen and Ink Sailor*, p. 116.

retained the somewhat old-fashioned form 'reformation' and sometimes argued by precedent, Middleton aimed for future-oriented institutional change. Historical change necessitated change in practices:

> The methods in use, however convenient they might have been in the Infancy of the Department, and to the management of a small Business, are by no means suitable to its present state, or to the vast sums of Money which continually pass through it.[170]

The reform agenda continued to revolve around the authority of the Comptroller. Middleton refined his concept of authority by adding 'power of control' and 'responsibility':

> Incredible sums, which under the present unmethodical Practice must pass almost wholly without Inquiry may be chequed & saved to the Public; and if, together with such Reformation, a controuling Power and consequent Responsibility were lodged with the Head of the Office, sufficient to conduct and give Energy to this great Machine, and to correct the many abuses, under which at present it labors.[171]

The main conceptual addition was the reorganisation of the Navy Board into three committees – Correspondence, Accounts, and Stores – each of which supervised three commissions and several senior clerks. The Comptroller would preside over each committee and 'occasionally assist at all of them'. In order to be able to concentrate on his steering role, Middleton asked for a deputy comptroller, who would take over day-to-day tasks and represent him in his absence.[172] Whilst there were precedents for such a structure, e.g. the EIC's Court of Directors,[173] it constituted a radical break with established Navy practices.

Middleton developed a firm hold over the Fees Commissioners. After a year of cooperation, Francis Baring assured Middleton that his plans had become the core part of their recommendations:

170 Charles Middleton, Observations on the Navy Board Department, NMM, MID 14/6, n. pag.

171 Ibid.

172 Ibid.; Charles Middleton, Arrangement of Business at the Navy Board and in the Office of Correspondence with Observations for the Consideration of the several Committees, MID 14/10; id., Arrangement of Business for the Consideration of the Navy Board and its Committees, 1789, NMM, MID 14/11.

173 Huw V. Bowen, *The Business of Empire. The East India Company and Imperial Britain* (Cambridge, 2006), pp. 182–218.

> I am very happy to assure you that the material part of the system which you have recommended appears so satisfactory to my brethren as well as myself from a thorough conviction of the necessity of the case, that I am thoroughly persuaded we shall have no difficulty to adopt it.[174]

Although he continued to treat the introduction of regular salaries as secondary issues, Middleton finally dropped his request for exceptions in the later versions of the *Observations*. Middleton was able to convince the Fees Commissioners and he had Pitt's ear. However, his activities were met with strong resistance within the Navy. He complained to Pitt that

> as it was discovered that my opinions went to reformation of abuses; [...] I very early discovered a jealousy against myself, which I had never before experienced; a jealousy which, from the encouragement it has received by the doubtful postponing of the reports, has put me into such a new and awkward situation, as renders me unable to bring forward any matter, beyond the mere current business of office, without opposition or hazard of success.[175]

The vivid description was intended to convince Pitt to intervene, but it is plausible that Middleton's reforming endeavours fuelled the ongoing conflict within the Navy. As he lacked formal authority, Middleton was vulnerable to noncompliance or outright refusal of cooperation. The fact that he had been forced to drop his defence of fees certainly did not help his position with the clerks.

Resistance to Middleton's plans was not confined to the clerks. Rather, the higher echelons of the Navy administration shared the clerks' customary notions and forcefully brought them to bear. For the distinct institutional culture of the Navy, customary ways of working were a matter of great significance and, arguably, identity.[176] In July 1789, George Jackson (1725–1822), since 1768 Judge Advocate of the Navy and an experienced Navy administrator, composed a detailed counterstatement to the *Fourth Report* of the Fees Commission, which contained Middleton's central notions of reorganisation.[177] Jackson presented a historical sketch of the Royal Navy to argue by precedent. According to Jackson, the Navy Board had been

[174] Baring to Middleton, 3 December 1787, in Laughton (ed.), *Letters and Papers*, p. 287.
[175] Middleton to Pitt, 8 February 1790, in ibid., pp. 338–9.
[176] Douglas W. Allen, *The Institutional Revolution. Measurement and the Economic Emergence of the Modern World* (Chicago, 2012), pp. 106–45.
[177] Observations upon the Reform in the Navy Office. July 1789, in JCK/7, pp. 89–116.

instituted as a collegial council of distinct officers, in which the Comptroller was given precedence, but no superior authority.[178] Jackson's derivation of the normative force of the Navy's original ordinations is a text-book case of ancient constitution reasoning:

> It has been made to appear, that the Constitution of the Civil Department of the Navy was first formed in the Time of Edward the 6th, now nearly two Centurys [sic] and a half ago. It is then fair to conclude, that the Principle was digested, and formed on a Basis adapted and perfectly suited to its Object; otherwise the Practice would not have been continued so long;[179]

For Jackson, the ancient origins of the Navy's constitution established its normative character. To him, the Navy's constitution combined the superior faculties of its founders with the cumulative experience of its long existence. The allegation that it had endured for centuries without material alteration reinforced its claim to perfection. Jackson's argument thus directly reversed the understanding of history displayed by Middleton and the Fees Commissioners. In Jackson's eyes, the Navy Board should always act as a guardian of the old forms:

> Whenever Innovations were attempted, the Navy Board has regularly resisted them; always insisting, that to break in upon the Forms of Business, would be nearly as fatal as Neglect, and dangerous to the good government of the Civil Branch; and that Rules and Precedents in great and extensive Affairs, are the only safe Arguments which can justify what is done. The more the Navy is increased, the more it seems a Foundation for a strict adherence to this Principle.[180]

Jackson thus transposed the ancient constitution argument to categorically justify resistance to change. Nothing could endanger the management of business as much as confusion; and confusion must, by necessity, be the result of the proposed reforms. The abolition of fees may seem 'in Appearance very captivating,' he conceded, but in many situations it was absolutely acceptable for a merchant to pay for the acceleration of business.[181] The cases of abuse did not warrant placing clerks and merchants

[178] George Jackson, Observations upon the Reform in the Navy Office, July 1789, in NMM, JCK/7, pp. 92–3.

[179] Ibid., p. 96.

[180] Ibid., p. 98.

[181] Ibid., p. 109.

under a general suspicion. After all, anyone could issue a complaint to the Navy Board.[182]

Middleton's foremost opponent was Lord Howe, who felt threatened by Middleton's efforts. Writing to Pitt in September 1787, Howe exerted his full authority against his unruly Comptroller. Howe, too, invoked the established constitution of the Navy:

> I cannot but totally differ in all Sir Charles's Ideas of giving more authority to the Comptroller of the Navy than he will derive from the countenance of the Admiralty. That general position is consonant to the constitution of the Navy Board and consistent with the soundest policy.[183]

Unlike Jackson, Howe did not engage with Middleton's reform reasoning, instead simply denying precedents of allegedly stronger positions of past Comptrollers. Howe threatened to veto Middleton's promotion to the rank of admiral due by seniority unless Middleton gave up the Comptrollership.[184] In the end, Middleton won the day. Pitt took his side and dismissed Howe, whose position in Cabinet was fragile. As successor, Pitt appointed his own brother John Pitt, second Lord Chatham (1756–1835), who duly confirmed Middleton's admiral rank in the Comptroller's office.[185]

After the completion of the Fees Commissioners' report on the Navy Office in February 1788, Middleton and the Pitt brothers were in close communication on details of the reform plan.[186] However, before any reform could be enacted, the Regency Crisis brought government to a near standstill. With the King unable to sanction orders of council and no regent in place, little could be done. The King recovered in March 1789, but Middleton's window of opportunity had passed.[187] Although he continued to urge both Pitt brothers on, neither the Prime Minister nor the First Lord would support any large-scale reform of the Navy anymore. When it became clear that nothing would be done, Middleton resigned in March 1790.[188]

With the British entry in the Wars of the Coalition in 1793, workload and fees exploded once again. Middleton's successor, Henry Martin (1733–94),

[182] Ibid., p. 110.

[183] Howe to Pitt, 22 September 1787, in TNA, PRO 30/8/148, fols. 215–16, quote on 216^{r}.

[184] Howe to Pitt, 25 September 1787, in PRO 30/8/148, fols. 217–18, quote on 217^{v}.

[185] Ehrman, *Years of Acclaim*, p. 315; Breihan, 'Commission on Fees', p. 67.

[186] Ibid., pp. 67–8; Morriss, *Naval Power*, p. 136.

[187] Ehrman, *Years of Acclaim*, pp. 315–17.

[188] Middleton to Pitt, 8 February and 15 March 1790, in Laughton (ed.), *Letters and Papers*, pp. 337–47.

who did not possess his predecessor's capacity for work, was disburdened by the appointment of a deputy comptroller. Martin's successors received higher salaries than the other Navy Commissioners.[189] In the aftermath of Middleton's reform efforts, the position of Comptroller would thus be strengthened after all.

The Admiralty Board finally considered the Fees Commissioners' report on the Navy Office in 1796 and endorsed many of Middleton's central propositions.[190] The answer unreservedly fell in with the Fees Commissioners' line on salaries and introduced a fees-fund to defray the increased salaries and regulated pensions. Clerks were forced to deposit a security and were banned from privately profiting from any contract they were concerned with. The most striking measure was the introduction of a functionally defined committee structure. As Middleton had proposed, the Comptroller presided over each committee and was even endowed with a superintending power and a secret service fund. Whilst the regulation considerably strengthened the Comptroller, his authority did not come close to what Middleton had intended. The Comptroller remained responsible to the Navy Board, and his only extra weight was the deciding vote in case of ties.[191]

The Admiralty Board's answer introduced far-reaching changes along the lines of economical office reform and made no exceptions for customary practice or vested privilege. However, the answer lacked reformatory fervour. Instead of engaging with the report's general reasoning, the Admiralty Board simply stated that 'we agree in Opinion with the Commissioners in many of the important Points contained in their Report.'[192] There is a conspicuous lack of economical language of reform. The answer did not indicate 'reforms', merely 'regulations'. Nor did it discuss its subject matter in terms of 'system' or 'principles'. The loudest omission is 'economy', which neither appears as a word nor as a regulating idea. The answer did not relate to retrenchment or to an overarching idea of improvement, but rather seems to pay service to conservative, though not explicitly patrimonial, positions. The introduction of committees, for instance, 'should not be understood as intended to disturb in other Respects the present Form of each Department.'[193]

189 J. M. Collinge, *Navy Board Officials 1660–1832* (London, 1978), p. 10.

190 Admiralty Board to the Lords of the Committee of His Majesty's Most Honourable Pricy Council, 2 May 1796, Finance Committee, 'Seventeenth Report', *SP 109* (Wilmington, 1975), 145–89, pp. 159–65.

191 Admiralty Board to the Lords of the Committee, 2 May 1796, in ibid., pp. 160–1.

192 Ibid., p. 160.

193 Ibid., p. 161.

It has been argued that the Admiralty answer on the Navy Board may have been pushed by Middleton himself.[194] However, Middleton had resigned from his new position as First Naval Commissioner once more in October 1795 after quarrels with Lord Spencer (1758–1834), who had succeeded Chatham as First Lord in December 1794 in a Cabinet reshuffle. Without prior Navy service, Spencer had no personal stake in customary Navy practice.[195] Rather, the Admiralty's answer to the Fees Commissioners' report responded to the internal situation and the necessities of war. Middleton's vigorous efforts for reform had led to a polarisation of opinion within the Navy. The ongoing war efforts needed an effective Navy Office and internal conflicts would have been dangerous. Lord Spencer attended the special committee of the Privy Council when it endorsed the answer without making any changes.[196] The reform of the Navy Office did not mark a large-scale reform effort within the Navy, but remained a singular measure at a point of time when administrative reform played hardly any role in Parliament or in government circles.

During the first years of Pitt's ministry, administrative reform was not a priority, but measures were implemented in small steps as long as they did not conflict with financial consolidation or cause political contestation. Michael Duffy has argued that, notwithstanding the patchwork character of the measures, Pitt's ministry still effected the most reform results of any ministry of the eighteenth century.[197] It was also the first ministry after the Economical Reform Debates that lasted long enough to do so. Pitt never pushed administrative reforms himself, but he did lend a reasonable measure of support to proactive reformers during the first years of his ministry. Towards the end of the 1780s, however, he ceased his efforts. Interpretations on this sudden reversal of policy vary. John Ehrman holds that Pitt had simply shifted priorities. John Breihan attributes the change of policy to the aftermath of the Post Office scandal that coincided with the Regency Crisis.[198] In fact, economical reform had never been a priority for Pitt to start with and the crises painfully revealed that his ministry continued to be vulnerable. From his conservative constitutional understanding, Pitt made sure to defend the prerogatives of the executive against parliamentary encroachment. Pitt fought hard to prevent a regency by the Prince of

194 Morriss, *Royal Dockyards*, p. 192.

195 Malcolm Lester, 'Spencer, George John, second Earl Spencer (1758–1834)', *ODNB*.

196 Privy council minute of 8 June 1796, TNA, PC 4/7, n. pag. The other attendees were Lord Chatham, now Lord President of the Privy Council, William Eden, Dudley Ryder, Charles Jenkinson, and Charles Townshend.

197 Duffy, *Younger Pitt*, p. 95.

198 Ehrman, *Years of Acclaim*, p. 317; Breihan, 'Commission on Fees', pp. 76–81.

Wales, who was close to Fox and anyways disturbed the relative quiescence about the Civil List by accruing massive debts due to his excessive lifestyle. The last thing that Pitt needed was another parliamentary controversy over the Crown. Additionally, the playing field was changed by the ramifications of the French Revolution. Fearing 'English Jacobins,' the government grew increasingly authoritarian and cracked down hard on political societies or radical ideas. This authoritarian turn also affected administrative reform that was, after all, closely connected to parliamentary reform. When Britain entered the War of the First Coalition in 1793, administrative reform faded into the background. However, by the late 1790s, Pitt's personal reform aura was subsiding. With war expenditure soaring and well-known administrative defects remaining unfixed, the topic would return to the political stage after 1796 with a vengeance.

5

British India: Enforcing Reform

In the nineteenth century, the colonial administration in British India would serve as a model for the British Civil Service. The foundations of the world's first 'Civil Service' were already in place by 1800. Yet, from the 1760s until into the 1790s, the administration of British India had been synonymous with corruption and maladministration. Between the assumption of territorial rule by the British East India Company (EIC) in 1757 and the end of the eighteenth century, the colonial administration underwent several transformations. Decisive economical reforms took place in 1788 and they were based on the recommendations of the Commissioners for Examining the Public Accounts. British India provides the prime example of a consistent administrative reform process in the eighteenth century.

The administrative reforms in British India were embedded in a larger transformation of the colonial government. With the assumption of territorial sovereign rights in 1757, a merchant company turned into a territorial government, but it continued to be managed as a joint-stock company. Neither the Company structures nor the Company staff were prepared for their new tasks. Accordingly, the EIC came under massive pressure and the shareholders' unrealistic expectations of returns added to widespread internal uncertainty. Twice, in 1772 and in 1784, the EIC faced bankruptcy. The British state intervened in both cases, regulated the Company, and successively assumed executive control. The British territories in India repeatedly came under military threat, so that the continued existence of the dominion was far from safe. Even more so than in Britain, the reforms in India took place against the backdrop of permanent crisis. Throughout the second half of the eighteenth century, administrative reforms in British India were first and foremost instruments of crisis management.

The transition from the tenure of Warren Hastings as Governor General (1773–85) to that of Charles Cornwallis (1786–93) marked a pivotal change in colonial governance. Warren Hastings was committed to establishing a sovereign Company state. By command of the EIC leadership in London, Hastings installed Company personnel in the revenue administration, but he also sought continuity with the 'ancient Mughal constitution'.

Administrative reforms carried out in the course of his tenure followed the principle of trial and error. Cornwallis, by contrast, focused on systematic administrative reforms along the lines of CEPA, whose methods he knew well. In the deliberate application and consistent implementation of the reforms within only one year, he expanded on CEPA's work. Under Charles Cornwallis, the systematically reformed administrative apparatus became a cornerstone of colonial government. After 1798, Governor General Richard Wellesley continued the 'Cornwallis System' and took it to the extreme. While he pursued a policy of military expansion, Wellesley internally relied on extreme discipline and efficiency. The successive implementation of rationalist administrative reforms took place in parallel with a process of alienation of the colonial rulers from the Indian population. At the time of Hastings, India could still be conceptualised as an advanced civilisation whose inhabitants had long suffered from despotism. During Cornwallis' and Wellesley's tenures, the regime increasingly uncoupled itself from the local population and stigmatised Indians as inherently corrupt.

Cornwallis and succeeding Governors General had quasi-despotic authority at their disposal. The agency of these central actors should not be underestimated. Although there was inertia and resistance within the ranks of the Company, the Governors General laid down the main lines from a position of power. In the case of Cornwallis, his particular agency resulted not only from his authority but also from his specific knowledge. While the Company leadership in Britain at most reacted passively to the economical reform discourse, Cornwallis brought the new administrative reform ideas to fruition.

The administrative reform processes are a good example of the complex networking that connected the colonies with the metropolis. In Britain, the colonial situation was always perceived through the filter of domestic discourses. India represented the promise of wealth and simultaneously a cesspit that threatened to corrupt the empire. Gradually, the number of agents boasting some expertise grew, but the overarching discourse was dominated by simplistic assumptions and philosophical questions. For most contexts, presupposing a relation of a periphery subordinate to the centre would be fundamentally wrong. The situation on the ground was always the decisive factor for decision-making. However, the notion that India served as a mostly disconnected laboratory of the empire is also flawed. The framework conditions imposed by the metropolitan centre may have been repeatedly undermined on the ground, but they still showed formative effects. In this setup, much came down to the experiences and connections of individual actors, whose fluctuation and diverse correspondences bound the empire together. The administrative reforms in British India were not conceived in London or modelled on an existing British example, nor did they emerge in India independently of Britain. Rather, the actors on the ground made use of British state-of-the-art administrative reform concepts in order to better handle the local crisis situation.

India in British Debates on Corruption

As of the late 1760s, British India figured prominently in the British discourse on corruption. The Indian case touched all aspects of the discourse: corruption of officers, the corrupt influence of the Crown and the elite, moral corruption, as well as constitutional corruption. Indian administrative issues became affairs of state. This is hardly self-evident as Indian affairs concerned the EIC that was, after all, a privately owned joint-stock corporation operating in Asia on the basis of a Crown charter. Yet, Indian trade had always entailed a national diplomatic dimension. By the middle of the eighteenth century, the British and French acted out their antagonism on the subcontinent. As two great powers among many others, the respective East India Companies participated in prolonged power struggles within the framework of the Mughal Empire. These games of changing local alliances were intertwined with the Anglo–French rivalry that was carried out by private forces and European-trained sepoy units, as well as regular forces. The Third Carnatic War (1757–63) can be considered an extension of the Seven Years' War into Indian territories and waters.[1]

The public national angle on Indian affairs was thus already established when the EIC became a territorial power in Bengal. In a series of struggles that reached their climax in the Battle of Plassey in 1757, the Company first became the power behind the throne of the Nawab (the prince of Bengal) and finally forced the Nawab into dependency. A final attempt to expel the British even involved the Mughal Emperor Shah Alam II (1728–1806), but this alliance suffered defeat in the Battle of Buxar in 1764. In the following year, the Emperor, now in dire need of allies, granted the Company the *diwani*, a privilege comprising taxation rights and civil jurisdiction of Bengal in exchange for a yearly tribute. By the logic of the Mughal Empire, the *diwani* entailed only a limited set of rights granted to the *de facto* power in Bengal, but the officers of the EIC now considered themselves territorial rulers of Bengal, a claim that they backed with military power.

1 Cf. e.g. Seema Alavi (ed.), *The Eighteenth Century in India* (Oxford, 2002); Meurer, 'State-Building'; Daniel A. Baugh, *The Global Seven Years War, 1754–1763. Britain and France in a Great Power Contest* (Harlow, 2011).

Though formal questions of sovereignty were complicated both in British and Mughal legal terms, the Company became, for all practical concerns, a territorial power in India.[2]

The granting of the *diwani* plunged the EIC into a series of political, economic, and administrative crises. There were also repercussions in England, where India became a topic of political dispute.[3] Robert Clive (1725–74), the Governor of Bengal, presented the takeover in Bengal to ministry and Parliament as a *fait accompli*, which he sweetened by optimistically calculating a yearly surplus of 1.6 million pounds from land taxes. This calculation not only overestimated the revenue, but, more crucially, vastly underestimated the administrative challenge of territorial rule; a challenge for which the merchant company was ill-prepared.[4] For Parliament and especially for the ministry of William Pitt, Lord Chatham, the prospect of substantial Indian revenues came as a godsend. The national debt had already reached an alarming level by the end of the Seven Years' War. Chatham took the view that the right to taxation belonged to the Crown since Bengal had been acquired by British military conquest. In the polarised political situation of the 1760s, this claim directly tied into contestations of Crown influence. A potentially huge source of Crown revenue beyond parliamentary fiscal control was anathema to the opposition and many independents. Eventually, a compromise was reached. The Company would pay an annual blanket sum of £400,000, but kept the trading monopoly and its exclusive jurisdiction in India. The complicated legal question of sovereignty and the relationship between state and Company remained unresolved.[5]

As a result of this compromise, the grave difficulties related to the revenue collection in Bengal were consequently considered private problems of the Company. Soon, news of mismanagement, exploitation, and rampant corruption in British India reached London. The Company lacked qualified staff to build up an effective administrative apparatus and the initial

2 Peter J. Marshall, *Bengal: The British Bridgehead. Eastern India, 1740–1828* (Cambridge, 1987), pp. 89–92.

3 Ibid.; Lucy S. Sutherland, *The East India Company in Eighteenth-Century Politics* (Oxford, 1952).

4 Huw V. Bowen, 'British India, 1765–1813: The Metropolitan Context', in Peter J. Marshall (ed.), *The Eighteenth Century*, The Oxford History of the British Empire, repr. (Oxford, 2006), 530–51, pp. 530–4; id., *Revenue and Reform. The Indian Problem in British Politics 1757–1773*, 2nd edn. (Cambridge, 2002), pp. 9–14.

5 Robert Travers, *Ideology and Empire in Eighteenth-Century India. The British in Bengal* (Cambridge, 2007), pp. 43–9. Also cf. the partly outdated account of Henry H. Dodwell, 'The Development of Sovereignty in British India', in Henry H. Dodwell (ed.), *Cambridge History of India*, vol. 5, *British India 1497–1858* (Cambridge, 1929), 589–608.

revenue estimates proved to be overly optimistic. Furthermore, Company servants used their positions of power for personal enrichment, leading to substantial losses. The tax yield dwindled with each passing year.[6] The Company fell into crisis when Bengal was hit by famine in 1769/70. Not only did the Company-government fail to bring relief, the pressure of taxation aggravated the situation. Estimates vary, but many millions of inhabitants – up to a third of the Bengal population – fell prey to the devastating famine.[7]

The Company's metropolitan structure and institutions as a stock company were just as ill-prepared for coping with the new situation as the agents on the ground. The course of events politicised the General Court of the EIC, the assembly of the Company's shareholders in London. For a time, this shareholder assembly played a prominent role in British politics, a role for which its rules of procedure were unfit.[8] News of the *diwani* plunged the metropolitan administration of the Company into chaos. Stock prices surged to previously unknown heights. New shareholders typically expected military victories to result in high dividend payments. The changed composition of shareholders drastically impacted the General Court. Formerly, few decisions had been put to the ballot; now, contested votes became the rule. Previously, directors had served long terms, now they were at the mercy of rapidly changing factions in the General Court. The lack of continuity complicated the formation of working routines in committees and the Court of Directors, and generally hampered long-term planning.[9]

Managing procedures in India from Britain had always been a strenuous task. Few directors had any first-hand experience in India and messages between England and India took at least half a year to be delivered. With the politicised institutions and market-dependant decision-making, the Company's command failed to develop a profound understanding of the rapidly changing situation in Bengal.[10] The directing of overseas affairs confined itself to a series of increasingly panic-driven responses to outdated

6 Michael Mann, *Bengalen im Umbruch. Die Herausbildung des britischen Kolonialstaates 1754–1793* (Stuttgart, 2000), pp. 135–40.

7 David Arnold, 'Hunger in the Garden of Plenty. The Bengal Famine of 1770', in Alessa Johns (ed.), *Dreadful Visitations: Confronting Natural Catastrophe in the Age of Enlightenment* (New York, 1999), 81–111.

8 Huw V. Bowen, 'The "Little Parliament". The General Court of the East India Company, 1750–1784', *The Historical Journal*, 34:4 (1991), 857–72.

9 Huw V. Bowen, *The Business of Empire. The East India Company and Imperial Britain* (Cambridge, 2006), pp. 84–117; Philip Lawson, *The East India Company. A History* (Harlow, 1993), pp. 109–10.

10 Bowen, *Revenue and Reform*, pp. 30–47.

and badly understood intelligence. While revenue continued to decrease, military expenditure soared with the costs of defending a huge territory. Despite a stunning accumulation of debt, dividends remained high, because the directors feared a crash of stock prices. When a financial crisis hit London in 1772, the Company was no longer solvent. It was this crisis that finally resulted in state regulation of the Company.[11]

On the one hand, the Regulating Act of 1773[12] aimed to strengthen the Company's position both in England and India; on the other, it subjected the Company to a tentative form of state control. The act limited the influence of speculators and extended the directors' tenures to four years in order to improve continuity. The ministry gained access to Indian correspondence, though the act made no arrangements for the assessment of this information.[13] The governor of Bengal became the Crown-appointed Governor General for all British affairs in India. The governing Council of India served as a check to the Governor General's authority. The majority of its members were appointed by the Crown as well, as were the judges of the supreme court of India. Finally, the act explicitly interdicted any further territorial expansion.[14]

The task of building up an administrative system in Bengal fell to Warren Hastings (1732–1818), the experienced governor in Calcutta, who became the first Governor General. Initially, the Company had only installed Company personnel in the highest positions of the existing Mughal institutions. This 'double system' was considered to have failed and Hastings received the order from the Court of Directors to 'stand forth as the diwan'[15] – revenue administration was to be fully conducted by Company servants. Hastings' tenure laid many foundations for British rule. However, the establishment of a stable state-system failed, at least in the short-run. Reports of gross corruption did not recede, nor did the EIC quite recover financially. There was a sense of crisis as the Company came under pressure in the Second Anglo-Mysore War after 1780 and, as a consequence, again struggled with

11 Mann, *Bengalen im Umbruch*, pp. 121–34.

12 Officially 'An Act for establishing certain Regulations for the better Management of Affairs of the East India Company, as well in India as in Europe', 13 Geo III, c. 63. Bowen, *Revenue and Reform*, pp. 169–86.

13 Vincent T. Harlow, *The Founding of the Second British Empire 1763–1793* (London, 1964), pp. 64–8.

14 Lawson, *East India Company*, pp. 124–35.

15 General Letter to Governor and Council, 28 August 1771, in M. E. Monckton-Jones, *Warren Hastings in Bengal* (Oxford, 1918), p. 136.

debt.[16] Towards the end of his tenure, Hastings' reputation in England was certainly not at its best.

Ongoing reports of corruption in British India acquired explosive force thanks to the Economical Reform Debates of 1780. The British discussions about India and the Governor General revolved around the same concepts as these debates: corruption, influence, economy, and despotism. Newspapers gleefully presented shocking examples of misdemeanours and undue enrichment. From the 1770s, the EIC's rule in British India became a prime example of corruption and maladministration. There was a widespread fear that the Indian dominion harboured dangers for the British constitution at home. Robert Clive and Warren Hastings were portrayed as 'nabobs' – ambitious and corrupt individuals out to enrich themselves. Armed with the treasures of the East and out of control, they were imagined to be buying out the constitution.[17]

Indian politics was mostly shaped by the two rivalling committees charged with the Indian situation: the Select Committee responsible to parliament, in which Burke was the central figure, and a Secret Committee managed by Henry Dundas that answered to the Crown.[18] However, as John Cannon remarked, their reports 'were no substitute for a thorough review of the administrative arrangements'[19] in India. By 1783, financial intervention and renewed government regulation again appeared to be the only remaining options to save the Company from bankruptcy and expulsion from Bengal. This situation resulted in the spectacular failure of James Fox's East India Bill in 1783 and the subsequent collapse of the Fox–North coalition. The political constellation at this time was unique, as there was open hostility between King George and the two leading politicians of the ministry, Charles James Fox, the polemic Whig leader George had long despised, and Lord North, the King's former champion, whom he now accused of betrayal. Fox's Bill, largely prepared by Burke, proposed to solve the Indian crisis by placing the direction of Indian affairs in the hands of a commission in London, effectively nationalising the Company. The first nominees for this commission were knowledgeable in Indian affairs, but undeniably strong supporters of Fox. The bill was therefore open to the

16 Peter J. Marshall, *The Making and Unmaking of Empires. Britain, India, and America c.1750–1783* (Oxford, 2005), pp. 366–70; Jon E. Wilson, *The Domination of Strangers. Modern Governance in Eastern India, 1780–1835* (Basingstoke, 2008), pp. 47–9.

17 Tillman W. Nechtman, *Nabobs. Empire and Identity in Eighteenth-Century Britain* (Cambridge et al., 2010); Michael Edwardes, *The Nabobs at Home* (London, 1991).

18 Cf. Sutherland, *East India Company*, pp. 361–74; John Cannon, *The Fox-North Coalition. Crisis of the Constitution, 1782–4* (Cambridge, 1969), pp. 107–8.

19 Ibid., p. 107.

critique that it would vest the Indian interest firmly into a small circle of Foxites. William Pitt denounced the bill as 'nothing more on the one side than absolute despotism and on the other side the most gross corruption',[20] thus summing up the arguments of undue influence and expropriation of the Company's property rights. Still, the vote passed the Commons and would have passed the Lords, had King George not intervened by threatening that he would consider any peer who voted in favour his enemy. Consequently, the Bill was defeated and George used this defeat as a pretext to dismiss the Fox–North ministry and to appoint Pitt as the new Prime Minister.[21]

With the unique political fault lines removed, Pitt's India Act passed with relative ease in 1784. While Fox's Bill had centred on patronage, Pitt's India Act[22] focused on authority. In place of the shareholders, the act established a Board of Control composed of Cabinet members and the Privy Council, including the Prime Minister. The Board's president became a Minister for Indian Affairs in all but name. Moreover, the act invested the Governor General of India with considerable executive powers over all three presidencies and a veto in the India Council. The new arrangement stayed in effect with no cardinal changes until the formal government takeover in 1858.[23]

Clive's golden promises had been dispelled. After the 1770s, India policy aimed at financial and geopolitical stability, and quiescence concerning corruption. To bring these aims about had been Hastings' chief assignment. It was also the chief assignment of Charles Cornwallis, who succeeded Hastings as Governor General after Pitt's India Act in 1786.[24] Company institutions and the British government tried to maintain their say in decisions, but, due to the physical distance between England and India, the execution of these goals was largely left to the agents in India.

Warren Hastings and India's Ancient Constitution

The call to stand forth as *diwan* and the Regulating Act initiated a phase of intense state-building. In the 1770s, there were neither theories nor precedents for the conception and implementation of a revenue system.

[20] Quoted in ibid., p. 115.

[21] Ibid., pp. 109–10.

[22] Officially 'An Act for the better Regulation and Management of Affairs of the East India Company, and of the British possessions in India', 24 Geo III, c. 25.

[23] Mann, *Bengalen im Umbruch*, pp. 281–321; Lawson, *East India Company*, pp. 123–5.

[24] Christopher A. Bayly, *Imperial Meridian. The British Empire and the World, 1780–1830* (London, 1989).

The EIC personnel was defined by the practice of the covenant, an oath of service that every proper Company servant took.[25] With the *diwani*, these merchant-officers were called upon to administer territorial rule, yet technically, they still acted in a private capacity. Governmental tasks such as police, the judiciary, and revenue administration were simply added to their trading business. Warren Hastings' various regulations appear inconsistent at first glance. In fact, they followed from a coherent approach to state-building and the adaption of the ancient constitution to the Indian situation.

Hastings' vision of Bengal stemmed from a British imperial perspective. He described his task as 'the dominion of an extensive kingdom, the collection of a vast revenue, the command of armies, and the direction of a great political system.'[26] This very much sums up the domain of a sovereign state, even though Hastings was painfully aware that neither Britain nor the Company formally laid claim to that sovereignty.[27] Hastings repeatedly voiced his fear that without a strong central authority, 'the government, for want of a power to preside and rule it, must fall into anarchy.'[28] While Hastings was dealing with the Company and the British government on this formal matter, he was already beginning to shape his vision of the Company based on factual sovereignty. After all, Company government was backed by military power ensuring that the rule was rarely challenged openly.[29] Hastings marked this claim to factual sovereignty clearly: '[e]very intermediate power is removed, and the sovereignty of this country wholly and absolutely vested in the Company.'[30]

That Hastings based his governance on this statement of sovereignty does not imply that he envisioned the transfer of a British model. Nor

25 Akshoy K. Ghosal, *Civil Service in India under the East India Company. A Study in Administrative Development* (Calcutta, 1944), pp. 415–36.

26 Warren Hastings to George Colebrooke, 7 March, 1773, in G. R. Gleig (ed.), *The Memoirs of the Life of the Honourable Warren Hastings, First Governor General of India. Compiled from Original Papers*, vol. 1 (London, 1841), 288–293, quote on p. 290.

27 Neil Sen, 'Warren Hastings and British Sovereign Authority in Bengal, 1774–80', *Journal of Imperial and Commonwealth History*, 25:1 (1997), 59–81, p. 66.

28 Warren Hastings to George Colebrooke, 7 March, 1773, in Gleig (ed.), *Memoirs*, vol. 1, p. 290.

29 Dodwell, 'Sovereignty in British India'; Sen, 'British Sovereign Authority'; Christopher A. Bayly, 'The British Military-Fiscal State and Indigenous Resistance. India 1750–1820', in Lawrence Stone (ed.), *An Imperial State at War: Britain from 1689 to 1815* (London, 1994), 322–54.

30 Warren Hastings to George Colebrooke, 7 March 1773, in Gleig (ed.), *Memoirs*, p. 293.

did he propose to conceptualise and introduce a new state system from scratch. Rather, he claimed continuity with Mughal institutions, or rather their hypothetical pure form: an ancient Mughal constitution. Hastings had lived in India for more than twenty years and mastered several South-Asian languages. He admired Indian culture and engaged in the patronage of Indian art. Moreover, he remembered the well-run administration of the Nawab Alivardi Khan (1671–1756) in the time before the British ascent.[31] Hastings therefore proposed that the Company state be based on what he perceived to be the 'first principles' of Mughal rule:

> The remedy which I would recommend [...] is obvious and simple. It is not to introduce fresh innovations but to restore the government to its first principles. [...] Many correspondent Regulations will be necessary, but not one perhaps which the original constitution of the Mogul Government hath not before established or adopted, & thereby rendered familiar to the People.[32]

In order to form a stable state, institutions thus needed to correspond to customary practices and ideas. In British ancient constitution thinking, the common law constituted a pillar of continuity for the constitution and also for British ethnic identity as a whole.[33] Analogously, Hastings' approach entailed a comprehensive inquiry into Hindu and Muslim legal traditions focusing not so much on the codification of positive law, but on the alleged essence of the Mughal (or Indian) constitution in a rather broad sense. Orientalists translated Muslim as well as Hindu legal documents and structured the results through the lens of English legal thought. This inquiry marks the beginning of early British Orientalism and its tendency to enshrine ancient legal texts resulting in a static picture not only of Indian law and religion but also of Indian society and culture.[34]

31 Lawson, *East India Company*, p. 114; Peter J. Marshall, 'Warren Hastings as Scholar and Patron', in Anne Whiteman (ed.), *Statesmen, Scholars and Merchants* (Oxford, 1973), 242–62; Travers, *Ideology and Empire*, p. 106.

32 Warren Hastings to George Colebrooke, Chairman of Court of Directors, 26 March, 1772, in Monckton-Jones, *Warren Hastings in Bengal*, pp. 150–1.

33 John G. A. Pocock, *The Ancient Constitution and the Feudal Law. A Study of English Historical Thought in the 17. Century*, reissued (Cambridge, 1987 [1957]), pp. 229–351; Colin Kidd, *British Identities before Nationalism. Ethnicity and Nationhood in the Atlantic World, 1600–1800* (Cambridge, 1999), pp. 83–98.

34 Rosane Rocher, 'British Orientalism in the Eighteenth Century. The Dialectics of Knowledge and Government', in Carol A. Breckenridge (ed.), *Orientalism and the Postcolonial Predicament: Perspectives on South Asia* (Philadelphia, 1993), 215–44; Philip B. Wagoner, 'Precolonial Intellectuals and the Production of

While Hastings respected the 'ancient Mughal constitution', he understood it in terms of 'asiatic despotism'. The concept of (Asiatic/oriental) despotism, popularised by Montesquieu, combined descriptive and pejorative semantics and the distinction was often blurred. In its constitutional sense, 'despotism' denoted a system of government in which the ruler held absolute sovereignty and in which no private property rights existed. At the same time, this form of government – commonly associated with Turkey and South Asia – served as a negative counter model for discussions on European states. Despotism was associated with slavery and rule by fear, and was rejected by the majority of contemporary authors. Reasoning with the despotic character of the Mughal constitution served both as a motivation (or pretext) and as the constitutional basis for legal intervention because the EIC had supposedly inherited a form of absolute 'despotic' sovereign authority from the Mughal emperor.[35]

Hastings' assignment to erect an administration and to fight corruption predated the Regulating Act of 1773. Fearing government intervention, the EIC leadership in London had actually started towards reform in 1769. The directors formed a high-ranking commission of supervisors, which they sent to Bengal endowed with the highest authority. However, the ship carrying these supervisors was lost at sea. The instructions originally issued to the commission convey an impression of the directors' perspectives. In the instructions, questions of revenue administration, corruption, and the Bengali population were entwined with geopolitical and military considerations. They do not express any consistent administrative ideas.[36] Problems with the servants' conduct were phrased either generally as 'maladministration' or, more often, as 'abuses' which needed to be 'reformed'. The instructions used 'reform' in the sense of remedying individual cases of unjust practice, i.e. reform to a morally better practice. Whilst this concept of reform aimed to remedy individual problems, it did not preclude innovation, but this aspect was hardly at the forefront either. For example, the instructions ordered the 'nature and constitution' of the courts 'to

Colonial Knowledge', *Comparative Studies in Society and History*, 45:4 (2003), 783–814; Travers, *Ideology and Empire*, pp. 115–32, 181–206.

35 Melvin Richter, 'Despotism', in Philip P. Wiener (ed.), *Dictionary of the History of Ideas: Studies of Selected Pivotal Ideas* (1973), vol. 2, 1–18; Bernard S. Cohn, *Colonialism and its Forms of Knowledge. The British in India* (Princeton, 1996), pp. 62–5; Travers, *Ideology and Empire*, pp. 104–7, 115–26.

36 Instructions to Commissioners, 15 September 1769, in Monckton-Jones, *Warren Hastings in Bengal*, pp. 127–30; also see Letter to the Commissioners, 23 March, 1770, in ibid., pp. 130–3.

be reformed and altered if necessary.'[37] Warren Hastings sometimes used 'reform' in the sense of institutional change, but mostly his use of the term carried moral connotations. When he stated that 'I never called myself a Reformer nor lamented that all men were not so virtuous and disinterested as myself' he meant to convey that he was not a hypocritical moralist judging the conduct of his fellow Company servants.[38]

Originally, Hastings would have preferred to stay with the double system of revenue collection, with Company servants only involved in the Bengali structures on the very highest level, because he feared that 'to admit other Europeans would open the door to every kind of rapine and extortion. Men of the basest kind and worst principles would creep into office.'[39] The problem, according to Hastings, lay in the overload and intermingling of duties. Adding the entire revenue administration to the fray would only aggravate matters. Revenue collection was the corrupting field of activity *par excellence.* Exchanging Bengali officers with Company personnel would invite abuses at the expense of the population.[40] The Court of Directors did not share Hastings' doubts. Seeing the revenue decrease, the directors became convinced that the decrease was caused by the allegedly 'corrupt nature' of Bengali officers. With the request to stand forth as *diwan,* the directors forced Hastings to fundamentally restructure the revenue.

> It is therefore our Determination to stand forth as Dewan and by the Agency of the Company's servants to take upon ourselves the entire Care and Management of the Revenues. [...] [W]e trust that in the Office of Dewan you will adopt such Regulations and pursue such Measures as shall at once ensure to us every possible Advantage and free the Ryotts from the Oppressions of the Zemindars and petty Tyrants under which they may have been suffered to remain from the interested Views of those whose Influence and Authority should have been exerted for their Relief and Protection.[41]

The order to stand forth as *diwan* operated on assumptions of Asiatic despotism. It depicted the *zamindars* (landholder-nobles) as culprits of tyranny against the *ryotts* (peasants) and of the waning revenues. In compliance with the order, Hastings removed Muhammad Reza Khan

37 Monckton-Jones, *Warren Hastings in Bengal*, p. 128. My emphasis.

38 Quoted in Keith Feiling, *Warren Hastings* (London, 1966), p. 161.

39 Warren Hastings, Proposed Regulations, undated [likely spring 1772], in Monckton-Jones, *Warren Hastings in Bengal*, pp. 163–5, p. 156.

40 Ibid.

41 General Letter to Governor and Council, 28 August 1771, in ibid., pp. 135–9, quote on p. 136.

(c.1717–91), who had presided over revenue collection and criminal justice as a relatively independent minister, from office. The conception of a revenue system concerned much greater issues than mere administrative reforms of Company offices. It affected the very foundations of Bengal society as formal relationships of taxation would supersede more complex relationships of rank and social responsibilities, while agrarian law instruments fundamentally changed the distribution of wealth.[42]

Hastings' measures show the Janus-faced logic of Asiatic despotism and factual company sovereignty. He enforced the auctioning of taxation rights per district for a period of five years to establish a market that would maximise the revenue. The right to taxation was part of the hereditary privileges of the *zamindars*, whose exact status and function in the Mughal constitution eluded colonial systematisation.[43] Comparing the Mughal constitution to a form of European medieval feudalism, Hastings asserted that there was no understanding of (freehold) property in India; all the land ultimately belonged to the Mughal emperor. The Company claimed the right to reallocate the taxation privileges by succession. Hastings substantiated the reorganisation with the despotic nature of the nawabi system, in which the *zamindars* had allegedly been 'left at liberty to plunder all below them'.[44] The collocation of the need for an increase in the revenue with the claim of protecting peasants against despotic nobility is a characteristic rhetorical feature that Hastings shared with the directors.

Along with the agrarian constitution and the system of taxation came the need for the reorganisation of revenue administration, more or less from scratch. Hastings maintained no illusions as to the Company's situation:

> The new Government of the Company consists of a confused heap of undigested materials, as wild as the chaos itself. The powers of government are undefined; the collection of the revenue, the provision of the investment, the administration of justice (if it exists at all), the care of the police are all huddled together, being exercised by the same hands.[45]

42 Majed A. Khan, *The Transition in Bengal 1756–1775. A Study of Saiyid Muhammad Reza Khan* (Cambridge, 1969); Wilson, *Domination of Strangers*, pp. 19–44; Ranajit Guha, *A Rule of Property for Bengal. An Essay on the Idea of Permanent Settlement*, 2nd edn. (New Delhi, 1982); Sirajul Islam, *The Permanent Settlement in Bengal. A Study of its Operation 1790–1819* (Dacca, 1979).

43 John R. MacLane, *Land and Local Kingship in Eighteenth-Century Bengal* (Cambridge, 1993), pp. 27–44.

44 Public letter of Warren Hastings and Council to the Court of Directors, 3 November 1772, in Bisheshwar Prasad (ed.), *Fort William – India House Correspondence and other Contemporary Papers Relating thereto*, vol. 6, 1770–1772 (Delhi, 1960), p. 420.

45 Hastings to Richard Barwell, 22 July 1772, in Gleig (ed.), *Memoirs*, p. 317.

There was no precedent for the erection of the administrative organisation of revenue collection. Hastings' regulations alternated widely between centralisation and decentralisation. In the former system, local Company 'supervisors' had served to provide a certain transparency to the revenue collection of the double system. In 1772, these supervisors became 'collectors' overseeing the revenue on a regional level. A variety of regulations were put in place to avoid Hastings' well-founded fear of corruption. The initial step was a separation of the mercantile from the revenue branches. Collectors were forbidden to hold land in their districts, nor were they allowed to engage in private trading or accept any form of gift. In place of the erstwhile council of revenue at Murshidabad, the Treasury (Khalsa) in Calcutta took over the superintendence of the revenue, under the direction of the president (the Governor General) and council in their new capacity as auditors of the *diwani*.[46]

The new arrangement did not last long. The all-important indicator of success or failure for Hastings and the Company directors was the revenue amount and this figure continued to dwindle. The auctioning off of revenue rights had seriously disrupted the structures at the localities, with new, often absent holders of revenue titles facing a similar lack of knowledge as the British. However, blame for the apparent failure fell on the collectors, who frequently circumvented the ban on profiteering. In April 1773, the directors ordered the withdrawal of the collectors and for 'some other plan' to be introduced.[47] To build up the necessary knowledge base, Hastings initiated six provincial councils in January 1774 to supervise the collectors.[48] Even though they did not solve any problems but rather added to the costs, these councils remained in place until, in 1781, a 'permanent' plan centralised revenue collection under a newly established Committee of Revenue at Calcutta directing the disempowered collectors.[49] The discontinuation of the provincial councils led to some savings, but the Committee of Revenue failed to effect control over the collection.[50]

In the reform process outlined above, lack of knowledge and lack of control went hand in hand. In 1776, Hastings pushed through a survey of the so-called Amini Commission that strongly relied on 'amins', i.e. Indian

[46] Warren Hastings to Josias Dupré, 6 January 1773, in Gleig (ed.), *Memoirs*, p. 268; Ghosal, *Civil Service in India*, pp. 136–46.

[47] General letter of 7 April 1773 to Bengal, quoted in ibid., pp. 148–9.

[48] Hastings to Laurence Sulivan, in Gleig (ed.), *Memoirs*, pp. 383–4.

[49] Lewis S. S. O'Malley, *The Indian Civil Service 1601–1930* (London, 1965), p. 24.

[50] Cf. Letter to Major Scott, 28 April 1781, in Gleig (ed.), *Memoirs*, pp. 357–8.

officers.[51] The resulting report was finished in March 1778 and provided the hitherto most detailed knowledge on land value and Mughal institutions. The report served as a basis for subsequent revenue realignments. Similar to the earlier surveys and the ongoing orientalist investigation into Mughal and 'Hindoo' law, the Amini Commission exclusively aimed to get a grasp on the ancient Mughal constitution, especially by means of old taxation lists. The workings of the Company offices did not come under scrutiny.[52] Hastings attributed the problems of revenue administration to the absence of a formal and effective constitution in Bengal:

> Many of my letters to the Company [...] have treated of the disorders and irregularities of the service, but these I have always attributed (and in my heart I still do) to a defective constitution, not to a depravity of principle in the servants of the Company.[53]

The colonial government thus rarely examined individual offices, but rather issued detailed regulations for the collectors, to little effect. Most actions applied on the level of the individual offices aimed at the general goal of retrenchment. Salaries were cut and private business opportunities checked where possible. Hastings' expression of sympathy did little to pacify the servants, many of whom had followed Clive's lure of financial fortune to India. As early as 1772, the young John Shore (1751–1834) wrote to his mother:

> The road to opulence grows daily narrower, and is more crowded with competitors, all eagerly pressing towards the goal, though few arrive there. [...] The Court of Directors are actuated with such a spirit of reformation and retrenchment, and so well seconded by Mr. Hastings, that it seems the rescission of all our remaining emoluments will alone suffice it. The Company's Service is in fact rendered an employ not very desirable.[54]

While the gold-rush days of Clive may have been over, Company salaries remained relatively high and officers hardly faced systematic reform.

51 B. B. Misra, *The Central Administration of the East India Company 1773–1834* (Manchester, 1959), p. 122; Mann, *Bengalen im Umbruch*, pp. 191–2.

52 R. B. Ramsbotham, *Studies in the Land Revenue History of Bengal 1769–1787* (London, 1926), pp. 99–130.

53 Warren Hastings to Laurence Sulivan, 21 March, 1776, in Gleig (ed.), *Memoir*, 28–42, p. 40.

54 John Shore to his Mother, 1 April 1772, in Teignmouth (ed.), *Memoir of the Life and Correspondence of John Lord Teignmouth* (London, 1843), 34–47, p. 39.

Nevertheless, the measures put a strain on the atmosphere within the ranks of the Company.

The sometimes frenzied search for workable systems of revenue administration, judiciary, police, and trade characterised Hastings' tenure. Faced with the decreasing revenue, measures were constantly revised and sometimes completely changed directions. In his official correspondence, Hastings tended to conceal how much the colonial government was groping in the dark, but he was aware that the reforms were a matter of trial and error:

> Your observation upon the impossibility of obtaining a perfect system is perfectly just. In many cases we must work as an arithmetician does with his Rule of False. We must adopt a plan upon conjecture, try, execute, add, and deduct from it, till it is brought into a perfect shape.[55]

In the eyes of his critics, Hastings' actions seemed neither pragmatic nor purposeful. The changing directions of reforms and harsh contemporary criticisms have coloured how historians have evaluated Hastings, in general painting him as a pragmatic leader lacking systematic thinking.[56] Whether a more consequential policy would have led to stability or increased revenue yield will remain open to question. In a situation characterised by a lack of expertise, colonial governance was bound to be reactive. Hastings consistently interpreted problems in view of his constitutional understanding, he shared a patrimonial notion of history that was palpable in the construction of the ancient Mughal constitution, and he generally framed reforms as the return to a hypothetical former state. At the same time, the idea of inherited despotic sovereignty legitimised supposedly beneficent interventions. While Hastings repeatedly changed the structure of colonial administration, the offices by themselves played only a subordinate role in his conceptualisations.

Charles Cornwallis and the Principles of 'True Economy'

Lord Charles Cornwallis succeeded Warren Hastings in 1786 as the first Governor General after Pitt's India Act. Cornwallis is credited with establishing the fundamentals of Company government as it stood until the Indian Rebellion of 1857. For better or worse, Cornwallis' tenure stabilised the critical colonial situation. After leaving India in 1793, Cornwallis first

55 Warren Hastings to Richard Barwell, 22 July 1772, in Gleig (ed.), *Memoirs*, p. 316.

56 Cf. Travers, *Ideology and Empire*, p. 100; Lawson, *East India Company*, p. 113.

became Master General of the Ordnance and later Lord Lieutenant of Ireland, where he quelled the rebellion and prepared the union. In 1801 and 1802, he negotiated the Peace of Amiens for Britain. In the course of this career, Cornwallis emerged as the foremost crisis manager of the British empire. This career is all the more remarkable because, in 1781, Cornwallis had been the general whose surrender at Yorktown heralded the rather inglorious end of the American Revolutionary War.[57]

Both official circles and the wider public accepted Cornwallis' account that the defeat at Yorktown had been beyond his control. This acceptance necessarily shifted blame towards Henry Clinton (1730–95), the Commander-in-Chief in America, who had been in charge of the overall strategy. When Clinton returned to England in 1782, half a year after Cornwallis, he publicly tried to shift blame back to Cornwallis and thereby started the so-called Clinton–Cornwallis Controversy, a war of words between the two generals. When Clinton's initial attempts failed, his attacks grew increasingly bitter and rather less coherent.[58] The Clinton–Cornwallis controversy merits attention because it was entangled with the discourse on administrative reform. In June 1782, CEPA published their *Seventh Report* that dealt with the logistics of the American Revolutionary War. The report disclosed embezzlements and profiteering on an enormous scale and generally condemned the Army leadership. However, the report emphatically commended Cornwallis for putting a stop to abuses under his command.[59] In 1784, Clinton composed a public letter to CEPA and bitterly complained that the report wrongly blamed him; that he should have been heard and that he was owed the credit for Cornwallis' measures.[60] Even though there were few arguments in his favour, Clinton persisted, ultimately drawing more attention to his own failings than restoring his reputation. Cornwallis decided that Clinton's attacks were 'not worth any serious notice' and did not deign to answer.[61]

57 Christopher A. Bayly and Katherine Prior, 'Cornwallis, Charles, first Marquess Cornwallis (1738–1805)', *ODNB*.

58 Cf. Richard Middleton, 'The Clinton-Cornwallis Controversy and Responsibility for the British Surrender at Yorktown', *History. Journal of the Historical Association*, 98:331 (2013), 370–89.

59 CEPA, 'Seventh Report, 18 June 1782', *JHC 38: 31 October 1780 to 10 October 1782*, col. 1066–112, col. 1069–72.

60 Henry Clinton, *A Letter from Lieut. Gen. Henry Clinton, K.B. to the Commissioners of Public Accounts, relative to Some Observations in their Seventh Report, which may be judged to imply Censure on the late Commanders in Chief of His Majesty's Army in North America* (London, 1784).

61 Charles Cornwallis to his friend Alexander Ross, 13 June 1784, in Charles Ross (ed.), *Correspondence of Charles, First Marquis Cornwallis*, vol. 1 (London, 1859), pp. 176–7.

The work of Burke's Select Committee and Dundas' Secret Committee had drawn attention to the difficult situation in India. While the two committees did not agree on a solution, they shared the conviction that serious reforms were needed to stop the ongoing mismanagement. Cornwallis fit the image of a new imperial virtue that would cleanse Company corruption under the auspices of economical reform.[62] Politically independent, Cornwallis was respected across party lines for his integrity and patriotic sense of duty. Moreover, he had a proven record of successful military logistics that was confirmed by CEPA. As early as 1782, Shelburne had offered the Governorship to Cornwallis and Pitt renewed this offer in 1784. Cornwallis only accepted a third offer on the condition that he would have both military high command in India and the power to overrule the India Council.[63]

When Cornwallis finally took command in India in 1786, he was endowed with quasi-despotic power; the very authority Hastings had asked for time and again. Moreover, he could count on the full support of Pitt and of Henry Dundas, who presided over the newly instituted Board of Control. Cornwallis formed a civil working relationship with the Company's Court, but he corresponded more regularly with the Board of Control or directly with Dundas and occasionally with Pitt himself. For concrete Indian expertise, Cornwallis relied on a small circle of advisors: George Barlow (1762–1847) as his personal secretary, Charles Grant (1746–1823) for commercial affairs, Accountant General William Larkins (died 1800), and most of all John Shore as an expert on Indian revenue, who briefed the Governor General during the journey to India.[64]

In the autumn of 1786, Cornwallis arrived in India and took over government from the interim Governor General John Macpherson (1745–1821). He found a Company establishment in crisis. A rebellion in Benares had shaken internal stability whilst the Company was simultaneously being pressed by the Marathas (First Anglo-Maratha War, 1775–82) and Mysore (Second Anglo-Mysore War, 1780–4). The dissatisfactory peace settlements suspending these conflicts did not seem stable at all. Tipu Sultan (1751–99) at Mysore, in particular, commanded a strong army and could rely on French support. The military threats, constant pressure for retrenchment, and internal instability weighed heavily on the Company. As Jon Wilson has shown, the situation created an ever-present mood of anxiety in the Company ranks in the 1780s.[65] While the threat of war was omnipresent, the first

62 Bayly, *Imperial Meridian*, pp. 109–15, 194–6.

63 Richard Middleton, *Cornwallis. Soldier and Statesman in a Revolutionary World* (New Haven, 2022), pp. 115–36.

64 Penderel Moon, *The British Conquest and Dominion of India* (London, 1989), pp. 229–32.

65 Wilson, *Domination of Strangers*, pp. 47–9, 210–22.

three years of Cornwallis' tenure fell into an interim period of peace before the beginning of the Third Anglo-Mysore War (1789/90–92). It was during these initial years of peace that Cornwallis enforced systematic administrative reforms.

The introduction of Cornwallis' new colonial government is usually dated to the year 1793. Various momentous reform processes converged in this year, which resulted in the *Regulations for Bengal*, the so-called 'Cornwallis Code'.[66] In addition to the permanent settlement of the revenue, the Cornwallis Code regulated the judiciary, police, public policy, and administrative issues. However, the decisive actions regarding administrative reform took place earlier in Cornwallis' tenure. After some months of preparations, the bulk of the administrative reforms were enacted in the span of only one year, from January 1788 to January 1789. These reforms were conceived, coordinated, and directed in the Secret and Separate Department of Reform (SSD), which consisted of the Governor General and the India Council. By establishing this distinct department, the India Council set administrative reform as its key agenda for 1788. The Governor General and Council allocated a full day each week to the matter.[67]

On 10 January 1789, the day after the SSD completed its final report to the Court of Directors, John Shore wrote individually to one of the directors. In his letter, Shore confidently asserted the success of the reforms by comparing them to recent administrative reforms in Britain:

> I wish it were possible to make a fair examination between the measures of this Government and that of Britain. Let the Reports of the Committees appointed to investigate the National Accounts be examined; and you will find, that for one sinecure place in Bengal, there are ten in England. Indeed, it would now, I believe, be difficult to point out any salary here for which some equivalent duty is not exacted.[68]

The message was clear: contrary to the British government, the colonial government in Bengal had successfully concluded general administrative reforms. For two decades, the EIC had been vilified for its corruption. Directly after concluding a full-blown reform programme and flush with satisfaction from the accomplished effort, it must have been gratifying for Shore to reverse the criticism: Britain, not Bengal, now had to do its homework. The remark shows that the Bengal government was aware of CEPA.

66 Richard Clarke (ed.), *The Regulations of the Government of Fort William in Bengal in force at the end of 1853*, vol. 1, *Regulations from 1793 to 1805* (London, 1854).

67 Letter to Court, 9 January 1789, § 2, in Syed H. Askari (ed.), *Fort William – India House Correspondence*, vol. 16: *Foreign, Secret and Political, 1787–1791* (Delhi, 1976), p. 204; Ghosal, *Civil Service in India*, p. 223.

68 John Shore to Nathanial Smith, 10 January, 1789, in Teignmouth (ed.), *Memoir*, p. 165.

That Shore slightly misnames them could be an indicator that he was not too intimately acquainted with the reports himself. Cornwallis, by contrast, had been actively involved with CEPA.

In preparation of the *Seventh Report*, CEPA had interrogated Cornwallis twice, on 27 February and 1 March 1782.[69] In particular, they applauded two of Cornwallis' general orders addressing some of the worst abuses of Army administration in the American Revolutionary War. The Quartermasters General had bought horses and wagons privately and then hired them out to themselves at exorbitant rates in their official capacity, whilst Commissaries General had been prone to internally charging for seized supplies. The first order determined that locally acquired wagons, horses, and stores should be purchased on public accounts and banned Army officers from private profiteering. The second order tightened the obligation of accounting for purchases by means of correct vouchers. CEPA calculated that the fraudulent hiring of wagons alone had induced the unnecessary costs of £417,000, 'the Whole of which might have been saved, had the Mode contained in the Orders of the 23rd of December 1780 been at first accepted.'[70]

In India, the reforms directed in the SSD followed from systematic economical reasoning. Cornwallis designed the Department's approach to reform by adapting his knowledge of the current British administrative discussion to the situation of the EIC. At the first meeting of the SSD on 31 January 1788, Cornwallis introduced a clear set of principles for all subsequent reforms:

> First. That the Offices for conducting the business of this Government be as few as possible, and no more than the public business requires.
> Second. That the Establishment of Writers and inferior servants in each Office be regulated by the business in it.
> Third. That the salary and allowance to every Officer of Government be proportioned to the responsibility of the office he holds, and the unavoidable expences of the situation.
> Fourth. That the allowances annexed to the principle and most responsible Offices be such as will enable the possessors of them, with proper oeconomy to return to Europe with a competency in a moderate period of service.

69 CEPA, 'Seventh Report,' pp. 1075–6 (Appendix no. 5).

70 Ibid., pp. 1069–72, quote on pp. 1071–2. Cornwallis' orders are included in the report as Appendix no. 33. Cf. ibid., p. 1109.

Fifth. That salaries to the inferior Officers & Servants of Government be equal to their subsistence.
Sixth. That no Company's Servant be allowed to hold an Office under two different Departments.
Seventh. That all the principal Offices be held by Company's Servants.
Eighth. That it be declared and understood that no Officer of Government is to derive any advantages from his office or situation beyond those authorized and allowed.
Ninth. That in the application of the preceding Principles, the strictest Oeconomy compatible with them be adopted.[71]

The principles encapsulate the central creeds of an economical understanding of office. They provided the overarching orientation of a systematic reform regulating each office – including subordinate places – but also aimed to improve their overall structure. The number and configuration of the offices followed from the 'public business,' i.e. its duties or functions. There would be no place for sinecures of any kind. All officers should receive regular salaries and the amount of these salaries should mirror the hierarchy.

Beyond these basic points, the principles responded to the specific situation in British India. The reforms were to put an end to the proverbial corruption and profiteering of Company servants. The principles accordingly aimed at enforcing compliance. In British India, Company servants not only compromised their positions by accepting fees and extorting bribes, they also abused their functions to boost their private trading activities. Cornwallis' eighth principle reacted to such abuses by generally banning all forms of private profit beyond official remuneration. Its comprehensive claim reversed the burden of proof. It would no longer suffice for Company servants to heed explicit interdictions or to separate their official and private capacities. Rather, the eighth principle reduced servants to expressly allowed gains. It would have been naïve to suppose that such a ban would have a large effect on its own; none of the preceding interdictions had. Yet, this principle provided a handle to stop even slightly suspicious practices without further substantiation.

The principles restricted servants to regular remuneration, but they also show deliberations on these remunerations that went beyond the ideas of CEPA. Salaries should provide a positive incentive that would

[71] Governor General and Council to Court of Directors, 9 January 1789, in BL, IOR/H/369, pp. 426–7.

serve as a counterpart to the strict enforcement of compliance. Ranking officers should look forward to generous profits, although they were bound to keeping 'proper economy'; the proverbial pomposity and dissipation of nabobs would not be encouraged. That salaries increased with the responsibilities and hierarchy implied the prospect of advancing up a career ladder. Given the high mortality rate of British officers in India, this prospect was much more palpable in India than in Britain.[72] Contrary to the Accounts and Fees Commissioners in Britain, Cornwallis did not restrict regular remuneration to the salary, but explicitly added allowances corresponding to the responsibilities and expenses of office. A ranking officer's station and social roles were inseparable from the functional definition of a given place and involved 'unavoidable expences of the situation'. Higher positions came with social responsibilities necessitating a representative (though not lavish) lifestyle and social interactions, e.g. the hosting of soirées. Together with principle five, binding the emolument of the lower echelons to their subsistence, the statement also objectified the cost of living. In his explanation, Cornwallis referred to the high cost of housing in Calcutta.[73] In this view, salaries and allowances partly depended on external, changeable factors. This idea went further than the British discussions, even though in Britain ignoring decades of inflation had contributed to the escalation of the extraordinaries and the over-indebtedness of the Civil List.

The ninth principle appertaining to economy stands out because it bears on all preceding rules. 'Economy' was the key term in the British reform discourse, but its meaning was ambiguous. This ambiguity was also at the heart of Cornwallis' usage of the term. To start with, the ninth principle suggests frugality, but simultaneously restricts this aspect. The principle aimed to acknowledge economically sound operations rather than endorse economy as an end in itself. This reservation was deliberate. In a preliminary report on the progress of the reforms, Cornwallis explained his priorities: 'Important however as the object of economy must be admitted to be, I confess that I considered it as of a secondary nature to that of establishing

[72] Peter J. Marshall, *East Indian Fortunes. The British in Bengal in the Eighteenth Century* (Oxford, 1976), pp. 214–20.

[73] Minute of the Secret and Separate Department, 31 January 1788, in A. Aspinall (ed.), *Cornwallis in Bengal. The Administrative and Judicial Reforms of Lord Cornwallis in Bengal* (Manchester, 1931), p. 37.

useful arrangements for employing and facilitating the dispatch of business at the Public Offices.'[74]

The qualified formulation of the principle of economy resulted from an ongoing disagreement between Cornwallis and the directors as well as the ministry on the question of salaries. The Company directors had urged the Bengal leadership towards the maximisation of financial yield ever since the 1760s and they continued to do so. Cornwallis, by contrast, regularly emphasised economical principles over retrenchment. Rather than cutting the salaries of Company servants, Cornwallis raised them substantially. He argued that only the prospect of making a 'moderate fortune' by legal means would deter servants from turning to corrupt and illicit profiteering. Three of his nine reform principles followed this trajectory. The dispute on economy permeated Cornwallis' correspondence with London from the beginning of his tenure. For instance, Cornwallis raised the issue in a letter to the Chairman of the EIC in December 1787, while laying claim to initial reform successes:

> I have been a most rigid oeconomist, in all cases where I thought rigid oeconomy was true oeconomy. I abolished sinecure places, put a stop to jobbing agencies and contracts, prevented large sums from being voted away in Council for trumped-up charges; and have been unwearied in hunting out fraud and abuse in every department. [...] But I shall never think it a wise measure in this country, to place men in great and responsible situations, where the prosperity of our affairs must depend on their exertions as well as integrity, without giving them the means, in a certain number of years, of acquiring honestly and openly a moderate fortune.[75]

To Cornwallis, indiscriminate retrenchment apparently constituted false economy. Whilst he assertively subscribed to economical reform, Cornwallis argued along the lines of CEPA and the Fees Commissioners to vindicate his own priorities.

This active engagement with economical reform sets Cornwallis' tenure apart from his predecessors'. After 1780, the language of economical reform had also entered the letters from London. However, this shift was only a change in vocabulary. The directors had demanded retrenchment throughout the 1770s. Given the enormous financial pressure of the early 1780s, they only intensified these demands. The fact that the directors started to phrase their calls for retrenchment as the need for 'strict economy' did not

[74] Charles Cornwallis to Court of Directors, 8 November 1788, in Ross (ed.), *Correspondence*, vol. 1, p. 541.

[75] Charles Cornwallis to John Motteux, 16 December, 1787, in ibid., p. 307.

constitute a change of policy. The letters of the Hastings and Macpherson governments similarly mimicked this vocabulary to demonstrate their efforts. In the transitional plan of 31 January 1785, just days before Hastings left for England, the Governor in Council described their efforts as the 'Investigation of the Establishments in the different Offices of your Government for the purpose of effecting a Reduction of Expence'. Public interest would be pursued by 'reducing the Expences of every Department, without Favor or Partiality within the Strictest Limits of Oeconomy.'[76]

Naturally, this policy of general cutbacks was unpopular among Company servants. Cornwallis' changed stance on the question of salaries has therefore been attributed to the influence of well-placed servants, notably of Charles Grant in the Commercial Department, who had started to lobby for higher salaries in 1786.[77] However, it was Cornwallis who established the increase of salaries as the pivotal point when he personally introduced the reform principles in the SSD on 31 January 1788:

> The first principle that every State should wish to adopt is to secure the honesty of its servants; to place people in situations of great temptation and responsibility without allowing them an adequate recompense, is a principle of false economy which will ever in the end prove most expensive. [...] Distress will overcome principle, and although no argument can justify an immoral action, yet reason and humanity will plead in favour of distress and temptation.[78]

That adequate emoluments might be necessary to prevent corruption was by no means an innovative argument. Nevertheless, these elucidations strikingly resemble CEPA's treatment of equivalent questions. They had touched upon the dangers of a conflict of public and private interest in situations of temptation in their *Seventh Report* in the context of Cornwallis' general order:

> We do not mean to suggest these as Impositions, that have all been actually committed upon the Public, but as Consequences that will follow, whenever the Temptation is powerful enough to overcome the

76 Governor in Council to the Court of Directors, 31 January, 1785, in C. H. Philips and B. B. Misra (eds.), *Fort William – India House Correspondence*, vol. 15, *Foreign and Secret 1782–1786* (Delhi, 1963), pp. 346–7.

77 Ainslie T. Embree, *Charles Grant and British Rule in India* (London, 1962), pp. 100–1.

78 Secret and Separate Department, minute of 31 January, in Aspinall, *Cornwallis in Bengal*, p. 36.

> Sense of Duty, and where the Opportunities of yielding to the Temptation are so frequent and so obvious.[79]

CEPA considered temptation as an empirical fact that they took into account when revising a system. In the eyes of the Commissioners, corruptibility could not be resolved by an appeal to personal virtues. Individual finger pointing or collective scolding did not, therefore, appear expedient; a point Cornwallis made as well. In their *Fifteenth Report,* CEPA presented their argument on salaries and temptation in a well-developed form:

> And this, we deem, is strictly consistent with sound Oeconomy, which manifests itself not by withholding from the efficient Servant of the Public a proper Return for his Service, and the fair Means of Support, but by suppressing useless Offices, reducing overgrown Emoluments, striking off unnecessary Expences, and modelling every Department upon such a Plan, that each Officer shall have a fit and sufficient Portion of Duty assigned to him, and all needless Superfluity in the Number of Officers maintained be rejected. [...][T]o admit the Pressure of Necessity, upon Situations exposed to frequent Temptation, and affording easy Opportunities of yielding thereto, can hardly be reconciled to Prudence or Humanity.[80]

It is this very line of argument and terminology that Cornwallis took up in his letter to John Motteux and in his explications in the SSD. Sound or true economy meant cutting unnecessary expenses, curbing abuses, and abolishing useless offices. However, he considered it false economy to put the axe to salaries indiscriminately, thereby inadvertently encouraging corruption among officials who were always exposed to temptation.[81]

Cornwallis not only adopted the arguments of CEPA, but also extended them by enlarging on the dialectics of incentive and punishment. Generous salaries and the prospect of career advancement provided a positive incentive for a deeper level of commitment and active zeal that regulations and prohibitions alone would never produce. The other side of the coin was punishment. Punishment was necessary, but it could only be effective if the servants had something to lose:

79 CEPA, 'Seventh Report', p. 769.
80 CEPA, 'Fifteenth Report', p. 30.
81 Governor in Council to Court of Directors, 3 November 1788, in Raghubir Sinh (ed.), *Fort William – India House Correspondence*, vol. 10, *1786–1788* (Delhi, 1972), pp. 622–3.

> If rigorous punishments be ordained as the penalties of every deviation from the strict line of rectitude, and the Government should depend upon these alone for enforcing honesty, the event will disappoint their expectations. [...] On the contrary, when a fair reward is allowed for labour and honesty, negligence and peculation should be deservedly punished with all the rigour which the law or the rules of the service can inflict.[82]

Cornwallis' treatment of reward and punishment as a means to affect behaviour was nothing new. The topic had figured prominently in the British debate on the penal law during the 1770s, notably in William Eden's *Principles of Penal Law*. To Eden, the threat of punishment was a necessary deterrent for the prevention of crimes. However, Eden doubted that fear was a stronger motivator than reward, and he rejected the idea that only the fear of punishment prevented men from committing crimes. Deterrents were only necessary as a safeguard against those who had lost their sense of duty. The severity of punishments should be proportionate to the severity of the crime, not to the facility or temptation to commit it. Well-balanced and reasonable laws would improve public virtue and thereby public utility.[83] Cornwallis' principles adapted such deliberations on the behavioural effect of positive incentives and appropriate sanctioning to the administrative system.

The reform programme of the SSD no longer addressed the Company offices by reference to the constitution, as Hastings' reforms had, but presupposed an interconnected system of offices. The SSD's final report highlighted this presupposition:

> The opportunity afforded by the revision of the Establishments suggested also to us the following objects [...] as immediately connected with the purposes of general arrangement.
> 1st Improvements in the mode of Keeping Public accounts.
> 2nd The Distribution of expenses under the heads of Establishments to which they properly belong, and
> 3rd The Establishment of regulations for Conducting the business in the different Offices where required.[84]

The report presented the office structure and accounting procedures as 'immediately connected'. While the reforms of both the establishment

82 Secret and Separate Department, minute of 31 January, in ibid., p. 36.

83 William Eden, *Principles of Penal Law*, 3rd edn. (London, 1775), esp. Chapters II and XXIV.

84 Askari (ed.), *India House Correspondence*, p. 205.

of offices and the financial accountability responded to demands from London, the proceedings might just as easily have been discussed in the context of taxation policy. After all, Pitt's India Act also demanded annual budgets to be submitted to Parliament. To make this connection meant to assume that public administration formed a coherent subject matter. The reform principles constituted a system in the sense of a well-grounded theory that informed all individual reform measures and thereby introduced consistency to formerly inconsistent establishments. A passage on the centralisation of the auditing process features both meanings of 'system'. Given the directors' insistence on retrenchment, the creation of a new civil auditor office necessitated particular justification:

> You may be assured that, at a time we were occupied on a System of reducing your Establishments as much as possible, we should not have proceeded to the Creation of a New Office without most Evident conviction of its Utility and Benefit. [...] [W]e are convinced that the appointment is an essential part of the general System.[85]

The SSD presented their reforms as a coherent theory that would improve the administrative system. The reform principles constituted a system of economy that emphasised utility over retrenchment.

Reforming the Company Offices

In the SSD, Cornwallis and the Council of India developed reform proposals and also enforced their implementation. The reforms consciously followed a particular method, which drew on CEPA's groundwork. To start with, the reforms of the Company offices needed a sound empirical basis:

> As preparatory to our arrangements, and as explanatory of them, Detailed Description of the Offices under each Department, and the mode in which Public business was conducted, are recorded upon our proceedings and to these we must beg leave to refer you, as particularly necessary to convey that information required for forming a competent Judgement of the principles laid down as the foundation of the proposed arrangements and of the consistency subsequently observed between the principles and their application in the different stages of the proceedings.[86]

[85] Ibid., p. 209.
[86] Ibid., p. 206.

This explanation may have served as a rhetorical strategy. The SSD confronted the Board of Directors with extensive and complicated materials to substantiate specific decisions. However, the reform process did indeed begin with the gathering of detailed empirical knowledge, which prepared for reform decisions for each office. In spite of the various surveys and circular requests during Hastings' tenure, the India government still lacked a sufficient information base. Hastings' surveys had focused on tax data or on information on local customs and laws, which had helped to substantiate the 'ancient Mughal constitution', but the surveys had never systematically considered the offices of the Company. The SSD gave up an initial categorisation of offices by structural criteria, because 'the want of materials & information' impeded this course of action.[87]

The SSD depended on answers from the concerned offices. Just like George Rose did in the Shelburne ministry, John Shore sent out letters requesting detailed information on offices, procedures, and accounts. In addition to these queries, the letters introduced Cornwallis' nine principles and invited the recipients to participate. The respective officers received the opportunity to justify establishments or contribute constructive reform suggestions, but they had no say in the decision-making. The answers show a variety of reactions to the request. Some departments simply delivered tabular representations of their establishments with generic covering letters. Others expressed profound unease with the queries. The official answer of the Adjutant General's office belongs to the former group.[88] However, Adjutant General Alexander Ross (1742–1827) personally composed a second letter to explain his difficulties in supplying the information:

> I have considered myself as responsible only for the due performance for the duties of my Office, and I have employed Writers and other occasional Aids, according to the different exigencies of my Business, but without thinking it of consequence to the Public to keep correct memorandums of their salaries or of the dates of their appointments, and having no individual to recommend for particular favor, I trust that the want of minute information upon this head will be no material disappointment to the Board.[89]

87 Ibid., pp. 206–12.

88 Statement of Business performed in the Adjutant General's Office with the present and proposed Establishment of Official Servants for conducting etc., 15 May, 1788, BL, IOR/H/369, pp. 55–8.

89 Adjutant General Alexander Ross, 21 May 1788, BL, IOR/H/369, p. 70.

While sounding somewhat unconcerned, Ross' justification reveals a patrimonial understanding of office, which was at odds with Cornwallis' principles. For Ross, the only point in question was his conduct as a senior officer. He accepted responsibility for his duties, but he considered it a private affair, whether or not to take recourse to the assistance of subordinate staff. The bold undertone underlying the letter is remarkable, because Alexander Ross was a personal friend of Cornwallis'. Ross had been Cornwallis' aide-de-camp at Yorktown and remained a confidant correspondent throughout Cornwallis' life, though they paused their private correspondence while Ross served under Cornwallis in India.[90]

Most subordinated writers were covenanted servants. Still, ranking officers like Ross were unwilling to consider these writers as regular officers in their own right. This patrimonial attitude was especially prevalent in the administration of the Army, which comprised both military and civilian positions. Another telling example is the statement of the Secretary to the Military Department and renowned botanist Robert Kyd (1746–93):

> I find myself in some measure at a loss to afford part of my Information now required strictly conformable to the Axiom premised in the first part of the Board's requisition Namely 'That the Establishments of Writers and inferior Servants in every public Office shall be regulated by the Business done in it', [...] my incapacity to anticipate the transaction which may occur [...] reduced me to the necessity of offering the present imperfect Information.[91]

The high fluctuation and versatility in business, Kyd argued, made the introduction of a regular establishment impossible. As a solution, he asked for 'a discretionary Power [...] [to] contract the monthly Establishment as the Business to be performed shall appear to him necessary'.[92] In other words, he suggested redefining and enlarging his personal authority in order to continue his habitual conduct. In the end, the SSD decided to effectively demote the position '[w]ith a view to a permanent and connected system', making it dependent on the Secretary General. However, '[t]he High Rank and respectable character of L[ieutenan]t Col[one]l Kyd induced us to postpone any immediate alteration in the office under his Controul.' The proposed change would be introduced later, 'upon a vacancy'.[93]

[90] B. H. Souldby, 'Ross, Alexander (1742–1827)', *ODNB*.

[91] Secret and Separate Consultations, BL, IOR/H/369, pp. 72–3.

[92] Ibid., pp. 73–4.

[93] Letter to Court, 9 January 1789, in Askari (ed.), *India House Correspondence*, pp. 206–7.

Ross and Kyd tried to use their personal status to resist inconvenient changes to their situations without engaging with the reform concept. Other officers employed reforming language to further their personal agenda. For instance, Joseph Price (c. 1727–96), Marine Storekeeper and Paymaster, positioned himself fully in favour of reform, but cautioned against unnamed officers, who might resist reforms:

> In an attempt to draw up future regulations on principles of oeconomy for a Marine Establishment that has been long standing, and in which stubborn local customs have taken deep root, the Support of Government will become necessary. Complaints from particular persons who may conceive themselves injured by the operations of a corrected System, may by their complaining teize [sic] Administration into a belief that the Remedy is worse than the disease.[94]

Price presented himself as an eager reformer and asked for support in asserting his position against internal adversaries, whom he presented as recalcitrant troublemakers. He asked for increased authority and the aggregation of several accounts in his hand. Price faithfully awaited 'the new regulation to declare what addition to the Monthly Salaries of the Marine Officers, commission on Stores or other Emoluments will be allowed to them as a reward for the faithful discharge of the Duties of their several Departments.'[95]

Price was an unlikely candidate for a disinterested reformer. He had been sailing rather adventurously as a free merchant in the employ of the Company for thirty years. In the early 1780s, Price had published controversial pamphlets in Britain and was temporarily confined after running into heavy debts. Only because of these debts had he accepted his current elevated but regular position in 1784 from Warren Hastings, to whom he personally owed a substantial amount of money. In light of his personal circumstances, Price's reform suggestions appear to be an attempt to increase gains from his office. Four years later, Price was attested insane and dismissed from his post.[96] Price's bold move may be an extreme example, but other officers mimicked the economical language in order to avert major cuts in their offices as well.

The reforms of the SSD followed a clear and swift process. The Secret and Separate Consultations show that Charles Cornwallis and John Shore were the prime movers. In addition, Accountant General William Larkins was

94 BL, IOR/H/369, p. 333.

95 BL, IOR/H/369, pp. 337–49, quote on p. 349.

96 Peter J. Marshall, 'Price, Joseph (c. 1727–1796)', *ODNB*.

closely involved in the department's work.[97] Independent of the offices' answers, John Shore assembled all centrally available information and accounts concerning these offices. William Larkins and Richard Johnson (1753–1807), a leading revenue accountant and orientalist, assisted Shore in this undertaking. The SSD used the resulting dossiers to assess the answers from the officers, to compare analogous establishments, and to identify abuses and defects. In a second step, the SSD developed a new establishment in accordance with Cornwallis' nine principles and decreed its implementation.[98] Decisions were generally taken by the India Council as a whole. While reforms would eventually need the sanction of the Court of Directors, the Court was not involved in the process. The Council sent the proceedings with a general explanation to London in November 1788 and the final report in January 1789.[99]

John Shore was the Council's expert on Indian revenue matters and consequently presided over the remodelling of the revenue offices. His first priority was the reorganisation of the Khalsa, the central revenue office.[100] The number of native Indian officers at the Khalsa and throughout the revenue administration was especially high. As early as 1782, Shore had drafted an internal memorandum on the alleged Indian 'national character', in which he propagated racist stereotypes, attributing various moral failures to the Hindoo and Muslim religions and to the acculturation of the population to despotism.[101] Shore's detailed, very negative opinions on Indians contributed to the decision to exclude native officers from higher Company service. Against this background, Shore's position towards the native officers of the Khalsa is, at first, somewhat surprising. He argued

97 See Askari (ed.), *India House Correspondence*, p. 204 for the preparations. For its ongoing work see especially the 'Arrangement proposed for conducting the Duties of the Auditor of Civil Accounts on the principles prescribed in the Orders of the Secret and Separate Department of 31st January 1788' of 5 May 1788 and Larkins' letter to Cornwallis read in the Secret and Separate Department on 23 May 1788, in BL, IOR/H/369, pp. 59–66 and 81–8. Cornwallis recommended Larkins to the Court of Directors. Cf. Letter to Court, 3 November 1788, in Sinh (ed.), *India House Correspondence*, p. 623.

98 Cf. e.g. the minute on the various Paymasters of the Army that encapsulates the entire process: Minute of the Secret and Separate Department, 9 October 1788, pp. 211–18, esp. pp. 217–18.

99 Letter to Court, 3 November 1788, in Sinh (ed.), *India House Correspondence*, pp. 622–3; Letter to Court, 9 January 1789, in Askari (ed.), *India House Correspondence*, pp. 203–37.

100 Cf. Misra, *Central Administration*, pp. 7–8.

101 John Shore: Remarks on the mode of administering Justice to the Natives in Bengal and on the Collection of the Revenues, in BL, IOR/P/50/58, pp. 382–414.

> that these Establishments of native Officers employed in the Public Accounts ought not to be diminished in Number, and I think their Salaries should be liberal. Their Labours are incessant, and it is not easy to supply or to find Men of sufficient ability for the Duties required of them.[102]

Extending the liberal salaries to the native officers seems to be at odds with his more general policy of exclusion, and even with the nine reform principles, but Shore responded to practical necessities. Many positions in the Khalsa required profound language skills and pertinent knowledge of local customs as well as Company rules. Qualified officers were hard enough to find among the native personnel, let alone among the British. Paradoxically, one reason for Shore's insistence on a high number of native officers at the Khalsa was that he did not trust them. Shore proposed to keep authenticated duplicates of all accounts in different departments. By this procedure, Shore argued, 'the Native Officers and Accounts in one Department will be Checks upon the others.' While Shore was confident that 'the Abuse of Influence and the Corruption attending it are by the Change of System greatly diminished,' he proposed an additional check. The Roy Royan (the presiding native officer at the Khalsa) should take an oath that any 'Instance of peculation, Extortion or Corrupt Practice' should expose him to religious disgrace or large financial penalties. Shore advised: 'Of the two I should from my knowledge of the Natives presume the latter obligation to be in general the most binding.'[103] Shore was following Cornwallis' general logic of reward and punishment in order to prevent corrupt practices. At the same time, he used the introduction of materially hurtful penalties to make a racist argument by insinuating that Indians lacked honour and religious candour.

Cornwallis himself concentrated on questions of emolument. Irregular remuneration by fees and gratuities was prevalent, even if the problem did not match the scale of the revenue administration in Britain. Cornwallis delivered several personal minutes on the substitution of fees and other forms of emolument by fixed salaries. For instance, he stopped all poundages on military supplies by a general argument that mirrored CEPA's condemnation of Army logistics in their *Seventh Report*: poundages created a motivation for wasteful dissipation of public money.[104] Cornwallis pre-

[102] John Shore: Minute on the Khalsa Establishment, 15 August 1788, in BL, IOR/H/369, pp. 155–63, quote on p. 155.

[103] Minute of John Shore, 9 October 1788, in BL, IOR/H/369, pp. 300–1.

[104] Minute of Charles Cornwallis, 18 August 1788, in BL, IOR/H/369, pp. 178–9; CEPA, 'Seventh Report.'

sented fixed salaries as a silver bullet that led to savings and also improved the conduct of Company servants:

> In the Arrangements […] the principle of Substituting avowed Salary to Fees, profits on Establishment whatever has been invariably adopted and I am convinced that the most essential benefits have been derived from it both to the Company and its Servants. To the Company it has made a large annual saving whilst it has contributed to give energy and dispatch to the Public business and it has relieved servants of the Company from the most dangerous and to Men of honor & integrity the most mortifying situation I mean that of being under the absolute necessity of taking some Emoluments which could not be publickly avowed.[105]

Cornwallis projected a positive image of the essentially honourable Company servant who rejoiced at being relieved from corrupting temptation. As proof in point, Cornwallis presented the commendable behaviour of George Barlow who had refused to accept the fees taken by his predecessors when he served as Collector of Customs at Calcutta. As a reward for outstanding merit, Cornwallis retrospectively granted Barlow a substantial salary.[106] This narrative of self-motivated virtuous behaviour leading to just rewards is dubious. It seems more likely that Cornwallis simply rewarded the loyalty and service of Barlow, who served as a sub-secretary to the Council of India and belonged to Cornwallis' closest associates. Such a personal reward did not fit well into the new system and would have been hard to defend in light of the Court of Director's insistence on austerity, whereas the official narrative exemplified the image of public-minded service and just leadership that Cornwallis meant to convey.[107]

The administrative reforms were carried out independently of the fundamental questions of revenue policy that led to the Permanent Settlement of 1793. This settlement did, however, mark a sea change of governance that also affected administration. Not so much because it brought along further slight changes of the office structure, but because it entailed the quite fundamental and unprecedented development in governance.[108] With the Cornwallis Code, regulations took on a law-like quality. Codified laws

[105] Minute of Charles Cornwallis, 30 June 1788, in BL, IOR/H/369, pp. 137–9, quote on p. 138.

[106] Ibid., p. 139.

[107] Cornwallis used a similar argumentation during his tenure as Lord Lieutenant of Ireland to commend a 'selfless' act of George Napier to Charles Abbot. Cf. chapter 7.

[108] Clarke (ed.), *Regulations.*

regulated everything from the size of paper to the proprietary constitution of Bengal. The 'obsession with the search for general, abstract rules'[109] as Jon Wilson has called it, became enshrined as one pillar of the colonial state and, particularly, of the Civil Service. The other pillar was attitude. Cornwallis emphasised the necessity of supplementing regulations with career prospects to encourage adherence to the rules, dedicated conduct, and zeal. His understanding of zeal was sober enough in the first place. Under the conditions of crisis and colonial anxiety, the Civil Service eventually became not only rationalistic but also secluded, elitist, and racist.[110]

Imperial Civil Service

On the surface, there was much continuity in policy between the tenures of Warren Hastings and Charles Cornwallis, but in fact, the change in governance was profound. The promulgation of the Cornwallis Code marked a decisive discursive break, which put an abrupt end to argumentations by means of the ancient Mughal constitution.[111] The application of British administrative theory had a more direct impact on colonial governance in India than it had in Britain, where complex decision-making processes and vested interests checked sudden changes. Cornwallis made a substantial contribution to this development by acting as the arbiter of the administrative ideas. CEPA's theory sat well with his sober and controlling attitude and helped to solve problems that had seemed impregnable before. In the process, Cornwallis turned from a military leader into an economical administrator – a new type of colonial agent.[112] However much the new colonial regime depended on Cornwallis' personal expertise for its erection, it proved stable after his departure. It is little surprising that the colonial government maintained its administrative approach during the subsequent tenure of John Shore (from 1793 to 1797), who had played an instrumental part in the reform process himself. More interestingly, Richard Wellesley, Earl of Mornington (1760–1842) took up and extended the Cornwallis system. Under Wellesley's uncompromising leadership, the Indian Civil Service turned into a rationalistic and elitist corps and a centrepiece of the imperialist colonial regime.

[109] Wilson, *Domination of Strangers*, p. 3.

[110] Ibid., pp. 45–74.

[111] Travers, *Ideology and Empire*, p. 251.

[112] Jon E. Wilson, 'The Silence of Empire, Imperialism and India', in David Craig and James Thompson (eds.), *Languages of Politics in Nineteenth-Century Britain* (London, 2013), 218–41, pp. 218–19.

Richard Wellesley had gained administrative experience as a junior Lord of the Treasury from 1786 to 1793 before transferring to Dundas' Board of Control for India. In this position, Wellesley became close to Cornwallis. Dundas and Pitt had planned to send Cornwallis to India for a second tenure in 1797, during which Wellesley would have served as Governor of Madras. Instead, Cornwallis went to Ireland as Lord Lieutenant and Wellesley went to India as Governor General in November 1797.[113]

Wellesley's tenure from 1797 to 1805 is mostly remembered as the starting point for military expansionism and the assertion of British dominion in India. In utter disregard for prohibitive orders from the Court of Directors, Wellesley waged wars of conquest, arguably motivated equally by a desire for personal glory as by strategic concerns. After defeating the Company's southern nemesis, Tipu Sultan, and ending French influence in India, Wellesley extended British dominance over most of the subcontinent. Wellesley's style of government suggests another strong break. His vice-regal splendour in ceremonial pageantry as well as the grandiose new building of Government House in Calcutta seem far off from Cornwallis' sober, if classicist-imperial style. In administrative matters, however, Wellesley continued and expanded on Cornwallis' legacy. He cultivated the spirit of the Civil Service as an elite corps characterised by its sense of duty, seclusion, and expert administrative knowledge. What is more, Wellesley initiated the inauguration of Fort William College in 1800, the first venture into the institutionalised education of civil servants in the English-speaking world.[114]

In reasoning for the inauguration of a Company college, Wellesley frequently referred to Cornwallis as the founder of a new system. For instance, Wellesley reminded the directors of 'the wise and benevolent system introduced by Lord Cornwallis, for the improvement of the internal government of the provinces immediately subject to the Presidency of Bengal' that was gradually expanded throughout British India.[115] For Wellesley, the 'Corn-

113 Christopher A. Bayly, 'Wellesley, Richard, Marquess Wellesley (1760–1842)', *ODNB*.

114 Moon, *Conquest and Dominion*, pp. 262–338.; John Bowen, 'The East India Company's Education of its Own Servants', *The Journal of the Royal Asiatic Society of Great Britain and Ireland*, 3/4 (1955), 105–23.

115 Wellesley to the Court of Directors, Notes with respect to the foundation of a College at Fort William, 10 July, 1800, in Montgomery Martin (ed.), *The Despatches, Minutes, and Correspondence, of the Marquess Wellesley, K.G. during his Administration in India*, vol. 2 (London, 1836), p. 325. Wellesley conveniently passed over resistance to this process among colonial servants. For the most noteworthy case of Madras, see T. H. Beaglehole, *Thomas Munro and the Development of Administrative Policy in Madras 1792–1818. The Origins of 'the Munro System'* (Cambridge, 1966).

wallis System' – as it was generally called – constituted the decisive step from trading company to sovereign government:

> In proportion to the extension of this beneficial system, the duties of the European civil servants of the East India Company are become of greater magnitude and importance [...] To dispense justice to millions of people of various languages, manners, usages and religions; to administer a vast and complicated system of revenue throughout districts equal in extent to some of the most considerable kingdoms in Europe; [...] these are now the duties of the larger proportion of the civil servants of the Company.[116]

This passage resembles Hastings' description of the extent of colonial sovereignty. However, Hastings' point was to draw attention to the factual sovereignty and state-like quality of Company territorial rule. Wellesley made the execution of public duties the defining feature of all Company servants. In contrast to Hastings, CEPA in Britain, and even Cornwallis, Wellesley could rely upon a term to identify the institutional setting of Company officers in a systematic view: 'Civil Service', a term that had originally distinguished the civil from the military branch of the Company, now consistently referred to the organised administrative apparatus of Company administration. Wellesley described the Civil Service as the executive arm of the Company, which applied policies and regulations but did not decide on them.

Even whilst applauding the Cornwallis System, Wellesley noticed a weakness in it. Not all servants were capable or willing to satisfy his standards.[117] Wellesley's remedy of choice was to remove these unwanted servants, compensating their loss of office by pensions. To Henry Dundas, Wellesley remonstrated against the 'false economy' of the directors, who had forbidden this line of action. His rationale indicates another semantic shift in the use of 'economy':

> Such persons have been suffered to retain their stations under the orders of the Court of Directors, prohibiting the grant of pensions of retreat to the civil service. This prohibition is contrary to true principles of economy. The inevitable operation of it has been to fix incapable persons in stations requiring efficiency; and the loss sustained by their negligencies or errors infinitely overbalances the expense of providing for them at the public charge.[118]

116 Wellesley to the Court of Directors, Notes with respect to the foundation of a College at Fort William, 10 July, 1800, in Martin (ed.), *Despatches*, vol. 2, p. 327.

117 Wellesley to Henry Dundas, 5 March, 1800, in ibid., pp. 231–4.

118 Ibid., p. 233.

Throughout the text, 'efficiency' was a key term for the definition of goals. Wellesley no longer used the word to designate an operative office as opposed to a sinecure, but to point to an ideal functioning in the context of a systematic cost–benefit calculation.[119] Cornwallis had argued with 'true economy' to justify high salaries against the imperative of retrenchment. He had insisted that structural problems, not immoral or incapable servants, lay at the heart of corruption and waste; it was therefore the system that needed reform. Wellesley reversed the terms. In his view, the system set the standard which every servant had to satisfy. Wellesley considered it false economy to suffer persons in office who fell short of expectations. Cornwallis had removed unnecessary offices; Wellesley looked to remove inadequate servants.

In addition to disposing of deviant servants, Wellesley aimed to increase the number of capable and conforming servants. In this context, 'qualification' became another key-term. In order to fulfil the needs of the colonial state, the system needed qualified personnel:

> [the system] has not been carried into execution with cordiality, zeal, and energy proportioned to its merits; it has received no aid of collateral institutions calculated to furnish a supply of men properly qualified to fill the several stations of judicature and revenue.[120]

Wellesley thus deduced his interest in qualification from a desire to perfect the Cornwallis System. The regularisation of affairs in the system led him to a level of abstraction that allowed the person themselves to be disregarded in favour of their qualifications. Government 'demands a constant, steady, and regular supply of qualifications'[121] – future junior servants figured as standardised skillsets with conforming morals. The foundation of Fort William College followed from the perceived need for an institutionalised system of selection and education of civil servants that would generate a steady supply of qualified servants:

> The efficiency of the service cannot wisely or conscientiously be left to depend on the success of individual or accidental merit, struggling against the defects of established institutions. [...] The nature of our establishments should furnish fixed and systematic encouragement to animate, to facilitate, to reward the progress of industry and virtue;

[119] 'efficiency, n.', *OED*. The first example for a similar usage in the Oxford English Dictionary stems from the 1850s and concerns engines.

[120] Martin (ed.), *Despatches*, vol. 2, pp. 231–2.

[121] Ibid., p. 339.

> and fixed and systematic discipline, to repress and correct the excesses of contrary dispositions.[122]

The selection and education of servants became just another abstract operation of the system. This level of depersonalisation evokes associations of Manchester in the heyday of industrialisation rather than of India at the dawn of the nineteenth century.

The envisaged curriculum of the college mirrored the reframing of legal and administrative assumptions during Wellesley's tenure:

> [the students] should be regularly instructed in the principles and system which constitute the foundation of that wise code of regulations and laws enacted by the Governor-General in Council for the purpose of securing to the people of this empire the benefit of the ancient and accustomed laws of the country, administered in the spirit of the British constitution.[123]

Only the codified, positive law of the Governor General in Council and the 'spirit' of the British constitution guaranteed the validity of ancient and accustomed laws. The ancient Mughal constitution yielded no legal normativity beyond the written result of orientalist law-making. Knowledge of 'the true and sound principles of the British constitution, [...] the general principles of ethics, civil jurisprudence, the law of nations, and general history' would qualify servants for 'the maintenance of order and good government.'[124]

The exposition of the curriculum also responded to the perceived need to install measures to counteract temptation and corruption. In place of Cornwallis' idea of making a fortune by legal means, Wellesley envisioned a regular career path with continual incentives: 'The spirit of emulation, in honourable and useful pursuits, should be kindled and kept alive by the continual prospect of distinction, and reward, of profit, and honour.'[125] Wellesley also took up the notion of the peculiar temptations and corrupting effects of the Indian station. In Wellesley's reasoning, these temptations no longer followed from the nature of the service. Rather, Wellesley pointed to the local climate and especially to the supposedly corrupt nature of Indians:

[122] Ibid., p. 338.
[123] Ibid., p. 330.
[124] Ibid.
[125] Ibid.

> Finally, their early habits should be so formed, as to establish in their minds such solid foundations of industry, prudence, integrity, and religion, as should effectually guard them against those temptations and corruptions with which the nature of this climate, and the peculiar depravity of the people of India, will surround and assail them in every station, especially upon their first arrival in India.[126]

During Hastings' tenure, the colonial leadership's image of the Indians had been neutral to positive; negative aspects such as corruptibility had mostly been ascribed to socialisation in a despotic constitution. The formulations of Shore and Cornwallis showed racist assumptions which essentialised vices as inherent Indian attributes. Wellesley went beyond this point by declaring a 'peculiar depravity of the people of India' as the main source of possible corruption among British servants. In this way, corrupt servants could be depicted as the victims of the very people at whose cost they misbehaved.

Wellesley did not wait for the directors' permission to implement his vision; nor was it forthcoming. On the contrary, the Court ordered the immediate annulment and shutdown of Fort William College in January 1802. Relations between the Court and Wellesley had been strained before; the college scheme only added to their enmity. The directors only engaged superficially with Wellesley's argument and mainly pointed to the high costs of the college scheme.[127] Most likely, they perceived the college as a direct attack on their patronage and control by a Governor General who regularly disregarded their explicit orders. Wellesley only complied sluggishly and partially to the order to close Fort William College. In the end, the college was allowed to remain, albeit only as a language training facility.

Wellesley's plan did result in an institutionalised form of administrative training in the end. In 1806, after Wellesley's tenure, the directors instituted a college in their immediate reach at Haileybury in Hertfordshire. Haileybury College experimented with admission by competitive examination which was followed by a meritocratic career path and thereby created a model that influenced discussions on the future British Civil Service in the wake of the *Northcote Trevelyan Report* of 1854.[128] Reports of student life at

[126] Martin (ed.), *Despatches*, vol. 2, p. 330.

[127] Court of Directors to Governor-General in Council, 27 January, 1802, in *Letters of the Marquis Wellesley. Respecting the College of Fort William* (London, 1812), pp. 58–63.

[128] Edward Hughes, 'Civil Service Reform 1853–5', *Public Administration*, 32:1 (1954), 17–51; Emmeline W. Cohen, *The Growth of the British Civil Service 1780–1939* (London, 1965), pp. 75–123; Jenifer Hart, 'The Genesis of the Northcote-Trevelyan

both colleges paint a picture that is rather different to Wellesley's vision of disciplined conduct. Nevertheless, the colleges became a cadre factory that added to the enclosed, elitist character of the Civil Service that continued in the Indian Civil Service after the dissolution of the Company and arguably even affected the postcolonial Indian Administrative Service.[129]

The administrative reforms conducted in British India under Cornwallis and his successors built on the groundwork provided by CEPA, but they were more than just an echo of the Economical Reform Debates. In India, British reform concepts were adapted and systematically implemented throughout the Company establishment. The concepts enabled the colonial leadership to check previously ineradicable problems of maladministration and to set the Company administration on a path to becoming a paragon of administrative efficiency. This remarkable feat did not at first reverberate in the British administrative discourse. In fact, for the remainder of the century, the reforms hardly appeared in the British debates on colonial India, even though corruption was still at the heart of these debates.

In the late 1780s and early 1790s, the British discourse on colonial India revolved around the impeachment trial of Warren Hastings (1787–1795). Edmund Burke, the driving force behind the impeachment, ascertained that the parliamentary trial was not confined to determining whether Hastings was guilty of mismanagement and corruption. Instead, Burke set the stage for an epic moral dispute on Britain's imperial vision. Burke posed the question of how Britain could reconcile rule of conquest with its liberal constitution. In the impeachment, the character of Warren Hastings and his conduct as Governor General mostly served as a foil for this fundamental argument.[130] Burke demonised Hastings as an arch-villain, who had 'corrupted his hands and sullied his government with bribes [and] used oppression and tyranny in the place of legal government.' In Warren Hastings, he held, 'all the frauds, all the peculations, all the violence, all the tyranny in India are embodied, disciplined and arrayed.'[131] Not only was the regime thoroughly corrupt, Burke argued, but it was openly despotic. Hastings did not deny that there were despotic aspects to Company rule but insisted that this despotism dated back to the ancient Mughal constitution, to which the Bengali population was accustomed. Only by continuing the

Report', in Gillian Sutherland (ed.), *Studies in the Growth of Nineteenth-Century Government* (London, 1972), 63–81.

129 O'Malley, *Indian Civil Service*, pp. 233–6.

130 Nicholas B. Dirks, *The Scandal of Empire. India and the Creation of Imperial Britain* (Cambridge, Mass., 2006).

131 Peter J. Marshall (ed.), *India: The Launching of the Hastings Impeachment 1786–1788*, The Writings and Speeches of Edmund Burke, 6 (Oxford, 1991), pp. 275, 287.

Mughal constitution, Hastings claimed, could Bengal gradually be lifted towards a more liberal constitution. In Burke's view, the British constitution pervaded the entire empire. Despotism was therefore as inacceptable in India as it was in Britain, and Burke forcefully declared that the exercise of despotism in India threatened to corrupt and bring down the whole British constitution. Thus, Burke targeted Hastings' governance not in terms of economical rationality but in reference to a differing version of the ancient constitution, i.e. the ancient, liberal constitution of Britain, which Hastings' alleged oriental despotic conduct threatened.[132]

Even though the impeachment centred on corruption, governance, and the nature of the colonial regime, the closely related aspects of administrative reasoning or economical reform hardly played a role. While Burke had helped inflame the Economical Reform Debates with his call for reform by principle, he never abandoned his essentially patrimonial rationality. In the public discourse of the 1790s, maladministration, corruption, and Indian governance could still be discussed in more or less the same terms as twenty years before.

As the trial dragged on, Burke grew more and more isolated. The relaxation of the Indian situation during Cornwallis' tenure contributed to the receding of public outrage and, arguably, public interest in the matter. On 9 April 1794, Cornwallis and Larkins, freshly returned from India, testified in favour of Hastings, strengthening the case of the defence.[133] Only days earlier, on 5 April, the City of London honoured Cornwallis. John Wilkes, his radical days long over, gave the laudatory speech at the occasion and included Hastings in the praise:

> The plan of a late Governor-General, the Saviour of India (Mr. Hastings), was examined with great care and attention, and adhered to with liberality. A better could not have been adopted. With wonderful ability he struggled through a mass of difficulties of a different kind, brought on in a most critical and perplexed situation of Indian affairs. He rose superior to the combined efforts of our Enemies, and preserved to us the Empire of the East, to be secured on the most permanent basis, and enlarged by Lord Cornwallis.[134]

132 Pavarala, 'Cultures of Corruption'.

133 Jeremy Bernstein, *Dawning of the Raj. The Life and Trials of Warren Hastings* (Chicago, 2000), p. 256. Cf. *The Times*, Thursday, 10 April 1794, p. 2; *The History of the Trial of Warren Hastings, Esq. Late Governor-General of Bengal, before the High Court of Parliament in Westminster-Hall, on an Impeachment by the Commons of Great-Britain, for High Crimes and Misdemeanours* (London, 1796), pp. 94–9.

134 'The Speech of Mr. Chamberlain Wilkes, when he presented the Freedom of the City of London to the Most Noble the Marquis Cornwallis', *The Sun* (21 April 1794).

The war with France had commenced and it was colonial heroes, no longer colonial villains, that the public demanded.[135] Wellesley profited from this change of public sentiment. While his wars of conquest violated Pitt's India Act and ignored the protests of the Board of Directors, they produced narratives of imperial glory, which resonated well with the intensifying patriotic discourse. Moreover, Wellesley's tenure marked a new vision for Britain of itself as an imperial power. As Wellesley saw it, firm rule combined with economical administration and strict anti-corruption measures amounted to a form of enlightened despotism that would control the presumed innate corruption of India. The Civil Service became the perfect tool to assert this programme of imperial domination and the objectification of colonial subjects. Most civil servants embraced their new role, as this role provided them with a source of confidence in the estranged and vulnerable colonial setting.[136]

[135] Marshall, Peter J., '"Cornwallis Triumphant". War in India and the British Public in the Late Eighteenth Century', in id., *Trade and Conquest: Studies on the rise of British Dominance in India* (Aldershot, 1993), XIV, 57–74.

[136] Linda Colley, *Britons* (New Haven, 2005), pp. 155–206; Jeremy Osborn, 'India and the East India Company in the Public Sphere of Eighteenth-Century Britain', in Huw V. Bowen, Margarette Lincoln, and Nigel Rigby (eds.), *The Worlds of the East India Company* (Woodbridge, 2002), 201–21; Bayly, *Imperial Meridian*, pp. 100–32; Wilson, *Domination of Strangers*, pp. 150–7.

6

Great Britain II: Assessing Reform

In 1797 and 1798, a parliamentary Finance Committee brought a fresh impetus to the reform discourse. This impetus was not what the Pitt ministry had intended. Against the backdrop of the ongoing wars, the ministry was still trying to keep the lid on economical reform issues. For Pitt, the Finance Committee constituted a small concession to the independents on whose votes he depended. That the Committee started a thorough stocktaking of the administrative reform process in Britain and pressured the government for new reforms resulted from the unexpected agency of Charles Abbot, the Committee's chairman. Abbot was a staunch reformer who was not afraid to provoke resistance.

Under Abbot's leadership, the Finance Committee set itself the task of examining to what extent the recommendations of the Accounts and Fees Commissioners had been implemented. The Finance Committee also updated the recommendations of the earlier reform commissions and adopted their principles. It expanded the approach to administrative reform in two ways. First, it further developed the reform principles, in particular by introducing statistical methods. The large-scale collection of standardised data in tabular form clarified the differences between the departments and opened up new questions. Second, the Finance Committee broadened the scope of the administrative reform principles to include the judiciary. The Finance Committee examined the courts of justice, and also included the judiciary in a broader sense, namely law enforcement and the prison system.

The inquiries of the Finance Committee enabled various actors to advance their personal reform agendas. Abbot did not shy away from using the Finance Committee to support his two stepbrothers, Jeremy and Samuel Bentham. Jeremy Bentham launched a new attempt to implement his plan of a novel penitentiary, whilst Samuel Bentham used the backing of the Finance Committee to get into a position that allowed him to fundamentally reshape the dockyards. In the Navy, reforms continued to spark internal contestations. However, the process gained a new dimension around 1800, because administrative reforms coincided with the beginnings of industrialisation. Samuel Bentham's technological and administrative economisation of the dockyards prefigured the epochal technological and social changes of the following decades.

After the inquiries of the Finance Committee, the systematic economical principles attained largely unchallenged validity in Great Britain. The reports of the earlier reform commissions became canonical and authoritative templates, which were open to interpretation. In the administrative discourse, agents based their arguments on economy and utility, while the ancient constitution and customary arguments hardly played a role anymore. However, the uncontested validity of economical reform principles did not automatically result in their application in the sense of a systematic reform of state administration.

The Finance Committee of 1797–8

After the Post Office scandal of 1787, administrative issues faded from the spotlight of parliamentary debate. During the winter of 1788/9, the government was effectively paralysed by the Regency Crisis. Only a few months after the recovery of the King, the onset of the French Revolution rendered any previous political agenda obsolete. After the publication of Edmund Burke's *Reflections on the Revolution in France* in 1790, the revolution controversy dominated the public discourse. Burke emphatically warned against the spreading of the revolution that, he argued, would destroy property rights and shatter the very foundations of society. For Burke, the root of the revolutionary evil was an ideological application of abstract ideas, which threatened the fabric of society. Burke argued for an emotionally based traditionalism that amounted to a powerful reformulation of ancient constitution convictions. In the *Reflections*, Burke openly attacked philosophical radicals such as Richard Price, who celebrated the events in Paris as a triumph over tyranny and confirmation of his belief in general progress towards more liberty and science. Famously, Thomas Paine, Mary Wollstonecraft (1759–97), and others reacted to Burke's attack by calling for human rights and powerfully endorsing utilitarian ideas and arguments based on natural law. A fear of spreading revolution soon determined the ministry's domestic policy as well as its foreign policy. Suspicious of English Jacobins, the ministry went after radicals with might and main. Even if the radicals mostly prevailed in court, the following patriotic surge pushed them to the margins of the discourse. With the founding of the United Irishmen in 1792, the danger of revolutionary uprising in Ireland seemed all the more acute. The fact that economical reform had been discussed in conjunction with parliamentary reform throughout the 1780s did not help the cause either.[1] With the start of the French Revolutionary War in 1793, the British state entered war mode once more. Again, government spending exploded. Reforms which were potentially disruptive and did not even promise short-term savings were hardly on top of the political agenda.

When economical reform did come up in Parliament during the 1790s, it was almost exclusively brought up by independents who expressed concerns with the state of public finances and pressed for retrenchment. Thomas Gilbert and the former Bank of England director John Harrison (1738–1811) breached the tacit consensus on the property theory of office by repeatedly calling for the taxation of patent offices. Harrison went as far as to propose a 50% tax on sinecure emoluments. Pitt mostly tried to appease independent interests and conceded a number of minor issues. Whilst Pitt drew criticism from both Foxites and George III for his stance, this 'pattern of defeat and retreat'[2] helped Pitt to maintain his majority and to preclude potentially dangerous reform debates, until economical reform came back with a vengeance in 1796.[3]

On 2 May 1796, Shelburne recalled several recommendations of CEPA that the ministry had failed to act on and called the ministry out on the wanton increase of Crown influence.[4] In the previous year, Shelburne had reconciled with Fox, and so the Foxites joined Shelburne's attack. The Whigs thus renewed the temporary alliance of 1780 and raised the alarm on the dangers of national bankruptcy. Public finance and administrative issues were once more debated in the same breath. The ministry shrugged off the Whig initiative as a tactical move until the Whigs' premonitions proved true early in the following year. Large-scale investment in housing schemes in North America had the makings of a financial bubble. In the ensuing nervousness of the stock market, rumours of an impending French invasion led to a panicked run on bank accounts, to which the ministry reacted by issuing a bank stoppage, on 27 February 1797, by order of council

1 Boyd Hilton, *A Mad, Bad, and Dangerous People? England, 1783–1846* (Oxford, 2006), pp. 57–91.

2 John R. Breihan, 'Economical Reform, 1785–1810', unpublished PhD thesis (Cambridge, 1977), p. 131.

3 Ibid., pp. 117–43; John R. Breihan, 'William Pitt and the Commission on Fees, 1785–1801', *Historical Journal*, 27:1 (1984), 59–81, p. 63; Philip Harling, *The Waning of 'Old Corruption': The Politics of Economical Reform in Britain, 1779–1846* (Oxford, 1996), pp. 170–3.

4 Parl. Reg., 45. 1796, pp. 277–89.

temporarily interdicting cash disbursements. The crisis of public credit took weeks to subside.[5]

Against the backdrop of public anxiety, John Harrison announced his intention to move for a committee to reduce sinecures and useless offices. At the same time, independent members demanded committees on the bank stoppage and on more general issues of public finance. Pitt once more reacted in a conciliatory manner and presented the prospect of a parliamentary finance committee.[6]

Pitt's Finance Committee received a threefold designation. The act of appointment charged the select committee firstly to provide an overview of the public debts and mark the amount that had accumulated in the preceding four years. Secondly, the act ordered the committee to note the progress of debt-reduction since the installation of Pitt's sinking funds in 1786. The offices came in only as a third head of the statute, which requested the committee to

> consider what Regulation and Checks have been applied, in order to control the several Branches of the Public Expenditure, and also, what Increase or Diminution has taken place, since the Year 1782, in the Number, or in the Account, of the Salaries and Emoluments of different Public Offices' and propose additional measures for their reduction, 'without Detriment to the Public Service.[7]

The act mirrors the pressure of the independents for retrenchment. The fifteen appointed members of the Finance Committee included majority, independent, and opposition interests. The two joint Paymasters of the Forces, Thomas Steele (1753–1823) and Dudley Ryder (1762–1847), were staunch Pittites. Ryder had chaired the Finance Committee of 1791 and regularly sat in the Select Committee of the Privy Council on the Fees Reports. Charles Philip Yorke (1764–1834), the second son of a former Lord Chancellor and brother to the Earl of Hardwicke, supported the ministry as well. Whilst Fox's candidacy was voted down, John Harrison added a prominent opposition voice to the roster. The chairman, Charles

5 Breihan, 'Economical Reform,' pp. 143–6; John Ehrman, *The Younger Pitt*, vol. 3, *The Consuming Struggle* (London, 1996), pp. 5–12; Bruce H. Mann, *Republic of Debtors. Bankruptcy in the Age of American Independence* (Cambridge, Mass., 2002), pp. 198–214.

6 Breihan, 'Economical Reform,' pp. 151–5; Ehrman, *Consuming Struggle*, pp. 40–3; Parl. Hist., 33, col. 77–107.

7 *JHC* 52, 12 July 1796 to 5 October 1797, col. 393.

Abbot (1757–1829), counted among the independents.[8] It was due to the unexpected commitment of Charles Abbot that the Finance Committee of 1797–8 rose to become the hitherto most comprehensive inquiry into the situation of public offices.

Charles Abbot's Administrative Statistics

Charles Abbot had only entered Parliament in 1795 following a legal career both as a practitioner and an academic. Abbot held a semi-sinecure as Clerk of the Rules at King's Bench. Instead of leaving the office's duties to a deputy, he used the position to reorganise and index the court records and published two treatises on rules, procedures, and practices at King's Bench and the Welsh courts.[9] In Parliament, Abbot used his expertise to propose improvements and to chair committees on legislative procedures.[10] Abbot counted among the Crown-friendly independents who generally voted with the ministry and he enthusiastically supported the controversial Seditious Meetings Bill that was the centrepiece of the ministry's authoritarian reaction towards radicals.[11] Whilst he disapproved of radical positions, Abbot did not agree with Burke's nostalgic vision of society either. Rather, his positions were in tune with the many loyalist pamphlets, which dismissed radical ideas from a decidedly modernist standpoint. These pamphlets depicted Paine and other radicals as levellers, who aimed to impose an economic egalitarianism that would endanger the foundations of the commercial society.[12] Respected and competent, Abbot seemed to suit the ministry's need for an uncontroversial chairman who might help to cool down the debate. Abbot bore no particular sympathies towards the opposition. However, his political independence cut both ways and his concern for improvement was genuine. In part, this particular concern for improvement stemmed from Abbot's upbringing. His father had died in 1760 and his mother remarried soon after. Abbot grew up under the stern guidance of his stepfather Jeremiah Bentham, and as a stepbrother to Jeremy and

8 Ibid., col. 392–3.

9 Charles Abbot, *Rules and orders on the plea side of the court of King's Bench beginning in Easter Term, 1731, and ending in Trinity Term, 1795. With preface and index* (London, 1795).

10 Clare Wilkinson, 'Abbot, Charles, first Baron Colchester (1757–1829)', *ODNB*.

11 Jennifer Mori, *Britain in the Age of the French Revolution, 1785–1820* (Harlow, 2000), pp. 92–101.

12 Gregory Claeys, 'The French Revolution Debate and British Political Thought', *History of Political Thought*, 11:1 (1990), 59–80.

Samuel Bentham. Especially close to the latter, Abbot corresponded with both brothers throughout his life.

Abbot applied himself to the Finance Committee with fervour, using his chairmanship to lead and arguably even dominate its proceedings. The Committee worked five days a week for at least six hours. According to his diary, Abbot himself often worked for thirteen hours at a time, pausing only for dinner.[13] Apart from drawing up many reports by himself and providing opening and closing remarks for all reports, he also coordinated and redacted, sometimes thoroughly reworking the reports which the other Committee members prepared in parallel.[14]

Abbot interpreted the act of appointment as a mandate for a comprehensive review of the administrative system. Whilst the Finance Committee approached the assignments directly regarding state finance first, these issues only filled five reports, followed by thirty-one reports on administrative questions. This comprehensive approach became the preeminent feature of the Finance Committee's investigation. The first three reports on the public debt and general financial topics were supportive of the ministry, but the following reports on the public offices took an openly critical stance. For Abbot, the results of the Accounts and Fees Commissions defined the benchmarks for the state of administrative reform. Each report of the Finance Committee first listed the respective recommendations of these commissions and specified the degree of their implementation. Secondly, the reports stated the development of a given establishment in terms of personnel and costs after 1782. In conclusion, the Finance Committee added their own recommendations based on 'the same Maxims of political Prudence and Oeconomy, which were so clearly stated, and so constantly urged by the Commissioners of Accounts and Inquiry.'[15]

At the end of July 1797, the Finance Committee presented their remarks on its first twenty-two reports. In these remarks, sinecures served as an important point of reference for Abbot's general thoughts on offices.[16] Abbot's explicit definition of a sinecure also applied to efficient offices, at least implicitly: 'A Sinecure, in the Opinion of your Committee, is to be considered only as a Pension with an ostensible Office annexed to it.'[17] In other words, sinecures were not offices at all, but rather pensions in the guise of an office. Abbot thus echoed CEPA's point that offices were defined

13 Charles Colchester (ed.), *The Diary and Correspondence of Charles Abbot, Lord Colchester. Speaker of the House of Commons 1802–1817*, vol. 1 (London, 1861), p. 115.

14 Breihan, 'Economical Reform', pp. 158–9.

15 Finance Committee, 'Fourth Report', *SP 107*, 189–329, p. 193.

16 Finance Committee, 'Twenty-second Report', *SP 109*, 509–617, pp. 526–7.

17 Ibid., p. 527.

by their public duties. Due to the obfuscation of their nature, Abbot argued, sinecures were especially liable to abuse. He therefore called for a general abolition of sinecures and the consolidation of offices whose duties were necessary but infrequent. However, he made an exception for some particular 'Sinecure Offices of high Rank [...] for the Reward of personal Services, or, to secure an honourable Retreat to Persons who are entitled to Marks of Public Favour by long and meritorious Discharge of the Duties of high Office.'[18] Abbot's defence of some of the most notorious sinecures stands out as a breach of the reasoning found throughout the remarks, which otherwise insisted on functional logic and transparency. Abbot bracketed out the elitist instrument of distinction from economical reform.[19]

In the report's concluding remarks, Abbot also reflected on the established practice of compensation for abolished offices. Instead of compensation with lifetime pensions, he suggested

> to make suitable COMPENSATIONS to all such Persons, until Opportunities shall occur of placing them in other Official Situations, of Duties in some Degree similar, and of Profits proportionate to the fair and ordinary Emoluments of their former Offices, as far as it may be practicable; a due Attention to Public Oeconomy requiring that the earliest Means should be taken for making such Arrangements.[20]

The scheme rested on two remarkable assumptions, which challenged the tacit consensus on the property theory of office. Firstly, Abbot implied that office-holders could be transferred between offices and, secondly, that an adequate surrogate position satisfied any obligation. Possible claims to compensation remained a legal grey area, but they necessarily depended on the definition of office. If an office was a public trust that depended on the execution of useful duties, there could be no claim to compensation without duties. The second part of each Finance Committee report listed all changes in the establishments after 1782. The tables provided just the information that could be used to assess potential reform measures and retrenchments. Abbot suggested the introduction of annual accounts of all establishments. Regularly collecting this information, Abbot argued, 'may very materially conduce to the Ends of Public Oeconomy.'[21] Abbot's suggestions implied the necessity of reform as a continuous process.

18 Ibid.
19 Ibid., pp. 527–8.
20 Ibid., p. 526.
21 Ibid.

To Abbot, the reports of the Finance Committee were more than singular empirical surveys. He endorsed CEPA's claim that the same principles *mutatis mutandis* applied to all departments. In the preliminary remarks to the *Fourth Report,* which introduce the Finance Committee's inquiry into the offices, Abbot implicitly reconstituted the administrative subject area by dividing the subjects of inquiry into three sections, i.e. collection, expenditure, and auditing.[22] The introduction to the first division of the system offered 'a preliminary View of the general Rate of Expense, incident to the whole System of Collection.' This overview consisted of a quantified comparison in tables, which specified the gross expense of collection in relation to the collected revenue expressed as a percentage. The tables compared the departments in terms of their cost-benefit ratio. The comparison comprised the period from 1789 to 1796 in order to contain 'equal Periods of Peace and War.'[23]

The new method immediately opened up new questions and insights. The quantified comparison assumed systemic homogeneity. However, Abbot pointed out that a number of offices were 'Establishment[s] of a mixed nature', because their duties went beyond the collection of revenue. For instance, the 'primary Functions' of the Hackney Coach Office, regulating and controlling hireable vehicles in London, were rather 'those of a Police Court.'[24] In fully equivalent offices, the results of the comparison revealed shocking differences. For instance, the expense ratio of the Scottish offices was twice or even three times as high as that of their English counterparts.[25] The new method not only allowed a comparison between departments, but also between the overall system of revenue collection and its international counterparts. Though information on these international counterparts was hard to obtain, the *Fourth Report* claimed that the expense of the British revenue 'does not much exceed Half the Expense [...] incurred in collecting the Revenues of France.'[26] Moreover,

> In Great Britain, every Farthing drawn from the Subject, on Account of the Public Revenues, and all Deductions therefrom, until the Net Produce is paid into the Exchequer and brought within the View of Parliament, can be ascertained with a mathematical Accuracy.[27]

22 Finance Committee, 'Fourth Report', p. 192.
23 Ibid., p. 193.
24 Ibid., p. 195.
25 Finance Committee, 'Fifth Report', *SP 107*, 331–409, pp. 335–6; Finance Committee, 'Eighth Report', *SP 108*, 203–73, pp. 211–12.
26 Finance Committee, 'Fourth Report', p. 197.
27 Ibid.

The statement sat well with Abbot's goal of assessing the progress of administrative reforms; the report presented transparency and mathematical accuracy as a source of national pride. The passage was, however, not from Abbot's own hand, but rather a quote from a document in the appendix to the *Fourth Report* that substantiated the whole comparison. The document's author was Thomas Irving (1738?–1800), who collaborated closely with Abbot.[28] Irving was one of the foremost statisticians in government service.

To characterise Irving as a statistician warrants some specification. The beginnings of modern statistics are usually dated to the early to mid-nineteenth century, while its predecessor, political arithmetic, is set to the late seventeenth and early eighteenth century. The period in between has long been characterised as a gap during which there was little interest in quantified information gathering. Recent history of science has put more emphasis on continuities and also on advances in statistical theory and practice during the second half of the eighteenth century.[29] This shift in the statistical approaches was closely connected to the Scottish form of utilitarian empiricism that looked for the specific conditions of social improvement. John Sinclair (1754–1835), a close friend of Irving's, was the first to use the term 'statistics' in English, in the context of the twenty-one volumes of his *Statistical Accounts of Scotland,* which he compiled throughout the 1790s. Sinclair's statistics focused on the 'quantum of happiness enjoyed by [a country's] inhabitants, and the means of its future improvement'.[30] Sinclair's statistical accounts fulfilled a suggestion of James Steuart, who had proposed a national survey of Scotland in his *Principles of Political Oeconomy.*

28 John J. McCusker, 'Colonial Civil Servant and Counter-Revolutionary. Thomas Irving (1738?–1800) in Boston, Charleston, and London' in id., *Essays in the Economic History of the Atlantic World* (London, 1997), 190–221.

29 Michael Donnelly, 'From Political Arithmetic to Social Statistics. How some Nineteenth Century Roots of the Social Sciences were implanted', in Johan Heilbron, Lars Magnusson, and Björn Wittrock (eds.), *The Rise of the Social Sciences and the Formation of Modernity: Conceptual Change in Context, 1750–1850,* (Boston 1996), 225–40, pp. 228–30; Joanna Innes, 'Power and Happiness. Empirical Social Enquiry in Britain, from "Political Arithmetic" to "Moral Statistics"', *Inferior Politics: Social Problems and Social Policies in Eighteenth-Century Britain* (Oxford, 2009), 109–75, pp. 109–10.

30 John Sinclair, *The Statistical Account of Scotland. Drawn up from the Communications of the Ministers of the Different Parishes* (Edinburgh, 1791–9). From 1785 Sinclair also published his seminal *History of the Public Revenue of the British Empire,* in which he analysed the state of the public debts, but did not touch on administrative issues. John Sinclair, *The History of the Public Revenue of the British Empire* (Dublin, 1785).

Irving's field was the statistics of trade. In various positions at the Boston Custom House, Irving had restructured the information on North American trade, leading to a first composite view of colonial commerce in the 1770s.[31] After some trials and tribulations in the wake of the American Revolution, Irving returned to Britain in 1783 and, in 1786, became Inspector General of Imports and Exports of Great Britain at the Customs Office. CEPA had classed the office as a sinecure and recommended its abolition.[32] Irving, however, worked intensely, compiling over eighty volumes of exhaustive tabular accounts on commerce and revenue for the use of the Treasury. He also gathered all data he could find about other European states. Irving's statistical accounts provided the basis for the quantitative comparisons conducted in the Finance Committee.[33]

Abbot appreciated this extensive set of empirical information and, particularly, the methodological impetus of statistics. Apparently, he was also impressed by Irving's affiliation with the Scottish empiricists:

> He [Irving] made himself acquainted with the financial details of the old Governments of France and Holland, by researches in these countries before the Revolution. He was well known to Adam Smith.[34]

Abbot apparently set great store by Scottish economical thinking for the inquiry into revenue collection. In the *Fourth Report* on the Customs, Abbot applauded the *Wealth of Nations* for its 'ablest writing' and 'an enlightened and extensive Observation of practical Details'.[35] Towards the end of the century, the ideas and language of Scottish political economy were gaining ground and they continued to provide methodological impetus for administrative reform.[36]

31 McCusker, 'Colonial Civil Servant'.

32 CEPA, 'Fourteenth Report', p. 20.

33 McCusker, 'Colonial Civil Servant', pp. 218–19.

34 Colchester (ed.), *Correspondence*, vol. 1, p. 97. How closely Irving and Smith were actually acquainted is hard to establish. Irving and Smith were certainly part of the same patronage network around Henry Scott, fifth Duke of Queensberry, and Irving's elder brother (who had died before Irving's birth) had attended Glasgow University together with Smith in the 1730s. McCusker, 'Colonial Civil Servant', p. 193.

35 Finance Committee, 'Fourth Report', pp. 214–15.

36 From 1778 to his death in 1790, Adam Smith himself served as Commissioner of Customs in Scotland. Cf. Ian Simpson Ross, *The Life of Adam Smith*, 2nd edn. (Oxford, 2010), pp. 388–52.

A Comprehensive Survey

The individual reports of the Finance Committee vary considerably in scale, depth, and tone. Rowland Burdon's (c.1757–1838) report on the Post Office was one of the sharpest. The report openly whipped the 'tardy Manner [...] in which their [the Fees Commissioners'] useful Suggestions were entertained [...] by those who were interested in the Continuance of the Abuses.'[37] Burdon's report also stands out because of its explicit use of mechanistic metaphors, which echoed Steuart's image of the government-machine in constant need of supervision:

> it is not enough to introduce Regulations of Dispatch, Security, and Economy; in order to maintain them, their Execution must be frequently examined and revised, and every Part of the complicated Movement must be regulated by Superintendants [sic] well informed in the Mechanism of the Whole, and regularly attentive to all the Parts.[38]

Notwithstanding their differences, the reports shared an economical vocabulary. 'Economy' itself was ever-present, both as an aspiration for reform and as a marker for appropriate principles. Similarly, 'system' served as the ubiquitous bracket to describe institutional setups: modes of working and accounting, interactions between single offices within a department, and the interplay of departments within the national revenue, 'the whole System of Collection.'[39] A system was defined by the operation of a small number of principles, which the Finance Committee sought to identify in order to suggest reforms. 'Principle(s)' appeared frequently in the reports, sometimes synonymously with 'maxims', to refer to the method of reform. The reform suggestions generally emphasised 'simplicity' and 'uniformity'. Similarly, they urged promotion of 'a systematic Unity in the Treasury Collection.'[40] The Finance Committee also used 'simplify' and 'simplification' as processual terms. 'Reform', which had faded from the spotlight in the reports of the Fees Commission, returned as a frequent marker for both the remedying of defects and, generally, for institutional change for the better. To quote just one example, the Finance Committee noted that the auditing at the Exchequer had 'undergone very important Reforms in the

[37] Finance Committee, 'Seventh Report', *SP 108*, 67–201, p. 161.
[38] Ibid., p. 97.
[39] Finance Committee, 'Fourth Report', p. 193.
[40] Ibid., p. 203.

last Sixteen Years.'[41] 'Improvement' appeared almost synonymously with 'reform' in its general sense. 'Regulations' denoted the concrete rules or orders of a department. The Finance Committee took up the term 'establishment' from the Fees Commission to invariably describe the endowment of a department in terms of places and salaries. Though it was a technical and seemingly neutral term, 'establishment' served to cement the functional perspective on offices by setting all offices, from board members to messengers or doorkeepers, on the same abstract footing. Together with its functions and regulations, the establishment defined a department, not the individual person at its helm. Finally, the use of 'public service' warrants attention. While its usage increased, 'public service' continued to denote the officers' actions, not the institutional system, e.g. in the formulaic disclaimer 'without detriment to the public service'.[42]

Due to the methodical comparison of current empirical findings with the recommendations of the Accounts and Fees Commissioners, historical arguments played only a minor role. Still, 'ancient' carried negative connotations while 'modern' implied improvement. In various cases, the Finance Committee juxtaposed deficient ancient institutions and well-working modern, economical institutions.[43]

Notwithstanding individual variations, the language of the reports was in tune with its message. The Finance Committee returned economical reform to centre stage. Lacking the authority to issue summons or administer oaths, the Finance Committee depended on the departments' returns. On the plus side, the Finance Committee represented Parliament. The Committee included independents, ministry supporters, and opposition Whigs alike and this unity added weight to economical reform. Moreover, the transparency of the reports heightened their effect. The Finance Committee used its power to name and shame and exposed non-compliant departments. In the *Seventeenth Report*, for example, the Finance Committee quoted the Admiralty Board, which justified its inaction by discounting the Fees Commissioners' recommendations as 'inadequate' and claimed salaries were 'by no means sufficient'. The Finance Committee commented: 'How far this may be deemed a satisfactory Explanation, Your Committee submit to the Judgement of the House.'[44]

The Finance Committee established the recommendations of the Accounts and Fees Commissions as benchmarks for reform and presented

41 Finance Committee, 'Twenty-second Report', p. 512.

42 E.g. Finance Committee, 'Tenth Report', *SP 108*, 319–33, p. 322.

43 Ibid., 3–65, p. 8.

44 Finance Committee, 'Seventeenth Report', pp. 147–8.

the failure to implement these recommendations as a deficiency in itself. Every report reviewed whether salaries had already been regularised, and suggested the introduction of fees funds if this was not the case. The Finance Committee also took up the Fees Commissions' call for a regularised pension system, though it dropped the fixed rate of 50% of the last salary. All reports sought to identify offices that could be abolished or consolidated. This examination of establishments poised for austerity received additional weight from the statistical sections of the reports, which specified and calculated the increase or decrease of places and expenditure per department from 1782. In many offices the committee members found wartime increases and recommended the abolition of places come peace.[45]

Judiciary, Police, and Convicts

After its prolongation in 1798, the Finance Committee widened its view beyond the scope of the Accounts and Fees Commissioners' reports to include the judiciary and issues of police. The courts of law had never faced administrative inquiries before.[46] When Abbot sent requests for accounts and establishments on 15 March 1798, the courts' reactions were not forthcoming.[47] Lloyd Kenyon (1732–1802), Lord Chief Justice and Abbot's superior at King's Bench, purportedly exclaimed: 'Sir, tell the House of Commons that I will not be yelped at by my own turnspit.'[48] In a private meeting, Lord Chancellor Wedderburn (1733–1805) tried to dissuade Abbot from the inquiry. Wedderburn did not deny that there were many defects within the courts. Rather he warned:

> that the public, which had hitherto considered the Courts of Justice with respect, would be led to suppose abuses, and treat them with disparagement; that all the details would be laid open to the public eye, which would begin to speculate upon points to which the Committee itself did not advert, or mean to attempt any charge, &c. &c.[49]

45 Finance Committee, 'Eighteenth Report', *SP 109*, 191–205, p. 194; Finance Committee, 'Twentieth Report', *SP 109*, 389–433, pp. 393–4.

46 Douglas W. Allen, *The Institutional Revolution. Measurement and the Economic Emergence of the Modern World* (Chicago, 2012), pp. 193–6.

47 Colchester (ed.), *Correspondence*, pp. 138–44.

48 Quoted in John Campbell, *The Lives of the Chief Justices of England*, vol. 4 (New York, 1878), p. 97.

49 Colchester (ed.), *Correspondence*, p. 48.

Wedderburn's argument played public interest against the alleged dangers of an unreliable public opinion. Appealing to Abbot as a supporter of the Seditious Meetings Bill, Wedderburn claimed a special status for the courts and presented political stability in times of war as the higher good. The *Twenty-Seventh Report* on the courts of justice reflected these premonitory contestations. Abbot stressed that the Committee had been 'more than commonly anxious' to make sure that measures would not result in 'detriment to the public service'.[50] His strategy was to counter the resistance of the courts by references to famous historical jurists, Francis Bacon (1561–1626) and Matthew Hale (1609–76):

> At the same Time, therefore, that in reviewing Establishments of such high Antiquity and Dignity, they cannot but acknowledge the Truth of the Observation made by Lord Bacon, that Time is the greatest of Innovators, and must be counteracted by human Counsel.[51]

Abbot's statement resembled the Account Commissioners' lip service to antiquity and dignity. With the reference to Francis Bacon, Abbot turned ancient constitution reasoning against itself. Reforms were necessary to counteract aberrations from the hypothetical original state. In the same vein, Abbot quoted Matthew Hale, the famous Restoration Chief Justice, to the point 'that the Amendment of Things amiss timely, may do very much good, and prevent very much Evil that may otherwise ensue.' Abbot added another quote of Hale's, who in reference to Exchequer sinecures had rhetorically asked: 'If these Officers are not necessary, why are they continued?'[52]

With the *Twenty-Eighth Report* on police and the convict system, the Finance Committee entered upon two more matters pertaining to the judiciary, which had been subject to intense public debate in the preceding years. To discuss police in the context of national-level regulation was to take a position in a contested discourse. The French loanword 'police' had increased in usage in the course of the eighteenth century, with its broadest meaning concerning (municipal) public health, morality, order, and law-abiding social coexistence. Its French origin was particularly present when the term was used in association with institutional and law-enforcement issues, and widely associated with absolutism. Critics referred to the

[50] Finance Committee, 'Twenty-seventh Report', *SP 111*, 41–315, p. 48.
[51] Ibid.
[52] Ibid., p. 49.

French example to portray police as a despotic threat to liberty.[53] On the other hand, especially in the fast-growing metropolis, the state of public safety and order was a cause for public concern. The entrepreneurial system of private thief-takers was prone to corruption and was evidently overwhelmed by the rising rate of crimes. The danger of public unrest loomed large, especially after the traumatic Gordon Riots of 1780. Henry Fielding's famous Bow Street Runners, established in 1749, remained a small public player in the partly corporate, mostly privately organised business of law enforcement.[54] In 1785, Pitt proposed a central police force, but his London and Westminster Police Bill failed because the City of London invoked the spectre of despotism to defend its corporate independence. Against the backdrop of the rising fear of English Jacobins, the ministry managed to pass the more limited Middlesex Justices Bill in 1792. The seven small offices introduced by the Bill just outside of the city's jurisdiction hardly constituted an impressive force to police a city of over a million.[55]

In the *Twenty-Eighth Report*, the Finance Committee presented an unconventional approach to police; a plan that directly proceeded from administrative reform issues. The report proposed the consolidation of the Hackney Coaches Office with the Hawkers' and Pedlars' Office into a single Board of Police Revenue. Thomas Irving's quantified comparison had called attention to the mixed nature of the old offices, which combined revenue and police functions.[56] Their revenue consisted of licensing fees for rent-coaches and street vendors, trades that were suspicious due to their role in smuggling and fencing. Far from separating the functions, the plan suggested to extend the jurisdiction of the proposed Board of Police Revenue to pawnbrokers and equally suspicious trades.[57] Moreover, the board would incorporate the seven offices and expand their authorities. In a remarkable double argumentation, the Finance Committee substantiated the plan both in reference to controlling crime as well as to the revenue:

53 Leon Radzinowicz, 'That Strange Word "Police". Cross-Currents in the Movement for the Reform of the Police' in id., *A History of English Criminal Law and its Administration from 1750*, vol. 3 (London, 1956), 1–13, pp. 1–8; Norman Gash, 'A Glaswegian Criminologist. Patrick Colquhoun, 1745–1820', in id., *Pillars of Government and Other Essays on State and Society: c. 1770–c. 1880* (London, 1986), 139–52, p. 141.

54 Allen, *Institutional Revolution*, pp. 208–11.

55 Clive Emsley, *The English Police. A Political and Social History* (Hemel Hempstead, 1991), pp. 15–20. The offices, designed on the model of the Bow Street Runners, consisted of but three magistrates and six constables each.

56 Finance Committee, 'Tenth Report'; Finance Committee, 'Eleventh Report', *SP 108*, 335–59.

57 Finance Committee, 'Twenty-eighth Report', *SP 112*, 3–215, pp. 31–2.

> It is no small Recommendation of this Proposition, that its Effect, as a Measure of Police, will be accompanied by an Increase of Revenue; an Increase which it is, however, less the Object of this Plan to procure, on account of its pecuniary Advantage, than for the Sake of the Check which will thereby be given to the improper Exercise of those Trades, which it is thought important to bring under a regular Mode of Inspection and Control.[58]

Two relatively marginal revenue offices provided the ground to attempt the institution of a central police department of hitherto unknown weight. The old offices held the authority to autonomously regulate the trades with which they were concerned. The new board would take up this power and add the means of enforcing its regulations. The board was designed as a disciplinary tool poised against the suspicious lower orders.[59]

The ambitious plan was the brainchild of Patrick Colquhoun (1745–1820), magistrate of the Shoreditch branch of the seven offices. Once a prominent Glaswegian merchant and commercial lobbyist, Colquhoun took the office on Dundas' recommendation in 1792 and advocated police reform from the outset.[60] In 1796, he published his comprehensive *Treatise on the Police of the Metropolis*[61] gaining him an honorary doctorate from the University of Glasgow and recognition as the architect of the modern police force in the older police historiography.[62] The book took up established arguments like Beccaria's insistence on proportionality of crime and punishment, but its main persuasive power came from a vivid presentation of prevailing immorality and crime in London, backed by statistics tables.[63] Colquhoun proposed extensive social regulation to increase morality and prevent crimes. He insisted on a uniform, public system of police to enforce such regulations by force and also by means of information-techniques like central registers of small trades and of known or suspected criminals. In his treatise, Colquhoun also pointed to the economic prospects of social engineering:

58 Ibid., pp. 5–6.

59 Peter Borsay, 'Urban Life and Culture', in Harry T. Dickinson (ed.), *A Companion to Eighteenth-Century Britain* (Malden, 2002), 196–207, pp. 205–7.

60 Ruth Paley, 'Colquhoun, Patrick (1745–1820)', *ODNB*.

61 Patrick Colquhoun, *A Treatise on the Police of the Metropolis. Explaining the Various Crimes and Misdemeanors which at Present are Felt as a Pressure upon the Community; and Suggesting Remedies for their Prevention* (London, 1796).

62 Cf. e.g. W. M. Lee, *A History of Police in England* (London, 1901), pp. 219–24. The epithet has since been challenged. Paley, 'Colquhoun, Patrick (1745–1820)'.

63 Colquhoun, *Treatise on the Police of the Metropolis*, for the reference to Beccaria cf. p. 12; Caesar Beccaria Bonesaria, *An Essay on Crimes and Punishments* (Edinburgh, 1778). Gash, 'Glaswegian Criminologist', pp. 139–52.

> With these combined advantages an infinite saving to the Nation would be experienced in useful labour, arising from the preservation of the morals of the lower orders of the people, and the consequent diminution of crimes. The money thus disbursed *á priori* would be returned one-hundred-fold *á posteriori*, in the result of the system, by counteracting the principles of criminality, and thereby reducing the enormous expense of punishments.[64]

Colquhoun relied on penalties and the extended usage of licensing-duties to exert (moral) control, catch criminals, and to finance rewards and premiums for the detection of crimes.[65] In the *Twenty-Eighth Report* of the Finance Committee, these approaches seamlessly blended with those of administrative reform. Policemen would receive regular salaries from a fund comprising fees, license duties, and penalties.[66] Colquhoun's ideas of police reform resonated with the administrative reform ideas of the Finance Committee. They also met in their empirical and systematic approach. Colquhoun had intended his treatise to be for practical usage, but he also drew on contemporary Scottish as well as continental scholarship, and the University of Glasgow recognised the treatise as a scientific contribution.[67] Empirical analysis and systematic reform went hand in hand. The Home Office, by contrast, dismissed the plans as impractical and the reliance on penalties and licensing fees as excessive. Abbot's Finance Committee opened up a new chance for Colquhoun to advocate for the scheme.

In addition to Colquhoun's ideas for the police, the *Twenty-Eighth Report* also advocated Jeremy Bentham's Panopticon-scheme to improve the penal system. The handling of convicts was a fiercely debated subject. Apart from short stays at correction houses or coercive detention in debtors' prisons, British judicial practice did not originally provide for prison sentences as a regular form of punishment.[68] The American Revolution had put a stop to the practice of transportation to the colonies. As a consequence, the existing prisons were overcrowded and generally in a shocking condition.[69]

64 Colquhoun, *Treatise on the Police*, p. 348.

65 Ibid., pp. 229–30.

66 Finance Committee, 'Twenty-eighth Report', p. 31.

67 Gash, 'Glaswegian Criminologist', pp. 139–41.

68 Michael Ignatieff, *A Just Measure of Pain. The Penitentiary in the Industrial Revolution, 1750–1850* (London, 1978), pp. 15–43.

69 For a case study see Joanna Innes, 'The King's Bench Prison in the Later Eighteenth Century. Law, Authority and Order in a London Debtors' Prison', in John Brewer and John A. Styles (eds.), *An Ungovernable People: The English and their Law in the Seventeenth and Eighteenth Centuries* (London, 1980), 250–98.

After 1776, the judiciary employed hulks – dismasted prison ships – as a cheap, though hardly more humane, alternative to jails.[70] The Penitentiary Houses Act of 1779 introduced convict labour as a viable form of punishment based on utilitarian deliberations.[71] Wrongdoers should be made useful to society. The act included the prospect that convict labour would refinance the costs of the running and, ideally, also the construction of penitentiaries in the long term. At first, however, no such penitentiary was forthcoming and, after 1787, the resumption of transportation sentences to the convict-colony of New South Wales in Australia considerably lessened the pressure to implement the act.[72] These developments took place against the backdrop of a complex public debate that touched on juridical, moral, medicinal, and hygienic, as well as societal and economic aspects.[73]

Jeremy Bentham's answer to the complex subject was the Panopticon. For a decade, Bentham worked hard to realise his vision of a penitentiary based on utilitarian principles. And for another decade, he fought for financial recompense for his considerable investment. Bentham had published his plan for the implementation of the Penitentiary Houses Act in general terms in 1791 and handed the ministry a formal proposal for its implementation soon after. Together with his brother Samuel, who contributed the engineering expertise, Bentham suggested building and running a visionary penitentiary as a government contractor. The famous design of the Panopticon was based on a round watch-tower, which the Bentham brothers had observed in Russia. A central tower allowed a small number of watchmen to monitor a maximum of convict-workers leading to a reduction of personnel costs. The convict-labour would effectively be farmed out to the Benthams. In terms of government-spending, Bentham promised to cut the costs per convict by at least 25% in comparison to the already cheap hulks. Henry Dundas, then Home Secretary, agreed to the plan in 1792 and Pitt equally gave his consent in 1793, though not in written form.[74]

70 Charles F. Campbell, *The Intolerable Hulks. British Shipboard Confinement, 1776–1857*, (Bowie, 1994).

71 19 Geo III, c. 74.

72 Alan G. L. Shaw, *Convicts and the Colonies. A Study of Penal Transportation from Great Britain and Ireland to Australia and other parts of the British Empire* (Carlton, 1977); Robert Hughes, *The Fatal Shore. A History of the Transportation of Convicts to Australia, 1787–1868* (London, 1987).

73 Cf. Ignatieff, *A Just Measure of Pain*, pp. 44–79. Though often criticised as essentially unfalsifiable, Foucault's derivation of the modern prison from Enlightenment ideas is still inspiring: Michel Foucault, *Discipline and Punish. The Birth of the Prison* (New York, 1977).

74 Janet Semple, *Bentham's Prison. A Study of the Panopticon Penitentiary* (Oxford, 1993), pp. 134–65.

As it turned out, the mandate from the ministry was only the start of a long and tedious affair, which, in the end, came to nothing. Bentham received an advance of £2,000 from the Treasury for his expenses, and a new bill passed in 1794 to substantiate the endeavour.[75] During the following years, Bentham negotiated for suitable premises near London, but was hindered by competing interests. By 1797, Bentham's efforts had reached a dead end and the ministry essentially hung the project out to dry. In this situation, the Finance Committee was a godsend to garner support for the scheme once more, especially as Bentham's personal connections to his stepbrother and further members of the Finance Committee promised a benevolent reception.[76]

The winter of 1797/8 was the ideal time to approach Abbot. The first phase of the Finance Committee's inquiry was completed, whilst preparations for the expected second phase had not yet begun. Though Jeremy Bentham's relationship to Charles Abbot was not nearly as close as Samuel's, the stepbrothers were on cordial terms. Abbot had provided assessments and occasional inside information for the project before.[77] It is not quite clear whether the idea of prompting the Finance Committee to include the Panopticon scheme originated with Bentham or with George Rose at the Treasury, who certainly supported this line of action.[78] Officially, the *Twenty-Eighth Report* presented a different narrative. According to the report, Colquhoun pointed the Finance Committee towards Bentham's plan when queried for ideas on the reduction of police expenses.[79] The Finance Committee then allegedly summoned Bentham for an interview that was included verbatim in the appendix of the report. Based on the interview, the Finance Committee claimed to have concluded that the plan was 'likely to be productive of the most essential Advantage, both in point of Oeconomy and Police'.[80] In fact, the report was drawn up in close cooperation between the committee member Reginald Pole-Carew (1753–1835) and

[75] Leonard J. Hume, 'Bentham's Panopticon. An Administrative History I', *Historical Studies: Australia and New Zealand*, 15 (1973), 703–21, p. 709.

[76] Ibid., pp. 714–17.

[77] Semple, *Bentham's Prison*, p. 199.

[78] Hume, 'Bentham's Panopticon', p. 716. Given the personal connections and the earlier correspondence between Abbot and Bentham, much still speaks for Leonard Hume's reading that Bentham used his personal ties to hijack the committee. Janet Semple has criticised the view in reference to statements in which Bentham voices scepticism as to that indirect approach. Cf. ibid., pp. 716–18; Semple, *Bentham's Prison*, pp. 203–4.

[79] Finance Committee, 'Twenty-eighth Report', p. 20.

[80] Ibid., p. 23.

Bentham and Colquhoun, with occasional input from Abbot.[81] The group also scripted the allegedly inquisitive interview together. Pole-Carew even prompted Bentham to formulate the questions in advance.[82]

As a consequence of the cooperation, the resulting argumentation is distinct from the other reports. Whilst the insistence on economy and transparency in accounting figured prominently in other inquiries, the very point of relying on private contractors and farming out convict labour was questionable in terms of administrative economy. Large-scale contracting had provoked critical examination before, as contracts had proven prone to abuse and were often wasteful. The *Twenty-Eighth Report* shows no signs of such doubts. Over long passages, the report makes societal and moral arguments related to debates on penal reform and utilitarian ideas rather than to administrative reform.[83]

It is interesting to note in this context that the report operates with two different concepts of 'reform'. On the one hand, 'salutary Reform' in the meaning of (institutional) improvement and, on the other hand, the older, moral sense of reform that was now restricted to concrete individuals or groups. Bentham's utilitarian plan aimed at 'employing and reforming Convicts'.[84]

Samuel Bentham and Navy Reform

The Finance Committee dedicated five reports to the civil departments of the Navy. The internal stalemate between the various boards and offices within the complicated power structure of the Navy had resulted in a less than enthusiastic implementation of the Fees Commissioners' recommendations. The Admiralty Board justified this state of affairs by a vague recourse to the ongoing war efforts. The Finance Committee was clearly dissatisfied, but it did not dispute this point. Rather, it endorsed the Fees Commissioners' older recommendations and requested comprehensive reform on the onset of peace.[85] Still, the Finance Reports had an impact

81 Semple, *Bentham's Prison*, pp. 212–17; Hume, 'Bentham's Panopticon', pp. 716–19.

82 Reginald Pole-Carew to Jeremy Bentham, 13 May 1798, in J. R. Dinwiddy (ed.), *The Correspondence of Jeremy Bentham*, vol. 6, *January 1798 to December 1801* (Oxford, 1984), p. 32.

83 Finance Committee, 'Twenty-eighth Report'; Leonard J. Hume, *Bentham and Bureaucracy* (Cambridge, 1981), pp. 165–209.

84 Finance Committee, 'Twenty-eighth Report', p. 32.

85 Finance Committee, 'Thirty-first Report', *SP 113*, 3–73, pp. 8–13; Finance Committee, 'Thirty-second Report', *SP 113*, 75–215, pp. 82–5.

on the administration of the Navy. This impact once more followed from personal connections. The Finance Committee granted support to Abbot's step-brother Samuel Bentham in an internal contention with the Navy Board about administrative reforms and technological innovations.

Samuel Bentham (1757–1831) had had a remarkable career. He had started his education with an apprenticeship as a shipwright at various dockyards. Simultaneously, he studied mathematics, while his older brother Jeremy tutored him on a wide variety of subjects. In 1779, Samuel went to Russia under the patronage of Grigory Aleksandrovich Potemkin (1739–91), favourite of Catherine the Great. For twelve years, Bentham worked there on ever greater naval, military, and industrial projects.[86] After his return to England and some years devoted to the Panopticon scheme and other projects, Bentham rejoined the Navy. On Middleton's intervention, Lord Spencer created the new office of the Inspector General of Naval Works to make use of Bentham's unique experience and ingenuity for engineering in March 1796.[87] The new office did not sit well in the Navy's civil administration. Bentham's office was attached to the Admiralty Board, while the technical facilities, which were the object of his work, fell under the authority of the Navy Board. Bentham soon bombarded the Navy Comptroller Andrew Hamond (1738–1828) with technical proposals and criticised deficiencies in a less than diplomatic manner. Annoyed at the encroachment into his work and the implied interference by the Admiralty Board, Hamond blanked Bentham.[88] To Bentham, the inquiry of the Finance Committee created an opportunity to try and force Hamond's hand.

The Finance Committee concerned itself with the creation of the new office in their *Seventeenth Report,* which addressed the Admiralty and Navy Boards. Given the general emphasis on entrenchment, the creation of new offices was a critical point of inquiry. However, in the case of Samuel Bentham's office, the Finance Committee offered nothing but encouragement, even though it confessed that it did not fully understand the scope of the office's duties. It seems clear that Abbot went out of his way to support Samuel Bentham's position at the Navy. In support of

86 Ian R. Christie, *The Benthams in Russia, 1780–1791* (Oxford, 1993); id., 'Samuel Bentham and the Russian Dnieper Flotilla 1787–1788', *The Slavonic and East European Review,* 50:119 (1972), 173–97; Catherine Pease-Watkin, 'Bentham, Samuel (1757–1831)', *ODNB.*

87 Appendix G5, Order of His Majesty in Council respecting the new Establishment of the Admiralty, 23 March 1796, in Finance Committee, 'Seventeenth Report', pp. 186–8.

88 Roger Morriss, *The Royal Dockyards during the Revolutionary and Napoleonic Wars* (Leicester, 1983), pp. 189–90.

this recommendation, Abbot provided a platitude about Britain being a maritime country at war and a reference to the scientific nature of the office and the expected technological progress, based solely on the original appointment given in the report's appendix.[89]

The cooperation between Abbot and Bentham intensified in the course of the *Thirty-First Report* which concerned the dockyards. The report reproduced extracts of a letter, in which Bentham expressed frustration about the Navy Board and hope for reasonable internal discussions of his suggestions.[90] Stating the purpose of his office, he detailed technological improvements and the design of 'certain Vessels for the Purpose of exemplifying various Ideas of Improvement'.[91] Bentham thus emphasised the technological improvements introduced by his office. Abbot used an interview to present Bentham rather as a general agent of reform in the employ of the Admiralty:

> [Q:] Is it your official Duty to propose any Measures of Improvement which may tend to Oeconomy in the Naval Service?
> [A:] I look upon it as my Duty to consider of all Matters of Improvement respecting His Majesty's Naval Establishments, according to the Tenor of my Instructions [...].[92]

The Finance Committee prompted Bentham to give his opinion on a number of issues, most notably on the organisation of the dockyards. Bentham proposed to put the respective dockyards 'to the immediate Discretion of a single Person, under the Guidance of such Regulations as the Admiralty may from Time to Time think proper to prescribe. [...] By such an Arrangement Dispatch as well as good Oeconomy would be very

89 Finance Committee, 'Seventeenth Report', p. 151; Appendix G5, Order of His Majesty in Council respecting the new Establishment of the Admiralty, 23 March 1796, in ibid., pp. 186–8.

90 Appendix D.5.a: Extract of Letter from the Inspector General of Naval Works, 5 April 1798, Finance Committee, 'Thirty-first Report', pp. 33–4. Also see Bentham's unabridged letter and the annexed table of 'Naval Works Proposed'. For each measure Bentham specified the 'Nature of the Work', its 'Original Utility', 'Estimated Expense', and 'Comparative Economy'. Samuel Bentham to Charles Abbot, 5 April 1798, in TNA, ADM 1/3525, n. pag.

91 Appendix D.5.a: Extract of Letter from the Inspector General of Naval Works, 5 April 1798, in Finance Committee, 'Thirty-first Report', pp. 33–4.

92 Appendix D.5.b: Extract of the Examination of Samuel Bentham, Esquire, Inspector General of Naval Works, 8 May 1798, ibid., pp. 35–8, quote on p. 35.

essentially promoted [...].'[93] The proposal came close to suspending the (unmentioned) Navy Board's authority for its largest branch. The Finance Committee unreservedly endorsed the implementation of Bentham's proposals.[94]

The collaboration with the Finance Committee provoked a severe rebuke from Lord Spencer. Spencer was annoyed because Bentham had circumvented him and carried Navy internals to the public.[95] However, Spencer could be appeased and he put Bentham in charge of finally drawing up a concept in response to both the Fees Commissioners' and the Finance Committee's reports. For the dockyard, Bentham indeed became the agent of administrative reform that the report had made him out to be.[96]

During the following two years, Bentham pursued both technological and administrative improvements for the dockyards. On the technological side, he oversaw the introduction of the first steam-powered sawmill and other industrial innovations.[97] On the administrative side, he developed a new system of administration for the dockyards based on Middleton's *Observations* and the various reports on Navy issues. In the process, Bentham repeatedly consulted Charles Abbot.[98] Early in 1800, Bentham circulated a preliminary concept for internal commenting. Hamond rejected the proposal and sent detailed objections to Lord Spencer, who passed the objections on to Bentham. In reaction, Bentham made an unprecedented move. He collated the objections and his own counterstatements and

93 Appendix D.5.b: Extract of the Examination of Samuel Bentham, Esquire, Inspector General of Naval Works, 8 May 1798, ibid., p. 33.

94 Ibid., p. 13.

95 Maria S. Bentham, *The Life of Brigadier-General Sir Samuel Bentham, K.S.G. Formerly Inspector-General of Naval Works Lately a Commissioner of his Majesty's Navy with the distinct Duty of Civil Architect and Engineer of the Navy* (London, 1862), p. 139.

96 John R. Breihan, 'The Addington Party and the Navy in British Politics 1801–1806', in Craig L. Symonds (ed.), *New Aspects of Naval History* (Annapolis, 1981), 163–89, p. 166.

97 Jonathan Coad's (non-academic) book on the industrial innovations at the Portsmouth dockyard gives an impressive account and indeed image of Bentham's pioneering technological accomplishments. Jonathan Coad, *The Portsmouth Block Mills. Bentham, Brunel and the Start of the Royal Navy's Industrial Revolution* (Swindon, 2005).

98 According to Bentham, Middleton had supplied him with a copy of his *Observations* he had revised after entering the Board of Admiralty. Samuel Bentham, *Answers to the Comptroller's Objections* (1800), p. 10. See Abbot's letters to Samuel Bentham of 12 September and 16 December 1799 as well as 20 May and 9 June 1800, BL, Add. Mss. 33542, fols 111, 160, 325, 334.

published them as *Answers to the Comptroller's Objections*. Over 127 pages, he detailed the internal discussions of the Navy to the public.[99]

The *Answers* formed a comprehensive reform concept for the administration of the dockyards that built on previous approaches. Due to the inclusion of Hamond's opposing view, the work also reflects the state of internal discussion within the Navy.[100] Both Hamond and Bentham attributed authority to Middleton's *Observations* as well as to the reports of the Fees Commission and the Finance Committee. Hamond declared that all reports had been 'perfectly satisfied with the general system by which the various operations are conducted' and insisted 'that nothing more was necessary than to correct the abuses pointed out.'[101] Hamond did not base his argument on customary practice, nor did he invoke the ancient constitution, but he treated deficiencies as discrete cases and equally addressed Bentham's points as singular measures.

Bentham countered by quoting the Fees Commissioners to the effect that 'we do not hesitate to declare our opinion that a new system is indispensably necessary' and justified his concept by claiming that his general principles were in tune with the reports.[102] A passage on the classification of officers demonstrates that Bentham's claim to be applying similar principles was plausible:

> As to the reason for classing the Master Workmen, the advantages of classification in any system seem obvious: and in the planning a system of management, I look upon the classing together all persons with respect to whom the same mode of treatment may be adopted, as a means of giving a degree of simplicity to the plan, and of uniformity to the management, such as could not fail of facilitating in various ways the dispatch of business.[103]

This dense application of the system-concept showed the characteristic features which CEPA had initially adapted from political economy. In the passage, Bentham presented simplicity and uniformity as desirable qualities of a system and prepared reforms that followed clearly articulated general principles. His new system chiefly aimed at the improvement of the operative business at the dockyards. While Bentham wrote at great length

99 Ibid.
100 For a Navy-centred appraisal of the concept see Morriss, *Naval Power*, pp. 151–60.
101 Bentham, *Answers*, pp. 2–4.
102 Ibid., pp. 4–7, quote on p. 4. Cf. Fees Commissioners, 'Ninth Report', p. 247.
103 Bentham, *Answers*, p. 65.

about waste and the cutting of costs, retrenchment was hardly the system's central point.[104]

The pivotal point of Bentham's system was the principle of individual responsibility. He quoted his own deliberations from the Finance Committee reports and insisted that even the Fees Commissioners had employed the term when arguing for a stronger position of the resident commissioners of the dockyards.[105] To Bentham, the dispersion of responsibility through collegial boards constituted 'the radical unsoundness of the whole system.'[106] Hamond praised the horizontal, mutual control exerted among offices and collegial boards in the old system:

> I have always considered the duties allotted to the several principal officers of a Dock Yard perfectly well adapted to the carrying on the service with regularity and dispatch (the Commissioners excepted), and that the check which the several departments have upon each other, are wisely ordered to correct abuses, and do not in any degree stand in the way of expediting the public service.[107]

Hamond defended the status quo by bringing forward a feasible argument framed in the functional logic of administration. The long establishment of offices and customary practice by itself no longer yielded strong arguments.

Against Hamond's point, Bentham stated that he was sceptical about the diffusion of responsibility. Bentham therefore presented individual responsibility as the central principle that he duplicated throughout the system, down to the clerks and storekeepers.[108] Middleton had criticised collegial boards by taking recourse to the principle of central authority. Focusing on responsibility instead of authority changed the picture. Bentham's system did not derive its strength from the central directing will, but from the individual efforts of the officers on all levels. The effects, Bentham argued, would far exceed the effects of any specific regulations. The officers would be motivated to acquire the necessary knowledge to act circumspectly and proceed in actively combatting abuses in their field of responsibility.[109] He emphasised differentiation over centralisation. For instance, he argued

[104] Ibid., pp. 90–102.

[105] Ibid., pp. 5–8; cf. Fees Commissioners, 'Sixth Report', p. 140. While the Fees Commissioners envisaged a strong position for the resident commissioner, they did not discuss responsibility as a principle.

[106] Bentham, *Answers*, p. 13.

[107] Ibid., p. 3.

[108] Ibid., pp. 120–5.

[109] Ibid., pp. 16, 87.

for the separation of operative duties and accounting under the operative principal's responsibility. As a consequence of the differentiation of duties, Bentham pointed to the significance of individual qualification together with responsibility. Officers should be

> placed under the direction of a superior, entrusted with authority to portion out that duty to each according to their particular personal qualifications [instead] as at present, charged two or three of them with a joint duty without subordination one to the other, and without any particular instructions for regulating the division of so multifarious a duty.[110]

In Bentham's view, the old system not only lacked stimulus for learning but also failed to effectively allocate the available qualifications.

Bentham also addressed the qualifications of artisans and especially of shipwrights, who enjoyed many privileges due to their unique expertise. Bentham's concept aimed to radically dismantle the customary master–apprentice relationship that regulated the shipwrights' training and provided the masters with direct power over their apprentices.[111] A naval seminary would introduce 'a system of education for those employed in the Navy as well as in the Dock Yards.' The resulting savings would 'more than compensate for the expense of this establishment.'[112] The system was equally designed to discipline the notoriously unruly shipwrights: 'I should conceive that the prospect of so great a number coming on to be capable of supplying their place, would not fail of rendering them likewise much more orderly and tractable.'[113] There was no place for customary artisan networks in Bentham's vision of a reformed and industrialised dockyard.

Bentham's strategy of publishing his programme worked out and he received the green light to prepare a formal concept, which Spencer submitted to the Privy Council on 31 January 1801. Nine years after the Privy Council's request for observations on the fees reports, this last answer was submitted. It was also the most detailed answer, as it reformulated Bentham's deliberations as answers to the Fees Commissioners' recommendations in no less than seventy points.[114] Only weeks after endorsing the concept,

110 Ibid., p. 17. For a more detailed view on Bentham's ideas on financial control, cf. Morriss, *Naval Power*, pp. 155–6.

111 For particulars of the system, cf. Knight, 'Dockyard Appointments', pp. 178–85.

112 Bentham, *Answers*, p. 111.

113 Ibid., p. 113.

114 Lords of the Admiralty to Special Committee, 31 January 1801, inserted into the Privy Council minutes of 11 May 1801, in TNA, PC 2/158, pp. 33–81.

Pitt resigned over the question of Catholic emancipation in Ireland and Spencer left office with him. The new First Lord of the Addington ministry, John Jervis, Earl of St. Vincent (1735–1823) was famous for his many naval victories and almost equally infamous as an unforgiving principal, who frequently enforced naval discipline by resorting to death sentences. After the Peace of Amiens in 1802, St. Vincent embarked on an equally ruthless reduction of Navy personnel and vowed to root out corruption. St. Vincent's uncompromising character and Samuel Bentham's rationalistic urge for reform came to harmonise well.[115]

Induced by the rising rates of contractors, St. Vincent confronted the Navy Board full-on. He initiated a commission of naval inquiry to bypass the Navy Board and pursue wrongdoers.[116] St. Vincent was generally suspicious of the civil branch and more interested in dominating and 'cleansing' the departments than in a systematic reform. Shortly after Bentham's plans were sanctioned, dockyard artificers went on strike at Plymouth (from 31 March 1801) and Sheerness (from 12 April) for higher wages. The protesters remained peaceful and could not be tried for treason even under the severe anti-Jacobin and anti-union statutes. To St. Vincent, the protests still constituted an insurrection, which he answered with mass dismissals. Afterwards, he fully supported Bentham's efforts to radically reorganise the dockyards.[117]

Bentham's reforms hit the artificers hard. In the *Answers to the Comptrollers Objections,* Bentham had advocated differentiation and individual responsibility to optimise the utility of the officers. His compartmentalising reorganisation of the work process aimed at optimising the utility of the new machines. In Bentham's approach, technological innovation and administrative reform were but two sides of the same coin. When he proclaimed to be introducing 'a general system of machinery'[118] to the dockyards, he referred to both. Bentham was reforming Britain's largest industrial complex and has to be counted among the pioneers of industrialisation with all its technical, organisational, and social implications. He was in communication with industrial pioneers of the private sector like the textile mass producers

[115] P. K. Crimmin, 'John Jervis, Earl of St Vincent, 1735–1823', in Richard Harding and Peter Le Fevre (eds.), *Precursors of Nelson: British Admirals of the Eighteenth Century* (London, 2000), 325–50; William J. Ashworth, '"System of Terror". Samuel Bentham, Accountability and Dockyard Reform during the Napoleonic Wars', *Social History,* 23:1 (1998), 63–79, pp. 63–5.

[116] Breihan, 'Addington Party', p. 168.

[117] Morriss, *Royal Dockyards,* pp. 121–6; Breihan, 'Addington Party', p. 167.

[118] Samuel Bentham, *Services rendered in the Civil Department of the Navy* (London, 1813), p. 164.

of Strutts and Arkwright and the Wedgwood porcelain magnates.[119] In his *Answers,* Bentham had emphasised individual responsibility over detailed regulations. In applying principles of industrial labour organisation to devise 'forms of accounts, calculated to exhibit the quantity of work really done, and the wages due accordingly', he introduced an excessive system of regulations and minuscule written accounting.[120]

Bentham's measures eliminated the customary work routine and social way of life of most artificers. The first steam-powered sawmill at Portsmouth started working in 1802. Immediately after, the vast majority of carpenters and sawyers were laid off. The reforms gave rise to frequent strikes and riots at the dockyards, which St. Vincent indiscriminately answered by dismissing all indicted and further suspicious artificers.[121] When an anonymous informer wrote to Henry Dundas in 1804 that 'a system of terror has prevailed in the dockyards', he reiterated an exasperated expression that had become common at the dockyards.[122]

Due to political developments, the hot phase of St. Vincent's and Bentham's reforms ended soon after. In May 1803, Britain again entered the, now, Napoleonic Wars. Pitt and his old guard of followers stormed the closet. The Pittites argued that the permanent conflicts with contractors and the continual unrest, along with the 'system of terror', significantly weakened the Navy and, thereby, Britain's readiness for war. When Pitt succeeded Addington in May 1804, Dundas took over as First Lord from St. Vincent and returned to the administrative approach of Middleton, who acted as his advisor and, later, successor. Dundas and Middleton instituted yet another statutory commission, which countermanded a number of St. Vincent's and Bentham's measures and strengthened the Navy Board again. However, the trend towards the industrialisation of the dockyards persisted.[123]

Samuel Bentham did not fit well into the new constellation. In the summer of 1805, he was sent to Russia to superintend the building of warships for the British Navy at Archangel. When he returned two years later,

119 R. S. Fitton and A. P. Wadsworth, *The Strutts and the Arkwrights 1758–1830. A Study of the Early Factory System* (Manchester, 1958), pp. 181–2; Ashworth, 'System of Terror', pp. 65–6, 70–1; Neil McKendrick, 'Josiah Wedgwood and Cost Accounting in the Industrial Revolution', *Economic History Review,* 23:1 (1970), 45–67.

120 Bentham, *Services rendered,* p. 5; Ashworth, 'System of Terror', pp. 73–9.

121 Morriss, *Royal Dockyards,* pp. 49–53; Carolyn C. Cooper, 'The Portsmouth System of Manufacture', *Technology and Culture,* 25:2 (194), 182–225; Breihan, 'Addington Party', p. 169.

122 Quoted in Ashworth, 'System of Terror', p. 65; for the ubiquity of the phrase see Breihan, 'Addington Party', p. 169.

123 Ibid., pp. 171–82; Morriss, *Naval Power,* pp. 171–4; id., *Royal Dockyards,* pp. 39–61.

he could only take seat as a subordinate commissioner at the Navy Board. His former independent office had been abolished. No longer in a position of power, Bentham turned to writing again, defending his measures in a comprehensive *Statement of Services Rendered* in 1813 and in a number of *Naval Essays* in the late 1820s.[124] By then, these texts were part of a larger debate on administrative issues in print: a new development for which Bentham had played a pioneering role.

Administrative Discourses

The reports of the Finance Committee temporarily returned administrative reform to the centre of the political debate. They triggered an intense, albeit short, phase of reform activity. They also provoked considerable resistance and opposition from vested interests. Abbot noted that 'Many people in & out of the House shewed … much ill will in consequence of our inquiries.'[125] However, the general political sentiment, especially in Parliament, welcomed the reports. The ministry and its direct followers were divided on the issue. Several politicians feared the consequences of public discussion of ongoing defects and abuses.[126] Pitt's confidant and later successor Henry Addington (1757–1844), who had worked with Abbot on legislative reforms before, took a more positive position and insisted that 'upon the whole Government has derived no inconsiderable degree of Credit' from the Finance Committee. Still, Addington intervened with Abbot in order to not include the politically dangerous Civil List in his projected subjects for inquiry.[127] Other Pittites generally agreed with the independent desire for retrenchment.

Pitt reacted to the reports and the sentiment in Parliament by making concessions. George Rose set a flurry of reform measures into motion in the following two years.[128] Some reforms concerned accounting procedures,

[124] Bentham, *Services rendered*; id., *Naval Essays, Or Essays on the Management of Public Concerns as Exemplified in the Naval Department; Considered as a Branch of the Business of Warfare* (London, 1828); id., *Naval Papers. And Documents Referred to in Naval Essays* (London, 1828); id., *Financial Reform Scrutinized* (London, 1830).

[125] Quoted in Breihan, 'Economical Reform', p. 171.

[126] Grey Cooper to Addington, 25 October, 1797, quoted in ibid., p. 173; John Hatsell to Addington, 4 October, 1797, quoted in Breihan, 'Economical Reform', p. 173.

[127] Henry Addington to Charles Abbot, 4 October, 1797, quoted in Breihan, 'Economical Reform', p. 174; ibid., pp. 181–2.

[128] Cf. e.g. William Pitt to George Rose, 26 January 1798 in Leveson Vernon Harcourt (ed.), *The Diaries and Correspondence of the Right Hon. George Rose*, vol. 1 (London, 1860), p. 211.

such as the introduction of Irving's format for Treasury finance reports in 1798. The Treasury, in turn, regulated the accounting procedures of the various revenue departments. The outdated calculations of Army and Navy estimates were finally put on a new footing. The ministry abolished some irregular emoluments, for instance the New Year's gifts at the Treasury itself. It also suppressed various sinecures and duly paid compensations. In an uncharacteristically strong move, the ministry reformed the establishment of the War Office against the resistance of its principal, Secretary at War William Windham (1750–1810), by order of council to do away with its fee-based emoluments. Nothing came of the Panopticon-scheme and Colquhoun's plan of a joint police board was discarded. However, the Hackney Coaches and Hawkers' and Peddlers' Offices were integrated into the Tax Office and the Salt Office into the Excise. Finally, Rose prepared seven bills to reform a number of aspects that needed legislative sanction.[129] Government made sure that the efforts did not go unnoticed. The Treasury Board's proceedings on the Finance reports, including many of Rose's letters, were printed and published within the parliamentary materials.[130]

As it turned out, fears the opposition might profit from a public discussion of administrative defects were unfounded. Fox argued that there was little point in economical reform without parliamentary reform. Together with his followers, he seceded from Parliament while looking for extra-parliamentary agitation, but his correspondence with Christopher Wyvill about a revival of the Association Movement came to nothing. The small rump of outspoken opposition Whigs remaining in Parliament called for retrenchment and raised the old spectre of ministerial extravagance without effecting major divisions.[131]

In reaction to independent ideas of sinecure-taxation and George Tierney's (1761–1830) rather radical idea of a tax on the Privy Purse, Pitt took up Addington's idea of a voluntary patriotic contribution to the war efforts. Moral pressure, especially on holders of prominent sinecures, ensured a high return. Pitt himself gave excessively, others, like Abbot or Addington, considerably. The King himself was finally coerced into contributing a third of his Privy Purse.[132] Pitt's own approach to the abiding theme of war finance was the first progressive income tax that, though controversial,

129 Breihan, 'Economical Reform,' pp. 177–8.

130 Sheila Lambert (ed.), *House of Commons Sessional Papers of the Eighteenth Century*, vol. 114, *Proceedings on the Finance Committee Reports 1798–1803* (Wilmington, 1975).

131 Leslie G. Mitchell, *Charles James Fox* (Oxford, 1992), pp. 136–57.

132 Ehrman, *Consuming Struggle*, pp. 107–9; Philip Ziegler, *Addington. A Life of Henry Addington, First Viscount Sidmouth* (London, 1965), pp. 79–81.

passed with surprising ease in December 1798. Between the strained war efforts, the income tax, and preparations for the Irish Union, Pitt worked to exhaustion. All tactical manoeuvres aside, administrative reform was hardly among Pitt's priorities.[133]

Whilst some of the administrative reforms begun in 1798 were carried out in 1799, the general impulse died down. Abbot continued to nag the Treasury and the ministry to continue the process. When Abbot finally entered a bill forcing delinquent accountants to pay interest, the ministry did not hinder its passing, but did not provide outspoken support either. By 1800, Treasury and ministry activity in the field of administrative reform had died down completely and parliamentary attention on the topic equally subsided. If it was indeed Pitt's strategy to ride out the discussions by making relatively minor concessions, as John Breihan claims, it worked out admirably well.[134]

In the 1790s, the political discourse continued to be determined by changing interests, political alliances, and short-term issues. When administrative issues were at centre stage, it was against the backdrop of the perceived threat of state bankruptcy and the persistent discourse on corruption. In the meantime, a separate administrative reform discourse was increasingly expanding its reach outside of the political arena. This discourse was determined by the scientific and economical approach that CEPA had pioneered. As early as 1794, for instance, a London printer published *The Former and Present State of the Principal Public Offices in this Kingdom*. The book compiled administrative information from the reports of the Accounts and Fees Commissioners as well as from additional public sources, mostly in the form of tables detailing the departments' offices, salaries, and fees.

In the short introduction, the unnamed editor praised the Accounts and Fees Commissions for making extensive administrative knowledge available to the public. The editor compared the two commissions by the – complementary – scales of their findings: 'The Reports of the Commissioners of Accounts diclos[ed] the whole system of the National Finances and the interior of many of the principal Offices of Government' and 'the important and dignified discussion of the Public Accounts of a great Empire at a period of the greatest National Expenditure ever known.' Regarding the Fees Commission, the editor pointed towards the 'details which it gives of the transactions of Office, the Duties and Attendence of Officers, the

133 Ehrman, *Consuming Struggle*, pp. 79–83, 260–5; A. Farnsworth, *Addington. Author of the Modern Income Tax* (London, 1951), pp. 12–18.

134 Breihan, 'Economical Reform,' pp. 186–8; cf. Duffy, *Younger Pitt*, pp. 92–5.

Compensation they receive from Governments and Individuals under various heads [...].'[135] The editor accentuated a central reform creed that CEPA had established against the prevailing discourse on corruption:

> Enquiries of this kind are not to be considered as mere Inquests into Abuses [...]: Regulation in future, not crimination for the past, is the object to be pursued. The conduct of the Officer may have been faultless, and yet the Office may admit of improvement.[136]

Distinguishing between office and office-holder apparently came easy to the editor, yet it was still a point worth making. These points served to prepare a fundamental argument on the critical importance of empirical information for any reform:

> It is important to know the real state of things, whether it be good or bad, whether the abuses be many or few, or none at all. Without such a knowledge, dark surmises fill the place of truth, and improvement is at a stand, even in those cases where it is most practicable; nor have we any answer to give to clamours of Reform, in those cases where alteration could be conductive to no good purpose.[137]

In order to substantiate this last point, the editor quoted the trenchant passage of CEPA's *Sixth Report*, according to which ancient offices, in particular, were 'entitled to the utmost respects, and that alterations in them should be well weighed.' Just like CEPA had, the editor paid lip service to tradition only to land a stinging blow to patrimonial argumentations. Not all reforms that were demanded made sense. But even a decision against a particular reform proposal needed corroboration by 'unquestionable evidence'[138] – reference to custom or the property theory of office no longer sufficed.

The Finance Committee partook in this administrative discourse, developed the reform approach further, and forcefully brought it to bear in Parliament. In doing so, the Finance Committee consolidated a normative ideal of economical reform based on their own reports as well as the reports of the Accounts and Fees Commissions. The recommendations contained in these reports were not necessarily then implemented. However, by 1800,

135 Ibid., pp. iii–iv.
136 Ibid., p. vii.
137 Ibid.
138 Ibid.

the inquiries and reform recommendations of the Accounts and Fees Commissions had clearly turned into authoritative texts which could not be ignored but which were open to interpretation.

7

Ireland: Struggling with Reform

This chapter is concerned with the attempted administrative reforms in Ireland in the wake of the parliamentary union of 1801. By means of the union, Westminster hoped to gain control of the critical situation in Ireland. The Irish Rebellion of 1798 and simultaneous French invasion attempts showed that Britain was vulnerable through its western flank. Moreover, a revolt spreading throughout the Irish troops would pose an existential threat to the entire Empire. The Acts of Union settled the integration of the Irish Peers and Commons into the Parliament of the United Kingdom in London. The acts did not settle the integration of the executive, i.e. of government and administration. In the aftermath of the union, the divergent administrative discourses of Britain and Ireland clashed.

The administrative history of the union is connected to the history of economical reform in Britain through its protagonists. In 1798, Charles Cornwallis went to Ireland as Lord Lieutenant to end the Irish Rebellion and to secure approval for the union in the Irish Parliament. Acting against his economical convictions, Cornwallis pulled all the patrimonial stops and bartered away offices on a grand scale among the Irish Ascendency, the Protestant elite that was the cornerstone of the British dominion over Ireland. The following year, Charles Abbot became Chief Secretary and received a mandate to implement the union by means of sweeping administrative reforms based on the principles of the Finance Committee. In spite of Abbot's position of power and his unrivalled administrative expertise, Abbot's reforms failed miserably against the resistance of the Irish elite. Abbot's methodical application of economical reform principles on a British model triggered incomprehension and resistance in Ireland that went beyond the mere vindication of privileges. The Irish elite pulled strings in London to fight back against the encroaching reformer and the entrenched resistance in Ireland directly impacted political disputes within the British Cabinet on the future government of Ireland. In the end, Westminster left the quasi-colonial government in place, but abruptly put an end to Abbot's economical reforms in 1802.

The Irish reforms constitute a unique case because they demonstrate the application of economical reform ideas for an attempted administrative integration on a national level. Due to geographical proximity and personal connections between the elites, the political discourses in Ireland and Great Britain were closely intertwined. However, the respective administrative discourses differed profoundly. In Ireland, an unperturbed patrimonial understanding of office prevailed. The prevalence of patrimonial notions made perfect sense because the patrimonial functions of the offices had been a crucial pillar for the political order in Ireland. The offices underpinned the dominance of the small Protestant elite over the Catholic majority, who remained excluded from offices and parliamentary seats due to their denomination. At the same time, patronage of the offices served to integrate this elite and ensure its loyalty to Westminster. The analysis of the Irish case shows the impact of tried and tested economical reform ideas in an administrative setting that was similar to Britain but had remained altogether unreformed.

Charles Cornwallis and the Price of the Union

Throughout the eighteenth century, the British government struggled to develop a clear political strategy for Ireland. The Irish situation was complicated. The relationship between the two kingdoms had never been fully clarified. While the Irish understood themselves as a sister kingdom to Great Britain, most British understood Ireland as a sort of colony. Under Poynings' Law of 1495, as well as the Declaratory Act of 1720, the British government and Parliament claimed almost unrestricted supremacy over Irish affairs. British dominion in Ireland relied on the Protestant elite, the Irish Ascendency, while the Catholic majority was barred from political and, at least in part, from economic and social participation. Officially, Catholics were also excluded from the military, even though, in practice, the number of Catholics in military service had steadily grown since the Seven Years' War. The Irish Parliament resembled early modern estates assemblies. It convened every two years to release additional funds, but could only claim subordinated legislation and no formal influence on the Irish executive at all. In 1782, the American Revolutionary War opened up an opportunity for the Irish Ascendency to strengthen Irish autonomy. The Irish Parliament gained (restricted) legislative powers in 1782, but it still lacked any direct influence on Dublin Castle, the government appointed by Westminster. In the new constitutional setup, the Lord Lieutenant resided permanently in Dublin, ran the government as a viceroy, and was responsible only to the

British Cabinet. The Constitution of 1782 also resulted in the elevation of the second executive position, the Chief Secretary, whose main task now was to manage the Irish parliamentary interest. The Catholic Relief Act of 1782 complemented the constitutional settlement.[1]

Against the backdrop of the Wars of Coalition, Westminster regarded the Irish situation as a risk to national security. Among the Catholic majority, revolutionary ideas fell on fertile ground. The Catholics shared their religion with France and they were not even virtually represented in the Irish Parliament. With the founding of the United Irishmen in 1791, a radical society came into existence which, to the chagrin of Westminster, transcended confessional boundaries and quickly spread among both the Protestant middle class and the Catholic majority. The grant of census-based active voting rights for Catholics in 1793 did little to quell the movement. Irishmen formed a huge contingent in the British imperial forces and the spectre of an insurrection within the troops in the midst of the struggle against France loomed large.[2] As the war went on, the threat of a French invasion added to the dangerous mix. Such fears proved well founded. Theobald Wolfe Tone (1763–98), the exiled head of the United Irishmen, travelled to France to invite a French intervention. In December 1796, France dispatched a considerable invasion force of 14,000 that was only prevented from landing by prolonged bad weather.[3]

To Pitt and his innermost circle, political union with Ireland combined with eventual Catholic emancipation appeared as the only feasible way to permanently contain the risk that Ireland represented. The plan was indebted to contemporary ideas, not least political economy. The proponents of union argued that a cessation of the constant quarrels manifesting in the Irish Parliament, local disputes, and religious strife would subside and commerce would increase prosperity; in consequence, the situation in Ireland would gradually pacify.[4] However, the Irish Parliament could hardly be expected to agree to its own dissolution, nor to agree to any further

1 Thomas Bartlett, *Ireland. A History* (Cambridge, 2010), pp. 143–90.

2 Thomas Bartlett, 'Ireland during the Revolutionary and Napoleonic Wars, 1791–1815', in James Kelly (ed.), *The Cambridge History of Ireland* (Cambridge, 2018), 74–101, pp. 74–8.

3 Robert B. McDowell, 'The Age of the United Irishmen. Revolution and the Union, 1794–1800', in T. W. Moody and W. E. Vaughan (eds.), *A New History of Ireland*, vol. 4, *Eighteenth-Century Ireland* (Oxford, 1986), 339–73, pp. 349–51.

4 Peter Jupp, 'Britain and the Union, 1797–1801', *Transactions of the Royal Historical Society*, Sixth Series, 10 (2000), 197–219, pp. 198–204; Stafford, *Case of Ireland*, pp. 139–72.

Catholic emancipation. Throughout 1797, the United Irishmen assembled a revolutionary army in secret, while a new invasion force gathered on the continent. Partly promoted by the United Irishmen and partly in reaction to martial laws imposed by the government, the Irish Rebellion commenced in May 1798. For some time, politicians in Britain and Ireland had privately discussed the option of a union. With the onset of the Irish Rebellion, the ministry decided to actively pursue this goal.[5]

Once again, William Pitt called on Charles Cornwallis to solve problems of empire. In Dublin, Lord Lieutenant John Pratt, Viscount Camden (1759–1840), was out of his depth. Cornwallis, who had declined the Lord Lieutenancy before, now accepted and went to Ireland in June 1798 as he had gone to Bengal in 1786: endowed with the double authority of political leadership and military high command. His assignment was similarly twofold. Pitt firstly charged Cornwallis with ending the rebellion and pacifying the island. Cornwallis' second order was to prepare the political union by securing a sufficient majority in the Irish Parliament at all costs. At his side was Robert Stewart, Viscount Castlereagh (1769–1822), who was confirmed as Chief Secretary.[6]

The main force of the rebellion had been broken in the battle of Vinegar Hill, on 20 June 1798, the day before Cornwallis arrived in Ireland. However, this victory alone would not suffice in attaining peace. During his first months in office, Cornwallis led the campaign against the remaining centres of resistance and persecuted rebel leaders. A small French expeditionary force of 1,100 soldiers landed in August, but was easily defeated because it failed to ignite another general rising, whilst the Navy intercepted French reinforcements at sea. In hope of pacification, Cornwallis followed a strategy of relative leniency. In consultation with Portland as Home Secretary, Cornwallis promised a general pardon for all but the leading rebels if they would renew their allegiance. Furthermore, he accepted the petition of seventy-eight ringleaders, who offered full confessions in return for the moderate sentence of banishment. Still, the trials resulted in 131 death sentences and at least three times that many banishments.[7]

Cornwallis needed to assert all of his personal authority at home in order to secure political backing for the policy of lenity, even though this

5 Ibid., pp. 199–200; Bartlett, *Ireland*, pp. 227–9.

6 Richard Middleton, *Cornwallis. Soldier and Statesman in a Revolutionary World* (New Haven, 2022), pp. 273–8.

7 Franklin B. Wickwire and Mary Wickwire, *Cornwallis. The Imperial Years* (Chapel Hill, 1980), pp. 224–30; Robert B. McDowell, *Ireland in the Age of Imperialism and Revolution 1760–1801* (Oxford, 1979), pp. 360–2.

course of action was in line with Pitt's policy. Cornwallis' loudest critics were, however, hardliners in Dublin, who accused Cornwallis of incompetence and weakness. Cornwallis' conciliatory advances towards the Catholic interest, hinting at eventual Catholic emancipation, especially enraged the Irish Protestant elite. Only the unabated support from London secured Cornwallis' political position in Ireland. The British leadership at Dublin Castle had often had the experience that, quasi-colonial authority notwithstanding, it was difficult to govern against the Protestant Ascendency, which held the key positions in society, monopolised most public offices, and maintained excellent connections with London.[8]

The Irish parliamentary majority for the union was equally controversial. Both among the public and the Protestant Ascendency, opinions were divided. After an initial phase of guarded reserve, Cornwallis and Castlereagh finally managed to gather prominent Irish figures to the pro-union camp, whose support in the battle of opinion was indispensable. Among this 'Dublin castle junto' was the Castle Under-Secretary Edward Cooke (c.1755–1820) as well as John Beresford (1738–1805), the Chief Commissioner of the Irish revenue. The central figure of the junto was Lord Chancellor John Fitzgibbon, Earl of Clare (1749–1802), who dominated the Irish House of Lords and fully supported plans for union, even though he was extremely averse to Catholic emancipation.[9] In September, union plans were leaked before preparations were finished. This mishap meant a loss of political initiative. The necessary coordination with Westminster prevented Cornwallis and Castlereagh from reacting promptly to the widespread anxieties caused by the information. Anti-unionists, especially in the judiciary, used their head start for a campaign in newspapers and pamphlets. Cornwallis and Castlereagh may have underestimated the onslaught. With a small majority, anti-unionists even passed a vote on 23 January 1799 that removed a pro-union passage from a parliamentary address to the Lord Lieutenant.[10]

After the January defeat, Cornwallis and Castlereagh woke to the difficulty of their task and made the preparation of union their priority. They decided not to address the matter during the current session of Parliament and shied away from initiating any kind of potentially contested legislation. They also shelved the overdue reform of the tithe system and the

8 G. C. Bolton, *The Passing of the Irish Act of Union. A Study in Parliamentary Politics* (Oxford, 1966), pp. 1–24.

9 Bartlett, *Ireland*, pp. 227–31.

10 Patrick M. Geoghegan, *The Irish Act of Union. A Study in High Politics, 1798–1801* (Dublin, 1999), pp. 54–76.

introduction of an income tax on the British model for the time being.[11] For the remainder of the year, Cornwallis and Castlereagh concentrated on extra-parliamentary activities aimed at securing a safe majority instead. One important area of activity was the battle for public opinion. With the help of the junto, they intensified the paper war by encouraging and circulating pro-union pamphlets and newspaper articles. Over the summer of 1799, Cornwallis undertook a number of goodwill tours through Ireland. Towards the end of the year, these measures checked the initial predominance of anti-union sentiment, and public opinion was again undecided.[12]

In the end, however, the Bill of Union would be passed by individual MPs, not by the general public. There were two ways to procure a majority. One was to secure or turn the opinions of MPs, the other was to try to twist the composition of the entire Lower House. The Dublin leadership pursued both by the ruthless exertion of all means at hand, namely threats, bribes, and the unrestrained use of patronage. Cornwallis' and Castlereagh's orders were to carry the union at any cost. They had use of an ample secret service fund, which, in violation of Burke's Civil Establishment Act and its Irish counterpart, amounted to more than £30,000.[13]

The uncompromising exertion of patronage provided by far the biggest form of leverage. As always, offices were its foremost form of currency. Offices could be used to buy votes. A particularly effective option was to grant profitable offices, which were incompatible with a parliamentary seat, to anti-union members.[14] Conversely, anti-union office-holders were dismissed in great numbers in June, not only to open up places for patronage, but also as an unmistakable warning to other officers not to cross the leadership. The operation created a difficult administrative legacy, because it filled many places with less-than qualified officers, confirmed expensive sinecures and generally reasserted a patrimonial system. The price of union became even higher because Cornwallis and Castlereagh made use of another questionable instrument in order to ensure the majority: in addition to available places, they traded in 'expectancies' of offices, i.e. promises of appointment to offices, meaning the person awarded this promise would

11 James Quinn, 'Dublin Castle and the Act of Union', in Michael Brown, Patrick M. Geoghegan, and James Kelly (eds.), *The Irish Act of Union, 1800: Bicentennial Essays* (Dublin, 2003), 95–107, pp. 103–4.

12 Ibid., p. 101; Cornwallis to Portland, 13 August 1799, Charles Ross (ed.), *Correspondence of Charles, First Marquis Cornwallis*, vol. 3 (London, 1859), p. 121.

13 Geoghegan, *Irish Act of Union*, pp. 84–7; David Wilkinson, '"How Did They Pass the Union?" Secret Service Expenditure in Ireland, 1799–1804', *History*, 82:266 (1997), 233–51.

14 Quinn, 'Dublin Castle', pp. 100–5.

be called in when a vacancy occurred. The secret list of these so-called 'union engagements' enumerates about 100 names with the respective promises of civil, military, and ecclesiastical offices, pensions, and honours.[15] The whole procedure was coordinated minutely with Portland at the Home Office, who ensured the backing of the Crown. Most of this work was done by Castlereagh and Edward Cooke.[16] The ploys worked and the union was passed both in Ireland and Britain by a comfortable majority and received royal assent on 2 July 1800.[17]

In the campaign, Cornwallis concentrated primarily on the most prominent targets himself, but he took full responsibility for all the government's operation and its consequences. Throughout the year 1800, Cornwallis repeatedly expressed his distaste for this line of action to his confidant Alexander Ross. The tone of these letters became increasingly depressed.[18] At the height of the campaign, Cornwallis likened himself to a devil from hell sowing corruption:

> My occupation is now of the most unpleasant nature, negotiating and jobbing with the most corrupt people under heaven. I despise and hate myself every hour for engaging in such dirty work, and am supported only by the reflection that without an Union the British Empire must be dissolved. When it is impossible to gratify the unreasonable demands of our politicians, I often think of two lines of Swift, speaking of the Lord-Lieutenant and the system of corruption
> 'And then at Beelzebub's great hall
> Complains his budget is too small.'[19]

Contemporaries then and historians since have taken up the cry and chastised both the British leadership and the Protestant Ascendency for their corruption. The assessment has changed with the publication of Geoffrey

15 List of Union engagements, in Michael MacDonagh (ed.), *The Viceroy's Post-Bag. Correspondence Hitherto Unpublished of the Earl of Hardwicke, First Lord Lieutenant of Ireland after the Union* (London, 1904), pp. 43–53.

16 Wilkinson, 'How Did They Pass'. Cf. the letters between Cornwallis, Castlereagh, and Portland in Ross (ed.), *Correspondence*, vol. 3.

17 Geoghegan, *Irish Act of Union*, pp. 97–129.

18 Cf. e.g. Cornwallis to Ross, 21 January, 28 January, 20 May, and 19 June 1799. Ross (ed.), *Correspondence*, vol. 3, pp. 39–40, 56, 100–1, 103–4.

19 Cornwallis to Ross, 8 June 1799, Ross (ed.), *Correspondence*, vol. 3, p. 102. The lines are taken from Jonathan Swift's poem *A Libel on the Rev. Dr. Delaney and His Excellency Lord Carteret* (1729): 'So, to effect his Monarch's ends,/From Hell a Viceroy devil ascends,/His budget with corruption crammed,/The contributions of the damned,/Which with unsparing hand he strows/Through courts and senates as he goes,/And then at Beelzebub's black hall/Complains his budget is too small.'

Bolton's now classic study of the union.[20] Bolton made the point that villainising historical agents who acted in accordance with the conventions of their day is detrimental to the historical understanding. After Bolton, most historians were content to vaguely point towards the conventions of the day.[21] Bolton's methodological warning against value judgements is as relevant today as it was then. However, in light of administrative history, assessments in this line fail to qualify and historicise contemporary standards. The abuse of the secret service fund necessitated a deliberate cover-up of financial transactions in the aftermath.[22] The government operation certainly followed on from an unbroken patrimonial rationality of using offices as coined patronage. But even though the instruments of political patronage may have been acceptable by themselves, the ruthless extent of their application exceeded the boundaries of convention. The most recent case of a politically motivated mass replacement of officers in Britain, the 'massacre of the Pelhamite Innocents' of 1762, had provided a rallying point for the opposition Whig ideology for decades. Far from conventional, it was considered a textbook case of the 'corrupt influence of the Crown' and a ruthless attack on parliamentary liberty. The older historiography explained away Cornwallis' expression of disgust at the operation by referring to his 'frank, honourable, soldier-like character.'[23] Recent historiography forgoes such value judgments, but still explains Cornwallis' scruples as a military-man's revulsion at dirtying his hands in the political arena. However, Cornwallis' characterisation of the Irish 'system of corruption' was first and foremost the reverse of the 'system of economy' he had worked to implement in Bengal. It was the qualified assessment of an agent, who knew the administrative standards of his day like few others.

Charles Abbot and the Business of the 'Real Union'

Following the two acts of union passed in 1800, the United Kingdom of Great Britain and Ireland came into existence on 1 January 1801.[24] However, when Pitt tried to push through the second part of his plan for Ireland, i.e. Catholic emancipation, King George brought his personal political weight

20 Bolton, *Passing of the Irish Act of Union*, pp. 221–2.

21 E.g. Geoghegan, *Irish Act of Union*, p. 87.

22 Wilkinson, 'How Did They Pass.'

23 Lecky, William Edward Hartpole, *A History of Ireland in the Eighteenth Century*, vol. 5 (London, 1892), p. 289.

24 In Britain the 'Union with Ireland Act,' 40 Geo III, c. 67 and in Ireland the 'Act of Union' 40 Geo III, [Ire.] c. 38.

to bear once more and vetoed the matter. Pitt would not recede from his position and resigned in January 1801 after seventeen years in office.[25]

Henry, Viscount Sidmouth succeeded Pitt as Prime Minister on 17 March 1801. Addington was a childhood friend of Pitt's and his loyal advisor. Nevertheless, he did not belong to Pitt's inner circle like Henry Dundas and William Wyndham Grenville. Rather, Addington had served as a rallying figure for a wide variety of politicians who were loyal to Pitt, but at times critical of Pitt's policies. In the conflict on Catholic emancipation, Addington tried to mediate between George III and Pitt and subsequently entered office with the backing of both. Neither Pitt nor Addington foresaw that half the Cabinet would decide to resign along with Pitt. These resignations left Addington with the difficulty of filling central posts, but also opened up the chance for a fresh start. Among those who had resigned were Cornwallis and Castlereagh, who had prepared and secured the passing of the union in the Irish Parliament and, like Pitt, were committed to the matter of Catholic emancipation. The new ministry was firmly set against any further concessions to the Catholics.[26]

Addington was challenged to spell out the political union with Ireland without Catholic emancipation and he needed to find new leadership to implement the union. The parliamentary debate on the union focused on the precise way to include the Irish peers and MPs into the two British Houses. Administrative questions played no role in these deliberations and the Irish departmental structure was initially left untouched. The pseudo-colonial dual government of Lord Lieutenant and the Chief Secretary was also retained. As viceroy, the Lord Lieutenant carried the higher rank. The Chief Secretary had been added in Elizabethan times as the Lord Lieutenant's chief of staff and right hand. However, in particular due to his duty to manage parliamentary interest, the Chief Secretary's position had gradually improved until he became the Lord Lieutenant's equal partner. Supported by an office in London, the Chief Secretary acted as the ministry's primary agent and sometimes even held Cabinet rank. Cornwallis' unmistakable primacy over Castlereagh had rather been an exception due to his personal influence as the ministry's crisis manager.[27]

Accordingly, Addington looked for a Chief Secretary first. In the course of putting together his ministry in February 1801, he approached Charles Abbot.[28] Abbot, who had originally had some hopes of succeeding Adding-

25 For a thorough weighing of the different interpretations of Pitt's reasons for resigning see Ehrman, *Consuming Struggle*, pp. 495–533 and Geoghegan, *Irish Act of Union*, pp. 208–26.

26 Bartlett, *Ireland*, pp. 240–2.

27 James Kelly, *Prelude to Union. Anglo-Irish Politics in the 1780s* (Cork, 1992), pp. 6–31.

28 Colchester (ed.), *Diary and Correspondence*, pp. 233–42.

ton as Speaker of the House of Commons, drove a hard bargain. In the end, Abbot became a Privy Councillor and received the Clerkship of the Pells. Having agreed to the post, it was Abbot who approached Philip York, Lord Hardwicke (1757–1834) for the Lord Lieutenancy in Addington's name. In agreement with the Prime Minister and in counsel with William Pitt, Abbot also drew up the private instructions for the Lord Lieutenant, which formed the guidelines of the Irish policy. Hence, Abbot took office as the first Chief Secretary after the union with self-confidence. As Abbot quoted Addington, 'the business would be to render the nominal union a real union.'[29] Building on his experience from the Finance Committee, Abbot planned to improve Irish administration on principles of administrative economy.

The mandate and agenda for the Lord Lieutenant and the Chief Secretary were laid down in the instructions, which comprised a public and a private part. The public instructions were somewhat anachronistically framed as a personal transferral of power from the King to his viceroy and they mirrored the uncertainties of the ministry's Irish policy.[30] Nevertheless, the instructions defined a preliminary setup regarding authorities, competencies, and responsibilities within the union that mirrored the state of discussion in the freshly constituted Cabinet.[31] Ireland remained a mostly autonomous unit governed by the Lord Lieutenant. The Lord Lieutenant retained his supremacy over the offices of the executive and the judiciary. His supremacy was restricted insofar as he was subject to orders from Britain and by threefold institutional subordination. In all financial matters, Dublin Castle depended on the approval of the British Treasury, whilst superintendence in all other civil matters lay with the Home Office, though the instructions did not spell out the exact distribution of power. The third restriction concerned the military. While the Lord Lieutenant retained certain duties with regard to fortifications and quartering, he held neither high command nor any military patronage.[32]

The twenty-first head of Hardwicke's public instructions made a number of general points regarding offices. The instructions renewed the ban on the sale of offices and of excessive fees. All Irish offices were to be held during pleasure only, a clear rejection of the property theory of office for Ireland.[33]

29 Ibid., p. 229.

30 Hoppen, 'Incorporating Union,' pp. 328–31.

31 The undefined legal status of Ireland within the new United Kingdom is apparent in the cumbersome denomination as 'that part of Our United Kingdom called Ireland,' which is used throughout the text. Cf. George III to Hardwicke, Public Instructions, 30 April 1801, in TNA, PRO 30/9/136, passim.

32 Ibid., fol. $6^{r/v}$.

33 Ibid., fols. 5^{v}–6^{r}.

Moreover, the instructions explicitly banned reversions. The old-fashioned term 'reversion' denoted the practice (or claim) of an office-holder or third party to determine the successor to an office, either by inheritance, patronage, or sale. The concept had played no role in the British debates of the preceding decades. Its use in the Irish context referred to the vestiges of the undertaker system in Ireland, by which a small number of power brokers had acquired the patronage to many offices in the name of the then mostly absent Lord Lieutenant.[34]

With regard to the administrative system, the instructions repeatedly deplored the general lack of information, especially in matters of revenue. The instructions demanded special scrutiny for the prevention of land tax fraud by means of a land survey and called for a general muster of the army and an inquiry in the conduct of the courts of justice. Moreover, the instructions tasked the Lord Lieutenant with compelling the Irish Treasury to transmit regular accounts and to pass them on to the British Treasury.[35] The public instructions show that the British government, now the government of the United Kingdom, lacked the information it had come to rely on. At the turn of the century, gathering 'statistical' information had become a widely accepted concern of the reason of state.

Whilst the public instructions formulated the initial principles of interaction between British and Irish departments, the private instructions delineated an economical reform programme:

> II. As to the Revenue
>
> In addition to the matters required by the several articles of your Public Instructions upon this head, you will inform yourself how far the collection of His Majesty's Revenues may be rendered more simple and less chargeable, without detriment to his service. And also how far the expenditure thereof may be more effectually checked and controlled. And you will transmit in writing, what shall appear to you as fit to be done therein, either by instituting a commission for stating and taking the public accounts of that part of the kingdom, or otherwise.[36]

[34] John Baker, *An Introduction to English Legal History*, 3rd edn. (London, 1990), pp. 312–14; S. J. Connolly, *Divided Kingdom. Ireland, 1630–1800* (Oxford, 2008), pp. 233–48; 'reversion, n.', *OED*.

[35] See heads 4 (Treasury Accounts), 5 (Land Survey), 8 (Muster), and 13 (Survey and Accounts of Castles and Forts). George III to Hardwicke, Public Instructions, 30 April 1801, in TNA, PRO 30/9/136.

[36] Ibid., p. 302.

The passage is clearly informed by the administrative reform experience in Britain, apparent in the formulated goals, as well as by its language. Only the last point raised a specifically Irish issue. Abbot's mandate for administrative reform left nothing to be desired.

Reforming by the Book

Hardwicke left for Ireland in early May 1801 and took over from Cornwallis, whilst Abbot remained in London for the session to manage Irish parliamentary affairs. Abbot carried a prolongation of martial law as well as the Irish Places Bill, which aimed to tighten the leadership's grip on Irish officials. The bill made offices in the Irish revenue incompatible with parliamentary seats and thereby excluded prominent members like John Beresford, the first Commissioner of the Irish revenue and effective leader of the Castle Party, from the House of Commons.[37] After the end of the session, Abbot followed Hardwicke to Ireland in early July and immediately initiated a large-scale programme of administrative reform.

Abbot and Hardwicke harmonised well. Philip Yorke, third Earl of Hardwicke, was born to one of the most prominent aristocratic families of England. His father had served as Lord Chancellor under Walpole, his brother Charles Philip was the current Secretary at War. Not a prominent politician himself, Hardwicke had originally been a Foxite, but supported Pitt continuously after 1785.[38] Shortly before Abbot left for Dublin, Hardwicke sent him a letter containing an agenda for Abbot's 'early attention':

> 1. The application as to Parliament House to some publick purposes, that may be useful both with a view to publick satisfaction & publick oeconomy. [...]
> 2. A Commission to Enquire into & report upon the state of the publick offices, as well as their expenditure of duties of the officers employed, upon the model of your Finance Reports. [...]
> 4. The consideration of some means to improve the Collection of the Revenue which is now miserable deficient, to diminish unnecessary expenditure. It occurs while I am writing that the enormous expence of the Staff ought to be diminished.[39]

37 41 Geo III, c. 52. Breihan, 'Economical Reform', p. 211.

38 J. M. Rigg, 'Yorke, Philip, third earl of Hardwicke (1757–1834)', *ODNB*.

39 Hardwicke to Abbot, 7 July 1801, in TNA, PRO 30/9/113, pp. 25–6.

Hardwicke thus fully embraced the administrative reform impetus for which Abbot stood. Their shared plan was to reduce costs by tightening the structure of offices, especially in the revenue. Conducting a survey on the current state of the offices had become an established method, a necessary first step in a process of reform that aimed at administrative improvement.

Abbot lost no time in the matter. In August, shortly after arriving in Dublin, he sent out a circular letter addressed to all Irish departments prompting them for detailed returns on office establishments, procedures, and accounts. The ductus of the letter was pressing, straight to the point, and very technical; a routine operation of an experienced administrative reformer:

> I have it in command from the Lord-Lieutenant to desire that you will transmit to me, with as little delay as possible, for the immediate information of His Excellency, a return of the establishment of your officers exactly corresponding with the enclosed form, and specifying correctly the information required in the respective columns thereof, when the headings severally apply to the establishment of your institution, or to any points connected therewith, and also to state the attendance and duties of the officers belonging thereto.[40]

The circular letter included a form in which all information should be inserted in columns. The form prompted detailed information on salaries, additional emoluments of office-holders, and working hours, and checked whether the offices were conducted in person. The inquiry was clearly modelled after the Finance Committee returns. Abbot also tried tapping into the kind of authority that had distinguished the inquiries of CEPA. He endowed the answers with an oath-like quality and held the departmental heads responsible by declaring 'that the return now required from you may be completed as if to be verified upon oath, and that it may be signed by the proper officer or officers.'[41]

For many departments, the request was the first communication which they received from the new Chief Secretary and returns took time. To Abbot, the letter was only a necessary first step, because systematic reforms relied on a suitable information base. Even looking back years later, Abbot complained about the departments' lack of enthusiasm:

> In consequence of general conversations with Mr. Addington, and also upon this point with Mr. Pitt before I left England, I issued circular orders in the month of August, calling upon all the departments

[40] Edward Gibson, *Pitt. Some Chapters of his Life and Times* (London, 1898), p. 273.
[41] Ibid.

> of Government, civil and military, in the Lord-Lieutenant's name, to make returns of their establishments, duties, salaries, &c., in the same manner I had practised in the British Parliament when Chairman of the Finance Committee. Several returns to these orders were made during the time of my Continuance in Ireland, but very reluctantly, and sometimes evasively. Those from the Customs and Excise were very imperfectly delivered, within a few days only of my departure from Dublin.[42]

It is not surprising that the departments frustrated Abbot's sense of urgency. The leading officers were hardly happy about the inquiries, which already hinted at larger interventions to come. Abbot made no secret out of his intention to reform. Even with goodwill, however, many Irish departments faced a difficulty. Unlike the British offices, the Irish offices had never before faced a comparable survey and the departments were badly prepared to deliver the desired information. Abbot did not appreciate such restraints and started requisitioning the returns the next month.[43] Abbot personally concentrated on the Excise, Customs, and Stamp offices. Starting in September, he bombarded these offices with requests for additional accounts, reports on details, and for proposals addressing individual defects.[44] In order to ensure their cooperation, he ordered board members to attend to their duties daily and demanded reports on the attendance of board members as copies of proceedings relative to the implementation of reforms and on a weekly basis.[45]

Abbot's measures concerned the whole bandwidth of deficiencies according to his economical understanding of administration. He aimed to unify and simplify accounting, to transfer money in the hands of officers to public accounts and to convert all fee-based emoluments into salaries. New regulations reduced holidays and aimed to enforce regular

42 Colchester (ed.), *Diary and Correspondence*, p. 280.

43 Cf.: Excise Department. Orders received from government since 25 July 1801, in TNA, PRO 30/9/168, n. pag. For the state of the offices see R. B. McDowell, *The Irish Administration, 1801–1914* (London, Toronto, 1964), pp. 20–1.

44 See the different lists of abstracts of Revenue correspondence: Excise Department. Orders received from government since 25 July 1801; Revenue Board. Orders of Government and Progress thereon, 23 July 1801 to 8 October (in fact covering the period till 8 January 1802); Orders from Government and Reports to be made August 1801 to January 1802; Correspondence with the Revenue Board since the 25. Day of May 1801, in TNA, PRO 30/9/168, n. pag. Copies of additional requests are included in TNA, PRO 30/9/137, pp. 1–40. For the Stamps Office see the various documents in TNA, PRO 30/9/152.

45 Letter to the Commissioners of Stamp Duties, directing several Regulations &c., 31 October 1801, in TNA, PRO 30/9/152, fols. 28–37; Revenue Board. Orders of Government and Progress thereon, 6 November, TNA, PRO 30/9/168, n. pag.

attendance throughout the departments. Abbot designed his measures to improve effectiveness, but most of all to assert control. His experience in the Finance Committee seemed to provide solutions to most problems. He simply applied British precedents:

> the principal object to which our exertions were directed was the regulation of the several offices of Revenue and Expenditure, and the accommodating all details of Finance as much as possible to the British model.[46]

The biggest lever for retrenchment would have been the reduction of establishments. On this issue, however, Abbot's hands were tied. The Irish departments included many sinecures and offices executed by deputies. Abbot could not touch these unnecessary offices because they made up the bulk of the 'union engagements' promised by Cornwallis and Castlereagh to secure the passing of the union. Abbot not only lacked the necessary power to dispose of the recently nominated officers, he was even compelled to fulfil the promised expectations by appointing nominees to vacancies in sinecures and efficient offices; nominees who were hardly qualified, let alone motivated or even loyal to government. Due to this inability to reform the higher offices, Abbot relied on the patronage of the lower echelons to exert control. In the Stamp Office, for instance, Abbot tried to force the Comptroller who had 'not been in the habit of conducting the Business of his own Office' to 'attend personally to the Duties of his Office'. At the same time, he promoted the first clerk, who had done the actual work, to the newly created office of a deputy controller.[47] While such solutions may have served to address some problems, they did not help to decrease costs. On a larger scale, Abbot split up the Irish revenue into two distinct Boards of Excise and Customs, but could not dismiss Beresford, who had presided over the old joint department, even though his position had become superfluous. Beresford was a central figure in the political networks of the Protestant Ascendency. The measure aimed at depreciating his powerbase and grip on the revenue, even though Abbot justified it only in terms of improved procedures.[48]

In September 1801, Abbot appointed a commission to inquire into the Board of Works and to develop proposals for improvement. The appointment of the three commissioners was modelled on CEPA. They were to make:

[46] Colchester (ed.), *Diary and Correspondence*, p. 280.

[47] Letter to the Commissioners of Stamp Duties, directing several Regulations &c., 31 October 1801, in TNA, PRO 30/9/152, fols. 28^{v}–29^{r}.

[48] Abbot to the Board of Revenue, 20 October 1801, in TNA, PRO 30/9/137, pp. 28–30.

> the fullest Investigation into the present Mode of conducting the Civil Expenditure of that Department, ascertaining by whose Authority Expences are incurred, how the Execution of the several services is examined and controlled, in what Manner are the Monies advanced are [sic] paid, and by whom and on what Voucher. [...]
>
> Having taken the whole into your mature Consideration, you will Report to me fully there upon for His Excellency's Information, and likewise point out such Alterations (if any) for the better Management of the Department as shall appear to you to be fit, and generally communicate your opinion upon the whole of this Important Subject.[49]

The powers necessary for such an inquiry had been practiced in Britain often enough. The commissioners received access to all relevant papers and the power to summon and interview officers, albeit without the power of administering oaths. Public money was the central point of reference of the inquiry. Contrary to British reform commissions, the instructions clearly emphasised financial authority over economy; these commissioners answered to Abbot only. In Ireland, Abbot preferred to keep full control and eschewed transparency.

The three commissioners brought with them varied backgrounds. Richard Annesley (1745–1824) had served as high sheriff of Down and sat on the Revenue Board, Sackville Hamilton (1732–1818) belonged to the Irish Privy Council. Colonel George Napier (1751–1804) had been installed as Comptroller of Army Accounts by Cornwallis. In this capacity, Napier had renounced all fees and had subsequently regulated the office.[50] At first, the inquiry seemed to be running well, as Hamilton reported after only two weeks.[51] However, soon the inquiry faced obstruction at every step.[52] In the end, the commissioners were not even able to agree on a joint report. In a long letter to Abbot, George Napier accused his colleagues of undermining the reform efforts. Napier was convinced that their motivation was prompted by the established power networks of the Ascendency:

> I confide in your candour to exculpate me from the contemptible inconsistency (not to apply a more severe Epithet) of opposing what I

49 Abbot to Sackville Hamilton, 28 September 1801, in BL, Add. Mss. 33108, fols. 63^{v}–64^{r}; also see Abbot to the Board of Works, 28 September 1801, ibid., fols. 65^{v}–66^{r}.

50 Roger T. Stearn, 'Napier, George (1751–1804)', *ODNB*. There is an interesting parallel to George Barlow, who, promoted by Cornwallis, had also renounced all fees belonging to his office in a seemingly voluntary way and was rewarded for the act by Cornwallis. See above, chapter 5.

51 Sackville Hamilton to Abbot, 11 October 1801, in TNA, PRO 30/9/113, p. 110.

52 The Board of Works would only produce its first full account in 1813. McDowell, *Irish Administration*, p. 21.

> really conceived would operate an improvement in the defective practice of the 'Civil Depart. of Works', namely from the petulant resentment at the Cavalier Treatment I have received from my Colleagues: [...] in Ireland zeal for the public service [...] must prove insufficient to overcome those well concerted Plans, and long established alliances, which in this country will continue to paralise the public exertions of a stranger when associated with the Disciples of the 'Old School'.[53]

Napier construed a battle line between disinterested reformers such as himself and a corrupt established cabal. It is of little consequence whether Napier's accusations were true – Hamilton assured Abbot of his cooperation.[54] Either way, the accusations provide an indication of the atmosphere of suspicion and political intrigue which formed the background to the ongoing reform process.

Abbot received anonymous letters endorsing reform and only little informed criticism.[55] Nor did Abbot invite an open discussion by his demeanour. The answers to Abbot's many requests were typically short and rarely contained criticism or even defence. This does not mean that there was no resistance; the opposite is true. However, resistance took the form of sluggish cooperation, while criticism of the reforms and Abbot's person was channelled through well-connected politicians directly to ministers in London.

Irritation and Resistance

At the centre of this opposition were the heads of the Castle Party. They were the very people who had formed a junto to help Cornwallis and Castlereagh carry the union: Undersecretary Edward Cooke, Lord Chancellor Clare, and John Beresford.[56] Edward Cooke had worked closely with Castlereagh, but evidently did not get along with Abbot; a dislike that was apparently mutual.[57] To Hardwicke, Cooke complained:

[53] George Napier to Abbot, 9 December 1801, in TNA, PRO 30/9/124, fols. 205^{r}–206^{r}.

[54] Sackville Hamilton to Charles Abbot, 19 February 1802, in TNA, PRO 30/9/113, p. 247.

[55] 'Publius' to Abbot, n.d. [January 1802], in TNA, PRO 30/9/110, fols. 66–9.

[56] Jupp, 'Britain and the Union', p. 200.

[57] Cooke to Castlereagh, 3 August 1801, in Charles Vane (ed.), *Memoirs and Correspondence of Viscount Castlereagh, Second Marquess of Londonderry*, vol. 4 (London, 1849), pp. 94–5; Colchester (ed.), *Diary and Correspondence*, p. 279.

> I never receive any thing but a Command. I have been used to different treatment from other persons superior to Mr. Abbot. I might have left this Country with advantage. I wish I had quitted it upon a change of Administration. Mr Pitt made proposals to me; I might have had the Situation Mr. Abbot has. I feel that I have a right to consideration.[58]

The Castle Party felt wronged: It was they who had facilitated the union and, instead of being allowed to reap its benefits, they felt they were being excluded and even attacked. Lord Chancellor Clare, most of all, was a rallying figure for the Protestant Ascendency. Clare did not mince his words. As soon as Abbot's circular letter was out, he wrote to the Home Secretary Thomas Pelham launching an all-out attack:

> Is there wisdom, justice, or policy in suffering this upstart prig to disgust and offend the gentlemen to whose support we are indebted for carrying the Union, before it has well been completed? I understand that Mr. Abbott, who commenced his official career by securing to himself a sinecure office in Ireland for life, has openly declared that he has come here for the sole purpose of effecting reformation in every department. Even if he were authorised to make such a declaration, how is the general inquisition which he has set on foot calculated to facilitate reformation? And if it were, how is his arrogance in the mode of carrying it into effect to be justified?[59]

Abbot's circular letter was anathema to Clare. Clare depicted Abbot's information gathering as a 'general inquisition', a direct attack on the legitimate Irish Protestant elite. Clare's only reference to administrative argumentation was the knock on Abbot's open flank, Abbot's acceptance of a sinecure on taking office. In his letters, Clare reminded Pelham that the Protestant Ascendency was the bedrock of British influence in Ireland and discredited Abbot personally by frequent allusion to Abbot's imperious, arrogant, and uncompromising conduct.

Clare's words did not fall on deaf ears. A change in the Cabinet significantly affected Irish policy-making. Thomas Pelham, second Earl of Chichester (1756–1826), replaced Portland as Home Secretary at the end of July 1801, soon after Abbot left London for Dublin. Pelham had served twice as

58 Verbatim transcription of a meeting between Mr. Cooke & L. Hardwicke, 31 August 1801, in TNA, PRO 30/9/123. Hardwicke afterwards wrote to Cooke politely, but refused to accept the criticism expressed in their conversation, which he correlated to both Abbot and himself. Hardwicke to Cooke, 11 September 1801, in TNA, PRO 30/9/113, fol. 64^{V}.

59 Clare to Pelham, 5 September 1801, in Gibson, *Pitt*, pp. 271–3, quote on p. 272.

Chief Secretary in Ireland, first in the Fox–North coalition and, changing affiliation, a second time from 1795 to 1798 under Pitt. Pelham's nomination did not follow Addington's preference, but rather constituted a concession to George III and his second son Frederick, the Duke of York (1763–1827).[60] Pelham succeeded Portland to a reduced Home Office portfolio, after the responsibility and patronage of the colonies had shifted to the War Office. On entering office, Pelham focused on Ireland instead and claimed full authority over Irish affairs. Consequently, Pelham's collaboration with Hardwicke and Abbot did not start out too well. Moreover, it was clear to them that Pelham was positively inclined towards Clare and Cooke, with whom they were in a state of open conflict.[61]

The third major player among the Irish opposition was John Beresford, the head of the Irish revenue, who had lost his seat in Parliament through Abbot's motion. Abbot's plans for dividing the joint revenue department into Excise and Customs directly threatened Beresford's position. Beresford was the only one to discuss the administrative side of Abbot's protracted reforms, though never with Abbot in person. As long as Abbot remained in Ireland, Beresford stayed at his country seat and avoided Dublin. Instead, Beresford wrote to the Secretary of War and the Colonies Robert Hobart, fourth Earl of Buckinghamshire (1760–1816) and to William Eden, Baron Auckland (1745–1814), the legal reformer who had joined Addington's ministry as Postmaster General. To Eden, Beresford expressed his shock at Abbot's creation of new offices to circumvent current lines of authority: 'By the letters which I receive, I verily believe the Government are gone mad; they are totally new modelling the Revenue, they have created new Offices, I hear, to the amount in Income of £4000 a year, and talk of many more.' After enumerating the new offices and assessing the new officers, he summed up with reference to the well-known quote of Juvenal: 'we are to have multiplication of Offices to watch one another, and who will watch the Watchers.'[62]

Hobart and Auckland evidently agreed in their condemnation of Abbot's conduct:

[60] Charles J. Fedorak, *Henry Addington, Prime Minister, 1801–1804. Peace, War, and Parliamentary Politics* (Akron, 2002), pp. 38–40; D. R. Fisher, 'Pelham, Thomas, second earl of Chichester (1756–1826)', *ODNB*.

[61] Cf. e.g. Hardwicke's letters to Abbot of 6 and 15 July 1801, TNA, PRO/30/9/113, pp. 20–3; 28–36.

[62] Beresford to Auckland, 11 October 1801, BL, Add. Mss. 34455, fols. 438–9, quotes on fol. 438. The quote from Juvenal's satires, 'quis custodiet ipsos custodes', implied tyrannical government.

> I quite agree with Beresford as to the folly of Abbots reform [...] & it is an additional proof to me that whatever that Gentleman undertakes he will contrive to do in the most offensive way possible. His return upon the face of it directed to all departments must be felt as a general censure upon a large body of Men, altho' he may force them for a time quietly to submit, you may be assur'd they will find the means ultimately of making Mr. Abbot pay for his Priggism and Impatience. A gradual Reform in the Public Offices in Ireland, with a view to a more steady & constant attention to business, might I think be usefull, but it should be effected by the suaviter in modo, & as little talked of as possible.[63]

Hobart did not repudiate Abbot's administrative objectives, but he excoriated Abbot's course of action, as it resulted in the alienation of the Irish elites. Hobart depicted administrative reform as desirable, but not essential. It was certainly not worth alienating major political allies in Ireland. Moreover, from his own experience, Hobart was quick to agree with Beresford's depreciation of Abbot's character. Auckland and Hobart frequently corresponded on Irish matters and they also strove to persuade others to their view. When Hobart took up the matter with the Prime Minister, he received a friendly answer:

> I return Lord Clare's letter, & am truly sorry that the conduct of the Irish Government towards him shou'd have been such as to provoke the resentment he seems to feel. In deprecating and disgusting him they have certainly mistaken the interests both of the existing administration & of the Publick, but he is totally incorrect in supposing that Mr. Addington approves much less abets what he calls the insolence of Mr. Abbot; & however chargeable he may be with having committed the original error of appointing that Gentleman to the Secretaryship, Lord Clare ought to know how difficult it is to remove him when he is once fairly in position.[64]

Unbeknownst to Abbot, his opponents in Ireland had brought their position to the attention of Cabinet at an early stage. In London, high-ranking politicians were ready to take up the case of the Irish Ascendancy.

63 Hobart to Auckland, 13 September 1801, in BL, Add. Mss. 34455, fols. 429^{v}–430^{r}.

64 Hobart to Auckland, dated 'Saturday Night' [presumably late September 1801], in BL, Add. Mss. 34455, fol. 464.

Negotiating the Administrative Union

The negotiations on the future Irish policy, the allocation of authorities, and the future of Abbot's administrative reforms took place throughout September 1801, in London. In these negotiations, Abbot was forced to rely on an emissary to act on his behalf. Abbot chose the Military Department Undersecretary Colonel Edward Baker Littlehales (died 1825). Littlehales had worked well with Cornwallis and he remained part of the inner circle of the leadership in Dublin in Hardwicke's tenure. Abbot's disadvantage comes as a blessing to historians. Littlehale's instructions for this mission and the ongoing correspondence with Abbot allow historians to assess the place of administrative concerns in the protracted negotiations about the future government and administration of Ireland.

Abbot provided Littlehales with a set of secret instructions specifying twenty-five points to be negotiated with the Prime Minister (Addington), the Treasury, the Home Secretary (Pelham), the Secretary at War (Charles Yorke), and the Commander in Chief (the Duke of York).[65] In addition, Littlehales' instructions comprised a memorandum with the positions of Hardwicke and Abbot on the executive and administrative settlement of Ireland. Littlehales was to pass this memorandum on to Addington and Pelham as a basis for negotiation. The memorandum essentially proposed to secure the status quo. Hardwicke and Abbot argued that the Lord Lieutenant necessarily relied on the Irish patronage in order to act from a position of strength. Otherwise, the memorandum warned, power would fall back to 'some of the principal individuals and families in Ireland, whose local passions and interests peculiarly disqualify them [...] from governing their countrymen.' Hardwicke and Abbot depicted the Protestant Ascendency as a secluded elite without public support. They advised that the Lord Lieutenant should be an Englishman, while prominent Irishmen should receive 'ostensible offices' in England in order to bind them to the 'parental influence which governs the country of the United Kingdom.'[66] This remarkable plan boils down to the use of sinecures for political reasons.

The plan sat rather uneasily with Abbot's subsequent deliberations on administrative reform. Abbot insisted on 'the expediency of my proceeding to regulate the collection of the public revenue in a more systematic, impartial, correct, and effectual manner than at present obtains [sic], without

[65] Secret Instructions to Colonel Littlehales, n.d. [end of August], in TNA, PRO 30/9/124, fols. 5–12.

[66] Instructions given to Colonel Littlehales, n.d. [end of August], in Colchester (ed.), *Diary and Correspondence*, p. 313.

individual severity or oppression.'[67] This point focused on patronage as a central means to control individuals and groups. Moreover, the reforms concerned the system itself and promised to establish control and achieve savings. In Abbot's presentation, the reforms were not open to discussion as such, with the only question he posed to the Prime Minister being which authority was needed to finalise the reforms. Abbot cautioned against the use of a parliamentary commission, which 'being placed beyond control, might digress into inquiries prejudicial to the interest of good government, and applicable to no useful purpose.'[68] Abbot was loath to relinquish control. Administrative reforms and Irish government in general instead depended on 'some latitude of action [that] should be recognised as belonging to the office of Lord Lieutenant.'[69] The paper called for what Cornwallis had enjoyed in India: quasi-despotic powers to govern and to reform all departments with a minimum of interference.

Littlehales' consultations with the War Office went most smoothly. These consultations exemplified the potential of administrative collaboration based on a shared understanding of principles. After a preliminary correspondence, Charles Yorke invited Littlehales to the War Office and provided him access to pertinent papers.[70] Littlehales reported to Abbot that

> a regulation is now in preparation which, I saw & think, if generally enforced in both Countries, will go essentially to simplify & controul the issues of public monies for military services: Mr. Yorke has directed the proper Officer to furnish me with a comparative statement of the mode of carrying on the duties of the War Department here with that which we followed: In assimilating the practice of the two Countries, as far as local circumstances will permit in the issues of public sums & in the necessary checks & controuls, it appears highly desirable that one system should be laid down and adhered to as to paylists & regulations.[71]

Yorke and Littlehales shared an understanding of reform methods and goals that was based on notions of administrative economy. They agreed on a swift incorporation of the military establishments, leaving only the question of implementation. An empirical evaluation and comparison of

67 Separate Instructions for conferring with Mr. Addington, n.d. [end of August], in TNA, PRO 30/9/124, fol. 4^{r}.

68 Ibid.

69 Ibid.

70 Littlehales to Abbot, 12 September 1801, in TNA, PRO 30/9/124, fol. 39^{v}.

71 Littlehales to Abbot, 16 September 1801, in TNA, PRO 30/9/124, fols. 55^{v}–6^{r}.

the offices in Britain and Ireland provided the necessary preparation for the unification into a single system. This system was supposed to be simpler than the current systems and provide better checks and controls in the appropriation of public money. These concerted preparations went so well because they took place under the best possible circumstances. Charles Yorke was positively inclined towards the Irish leadership. After all, he was Hardwicke's younger brother and a friend of Abbot's. Moreover, Yorke had been a member of the Finance Committee himself and he was therefore well acquainted with administrative reform theory. With regard to the military offices, there was only one point that Littlehales could not solve. Despite the support from the War Office, Prince Frederick refused to delegate parts of his Irish military patronage to the Lord Lieutenant.[72]

The man whose agreement and support meant most for Hardwicke and Abbot was the Prime Minister. Littlehales handed the memorandum to Addington and met with him several times. While the Prime Minister did not commit himself to decisions, the discussions at first seemed to bode well to Littlehales. Addington hinted that a major restructuring of Irish government was unlikely.[73] A typical formulation by Addington that Littlehales reported repeatedly was the Prime Minister's intentions to proceed on 'principles of the union'. These unspecified principles remained vague, after all, the acts of union had evidently not addressed questions of government and administration. After two weeks, Addington commented on the administrative reforms that Abbot had begun in Ireland. The comment will hardly have pleased Abbot. The Prime Minister acknowledged the existence of defects in the Irish administration and agreed on the desirability of administrative reform. However,

> Mr. Addington seemed rather apprehensive that there might possibly have been too much precipitancy used as to the enquiries that are now afloat into certain supposed abuses in the public departments in Ireland [...] those evils would gradually be cured or at a more distant period be effectually eradicated whereas at present a rapid adoption of a system of reform would not only disgust many of those who had supported the Union, but the Nation at large might be induced to feel that it was a manifestation of the intention of the Cabinet to act towards them in an harsh and rather oppressive manner, and that the adoption of any unusual measures even in regard to the conduct of

72 Littlehales to Abbot, 4 September 1801, ibid., fols. 29^{r}–33^{r}, quote on fol. 29; Littlehales to Abbot, 20 September 1801, ibid., fols. 59^{r}–59^{v}.

73 Littlehales to Abbot, 3 September 1801, TNA, PRO/30/9/124, fols. 21^{r}–5^{v}.

> public departments without a conference previously obtained with the King's servants seemed impolitic, & upon a principle of good will & cordiality, inexpedient.[74]

Addington had quite a clear idea of what Abbot's plans amounted to; he had, after all, discussed the issue with Abbot before appointing him as Chief Secretary. However, his statement on the ongoing reform process came down to a severe rebuke. Triggered, no doubt, by the Irish Ascendency's fierce opposition, by now taken up by members of the Cabinet, Addington could hardly overlook the political costs of Abbot's reforms. Addington thus criticised Abbot's line of action as too rash. The prompt and comprehensive reform Abbot had in mind was politically undesirable. It irritated influential persons and potentially also the public, who might have perceived large-scale changes on executive authority as acts of oppression. Instead, a policy of exemplary conduct in government combined only with small steps towards improvement might yield good results in the long run. The disagreement did not follow from different administrative understandings, but rather concerned the assessment of the political situation and the relative importance of reform.

Upon receiving Littlehales' recount of Addington's position, Abbot answered with a very different interpretation of the lines of conflict in Ireland. In Abbot's view, the Irish government only faced the hostility of an anti-unionist minority, and this hostility was really directed at the ministry in London: 'the Old System is at War with the Union System & battle is joined between them.' In spite of his perception of a war of systems, Abbot did not accept that his reforms played any role in the conflict:

> I am not aware of any apprehension which need be entertained from any precipitation to reform as no step has been yet taken but for ascertaining the actual state of the Civil & Military Offices in this Country – nor do I know of any persons likely to be offended if it should take place, except such as L[ord] C[lare], who nevertheless professes to speak of it as highly meritorious and L[ord] Shannon with others of his Character, I believe with more sincerity declare their wish that a fair exertion of authority may be used to put Ireland upon an English footing in its receipt & expenditure.[75]

74 Littlehales to Abbot, 16 September 1801, TNA, PRO/30/9/124, fols. 47^{r}–51^{v}, quote on fols. 49^{v}–50^{v}.

75 Abbot to Littlehales, 21 September 1801, TNA, PRO 30/9/124, fols. 75^{r}–6^{r}, quote on fol. 77^{r}.

Whether due to a misunderstanding or a calculated decision to deliver Littlehales this version, Abbot drew a line between administrative reform and the sphere of politics, where he located the real cause for political discontent. How could reform have caused any resentment, he argued, when he had not even really begun changing anything? Abbot's insistence that even Lord Clare did not openly argue against administrative reform may even have been accurate, but it seems unlikely that Abbot did not realise the enmity against his person and his reform agenda.

A Contest for Power

That negotiations with Pelham and the Home Office would prove to be difficult did not come as a surprise. In the first audiences, Pelham asked for comprehensive information, criticised the separate consultations with the War Office, and insisted that Irish affairs exclusively fell under the authority of the Home Office.[76] Apart from this rebuke, Pelham did not commit himself.[77] Three weeks into Littlehale's mission, Abbot vented his frustration in a letter to Littlehales:

> Why is the Use of Pen and Ink debarred to the Office up two-pair of stairs from Whitehall, so as to disable it from signifying what it stands in need of, instead of leaving us to conjecture, or taking the chance of our sending a Min[iste]r Plenipot[entiar]y to ask them what they are thinking about.[78]

Pelham was far from passive. Rather, he only held out on Littlehales and Abbot while he negotiated Irish policy in Cabinet. Pelham's position was directly opposed to Abbot's and Hardwicke's interests. On 26 September, Pelham finally put his cards on the table, as Littlehales reported the following day. The differences in opinion did not concern principles of administrative reform, but the distribution of power:

> I have no doubt of your having formed a just idea 'of the few political enemies with whom you may have to contend in Ireland,' and equally so in regard to the supposition here as to the precipitation to reform; it appears, however, that there is no such material difference in opinion

76 Littlehales to Abbot, 19 September 1801, TNA, PRO 30/9/124, fols. 63ʳ–70ʳ. This letter has been included in Colchester (ed.), *Diary and Correspondence*, pp. 314–17. There, it is falsely dated 9 September.

77 TNA, PRO/30/9/124, fols. 39ʳ–40ᵛ; 41ʳ–42ʳ.

78 Abbot to Littlehales, 22 September 1801, TNA, PRO 30/9/124, fol. 77ʳ.

> on this side of the water with you as to the latter point; the contention being confined to a previous communication, and to the mode, and to the period, not to the policy, necessity & expediency, which are fully conceded with an entire coincidence in his Excellency & your opinion upon the general view of the subject.[79]

Even while entering into open conflict with the Irish leadership, Pelham agreed with Abbot on the general idea of administrative reform. Like Addington, Pelham rather criticised Abbot's rash actions, which made him too many enemies and thereby caused political problems. Pelham claimed full authority over Irish matters and he was not inclined to discuss the matter with Abbot or his emissary. He merely passed on a written memorandum titled *Considerations upon the situation of the Lord-Lieutenant and his Chief Secretary*, which he had laid before the Cabinet in the preceding week.[80]

In the *Considerations*, Pelham argued that the union implied not only legislative but also executive incorporation. A strong viceroy had only been necessary as a constitutional counterweight to the Irish Parliament. In the United Kingdom, the arrangement made no sense anymore. On the principles of union, Pelham argued, there could only be one government in the United Kingdom. Within this government, Ireland belonged to the jurisdiction of the Home Office because the union had turned Irish affairs into domestic affairs.[81] The Home Office was supposed to hold full authority over the Irish executive and full authority meant the unconfined exercise of Irish patronage:

> Now, as it is generally understood that the Government of a Country resides wherever the power of selecting men for Official situations is exercised, it would seem, that appointments in general to Offices in Ireland ought as much as possible to appear, at least to originate, in the British Cabinet, or in some power in England immediately deriving from the source of all Patronage in the Empire.[82]

Pelham proposed to retain the office of Lord Lieutenant as the head of a 'strong, vigilant, and energetic local executive, directing its chief attention to the police of the country, but acting in immediate subordination to the

79 Littlehales to Abbot, 27 September 1801, PRO/30/9/124, fols. 99^{r}–106^{v}, quote on 105.

80 Thomas Pelham: Considerations upon the situation of the Lord-Lieutenant and his Chief Secretary, BL, Add. Mss. 35771, fols. 101^{v}–4^{r}.

81 Ibid., fols. 101^{v}–4^{r}. Hoppen, 'Incorporating Union', pp. 331–2.

82 Pelham, Considerations, BL, Add. Mss. 35771, fols. 101^{v}–2^{r}.

general executive government of the empire.'[83] The Lord Lieutenant would no longer be a viceroy, but rather a high office to deal with local affairs, public safety, and police, similar to county offices in England. Pelham did not mention the Chief Secretary at all and thereby implied that this office would be abolished.

Counterbalancing the loss of colonial patronage was certainly a strong motivation for Pelham, but his concept should not be reduced to a grab for personal influence. Pelham's argumentation follows from a consistent interpretation of union: one polity, one government. He pointed to the precedent of the union with Scotland. While there were many departments in Scotland, which mirrored their South-British equivalents, there was no independent Scottish government. Likewise, the Scottish parliamentary interest was managed, but there was no official office that would have implied Scottish subordination. Pelham's concept put a finger in the wound. The ministry did not follow a clear policy for implementing the union.

Pelham's intervention opened up a power struggle within the Cabinet to which Hardwicke and Abbot were forced to react. In October, they carefully drafted Hardwicke's *Counter Statement in Answer to the Paper of Considerations &c.* and sent it to London.[84] Hardwicke and Abbot pointed out that peace and order in Ireland were fragile. Therefore, they argued, historical deliberations and theoretical ideas on the nature of the union missed the point. The only relevant question was 'what may be the best practical mode of administering the Kings Government, in and for, this part of the United Kingdom.' By reforming the Irish departments on British reform principles, they would establish lasting control without a full amalgamation. Hardwicke and Abbot thus re-emphasised that a Lord Lieutenant, who was on the ground in Ireland, was in a position to apply the patronage more expediently than the Home Office in London, as he would have more intimate knowledge of local politics and networks. Hardwicke and Abbot renewed the 'undertaker gambit' and played on the fears and preconceptions of the Irish situation to delineate a gloomy scenario. The implementation of Pelham's plan would surrender the ministry 'to interested and irresponsible Individuals, by which means the true interests of the Country would be endangered, and instead a wholesome principle of faction, cabal, and party, would prevail throughout the Country, and excite the discontents of the

83 Ibid., fol. 103^{r}.

84 'A Counter Statement in Answer to the Paper of Considerations &c.', BL, Add. Mss. 35771, fols. 105^{r}–11^{v}.

people.'[85] At best, Irish government would fall prey to corrupt and factious local elites. At worst, he insinuated, Ireland would fall back into rebellion.

Writing in hindsight, Abbot held that the *Counterstatement* had convinced Addington to bury Pelham's plan: 'Mr. Addington and the majority of Cabinet, upon receiving the Lord-Lieutenant's answer to Lord Pelham's proposal, laid aside the discussion of the proposal, and it was never resumed.'[86] Pelham did not succeed with his plan in Cabinet, that much is true. Pelham, who had never been Abbot's choice, grew increasingly isolated. However, Addington did not support Hardwicke's and Abbot's plan either.[87] For the moment, Addington stayed with the provisional status quo in Ireland, but he closed down the Irish office in London and thereby seriously weakened Abbot's political agency. On 31 October, Henry Legge (born 1757), a member of this office, reported to Abbot that the shutdown was a direct result of Irish complaints about the reforms and added a warning:

> I believe it, even, to be in contemplation to remove you from your present office, as soon as another can be found which you would accept; & I cannot help suspecting that the orders you received to remain at Dublin instead of attending your parliamentary duty were issued in order to keep you in ignorance of, & perhaps, by those means, to facilitate, the arrangement for your change of situation.[88]

Legge's premonitions proved true. Abbot received no support for his reforms and Addington cut him out from his inner circle. Without his London office and banned from returning to London himself, Abbot could no longer manage the Irish parliamentary interest. Abbot used this involuntary relief to push for reforms in Ireland during the winter of 1801 to 1802, paying no regard to the Prime Minister's appeal to caution. When the opportunity presented itself, Addington took recourse to the plan Legge had heard about. Ironically, the death of Abbot's chief enemy in Ireland, Lord Clare, on 28 January 1802 provided this opportunity. John Mitford (1748–1830), the Speaker of the House of Commons, succeeded Clare as Lord Chancellor of Ireland and Addington offered the Speakership

85 Ibid., fols. 108^{r}–108^{v}; Hoppen, 'Incorporating Union', pp. 332–4.

86 Colchester (ed.), *Diary and Correspondence*, p. 278.

87 Hoppen, 'Incorporating Union', pp. 334–5.

88 Henry Legge to Charles Abbot, 31 October 1801, TNA, PRO 30/9/123, fols. 191–2, quote on fol. 191^{v}.

to Abbot. The Speakership was the position which Abbot had originally aspired to, so he accepted gladly and returned to London.[89]

Hardwicke continued as Lord Lieutenant until 1805, but the reforms were shut down. William Wickham (1761–1840), a former Undersecretary of Pelham's Home Office, succeeded Abbot as Chief Secretary and reversed Abbot's major reforms, such as the restructuring of the Revenue and Stamps Offices.[90] In 1805, 1815, and 1821 reform commissions addressed the Irish administrative situation. These commissions would follow in the tracks of administrative economy. Contrary to Abbot, these commissions relied on parliamentary backing and proceeded slowly.[91]

Abbot's measures followed from his expertise of economical administrative reform. He believed that the systematic implementation of the union on British principles would lead to significant improvement in Ireland. Abbot applied the conclusions of the Finance Committee and the methods developed and refined over two decades of administrative reform in Britain. In hindsight, Abbot's lack of appreciation for the diplomatic ramifications of such a major intervention into the Irish establishment may appear naive. However, Abbot had started his endeavour with the Prime Minister's backing and acted in agreement with the Lord Lieutenant. In a way, Abbot's starting position resembled the starting position of Cornwallis in Bengal.

Abbot failed because he made enemies of stakeholders with strong connections both in Ireland and in London. These stakeholders interpreted his actions as an open attack on their power base. Their harsh reactions show disappointment and shock, but also incomprehension towards Abbot's actions. Unlike the British departments, which had become used to dealing with countless surveys and regulations over the last two decades, the Irish administration had not been exposed to economical reform before. Rather, with the Protestant Ascendency acting as British suzerains in Ireland, the patrimonial functions of office had been at the forefront. Offices provided reward, distinction, rank, and power. They integrated the political elite. In preparation for the union, Cornwallis and Castlereagh played the patrimonial repertoire to its limit and intensely cooperated with personages like Clare, Beresford, and Cooke to do so. In light of this background, the extreme reactions of the Irish stakeholders made sense. To them, Abbot's actions constituted not only an affronting encroachment into their affairs, but also an almost incomprehensible breach of the customary code of

[89] Wilkinson, 'Abbot, Charles, first Baron Colchester (1757–1829)', *ODNB*.

[90] Elizabeth Sparrow, 'Wickham, William (1761–1840)', *ODNB*.

[91] McDowell, *Irish Administration*, pp. 21–3.

conduct. Abbot's critics in London took up the Irish complaints. Without Catholic emancipation, the ministry was forced to rely on the Ascendency.[92] Not one of Abbot's British adversaries criticised the concept and vision of the reforms, even when corresponding among themselves. On the contrary, these critics regularly emphasised their agreement in general terms. Instead, they criticised Abbot for his impolitic conduct that, in their view, lacked any sensitivity for the relative political significance of reforms. After two decades of economical reform, overtly patrimonial arguments had lost their cogency in Britain, but only the most fervent advocates of administrative reform could assume that the introduction of a system of economy into the offices was a political priority.

92 Bartlett, *Ireland*, p. 242.

Conclusion

In 1804, the Commissioners of Naval Inquiry triggered a scandal that shook the second Pitt ministry to its foundations. This scandal concerned Pitt's closest political companion Henry Dundas, now Viscount Melville. During his long tenure as Treasurer of the Navy (1783–1800), Dundas had not only left most of the duties to his deputy Alexander Trotter (1750–1830), but also tolerated the fact that Trotter systematically ignored basic regulations of the office. Trotter channelled the immense sums he accounted for through a private bank account, used the money to speculate in the stock market, and grew rich on the interest. Dundas had reformed the Treasurership of the Navy in 1785 by following the model of Burke's similar reform of the Army Paymastership. The inquiry revealed that Dundas had consistently disregarded the rules, which he himself had introduced. As the inquiry widened, the Commissioners of Naval Inquiry unearthed evidence suggesting that Pitt had similarly ignored reform legislation by systematically misappropriating money from the Civil List and permitting the Civil List to amass enormous debts without parliamentary approval.[1] The findings of the inquiry incited new debates on economical reform issues in Parliament. The debates once again revolved around corruption, secret influence, and ministerial extravagance. The lines of attack, which the Whig opposition had developed in the 1760s, were very much alive half a century later. A decade after the Hastings impeachment, Parliament sat once again in judgement over a prominent politician. Starting with the Melville impeachment, moral outrage fuelled a renewed interest in administrative reform that attempted to root out individual wrongdoers and submit them to exemplary punishment.[2] Had nothing changed since 1779?

1 Mark Knights, *Trust and Distrust. Corruption in Office in Britain and its Empire, 1600–1850* (Oxford, 2021), pp. 219–22; John R. Breihan, 'The Addington Party and the Navy in British Politics 1801–1806', in Craig L. Symonds (ed.), *New Aspects of Naval History* (Annapolis, 1981), pp. 175–8; John Ehrman, *The Younger Pitt*, vol. 3, *The Consuming Struggle* (London, 1996), pp. 752–80.

2 Philip Harling, *The Waning of 'Old Corruption'. The Politics of Economical Reform in Britain, 1779–1846* (Oxford, 1996), pp. 104–35; John R. Breihan, 'Economical Reform, 1785–1810', PhD thesis (Cambridge, 1977), pp. 256–399.

There was indeed a strong continuity, but it was mainly the continuity of the discrepancy between the political discourse on corruption and economical reform practice. The Melville impeachment in Parliament was a public spectacle that centred on corruption. However, over the next five years, six commissions of inquiry and seven select committees produced more than sixty reports based on the administrative principles developed since 1780. Whilst Parliament exposed and attacked individual offenders on moral grounds, the systematic reforms that followed from the outrage implemented economical ideas of administration. Administrative reforms thus depended on policy decisions, which still emerged from debates fuelled by moral critiques of corruption. Similar critiques would continue to drive policy throughout the first half of the nineteenth century via the great reform act of 1832, and only lost cogency after the repeal of the Corn Laws in 1846.[3]

Historical research on corruption seems to have produced a blind spot. Administrative arguments appear as mere appendices to political and social contestations. An intellectual history of administration can complement this incomplete picture. Debates on corruption were closely connected to administrative reform in theory and practice. The discourses depended on each other, often shared subjects and mutually affected each other's terms, but they were not identical. The more clearly the duties, authorities, and emoluments of offices were defined, the easier it became to identify malpractice. At the same time, malpractice was transformed from a moral deficiency into a mere violation of rules. Such results of administrative theory-making did not initiate a broad public debate on administrative issues. They necessarily modified the prevalent understanding of individual corruption, but, at first, hardly affected pervasive notions of 'old corruption'. However, administrative theory-making had a huge impact on administrative practice and officials' self-conceptions.

Historical research often assumes that the British administrative reforms after 1780 aimed at efficiency. The results of this study suggest a more differentiated reading. Granted, against the backdrop of the perceived crisis of state finances, the correlation of ends and means, of costs and results, was repeatedly formulated. The act that appointed CEPA in 1780 set this relation in normative terms. Subsequently, virtually all reform concepts promised that their implementation would result in a decrease of costs, at least in the long run. However, in the period under investigation, the condensed meaning of the term 'efficiency' was not yet in use.

3 Harling, *Waning of 'Old Corruption'*, pp. 136–254; Michael J. Turner, *The Age of Unease. Government and Reform in Britain, 1782–1832* (Stroud, 2000), pp. 179–257.

The normative signifier of the discourse was 'economy'. The terms are not synonymous, and this difference is important. Due to the background of crisis, the normative force of 'economy' was so strong that its relevance was rarely disputed. Instead, different actors based their arguments on widely different interpretations of what exactly economy amounted to and which of its aspects was most important in a given situation. In general, the Accounts and Fees Commissioners and the Finance Committee, as well as like-minded authors of particular reform papers, emphasised functional improvement and the overcoming of patrimonial structures over financial savings. This emphasis was sometimes explicit, for instance when Charles Cornwallis warned of 'false economy'. More often, the emphasis remained implicit. Differing understandings of 'economy' were therefore at the heart of the tension between administrative reasoning and the political debate, which generally emphasised retrenchment.

This book began with the notion that the inquiries of CEPA marked a clear threshold between pre-modern and modern administration. Even more frequently, the *Northcote Trevelyan Report* of 1854 is set as the beginning of the modern Civil Service. Such ideas overestimate the aspect of the entry exams and the immediate impact of the *Report*. By no means did the *Report* create the modern Civil Service over night. As this study shows, it is equally wrong to consider the mid-nineteenth century administrative apparatus as entirely unreformed and patrimonial. CEPA did not anticipate the *Northcote Trevelyan Report* or the Victorian Civil Service. However, they do mark a starting point for economical administrative thought. Administrative ideas continued to be refined between Parliament, government, countless reform commissions, and, increasingly, also in a printed discourse. Economical reform ideas endured into the nineteenth century even though 'reform' itself became a highly contested concept that marked the heated and, at times, bloody conflicts between the emerging labour movement and uncompromising High Tory governments. Administrative reformers such as George Harrison (1767–1841), the first Permanent Undersecretary of the Treasury, reacted by making a distinction between 'radical reform' – the demands for parliamentary reform by the labour movement, which they despised, and 'the legitimate object of rational reform', the ongoing 'gradual improvement in our system of jurisprudence or of civil government'.[4]

[4] George Harrison, *Fragments and Scraps of History* (London, 1834), p. 73; Meurer, 'Dawning of the Age of Reform', pp. 73–6.

Britain was the only country in which the administrative reforms of the nineteenth century ultimately resulted in a downsizing of the administrative personnel.[5] A case can be made that the enduring primacy of 'economy' with its inherent tension between administrative improvement and retrenchment was instrumental for this development. Getting to the bottom of this question will be a complex undertaking. Too often, nineteenth-century administrative reforms leading towards the fully bureaucratised state have simply been labelled as 'Benthamite'. Jeremy Bentham appears as a *deus ex machina*, whose name seems to suffice as a characterisation of a wide range of utilitarian persuasions. Given his close proximity to agents of late eighteenth-century administrative reform, the present study suggests rather to reverse the perspective and ask how the concrete administrative reform processes influenced Bentham's ideas.[6]

Teleological fallacies loom large in administrative history. Drawing a premature connection between late-eighteenth century ideas and modernity results in the assumption that administrative reforms automatically led to bureaucracy and efficiency. Such interpretations followed from the twentieth-century notion that bureaucracy was the logical end result of modern rationalisation. Similar to the way in which Francis Fukuyama presented liberal democracy as the final form of government, administrative historians assumed that bureaucracy was the end of administrative history.[7] This interpretation is no longer convincing, as administrative systems have been changing fundamentally since the Thatcherite reforms of the 1980s. This ongoing process is marked by the term 'new public management'. Public administration is no longer conceived along the lines of fixed organisation and regular hierarchies, but rather in terms of markets and networks. Mark Bevir's lucid analysis of this transformation reveals a striking parallel to the subject of this study. Once more, theories of the social sciences are adapted in the reform of public administration and gradually take hold. On the one hand, new institutional structures and official self-conceptions have since come to shape new practices. On the other hand, habits, vested interests,

5 Philip Harling, 'The Politics of Administrative Change in Britain, 1780–1850', in Erk V. Heyen (ed.), *Administration and Administrative Law in France and England (18th/19th c.)* (Baden-Baden, 1996), 191–212, pp. 192–7.

6 Leonard Hume's *Bentham and Bureaucracy* explains their genealogy from a plethora of eighteenth-century European ideas, but hardly relates to the contemporary reform process. Leonard Hume, *Bentham and Bureaucracy* (Cambridge, 1981).

7 Cf. Francis Fukuyama, *The End of History and the Last Man* (New York, 2006 [1992]).

and established ways of working remain an enduring force. Bureaucratical administration has not ended overnight.[8]

The reports of CEPA did not bring about a sudden switch to modern bureaucracy either but the Commissioners' theory had a considerable impact on subsequent reforms and administrative practice. The semantic analysis shows that both patrimonial and economical notions coexisted (and sometimes clashed) until well into the 1790s. In any case, the lines between patrimonial and economical reasoning were not clearly drawn. However, the general tendency saw economical reasoning increasingly gaining legitimacy, while patrimonial reasoning lost it. The great surveys and many smaller inquiries reiterated systematic assumptions. They forced actors in the departments to react to economical categories and to justify aberrations from best practice models, which the comparison of establishments revealed. After an initial phase of patrimonial bafflement, their individual stances mostly corresponded to their principals' proximity to the centre of power. Members of Pitt's Cabinet did not at first feel the need to engage with reform inquiries in a detailed manner and adhered to their patrimonial preconceptions. Actors further removed from the political power centre, for instance, the Clerks of the Roads at the Post Office, at least tried to frame their interests in an economical language, even though their understanding of economy had little in common with the administrative concepts developed by the commissions.

The administrative reforms in Britain, British India, and Ireland were closely connected. All three cases referred to the economical reform ideas developed by CEPA and subsequent inquiries. They took place in the framework of the British empire. Their protagonists shared the same cultural and constitutional backgrounds and they partook in interconnected personal networks. This study corroborates the conviction of recent research, which emphasises the importance of personal networks as a foundation of the British empire in the eighteenth and into the nineteenth century.[9] It is also against this background that Cornwallis' personal agency for the reforms in British India must be set so high. Crucial flows of knowledge and information took place not through institutions but through personal connections. The flows of information, however, were interest-driven and subjective, as the Irish case shows. In contrast to parliamentary reform, economical

[8] Mark Bevir, *A Theory of Governance* (Berkeley, 2013), pp. 129–66; for Bevir's empirical examples cf. e.g. Mark Bevir, *Governance. A Very Short Introduction* (Oxford, 2012).

[9] Natasha Glaisyer, 'Networking, Trade and Exchange in the Eighteenth-Century British Empire', *Historical Journal*, 47:2 (2004), 451–76; Zoë Laidlaw, *Colonial Connections 1815–45. Patronage, the Information Revolution, and Colonial Government* (Manchester, 2005).

reform had not been a major issue in Ireland before 1801. Nevertheless, the Irish case cannot be explained without this network character. Abbot failed because he ignored the entangled foundations of Anglo-Irish politics.

It is less easy to relate the three cases to contemporary developments in continental Europe. Jos Raadschelders has characterised the period from 1780 to 1820 as a watershed in European administrative history, as the 'administrative *Sattelzeit*'.[10] Raadschelders specifies a number of characteristic changes in administration: departmentalisation, the separation of office and office-holders, and the regularisation of salaries and pensions. These major changes, he argues, drew on conceptual roots that had been developed in the previous century and depended on contemporary constitutional developments such as the separation of public and private and of church and state, and the creation of written constitutions. Raadschelders claims that, varying forms and national backgrounds notwithstanding, these changes took place simultaneously throughout Europe.[11]

Even accepting a thesis of simultaneous emergence in reaction to complex social and constitutional developments, the question remains as to how these processes were entangled and how they may have affected each other. Surprisingly, even with the in-depth view the methodological framework of this study allowed for, few direct connections and transfers have become visible. Burke pointed to Necker's fiscal policies and reforms in his 1780 speech, but these deliberations were not taken up in subsequent discussions. Continental administrative practice or reasoning played hardly any role for the British actors, nor did their backgrounds suggest a particular familiarity with continental conditions. Robert Bernsee's study on bureaucratisation and the discourse on corruption in German territories allows a reverse view. Bernsee shows that Britain did serve as an example for administrative arguments in the first decades of the nineteenth century. German publicists like Adam Müller (1779–1829) or Heinrich Friedrich Karl vom und zum Stein (1757–1831) notably referred to Edmund Burke in order to argue against the pitfalls of new forms of administration and an overpowering state. They proposed decentralisation instead and to keep administration cheap by delegating duties to the local estates.[12] The German publicists in question thus did not draw on current British administrative

10 Jos C. N. Raadschelders, 'Changing European Ideas about the Public Servant. A Theoretical and Methodological Framework', in Fritz Sager and Patrick Overeem (eds.), *The European Civil Servant: A Shared Administrative Identity?* (Colchester, 2015), 15–34.

11 Ibid., pp. 11–12.

12 Robert Bernsee, *Moralische Erneuerung. Korruption und bürokratische Reformen in Bayern und Preußen, 1780–1820* (Gottingen, 2018).

ideas after all. Rather, they employed Burke's conservative ideas and their conventional view of the British constitution and British customary local administration without realising that in Britain, too, current administrative ideas favoured central, departmentalised, and systematic administration, whilst the local institutions praised by the Germans were increasingly regarded as patrimonial and corrupt relics. The development of administrative reform ideas in the two countries was not directly intertwined, but the debates on corruption and public welfare were.

British administrative reform ideas drew on scientific discourses, especially on utilitarian ideas and political economy. Contrary to administrative discourses, scientific discourses interacted across borders. The exchange among the pan-European *république de lettres* is well researched and has also been noted in the present study, for instance, with regard to Steuart's wide continental reception or John Sinclair's active engagement with continental statistics. In his studies on contemporary French administrative reforms, Èric Brian has emphasised their dependence on scientific discoveries. Brian has shown how, during the last decades of the *ancien régime*, academic and administrative circles touched at the Académie française. Nicolas de Condorcet (1743–94) and others adopted mathematical innovations for the needs of state administration. The results not only determined the methods of nascent demographical statistics and tasks bordering on engineering, such as road building; they also changed the overall epistemological foundations of administrative practice and, thereby, prepared the ground for the revolutionary and especially the Napoleonic reforms.[13]

The perspective you adopt determines what you can see. This book inquired into the genesis of administrative ideas and their significance for processes of reform. Emphasising agency, this book focused on a relatively short period and rejected teleological narratives of bureaucratisation. The results do not claim to represent the whole story. Structural-historical frameworks and path dependencies that become visible in the long-term perspective of historical sociology can be equally valid. When classifying macro-narratives such as clear paths to modernity or the formative power of unfolding industrial capitalism, one should be equally aware that a change in scale greatly alters the picture. The emerging administrative language prefigured forms and standards of subsequent reform processes, but it did not predetermine their direction.

[13] Éric Brian, *La mesure de l'Etat. Administrateurs et géomètres au XVIIIe siècle* (Paris, 1994); id., 'Mathematics, Administrative Reforms and Social Science in France at the End of the Eighteenth Century', in Johan Heilbron, Lars Magnusson, and Björn Wittrock (eds.), *The Rise of the Social Sciences and the Formation of Modernity: Conceptual Change in Context, 1750–1850* (London, 1996), 207–24.

Bibliography

Archives

British Library, London (BL)
Add. Mss. 33108 (Pelham Papers)
Add. Mss. 33542 (Bentham Papers)
Add. Mss. 34455 (Auckland Papers)
Add. Mss. 35731 (Hardwicke Papers)
Add. Mss. 35771 (Hardwicke Papers)
Add. Mss. 38307 (Liverpool Papers)
India Office Records
IOR/H/369 (Home Miscellaneous)
IOR/P/50/58 (Bengal Revenue Consultations)

Caird Library, National Maritime Museum, Greenwich (NMM)
JCK/7 (Jackson Papers)
MID 14/6 (Middleton Papers)
MID 14/11 (Middleton Papers)

The National Archives, Kew (TNA)
ADM 1/3525 (Admiralty Papers)
PC 1/19/27 (Privy Council Papers)
PC 1/20/31 (Privy Council Papers)
PC 1/24/43 (Privy Council Papers)
PC 2/138 (Privy Council Papers)
PC 2/142 (Privy Council Papers)
PC 2/158 (Privy Council Papers)
PC 4/5 (Privy Council Papers)
PC 4/7 (Privy Council Papers)
PRO 30/8/120 (Chatham Papers)
PRO 30/8/148 (Chatham Papers)
PRO 30/8/231 (Chatham Papers)
PRO 30/8/282 (Chatham Papers)
PRO 30/9/110 (Colchester Papers)
PRO 30/9/113 (Colchester Papers)
PRO 30/9/123 (Colchester Papers)
PRO 30/9/124 (Colchester Papers)
PRO 30/9/136 (Colchester Papers)

PRO 30/9/137 (Colchester Papers)
PRO 30/9/152 (Colchester Papers)
PRO 30/9/168 (Colchester Papers)
T 29/45 (Treasury: minute books)
T 29/52 (Treasury: minute books)

Royal Mail Archive, London (RMA)
POST 59/178 (Walsingham Papers)

William L. Clements Library, Ann Arbor, Michigan (WCL)
Shelburne Papers, vol. 101
Shelburne Papers, vol. 114
Shelburne Papers, vol. 115
Shelburne Papers, vol. 122
Shelburne Papers, vol. 125
Shelburne Papers, vol. 129
Shelburne Papers, vol. 135
Shelburne Papers, vol. 151
Shelburne Papers, vol. 162
Shelburne Papers, vol. 166
Shelburne Papers, vol. 168, boxes 1, 3, 4

Printed Sources

Abbot, Charles, *Rules and orders on the plea side of the court of King's Bench beginning in Easter Term, 1731, and ending in Trinity Term, 1795. With preface and index* (London, 1795).

The Annual Biography and Obituary. For the year 1822 (London, 1822).

The Annual Register, or a View of the History, Politicks, and Literature, for the Year 1763 (London, 1764).

Anson, William R. (ed.), *Autobiography and Political Correspondence of Augustus Henry Third Duke of Grafton. From Hitherto Unpublished Documents in the Possession of his Family* (London, 1898).

Askari, Syed H. (ed.), *Fort William – India House Correspondence*, vol. 16, *Foreign, Secret and Political, 1787–1791*, Indian Records Series (Delhi, 1976).

Aspinall, A. (ed.), *Cornwallis in Bengal. The Administrative and Judicial Reforms of Lord Cornwallis in Bengal, together with Accounts of the Commercial Expansion of the East India Company, 1786–1793, and of the Foundation of Penang, 1786–1793* (Manchester, 1931).

Beccaria Bonesaria, Caesar, *A Discourse on Public Oeconomy and Commerce* (London, 1769).

——, *An Essay on Crimes and Punishments. Translated from the Italian* (Edinburgh, 1778).

Bentham, Jeremy, 'A Fragment on Government', in H. Burns and H. L. A. Hart (eds.), *A Comment on the Commentaries and a Fragment on Government, The Collected Works of Jeremy Bentham. Principles of Legislation* (London, 1977), 393–501.

Bentham, Maria S., *The Life of Brigadier-General Sir Samuel Bentham, K.S.G. Formerly Inspector-General of Naval Works Lately a Commissioner of his Majesty's Navy with the distinct Duty of Civil Architect and Engineer of the Navy* (London, 1862).

Bentham, Samuel, *Answers to the Comptroller's Objections* (1800).

—, *Financial Reform Scrutinized. in a Letter to Sir Henry Parnell* (London, 1830).

—, *Naval Essays, Or Essays on the Management of Public Concerns as Exemplified in the Naval Department; Considered as a Branch of the Business of Warfare* (London, 1828).

—, *Naval Papers. And Documents Referred to in Naval Essays* (London, 1828).

—, *Services rendered in the Civil Department of the Navy* (London, 1813).

Bielfeld, Jacob F., *The Elements of Universal Erudition. Containing an Analytical Abridgment of the Sciences, Polite Arts, and Belles Lettres. By Baron Bielfeld, Secretary of Legation to the King of Prussia [...] Author of the Political Institutes, &c. Translated from the last Edition printed in Berlin. By W. Hooper, M.D.* (3 vols., Dublin, 1771).

—, *Institutions Politiques* (4 vols., Paris, 1760).

—, *Letters of Baron Bielfeld. Secretary of Legation to the King of Prussia [...] Author of the Political Institutes. Translated from German by Mr. Hooper* (4 vols., London, 1770).

Blackstone, William, *Commentaries on the Laws of England* (4 vols., Oxford, 1765–9).

Bolingbroke, Henry St. John, *A Dissertation Upon Parties* (London, 1735).

Burgh, James, *Political Disquisitions. Or an Enquiry into Public Errors, Defects, and Abuses* (2 vols., London, 1774–5).

Burke, Edmund, 'Speech on Economical Reform, 11 February 1780', in W. M. Elofson and A. Woods (eds.), *Party, Parliament, and the American War,* The Writings and Speeches of Edmund Burke, 3 (Oxford, 1996), 481–551.

—, 'Speech on Public Expenses, 15 December 1779', in W. M. Elofson and A. Woods (eds.), *Party, Parliament, and the American War,* The Writings and Speeches of Edmund Burke, 3 (Oxford, 1996), 466–76.

—, 'Thoughts on the Present Discontents', in Paul Langford (ed.), *Party, Parliament, and the American Crisis,* The Writings and Speeches of Edmund Burke, 2 (Oxford, 1981), 241–323.

Campbell, John, *The Lives of the Chief Justices of England,* vol. 4, 7th edn. (New York, 1878).

Clinton, Henry, *A Letter from Lieut. Gen. Henry Clinton, K.B. to the Commissioners of Public Accounts, relative to Some Observations in their Seventh*

Report, which may be judged to imply Censure on the late Commanders in Chief of His Majesty's Army in North America (London, 1784).

Clarke, Richard (ed.), *The Regulations of the Government of Fort William in Bengal in force at the end of 1853*, vol. 1, *Regulations from 1793 to 1805* (London, 1854).

Colchester, Charles (ed.), *The Diary and Correspondence of Charles Abbot, Lord Colchester. Speaker of the House of Commons 1802–1817* (3 vols., London, 1861).

Colquhoun, Patrick, *A Treatise on the Police of the Metropolis. Explaining the Various Crimes and Misdemeanors which at Present are Felt as a Pressure upon the Community; and Suggesting Remedies for their Prevention* (London, 1796).

Cross, Arthur L., *Eighteenth Century Documents Relating to the Royal Forests, the Sheriffs and Smuggling* (New York, London, 1928).

Dinwiddy, J. R. (ed.), *The Correspondence of Jeremy Bentham*, vol. 6, *January 1798 to December 1801, The Collected Works of Jeremy Bentham* (Oxford, 1984).

Eden, William, *Principles of Penal Law*, 3rd edn. (London, 1775).

Fitzmaurice, E. G. P. F. and Lansdowne, W. P. M., *Life of William, Earl of Shelburne, Afterwards First Marquess of Landsdowne: With Extracts from His Papers and Correspondence*, vol. 3 (1876).

The Former and Present State of the Principal Public Offices in the Kingdom; [...] *with Tables of the Established Fees Received in Most of the Said Offices* [...] (London, 1794).

Gibson, Edward, *Pitt. Some Chapters of his Life and Times* (London, New York, Bombay, 1898).

Gleig, G. R. (ed.), *The Memoirs of the Life of the Honourable Warren Hastings, First Governor General of India. Compiled from Original Papers*, vol. 1 (London, 1841).

Hale, Matthew, *A Short Treatise Touching Sheriffs Accompts* (1683).

Harcourt, Vernon Leveson (ed.), *The Diaries and Correspondence of the Right Hon. George Rose. Containing Original Letters of the Most Distinguished Statesmen of his Day* (2 vols., London, 1860).

Harrington, James, 'A System of Politics,' in John G. A. Pocock (ed.), *The Political Works of James Harrington*, Cambridge Studies in the History and Theory of Politics (Cambridge, New York, 1977), 833–54.

Harrison, George, *Fragments and Scraps of History* (2 vols., London, 1834).

Hathaway, W. S., *The Speeches of William Pitt*, vol. 1 (London, 1806).

'Historical Chronicle', *Gentleman's Magazine* (January 1780).

The History of the Trial of Warren Hastings, Esq. Late Governor-General of Bengal, before the High Court of Parliament in Westminster-Hall, on an Impeachment by the Commons of Great-Britain, for High Crimes and Misdemeanours (London, 1796).

Hobbes, Thomas, *Leviathan. Or the Matter, Forme and Power of a Commonwealth Ecclesiasticall and Civil* (Oxford, 1946 [1651]).

Holdsworth, W. S., *A History of English Law*, vol. 1 (London, 1903).

Hume, David, 'Of Commerce', in Eugene F. Miller (ed.), *Essays, Moral, Political, and Literary* (Indianapolis, 1987), 253–67.

——, 'On the Independency of Parliament', in Eugene F. Miller (ed.), *Essays, Moral, Political, and Literary* (Indianapolis, 1987), 42–6.

——, 'That Politics may be Reduced to a Science', in Eugene F. Miller (ed.), *Essays, Moral, Political, and Literary* (Indianapolis, 1987), 14–31.

——, *A Treatise on Human Nature* (Oxford, 1896 [1739]).

Lambert, Sheila, House of Commons Sessional Papers of the Eighteenth Century, vol. 35: Bills 1782–1783 and 1783–1784 (Wilmington, 1975).

Laslett, Peter (ed.), *John Locke: Two Treatises of Government. A Critical Edition with an Introduction and Apparatus Criticus* (Cambridge, 1960).

Laughton, John K. (ed.), *Letters and Papers of Charles, Lord Barham Admiral of the Red Squadron, 1758–1813*, Publications of the Navy Records Society (3 vols., London, 1907–11).

Letters of the Marquis Wellesley. Respecting the College of Fort William (London, 1812).

MacDonagh, Michael (ed.), *The Viceroy's Post-Bag. Correspondence Hitherto Unpublished of the Earl of Hardwicke, First Lord Lieutenant of Ireland after the Union* (London, 1904).

Marshall, Peter J. (ed.), *India: The Launching of the Hastings Impeachment 1786–1788*, The Writings and Speeches of Edmund Burke, 6 (Oxford, 1991).

Martin, Montgomery, *The Despatches, Minutes, and Correspondence, of the Marquess Wellesley, K. G. during his Administration in India* (2 vols., London, 1836).

Monckton-Jones, M. E., *Warren Hastings in Bengal* (Oxford, 1918).

Montesquieu, Charles Louis de Secondat de, 'De l'esprit des lois', in Roger Caillois (ed.), *Montesquieu. Oeuvres complètes*, vol. 2, Bibliothèque de la Pléiade (Paris, 1951), 973–1574.

Musgrave, William, *A collection of all the statutes now in force, relating to the revenue and officers of the Customs in Great Britain and the Plantations* (2 vols., London, 1780).

The New Annual Register. Or General Repository of History, Politics, and Literature for the Year 1796 (London, 1797).

Paine, Thomas, 'Common Sense', in Moncure D. Conway (ed.), *The Writings of Thomas Paine: 1774–1779* (New York, 1967), 69–120.

Prasad, Bisheshwar (ed.), *Fort William – India House Correspondence and other Contemporary Papers Relating thereto*, vol. 6, *1770–1772*, Indian Records Series (Delhi, 1960).

Price, Richard, 'Additional Observations on the Nature and Value of Civil Liberty, and the War with America', in David O. Thomas (ed.), *Richard Price:*

Political Writings, Cambridge Texts in the History of Political Thought (Cambridge, 1991), 76–100.

——, 'Britain's Happiness, and the Proper Improvement of it', in David O. Thomas (ed.), *Richard Price: Political Writings*, Cambridge Texts in the History of Political Thought (Cambridge, 1991 [1759]), 1–13.

——, 'Observations on the Nature of Civil Liberty, the Principles of Government, and the Justice and Policy of the War with America', in David O. Thomas (ed.), *Richard Price: Political Writings*, Cambridge Texts in the History of Political Thought (Cambridge, 1991 [1759]), 20–75.

Priestley, Joseph, 'Essay on the First Principles of Government', in J. T. Rutt (ed.), *Theological and Miscellaneous Works of Joseph Priestley* (New York, 1972), 1–144.

Roe, William, *The Private Memorandums of William Roe of Withdean in the County of Sussex 1775–1809*, Printed for Private Circulation (Brighton, 1928).

Ross, Charles (ed.), *Correspondence of Charles, First Marquis Cornwallis*, 2nd edn. (3 vols., London, 1859).

Russell, Francis, 'Report concerning the Revenues of the Crown in the Collection of Sheriffs in England and Wales, and the Manner of their Accounting in the Exchequer with Plans for the Increase of those Revenues, and Retrenchment of the present Expences of accounting for them, February 15th 1783', in Arthur L. Cross (ed.), *Eighteenth Century Documents Relating to the Royal Forests the Sheriffs and Smuggling* (New York, London, 1928), 165–233.

Sergeant, Thomas and Lowber, John C. (eds.), *Reports of Cases Argued and Determined in the English Courts of Common Law*, vol. 26 (Philadelphia, 1853).

Sinclair, John, *The History of the Public Revenue of the British Empire* (Dublin, 1785).

——, *The Statistical Account of Scotland. Drawn up from the Communications of the Ministers of the Different Parishes* (21 vols., Edinburgh, 1791–9).

Sinh, Raghubir (ed.), *Fort William – India House Correspondence*, vol. 10, *1786–1788*, Indian Records Series (Delhi, 1972).

Smith, Adam, *An Inquiry into the Nature and Causes of the Wealth of Nations*, The Glasgow Edition of the Works and Correspondence of Adam Smith, ed. by R. H. Campbell, A. S. Skinner and W. B. Todd (2 vols., Oxford, 1976 [1776]).

'The Speech of Mr. Chamberlain Wilkes, when he presented the Freedom of the City of London to the Most Noble the Marquis Cornwallis', *The Sun* (21 April 1794).

Statutes at Large (various vols).

Steuart, James, *An Inquiry into the Principles of Political Oeconomy*, ed. by Andrew S. Skinner (2 vols., Edinburgh, London, 1966 [1767]).

——, *An Inquiry into the Principles of Political Oeconomy. Being an Essay on the Science of Domestic Policy in Free Nations. In which are particularly considered Population, Trade, Industry, Money, Coin, Interest, Circulation, Banks, Exchange, Public Credit, and Taxes* (2 vols., London, 1767).

Teignmouth, *Memoir of the Life and Correspondence of John Lord Teignmouth* (2 vols., London, 1843).
Vane, Charles (ed.), *Memoirs and Correspondence of Viscount Castlereagh, Second Marquess of Londonderry*, vol. 4, *Concessions to Catholics and Dissenters; Emmets Insurrection* (London, 1849).
Wilkes, John, 'The North Briton No. 45, Saturday, April 23, 1763', *The Works of the Celebrated John Wilkes, Esq: Formerly Published under the Title of The North Briton*, vol. 2 (London, [1765]), 227–41.
Wyvill, Christopher, *Political Papers. Chiefly Respecting the Attempt of the County of York*, vol. 1 (York, 1794).

Reports of Commissions and Committees

Commissioners for Examining the Public Accounts (CEPA)

'First Report, 27 November 1780', *JHC 38: 31 October 1780 to 10 October 1782*, 74–85.
'Second Report, 31 January 1781', *JHC 38: 31 October 1780 to 10 October 1782*, 141–54.
'Third Report, 7 March 1781', *JHC 38: 31 October 1780 to 10 October 1782*, 247–70.
'Fourth Report, 9 April 1781', *JHC 38: 31 October 1780 to 10 October 1782*, 380–94.
'Fifth Report, 10 August 1781', *JHC 38: 31 October 1780 to 10 October 1782*, 572–92.
'Sixth Report, 9 February 1782', *JHC 38: 31 October 1780 to 10 October 1782*, 702–78.
'Seventh Report, 18 June 1782', *JHC 38: 31 October 1780 to 10 October 1782*, 1066–1112.
'Eighth Report, 12 December 1782', *JHC 39: 26 November 1782 to 24 March 1784*, 45–80.
'Ninth Report, 31 March 1783', *JHC 39: 26 November 1782 to 24 March 1784*, 325–44.
'Tenth Report, 2 July 1783', *JHC 39: 26 November 1782 to 24 March 1784*, 522–764.
'Eleventh Report, 5 December 1783', *JHC 39: 26 November 1782 to 24 March 1784*, 771–823.
'Twelfth Report, 11 June 1784', *JHC 40: 18 May 1784 to 1 December 1785*, 111–93.
'Thirteenth Report, 21 March 1785', *JHC 40: 18 May 1784 to 1 December 1785*, 653–747.
'Fourteenth Report, 27 January 1786', *JHC 41: 24 January 1786 to 14 December 1786*, 9–151.
'Fifteenth Report, 1 March 1787', *JHC 42: 23 January 1787 to 16 October 1787*, 7–264.

Commissioners on Fees

Reports of the Commissioners Appointed to Inquire into the Fees Gratuities Perquisites and Emoluments which Are or Have Been Lately Received in the Several Public Offices (London, 1793):

'First Report, Secretaries of State', ibid., 1–20.

'Second Report, Treasury', ibid., 22–36.

'Third Report, Admiralty', ibid., 37–54.

'Fourth Report, Treasurer of the Navy', ibid., 55–67.

'Fifth Report, Commissioners of the Navy', ibid., 68–104.

'Sixth Report, Dock Yards', ibid., 105–56.

'Seventh Report, Sick and Hurt Office', ibid., 157–68.

'Eighth Report, Victualling Office', ibid., 169–227.

'Ninth Report, Naval and Victualling Departments at Foreign Ports', ibid., 228–48.

'Tenth Report, Post Office', ibid., 249–312.

Finance Committee

Lambert, Sheila, *House of Commons Sessional Papers of the Eighteenth Century*, vols. 109–14: Proceedings on the Finance Committee Reports 1798–1803 (Wilmington, 1975).

'Fourth Report', *SP 107*. 1797 (Wilmington, 1975), 189–329.

'Fifth Report', *SP 107*. 1797 (Wilmington, 1975), 331–409.

'Sixth Report', *SP 108*. 1797 (Wilmington, 1975), 3–65.

'Seventh Report', *SP 108*. 1797 (Wilmington, 1975), 67–201.

'Eighth Report', *SP 108*. 1797 (Wilmington, 1975), 203–73.

'Tenth Report', *SP 108*. 1797 (Wilmington, 1975), 319–33.

'Eleventh Report', *SP 108*. 1797 (Wilmington, 1975), 335–59.

'Seventeenth Report', *SP 109*. 1797 (Wilmington, 1975), 145–89.

'Eighteenth Report', *SP 109*. 1797 (Wilmington, 1975), 191–205.

'Twentieth Report', *SP 109*. 1797 (Wilmington, 1975), 389–433.

'Twenty-second Report', *SP 109*. 1797 (Wilmington, 1975), 509–617.

'Twenty-seventh Report', *SP 111*. 1798 (Wilmington, 1975), 41–315.

'Twenty-eighth Report', *SP 112*. 1798 (Wilmington, 1975), 3–215.

'Thirty-first Report', *SP 113*. 1798 (Wilmington, 1975), 3–73.

'Thirty-second Report', *SP 113*. 1798 (Wilmington, 1975), 75–215.

Research Literature

Aimo, Piero, 'The History of Public Administration: Some Brief Reflections on an Uncertain Discipline', *Jahrbuch für europäische Verwaltungsgeschichte*, 14 (2002), 317–35.

Alavi, Seema (ed.), *The Eighteenth Century in India*, Oxford in India Readings (Oxford, 2002).

Allen, Douglas W., *The Institutional Revolution. Measurement and the Economic Emergence of the Modern World*, Markets and Governments in Economic History (Chicago, 2012).

Anderson, Gary M. and Tollison, Robert D., 'Sir James Steuart as the Apotheosis of Mercantilism and His Relation to Adam Smith', *Southern Economic Journal*, 51:2 (1984), 456–68.

Archer, Jayne E., Goldring, Elizabeth, and Knight, Sarah, *The Intellectual and Cultural World of the Early Modern Inns of Court* (Manchester, New York, 2011).

Arnold, David, 'Hunger in the Garden of Plenty. The Bengal Famine of 1770', in Alessa Johns (ed.), *Dreadful Visitations: Confronting Natural Catastrophe in the Age of Enlightenment* (New York, 1999), 81–111.

Ashworth, William J., '"System of Terror". Samuel Bentham, Accountability and Dockyard Reform during the Napoleonic Wars', *Social History*, 23:1 (1998), 63–79.

Aylmer, Gerald E., 'Bureaucracy', in Peter Burke (ed.), *The New Cambridge Modern History* (Cambridge, 1979), 164–200.

Baker, John H., *An Introduction to English Legal History*, 3rd edn. (London, Boston, 1990).

Bartlett, Thomas, 'Ireland during the Revolutionary and Napoleonic Wars, 1791–1815', in James Kelly (ed.), *The Cambridge History of Ireland* (Cambridge et al., 2018), 74–101.

——, *Ireland. A History* (Cambridge, 2010).

Baugh, Daniel A., *The Global Seven Years War, 1754–1763. Britain and France in a Great Power Contest*, Modern Wars in Perspective (Harlow, New York, 2011).

Bayly, Christopher A., *The Birth of the Modern World 1780–1914. Global Connections and Comparisons* (Malden, 2004).

——, 'The British Military-Fiscal State and Indigenous Resistance. India 1750–1820', in Lawrence Stone (ed.), *An Imperial State at War: Britain from 1689 to 1815* (London, New York, 1994), 322–54.

——, *Imperial Meridian. The British Empire and the World, 1780–1830*, Studies in Modern History (London, 1989).

——, 'Wellesley, Richard, Marquess Wellesley (1760–1842)', *ODNB*.

Bayly, Christopher A. and Prior, Katherine, 'Cornwallis, Charles, first Marquess Cornwallis (1738–1805)', *ODNB*.

Beaglehole, T. H., *Thomas Munro and the Development of Administrative Policy in Madras 1792–1818. The Origins of 'the Munro System'* (Cambridge, 1966).

Bernsee, Robert, *Moralische Erneuerung. Korruption und bürokratische Reformen in Bayern und Preußen, 1780–1820* (Gottingen, 2018).

Bernstein, Jeremy, *Dawning of the Raj. The Life and Trials of Warren Hastings* (Chicago, 2000).

Bevir, Mark, *Governance. A Very Short Introduction*, Very Short Introductions (Oxford, 2012).

—, *A Theory of Governance*, Studies in Governance (Berkeley et al., 2013).
Binney, John, *British Public Finance and Administration 1774–92* (Oxford, 1958).
Blanning, Timothy C. W. and Wende, Peter (eds.), *Reform in Great Britain and Germany. 1750–1850*, Proceedings of the British Academy, 100 (Oxford, 1999).
Bödeker, Hans E., 'Ausprägungen der historischen Semantik in den historischen Kulturwissenschaften', in Hans E. Bödeker and Mark Bevir (eds.), *Begriffsgeschichte, Diskursgeschichte, Metapherngeschichte*, Göttinger Gespräche zur Geschichtswissenschaft (Göttingen, 2002), 7–27.
Bolitho, Hector and Peel, Derek, *The Drummonds of Charing Cross* (London, 1967).
Bolton, Geoffrey C., *The Passing of the Irish Act of Union. A Study in Parliamentary Politics*, Oxford Historical Series (Oxford, 1966).
Bonwick, Colin, *English Radicals and the American Revolution* (Chapel Hill, 1977).
Borsay, Peter, 'Urban Life and Culture', in Harry T. Dickinson (ed.), *A Companion to Eighteenth-Century Britain*, Blackwell Companions to British History (Malden et al., 2002), 196–207.
Bourke, Richard, *Empire and Revolution. The Political Life of Edmund Burke* (Princeton, Oxford, 2015).
Bourne, J. M., *Patronage and Society in Nineteenth-Century England* (London, Baltimore, 1986).
Bowen, Huw V., 'British India, 1765–1813: The Metropolitan Context', in Peter J. Marshall (ed.), *The Eighteenth Century*, The Oxford History of the British Empire, repr. (Oxford, 2006), 530–51.
—, *The Business of Empire. The East India Company and Imperial Britain* (Cambridge, 2006).
—, 'The "Little Parliament". The General Court of the East India Company, 1750–1784', *The Historical Journal*, 34:4 (1991), 857–72.
—, *Revenue and Reform. The Indian Problem in British Politics 1757–1773*, 2nd edn. (Cambridge et al, 2002).
Bowen, John, 'The East India Company's Education of Its Own Servants', *The Journal of the Royal Asiatic Society of Great Britain and Ireland*, 3/4 (1955), 105–23.
Breihan, John R. 'The Addington Party and the Navy in British Politics 1801–1806', in Craig L. Symonds (ed.), *New Aspects of Naval History*. Selected Papers presented at the fourth Naval History Symposium, United States Naval Academy, 25–6 October 1979 (Annapolis, 1981), 163–89.
—, 'William Pitt and the Commission on Fees, 1785–1801', *Historical Journal*, 27:1 (1984), 59–81.
Brett, Annabel and Tully, James (eds.), *Rethinking the Foundations of Modern Political Thought* (Cambridge, 2006).

Brewer, John, *Party Ideology and Popular Politics at the Accession of George III* (Cambridge, 1976).

——, *The Sinews of Power. War, Money and the English State, 1688–1783* (London, 1989).

——, 'The Wilkites and the Law, 1763–74. A Study of Radical Notions of Governance', in John Brewer and John A. Styles (eds.), *An Ungovernable People: The English and their Law in the Seventeenth and Eighteenth Centuries* (London, 1980), 129–71.

Brian, Éric, *La mesure de l'Etat. Administrateurs et géomètres au XVIIIe siècle*, L'Évolution de l'humanité (Paris, 1994).

——, 'Mathematics, Administrative Reforms and Social Science in France at the End of the Eighteenth Century', in Johan Heilbron, Lars Magnusson, and Björn Wittrock (eds.), *The Rise of the Social Sciences and the Formation of Modernity: Conceptual Change in Context, 1750–1850*, Sociology of the Sciences. A Yearbook (Dordrecht, Boston, London, 1996), 207–24.

Broadie, Alexander (ed.), *Scottish Enlightenment. An Anthology* (Edinburgh, 1997).

Brockliss, Laurence, 'Science, the Universities, and Other Public Spaces. Teaching Science in Europe and the Americas', in Roy Porter (ed.), *Eighteenth-Century Science*, The Cambridge History of Science (Cambridge, 2016), 44–86.

Broomfield, J. H., 'Lord Sandwich at the Admiralty Board. Politics and the British Navy, 1771–1778', *Mariner's Mirror*, 51 (1965), 7–18.

Brown, Michael, Geoghegan, Patrick, and Kelly, James, *The Irish Act of Union, 1800. Bicentennial Essays* (Dublin et al., 2003).

Buchan, Bruce and Hill, Lisa, *An Intellectual History of Political Corruption*, Political Corruption and Governance (Basingstoke, 2014).

Bucholz, Robert O., 'Introduction', in J. C. Sainty and R. O. Bucholz (eds.), *Officials of the Royal Household 1660–1837*, part 1, *Department of the Lord Chancellor and Associated Offices*, Office-Holders in Modern Britain (London, 1997).

Burns, Arthur and Innes, Joanna (eds.), *Rethinking the Age of Reform. Britain 1780–1850*, (Cambridge, 2003).

Burns, J. H. and Hart, H. L. A., 'Introduction', in James H. Burns and H. L. A. Hart (eds.), *A Comment on the Commentaries and a Fragment on Government, The Collected Works of Jeremy Bentham. Principles of Legislation* (London, 1977), xix–li.

Butterfield, Herbert, *George III, Lord North and the People 1779–80*, 2nd edn. (London, 1969).

——, 'The Yorkshire Association and the Crisis of 1779–80', *Transactions of the Royal Historical Society. Fourth Series*, 29 (1947), 69–91.

Campbell, Charles F., *The Intolerable Hulks. British Shipboard Confinement, 1776–1857*, 2nd edn. (Bowie, 1994).

Cannon, John, 'Dunning, John, first Baron Ashburton (1731–1783)', *ODNB*.

——, *The Fox–North Coalition. Crisis of the Constitution, 1782–4* (Cambridge, 1969).

——, 'Lord Shelburne's Ministry, 1782–3. "A Very Good List"', in Nigel Aston and Clarissa C. Orr (eds.), *An Enlightenment Statesman in Whig Britain: Lord Shelburne in Context, 1737–1805*, Studies in Early Modern Cultural, Political and Social history (Woodbridge, 2011), 161–75.

——, 'Montagu, George, fourth duke of Manchester (1737–1788)', *ODNB*.

——, 'Petty, William, second earl of Shelburne and first marquess of Lansdowne (1737–1805)', *ODNB*.

——, 'Savile, Sir George, eighth baronet (1726–1784)', *ODNB*.

Canovan, Margaret, 'The Un-Benthamite Utilitarianism of Joseph Priestley', *Journal of the History of Ideas*, 45:3 (1984), 435–50.

Cash, Arthur H., *John Wilkes. The Scandalous Father of Civil Liberty* (New Haven, London, 2006).

Cheney, Paul, 'Constitution and Economy in David Hume's Enlightenment', in Carl Wennerlind and Margaret Schabas (eds.), *David Hume's Political Economy* (London, New York, 2008), 223–42.

Chester, Norman, *The English Administrative System 1780–1870* (Oxford, 1981).

Christie, Ian R., *The Benthams in Russia, 1780–1791* (Oxford, Providence, 1993).

——, 'Economical Reform and "The Influence of the Crown", 1780', *Myth and Reality in Late-Eighteenth-Century British Politics and Other Papers* (London, 1970), 296–310.

——, *The End of North's Ministry 1780–1782* (London, New York, 1958).

——, 'Myth and Reality in Late-Eighteenth-Century British Politics', *Myth and Reality in Late-Eighteenth-Century British Politics and Other Papers* (London, 1970), 27–54.

——, 'Samuel Bentham and the Russian Dnieper Flotilla 1787–1788', *The Slavonic and East European Review*, 50:119 (1972), 173–97.

——, *Wilkes, Wyvill and Reform. The Parliamentary Reform Movement in British Politics 1760–1785* (New York, 1962).

Claeys, Gregory, 'The French Revolution Debate and British Political Thought', *History of Political Thought*, 11:1 (1990), 59–80.

Clark, Peter, *British Clubs and Societies, 1580–1800. The Origins of an Associational World* (Oxford, 2000).

Coad, Jonathan, *The Portsmouth Block Mills. Bentham, Brunel and the Start of the Royal Navy's Industrial Revolution* (Swindon, 2005).

Cohen, Emmeline W., *The Growth of the British Civil Service 1780–1939* (London, 1965).

Cohn, Bernard S., *Colonialism and its Forms of Knowledge. The British in India*, Princeton Studies in Culture/Power/History (Princeton, 1996).

Colley, Linda, 'The Apotheosis of George III. Loyalty, Royalty and the British Nation 1760–1820', *Past and Present*, 102 (1984), 94–129.

——, *Britons*, 2nd edn. (New Haven, 2005).

Collinge, J. M., *Navy Board Officials 1660–1832*, Office-Holders in Modern Britain, vol. 7 (London, 1978).

Collingwood, Robin G., *The Idea of History* (London et al., 1956 [1946]).
Connolly, S. J., *Divided Kingdom. Ireland, 1630–1800*, Oxford History of Early Modern Europe (Oxford, New York, 2008).
Cooper, Carolyn C., 'The Portsmouth System of Manufacture', *Technology and Culture*, 25:2 (194), 182–225.
Corrigan, Philip and Sayer, Derek, *The Great Arch. English State Formation as Cultural Revolution* (Oxford, 1985).
Crane, Verner W., 'The Club of Honest Whigs. Friends of Science and Liberty', *William and Mary Quarterly*, 23:2 (1966), 210–33.
Crimmin, P. K., 'John Jervis, Earl of St Vincent, 1735–1823', in Richard Harding and Peter Le Fevre (eds.), *Precursors of Nelson: British Admirals of the Eighteenth Century* (London, 2000), 325–50.
Dalrymple, William, *The Anarchy. The Relentless Rise of the East India Company* (London et al., 2020).
Dickinson, Harry T., *Liberty and Property. Political Ideology in Eighteenth-Century Britain* (London, 1977).
—, 'Radicals and Reformers in the Age of Wilkes and Wyvill', in Jeremy Black (ed.), *British Politics and Society from Walpole to Pitt 1742–1789* (Basingstoke, Hampshire, 1990), 123–46.
—, 'Wyvill, Christopher (1738–1822)', *ODNB*.
Dickson, Peter G. M., *The Financial Revolution in England. A Study in the Development of Public Credit 1688–1756* (London, 1967).
Dirks, Nicholas B., *The Scandal of Empire. India and the Creation of Imperial Britain* (Cambridge, Mass., 2006).
Dodwell, Henry H., 'The Development of Sovereignty in British India', in Henry H. Dodwell (ed.), *Cambridge History of India*, vol. 5, *British India 1497–1858* (Cambridge, 1929), 589–608.
Donnelly, Michael, 'From Political Arithmetic to Social Statistics. How some Nineteenth Century Roots of the Social Sciences were Implanted', in Johan Heilbron, Lars Magnusson, and Björn Wittrock (eds.), *The Rise of the Social Sciences and the Formation of Modernity: Conceptual Change in Context, 1750–1850*, Sociology of the Sciences. A Yearbook (Dordrecht, Boston, London, 1996), 225–40.
Drummond, Mary M., 'Bowlby, Thomas', in Lewis Namier and John Brooke (eds.), *The House of Commons 1754–1790*, vol. 2 (London, 1964), 108–9.
Duffy, Michael, *The Younger Pitt*, Profiles in Power (Harlow, 2000).
Dziembowski, Edmond, 'Lord Shelburne's Constitutional Views in 1782–3', in Nigel Aston and Clarissa C. Orr (eds.), *An Enlightenment Statesman in Whig Britain: Lord Shelburne in Context, 1737–1805*, Studies in Early Modern Cultural, Political and Social History (Woodbridge, 2011), 215–32.
Eagles, Robin, '"Opening the Door to Truth and Liberty", Bowood's French Connection', in Nigel Aston and Clarissa C. Orr (eds.), *An Enlightenment Statesman in Whig Britain: Lord Shelburne in Context, 1737–1805*, Studies in Early Modern Cultural, Political and Social History (Woodbridge, 2011), 197–214.

Edwardes, Michael, *The Nabobs at Home* (London, 1991).

Ehrman, John, *The Younger Pitt*, vol. 1, *The Years of Acclaim* (London, 1969).

—, *The Younger Pitt*, vol. 3, *The Consuming Struggle* (London, 1996).

Ellis, Kenneth L., *The Post Office in the Eighteenth Century. A Study in Administrative History*, 2nd edn. (London, 1969).

Embree, Ainslie T., *Charles Grant and British Rule in India* (London, 1962).

Emich, Birgit et al., 'Stand und Perspektiven der Korruptionsforschung. Zugleich eine Antwort auf Heiko Droste', *Zeitschrift für historische Forschung*, 32 (2005), 233–65.

Emsley, Clive, *The English Police. A Political and Social History* (Hemel Hempstead, Herts., New York, 1991).

Farnsworth, A., *Addington. Author of the Modern Income Tax* (London, 1951).

Farrell, S. M., 'Wentworth, Charles Watson, second marquess of Rockingham (1730–1782)', *ODNB*.

—, 'Wentworth, Mary Watson, marchioness of Rockingham (bap. 1735, d. 1804)', *ODNB*.

Fedorak, Charles J., *Henry Addington, Prime Minister, 1801–1804. Peace, War, and Parliamentary Politics*, Series on International, Political, and Economic History (Akron, 2002).

Feiling, Keith, *Warren Hastings* (London, Melbourne, Toronto, 1966).

Fischer, Wolfram and Lundgreen, Peter, 'The Recruitment and Training of Administrative and Technical Personnel', in Charles Tilly (ed.), *The Formation of National States in Western Europe* (Princeton, London, 1975), 456–561.

Fisher, D. R., 'Pelham, Thomas, second earl of Chichester (1756–1826)', *ODNB*.

Fitton, R. S. and Wadsworth, A. P., *The Strutts and the Arkwrights 1758–1830. A Study of the Early Factory System* (Manchester, 1958).

Fitzpatrick, Martin, 'Joseph Priestley, Political Philosopher', in Isabel Rivers and David L. Wykes (eds.), *Joseph Priestley. Scientist, Philosopher, and Theologian* (Oxford, New York, 2008), 113–43.

Foucault, Michel, *Discipline and Punish. The Birth of the Prison* (New York, 1977).

Freeman, Ray, 'The Holdsworth and Newman Families in Dartmouth', Dartmouth History Research Group (1992) https://dartmouth-history.org.uk/dhrg-books/the-holdsworth-newman-families/.

Fruchtman, Jack, 'The Apocalyptic Politics of Richard Price and Joseph Priestley. A Study in Late Eighteenth-Century English Republican Millennialism', *Transactions of the American Philosophical Society*, 73:4 (1983), 1–125.

Fukuyama, Francis, *The End of History and the Last Man* (New York, 2006 [1992]).

Gash, Norman, 'A Glaswegian Criminologist. Patrick Colquhoun, 1745–1820', in Norman Gash, *Pillars of Government and Other Essays on State and Society: c.1770–c.1880* (London, 1986), 139–52.

Gambetta, Diego, 'Corruption. An Analytical Map', in Emmanuel Kreike and William C. Jordan (eds.), *Corrupt Histories*, Studies in Comparative History (Rochester, 2004), 3–28.

Geoghegan, Patrick M., *The Irish Act of Union. A Study in High Politics, 1798–1801* (Dublin, 1999).
Ghosal, Akshoy K., *Civil Service in India under the East India Company. A Study in Administrative Development* (Calcutta, 1944).
Glaisyer, Natasha, 'Networking, Trade and Exchange in the Eighteenth-Century British Empire', *Historical Journal*, 47:2 (2004), 451–76.
Goering, Timothy D., 'Concepts, History and the Game of Giving and Asking for Reasons: A Defense of Conceptual History', *Journal of the Philosophy of History*, 7 (2013), 426–52.
Goldie, Mark, 'The Reception of Hobbes', in J. H. Burns and Mark Goldie (eds.), *The Cambridge History of Political Thought, 1450–1700* (Cambridge, 1991), 589–615.
Gough, John W., 'Political Trusteeship', in J. W. Gough (ed.), *John Locke's Political Philosophy: Eight Studies* (Oxford, 1973), 154–92.
Grüne, Niels and Slanicka, Simona (eds.), *Korruption. Historische Annäherungen an eine Grundfigur politischer Kommunikation* (Göttingen, 2010).
Guha, Ranajit, *A Rule of Property for Bengal. An Essay on the Idea of Permanent Settlement*, 2nd edn. (New Delhi, 1982).
Haakonssen, Knud, *The Science of a Legislator. The Natural Jurisprudence of David Hume and Adam Smith* (Cambridge, 1981).
Harling, Philip, 'Equipoise Regained? Recent Trends in British Political History, 1790–1867', *The Journal of Modern History*, 75 (2003), 890–918.
—, 'The Politics of Administrative Change in Britain, 1780–1850', in Erk V. Heyen (ed.), *Administration and Administrative Law in France and England (18th/19th c.)*, Yearbook of European Administrative History, 8 (Baden-Baden, 1996), 191–212.
—, *The Waning of 'Old Corruption'. The Politics of Economical Reform in Britain, 1779–1846* (Oxford, 1996).
Harling, Philip and Mandler, Peter, 'From "Fiscal-Military" State to Laissez-Faire State, 1760–1850', *Journal of British Studies*, 32:1 (1993), 44–70.
Harlow, Vincent T., *The Founding of the Second British Empire 1763–1793* (London, 1964).
Harris, James A., *Hume. An Intellectual Biography* (Cambridge, 2015).
Hart, Jenifer, 'The Genesis of the Northcote-Trevelyan Report', in Gillian Sutherland (ed.), *Studies in the Growth of Nineteenth-Century Government* (London, 1972), 63–81.
Heilbron, Johan, 'Introductory Essay', in Tore Frängsmyr, Johan Heilbron, and Robin Rider (eds.), *The Quantifying Spirit in the Eighteenth Century* (Berkeley, Los Angeles, Oxford, 1990), 1–23.
Heilbron, Johan, Magnusson, Lars, and Wittrock, Björn, 'The Rise of the Social Sciences and the Formation of Modernity', in Johan Heilbron, Lars Magnusson, and Björn Wittrock (eds.), *The Rise of the Social Sciences and the Formation of Modernity: Conceptual Change in Context, 1750–1850*, Sociology of the Sciences. A Yearbook (Dordrecht, Boston, London, 1996), 1–34.

Hellmuth, Eckhart, 'Why does Corruption Matter? Reforms and Reform Movements in Britain and Germany in the Second Half of the Eighteenth Century', in Timothy C. W. Blanning and Peter Wende (eds.), *Reform in Great Britain and Germany: 1750–1850*, Proceedings of the British Academy (Oxford, 1999), 5–23.

Herzfeld, Michael, *The Social Production of Indifference. Exploring the Symbolic Roots of Western Bureaucracy* (New York, 1992).

Heyen, Erk V., 'Zum Amtsbegriff als Kernelement des Begriffs der öffentlichen Verwaltung. Überlegungen aus Anlaß eines Leidener Forschungsprojekts', *Jahrbuch für europäische Verwaltungsgeschichte*, 12 (2000), 265–79.

Hilton, Boyd, *A Mad, Bad, and Dangerous People? England, 1783–1846*, The New Oxford History of England (Oxford, 2006).

Hoesch, Matthias, 'Das Nutzenprinzip als neues Paradigma. Zur "Verfestigung" des Utilitarismus zwischen Hume und Bentham', in Christel Gärtner et al. (eds.), *Normative Krisen: Verflüssigung und Verfestigung von Normen und normativen Diskursen* (Tübingen, 2019), 137–60.

Hoon, Elizabeth, *The Organization of the English Customs System 1696–1787* (Newton et al., 1968).

Hont, Istvan, 'The Rhapsody of Public Debt. David Hume and Voluntary State Bankruptcy', in Istvan Hont (ed.), *Jealousy of Trade: International Competition and the Nation State in Historical Perspective* (Cambridge, Mass., London, 2005), 325–53.

Hoppen, K. T., 'An Incorporating Union? British Politicians and Ireland 1800–1830', *English Historical Review*, 123:501 (2008), 328–50.

Hoppit, Julian, *Britain's Political Economies. Parliament and Economic Life, 1660–1800* (Cambridge, 2017).

—, 'Checking the Leviathan, 1688–1832', in Donald Winch and Patrick K. O'Brien (eds.), *The Political Economy of British Historical Experience, 1688–1914* (Oxford et al., 2002), 267–94.

—, 'Economical Reform and the Mint, 1780–1816', *British Numismatic Journal*, 84 (2014), 177–90.

—, 'Political Arithmetic in Eighteenth-Century Britain', *Economic History Review*, 49 (1996), 516–40.

Hughes, Edward, 'Civil Service Reform 1853–5', *Public Administration*, 32:1 (1954), 17–51.

Hughes, Robert, *The Fatal Shore. A History of the Transportation of Convicts to Australia, 1787–1868* (London, 1987).

Hume, Leonard J., *Bentham and Bureaucracy*, Cambridge Studies in the History and Theory of Politics (Cambridge, 1981).

—, 'Bentham's Panopticon. An Administrative History I', *Historical Studies: Australia and New Zealand*, 15 (1973), 703–21.

Hutchison, T. W., *Before Adam Smith. The Emergence of Political Economy, 1662–1776* (Oxford, Cambridge Mass., 1988).

Ignatieff, Michael, *A Just Measure of Pain. The Penitentiary in the Industrial Revolution, 1750–1850*, The Critical Criminology Series (London, 1978).

Innes, Joanna, 'The British Way of Bildung. The Formation of George Rose, Secretary to the Treasury and Vicepresident of the Board of Trade 1782–1812', in Anke Fischer-Kattner et al. (eds.), *Schleifspuren: Lesarten des 18. Jahrhunderts* (München, 2011), 204–15.

——, 'The Domestic Face of the Military-Fiscal State. Government and Society in Eighteenth-Century Britain', in Lawrence Stone (ed.), *An Imperial State at War: Britain from 1689 to 1815* (London, New York, 1994), 96–127.

——, 'Forms of "Government Growth", 1780–1830', in David Feldman and Jon Lawrence (eds.), *Structures and Transformations in Modern British History* (Cambridge, New York, 2011), 74–99.

——, 'The King's Bench Prison in the Later Eighteenth Century. Law, Authority and Order in a London Debtors' Prison', in John Brewer and John A. Styles (eds.), *An Ungovernable People: The English and their Law in the Seventeenth and Eighteenth Centuries* (London, 1980), 250–98.

——, 'Politics and Morals. The Reformation of Manners Movement in Later Eighteenth-Century England', in Eckhart Hellmuth (ed.), *The Transformation of Political Culture: England and Germany in the Late Eighteenth Century* (Oxford, 1990), 57–118.

——, 'Power and Happiness. Empirical Social Enquiry in Britain, from "Political Arithmetic" to "Moral Statistics"', *Inferior Politics: Social Problems and Social Policies in Eighteenth-Century Britain* (Oxford, 2009), 109–75.

——, '"Reform" in English Public Life. The Fortunes of a Word', in Arthur Burns and Joanna Innes (eds.), *Rethinking the Age of Reform: Britain 1780–1850* (Cambridge, 2003), 71–97.

——, 'State, Church and Voluntarism in European Welfare, 1690–1850', in Hugh Cunningham and Joanna Innes (eds.), *Charity, Philanthropy, and Reform: From the 1690s to 1850* (Basingstoke, 1998), 15–65.

Innes, Joanna and Burns, Arthur, 'Introduction', in Joanne Innes and Arthur Burns (eds.), *Rethinking the Age of Reform: Britain 1780–1850* (Cambridge, 2003), 1–70.

Islam, Sirajul, *The Permanent Settlement in Bengal. A Study of its Operation 1790–1819* (Dacca, 1979).

Jackson, Clare, 'Progress and Optimism', in Martin Fitzpatrick (ed.), *The Enlightenment World* (London, New York, 2004), 177–93.

Jacob, Margaret C., *The Cultural Meaning of the Scientific Revolution*, New Perspectives on European History (New York, 1993).

Jupp, Peter, 'Britain and the Union, 1797–1801', *Transactions of the Royal Historical Society*, Sixth Series, 10 (2000), 197–219.

——, *The Governing of Britain, 1688–1848. The Executive, Parliament and the People* (London, New York, 2006).

——, 'The Landed Elite and Political Authority in Britain, ca. 1760–1850', *Journal of British Studies*, 29:1 (1990), 53–79.

Kaplan, Steven L. and Reinert, Sophus A., 'The Economic Turn in Enlightenment Europe', in Steven L. Kaplan and Sophus A. Reinert (eds.), *The Economic Turn: Recasting Political Economy in Enlightenment Europe* (London, 2019), 1–33.

Keir, D. L., 'Economical Reform, 1779–1787', *Law Quarterly Review*, 50 (1934), 368–85.

Kelly, James, *Prelude to Union. Anglo-Irish Politics in the 1780s* (Cork, 1992).

Kemp, Betty, 'Crewe's Act, 1782', *English Historical Review*, 68 (1953), 258–63.

Khan, Majed A., *The Transition in Bengal 1756–1775. A Study of Saiyid Muhammad Reza Khan* (Cambridge, 1969).

Kidd, Colin, *British Identities Before Nationalism. Ethnicity and Nationhood in the Atlantic World, 1600–1800* (Cambridge, 1999).

Knight, Roger J. B., 'Sandwich, Middleton and Dockyard Appointments', *Mariner's Mirror*, 57 (1971), 175–92.

Knights, Mark, 'Anticorruption in Seventeenth- and Eighteenth-Century Britain', in Ronald Kroeze, André Vitória, and Guy Geltner (eds.), *Anticorruption in History: From Antiquity to the Modern Era* (Oxford, 2018), 181–95.

——, *Trust and Distrust. Corruption in Office in Britain and its Empire, 1600–1850* (Oxford, 2021).

Kobayashi, Noboru, 'On the Method of Sir James Steuart's Principles of Political Economy', in Ramón Tortajada (ed.), *The Economics of James Steuart* (London et al., 1999), 102–20.

Koselleck, Reinhart, 'Einleitung', in Otto Brunner, Werner Conze, and Reinhart Koselleck (eds.), *Geschichtliche Grundbegriffe: Historisches Lexikon zur politisch-sozialen Sprache Deutschlands*, vol. 1 (Stuttgart, 1972), XIII–XXVII.

Kramnick, Isaac, 'Republicanism Revisited. The Case of James Burgh', Proceedings of the American Antiquarian Society, 102:1 (1992), 81–98.

Kroeze, Ronald, Vitória, André, and Geltner, Guy, 'Introduction. Debating Corruption and Anticorruption in History', in Ronald Kroeze, André Vitória and Guy Geltner (eds.), *Anticorruption in History: From Antiquity to the Modern Era* (Oxford, 2018), 1–17.

Laboucheix, Henri, *Richard Price as Moral Philosopher and Political Theorist* (Oxford, 1982).

Laidlaw, Zoë, *Colonial Connections 1815–45. Patronage, the Information Revolution, and Colonial Government* (Manchester, 2005).

Langford, Paul, *Public Life and the Propertied Englishman 1689–1798*. The Ford Lectures Delivered in the University of Oxford 1990 (Oxford, 1991).

Laudan, Rachel, 'The "New" History of Science. Implications for Philosophy of Science', *Proceedings of the Biennual Meeting of the Philosophers of Science Association*, vol. 2 (1992), 476–81.

Lawson, Philip, *The East India Company. A History*, Studies in Modern History (Harlow, 1993).

Lecky, William Edward Hartpole, *A History of Ireland in the Eighteenth Century*, vol. 5 (London, Bombay, Calcutta, 1892).

Lee, W. M., *A History of Police in England* (London, 1901).

Lester, Malcolm, 'Spencer, George John, second Earl Spencer (1758–1834)', *ODNB*.

Lieberman, David, *The Province of Legislation Determined. Legal Theory in Eighteenth-Century Britain* (Cambridge, 1989).

Lobban, Michael, *The Common Law and English Jurisprudence* (Oxford, 1993).

MacDonagh, Oliver, 'The Nineteenth-Century Revolution in Government. A Reappraisal', *Historical Journal*, 1:1 (1958), 52–67.

MacIntyre, Alasdair C., *After Virtue. A Study in Moral Theory* (London et al., 1981).

MacLane, John R., *Land and Local Kingship in Eighteenth-Century Bengal*, Cambridge South Asian Studies, 53 (Cambridge, 1993).

Maitland, Frederic W., 'The Crown as Corporation', in H. D. Hazeltine, G. Lapsley and P. H. Winfield (eds.), *Frederic W. Maitland: Selected Essays* (Cambridge, 1936), 104–27.

——, 'Introduction', in Frederic Maitland (ed.), *Otto Gierke: Political Theories of the Middle Age* (Cambridge, 1913), vii–lxxx.

——, 'Trust and Corporation', in H. D. Hazeltine, G. Lapsley and P. H. Winfield (eds.), *Frederic W. Maitland: Selected Essays* (Cambridge, 1936), 141–222.

Mann, Bruce H., *Republic of Debtors. Bankruptcy in the Age of American Independence* (Cambridge, Mass., 2002).

Mann, Michael, *Bengalen im Umbruch. Die Herausbildung des britischen Kolonialstaates 1754–1793* (Stuttgart, 2000).

Marciano, Alain, 'Benevolence, Sympathy, and Hume's Model of Government. How Different is New Political Economy from Classical Political Economy?', in Steven G. Medema and Peter J. Boettke (eds.), *The Role of Government in the History of Economic Thought*, History of Political Economy (Durham, 2005), 43–70.

Marshall, Peter J., *Bengal: The British Bridgehead. Eastern India, 1740–1828*, The New Cambridge History of Indian States and the Transition to Colonialism, 2 (Cambridge, 1987).

——, '"Cornwallis Triumphant". War in India and the British Public in the Late Eighteenth Century', in Peter J. Marshall, *Trade and Conquest: Studies on the Rise of British Dominance in India* (Aldershot, Brookfield, 1993), XIV, 57–74.

——, *East Indian Fortunes. The British in Bengal in the Eighteenth Century* (Oxford, 1976).

——, *The Making and Unmaking of Empires. Britain, India, and America c.1750–1783* (Oxford, 2005).

——, 'Price, Joseph (c.1727–1796)', *ODNB*.

——, 'Warren Hastings as Scholar and Patron', in Anne Whiteman (ed.), *Statesmen, Scholars and Merchants* (Oxford, 1973), 242–62.

McCusker, John J., 'Colonial Civil Servant and Counter-Revolutionary. Thomas Irving (1738?–1800) in Boston, Charleston, and London', *Essays in the Economic History of the Atlantic World*, Routledge Studies in International Economic and Social History (London, New York, 1997), 190–221.

McDowell, Robert B., 'The Age of the United Irishmen. Revolution and the Union, 1794–1800', in T. W. Moody and W. E. Vaughan (eds.), *A New History of Ireland*, vol. 4, *Eighteenth-Century Ireland* (Oxford et al., 1986), 339–73.

—, *Ireland in the Age of Imperialism and Revolution 1760–1801* (Oxford, New York, 1979).

—, *The Irish Administration, 1801–1914*, Studies in Irish History, Second Series, 2 (London, Toronto, 1964).

McKendrick, Neil, 'Josiah Wedgwood and Cost Accounting in the Industrial Revolution', *Economic History Review*, 23:1 (1970), 45–67.

Melikan, R. A., 'Pigott, Sir Arthur Leary (1749–1819)', *ODNB*.

Meurer, Sebastian, 'Approaches to State-Building in Eighteenth Century British Bengal', in Antje Flüchter and Susan Richter (eds.), *Structures on the Move: Technologies of Governance in Transcultural Encounter*, Transcultural Research. Heidelberg Studies on Asia and Europe in a Global Context (Heidelberg et al., 2012), 219–41.

—, 'The Dawning of the Age of Reform. Epistemic and Semantic Shifts in Georgian Britain', in Susan Richter, Thomas Maissen, and Manuela Albertone (eds.), *Languages of Reform in the Eighteenth Century: When Europe Lost its Fear of Change* (New York, 2020), 62–84.

Middleton, Richard, 'The Clinton-Cornwallis Controversy and Responsibility for the British Surrender at Yorktown', *History. Journal of the Historical Association*, 98:331 (2013), 370–89.

—, *Cornwallis. Soldier and Statesman in a Revolutionary World* (New Haven, 2022).

Misra, B. B., *The Central Administration of the East India Company 1773–1834* (Manchester, 1959).

Mitchell, Leslie G., *Charles James Fox* (Oxford, 1992).

Moon, Penderel, *The British Conquest and Dominion of India* (London, Bloomington, 1989).

Mori, Jennifer, *Britain in the Age of the French Revolution, 1785–1820* (Harlow, 2000).

Morriss, Roger, 'Middleton, Charles, first Baron Barham (1726–1813)', *ODNB*.

—, *Naval Power and British Culture, 1760–1850. Public Trust and Government Ideology* (Aldershot, Burlington, 2004).

—, *The Royal Dockyards during the Revolutionary and Napoleonic Wars* (Leicester, 1983).

Murphy, Anne, *Virtuous Bankers. A Day in the Life of the Eighteenth-Century Bank of England* (Princeton, 2023).

Namier, Lewis, *The Structure of Politics at the Accession of George III*, 2nd edn. (London, New York, 1963 [1929]).

Nechtman, Tillman W., *Nabobs. Empire and Identity in Eighteenth-Century Britain* (Cambridge et al., 2010).

Nisbet, Robert, *History of the Idea of Progress* (London, 1980).

Norris, John, *Shelburne and Reform* (London, New York, 1963).

North, Douglass Cecil and Weingast, Barry R., 'Constitutions and Commitment. The Evolution of Institutions Governing Public Choice in Seventeenth-Century England', *Journal of Economic History*, 49 (1989), 803–32.

O'Brien, Karen, *Narratives of Enlightenment. Cosmopolitan History from Voltaire to Gibbon*, Cambridge Studies in Eighteenth-Century English Literature and Thought, 34 (Cambridge, New York, 1997).

O'Gorman, Frank, *The Long Eighteenth Century. British Political and Social History 1688–1832*, The Arnold History of Britain (London, 1997).

—, 'The Myth of Lord Bute's Secret Influence', in Karl W. Schweizer (ed.), *Lord Bute: Essays in Re-Interpretation* (Leicester, 1988), 57–81.

Olson, Richard, 'The Human Sciences', in Roy Porter (ed.), *Eighteenth-Century Science*, The Cambridge History of Science (Cambridge, 2016), 436–62.

O'Malley, Lewis S. S., *The Indian Civil Service 1601–1930*, 2nd edn. (London, 1965).

Orbell, John, 'Lord Shelburne, Finance, and Sir Francis Baring', in Nigel Aston and Clarissa C. Orr (eds.), *An Enlightenment Statesman in Whig Britain: Lord Shelburne in Context, 1737–1805*, Studies in Early Modern Cultural, Political and Social History (Woodbridge, 2011), 97–113.

Osborn, Jeremy, 'India and the East India Company in the Public Sphere of Eighteenth-Century Britain', in Huw V. Bowen, Margarette Lincoln, and Nigel Rigby (eds.), *The Worlds of the East India Company* (Woodbridge, Rochester, 2002), 201–21.

Ottaway, Marina, 'Rebuilding State Institutions in Collapsed States', *Development and Change*, 35:5 (2002), 1001–23.

Oxford English Dictionary: s.v. 'bureaucracy, n.', 'economy, n.', 'efficiency, n.', 'reversion, n.', 'system, n.', *OED*.

Paley, Ruth, 'Colquhoun, Patrick (1745–1820)', *ODNB*.

Parris, Henry, *Constitutional Bureaucracy. The Development of British Central Administration since the Eighteenth Century* (London, 1969).

—, 'The Nineteenth-Century Revolution in Government. A Reappraisal Reappraised', *Historical Journal*, 3:1 (1960), 17–37.

Pavarala, Vinod, 'Cultures of Corruption and the Corruption of Culture. The East India Company and the Hastings Impeachment', in Emmanuel Kreike and William C. Jordan (eds.), *Corrupt Histories*, Studies in Comparative History (Rochester et al., 2004), 291–336.

Pease-Watkin, Catherine, 'Bentham, Samuel (1757–1831)', *ODNB*.

Philips, C. H. and Misra, B. B. (eds.), *Fort William – India House Correspondence*, vol. 15, *Foreign and Secret 1782–1786*, Indian Records Series (Delhi, 1963).

Phillips, Amanda, 'Neave, Caroline Hannah (1781–1863)', *ODNB*.

Phillips, John A., 'The Structure of Electoral Politics in Unreformed England', *Journal of British Studies*, 19:1 (1979), 76–100.

Phillips, N. C., 'Edmund Burke and the County Movement, 1779–1780', *English Historical Review*, 76 (1961), 254–78.

Pocock, John G. A., *The Ancient Constitution and the Feudal Law. A Study of English Historical Thought in the 17. Century*, reissued (Cambridge, 1987 [1957]).

—, 'The Concept of Language and the metier d'historien. Some Considerations on Practice', *Political Thought and History: Essays on Theory and Method*, repr. (Cambridge, 2010), 87–105.

—, 'Modes of Political and Historical Time in Early-Eighteenth-Century England', *Virtue, Commerce, and History: Essays on Political Thought and History, Chiefly in the Eighteenth Century*, repr. (Cambridge, 2002), 91–102.

—, 'Political Thought in the English-Speaking Atlantic, 1760–1790, Part 2: Empire, Revolution and the End of Early Modernity', in John G. A. Pocock, *The Varieties of British Political Thought, 1500–1800* (Cambridge, 1993), 283–317.

—, *Political Thought and History. Essays on Theory and Method*, repr. (Cambridge, 2010).

Porter, Roy, *The Creation of the Modern World. The Untold Story of the British Enlightenment* (London, New York, 2000).

—, 'Introduction', in Roy Porter (ed.), *Eighteenth-Century Science*, The Cambridge History of Science (Cambridge, 2016), 1–20.

Prest, Wilfrid, 'Blackstone, Sir William (1723–1780)', *ODNB*.

Quinn, James, 'Dublin Castle and the Act of Union', in Michael Brown, Patrick M. Geoghegan, and James Kelly (eds.), *The Irish Act of Union, 1800: Bicentennial Essays* (Dublin, Portland, 2003), 95–107.

Raadschelders, Jos C. N., 'Changing European Ideas about the Civil Servant. A Theoretical and Methodological Framework', in Fritz Sager and Patrick Overeem (eds.), *The European Civil Servant: A Shared Administrative Identity?* (Colchester, 2015), 15–34.

—, *Public Administration. The Interdisciplinary Study of Government* (New York, 2011).

Radzinowicz, Leon, 'That Strange Word "Police". Cross-Currents in the Movement for the Reform of the Police' in id., *A History of English Criminal Law and its Administration from 1750*, vol. 3 (London, 1956), 1–13.

Ramsay, Nigel, 'Astle, Thomas (1735–1803)', *ODNB*.

Ramsbotham, R. B., *Studies in the Land Revenue History of Bengal 1769–1787* (London, 1926).

Rashid, Salim, 'Smith, Steuart, and Mercantilism: Comment', *Southern Economic Journal*, 52:3 (1986), 843–52.

Reich, Jerome R., *British Friends of the American Revolution* (Armonk, 1998).

Reitan, Earl A., 'The Civil List in Eighteenth-Century British Politics. Parliamentary Supremacy versus the Independence of the Crown', *Historical Journal*, 9 (1966), 318–37.

—, 'From Revenue to Civil List, 1689–1702. The Revolution Settlement and the "Mixed and Balanced" Constitution', *Historical Journal*, 13:4 (1970), 571–88.

——, *Politics, Finance, and the People. Economical Reform in England in the Age of the American Revolution, 1770–92* (New York, 2007).

Richter, Melvin, 'The Comparative Study of Regimes and Societies', in Mark Goldie and Robert Wokler (eds.), *The Cambridge History of Eighteenth-Century Political Thought* (Cambridge, 2006), 147–71.

——, 'Despotism', in Philip P. Wiener (ed.), *Dictionary of the History of Ideas: Studies of Selected Pivotal Ideas,* vol. 2 (1973), 1–18.

Richter, Susan, Meurer, Sebastian, et al., 'Introduction: Languages of Reform and the European Enlightenment', in Susan Richter, Thomas Maissen, and Manuela Albertone (eds.), *Languages of Reform in the Eighteenth Century: When Europe lost its Fear of Change* (New York, 2020), 1–26.

Rigg, J. M., 'Yorke, Philip, third earl of Hardwicke (1757–1834)', *ODNB.*

Robertson, John, 'The Scottish Contribution to the Enlightenment', in Paul Wood (ed.), *The Scottish Enlightenment: Essays in Reinterpretation* (Rochester, NY, 2000), 37–62.

Rocher, Rosane, 'British Orientalism in the Eighteenth Century. The Dialectics of Knowledge and Government', in Carol A. Breckenridge (ed.), *Orientalism and the Postcolonial Predicament: Perspectives on South Asia,* South Asia Seminar Series (Philadelphia, 1993), 215–44.

Roitman, Janet L., *Anti-Crisis* (Durham, 2014).

Rosen, Frederick, *Classical Utilitarianism from Hume to Mill* (London, 2003).

Roseveare, Henry, *The Treasury. The Evolution of a British Institution* (London, 1969).

——, *The Treasury 1660–1870. The Foundations of Control* (London, New York, 1973).

Sager, Fritz and Overeem, Patrick (eds.), *The European Civil Servant. A Shared Administrative Identity?* (Colchester, 2015).

Sainsbury, John, *Disaffected Patriots. London Supporters of Revolutionary America, 1769–1782* (Kingston, 1987).

Schabas, Margaret, *The Natural Origins of Economics* (Chicago, 2005).

Schofield, Robert E., *The Enlightenment of Joseph Priestley. A Study of his Life and Work from 1733 to 1773* (University Park, 1997).

Schultz, Bart, *The Happiness Philosophers. The Lives and Works of the Great Utilitarians* (Princeton, 2017).

Scott, Hamish M., 'Britain's Emergence as a European Power, 1688–1815', in Harry T. Dickinson (ed.), *A Companion to Eighteenth-Century Britain* (Malden et al., 2002), 431–46.

——, 'The Fiscal Military State and International Rivalry during the Long Eighteenth Century', in Christopher Storrs (ed.), *The Fiscal Military State in Eighteenth-Century Europe. Essays in Honour of P. G. M. Dickson* (Aldershot, Burlington, 2008), 23–54.

Semple, Janet, *Bentham's Prison. A Study of the Panopticon Penitentiary* (Oxford, 1993).

Sen, Neil, 'Warren Hastings and British Sovereign Authority in Bengal, 1774–80', *Journal of Imperial and Commonwealth History,* 25:1 (1997), 59–81.

Shank, J. B., 'Crisis: A Useful Category of Post-Social Scientific Historical Analysis?', *American Historical Review,* 113:4 (2008), 1090–9.

Shaw, Alan G. L., *Convicts and the Colonies. A Study of Penal Transportation from Great Britain and Ireland to Australia and other parts of the British Empire* (Carlton, 1977).

Sheehan, Jonathan and Wahrman, Dror, *Invisible Hands. Self-Organization and the Eighteenth Century* (Chicago, 2015).

Siskin, Clifford, 'The Problem of Periodization: Enlightenment, Romanticism and the Fate of System', in James Chandler (ed.), *The Cambridge History of English Romantic Literature* (Cambridge et al., 2009), 101–26.

Skinner, Andrew S., 'Introduction. Sir James Steuart and the Jacobite Connection', in Ramón Tortajada (ed.), *The Economics of James Steuart* (London, 1999), 1–23.

Skinner, Quentin, 'Meaning and Understanding in the History of Ideas', *History and Theory,* 8:1 (1969), 3–53.

—, *Visions of Politics,* vol. 1, *Regarding Method* (Cambridge, 2002).

Slack, Paul, *From Reformation to Improvement. Public Welfare in Early Modern England* (Oxford, New York, 1999).

Smith, Alfred H., *County and Court. Government and Politics in Norfolk, 1558–1603* (Oxford, 1974).

Smith, Anthony D., 'State-Making and Nation-Building', in John A. Hall (ed.), *States in History* (Oxford, 1986), 228–63.

Souldby, B. H., 'Ross, Alexander (1742–1827)', *ODNB.*

Spadafora, David, *The Idea of Progress in Eighteenth-Century Britain* (New Haven, 1990).

Sparrow, Elizabeth, 'Wickham, William (1761–1840)', *ODNB.*

Stafford, James, *The Case of Ireland. Commerce, Empire and the European Order, 1750–1848,* Ideas in Context, 138 (Cambridge, 2022).

Stearn, Roger T., 'Napier, George (1751–1804)', *ODNB.*

Stollberg-Rilinger, Barbara, *Der Staat als Maschine. Zur politischen Metaphorik des absoluten Fürstenstaats,* Historische Forschungen, 30 (Berlin, 1986).

Storrs, Christopher, *The Fiscal Military State in Eighteenth-Century Europe. Essays in Honour of P. G. M. Dickson* (Aldershot, Burlington, 2008).

Sturgis, James, 'Carleton, Guy, first Baron Dorchester (1724–1808)', *ODNB.*

Sutherland, Lucy S., *The East India Company in Eighteenth-Century Politics* (Oxford, 1952).

Talbott, John E., *The Pen and Ink Sailor. Charles Middleton and the King's Navy, 1778–1813,* Cass Series Naval Policy and History, 6 (London, 1998).

Teichgraeber III, Richard F., '"Less Abused than I had Reason to Expect". The Reception of The Wealth of Nations in Britain, 1776–90', *Historical Journal,* 30:2 (1987), 337–66.

Thiessen, Hillard von, 'Normenkonkurrenz. Handlungsspielräume, Rollen, normativer Wandel und normative Kontinuität vom späten Mittelalter bis zum Übergang zur Moderne', in Arne Karsten and Hillard von Thiessen (eds.), *Normenkonkurrenz in historischer Perspektive, Zeitschrift für Historische Forschung*, Beihefte (Berlin, 2015), 241–86.

Thomas, David O., *The Honest Mind. The Thought and Work of Richard Price* (Oxford, 1977).

Thomas, Peter D. G., *John Wilkes, a Friend to Liberty* (New York, 1996).

Tilly, Charles, 'Reflections on the History of European State-Making', in Charles Tilly (ed.), *The Formation of National States in Western Europe* (Princeton, London, 1975), 3–84.

Tompson, Richard S., 'Gilbert, Thomas (bap. 1720, d. 1798)', *ODNB*.

Torrance, John, 'Sir George Harrison and the Growth of Bureaucracy in the Early Nineteenth Century', *English Historical Review*, 83:326 (1968), 52–88.

——, 'Social Class and Bureaucratic Innovation. The Commissioners for Examining the Public Accounts 1780–1787', *Past and Present*, 78 (1978), 56–81.

Travers, Robert, *Ideology and Empire in Eighteenth-Century India. The British in Bengal*, Cambridge Studies in Indian History and Society, 14 (Cambridge, 2007).

Trevor-Roper, Hugh, 'The Scottish Enlightenment', *Blackwood's Magazine*, 322 (1977), 371–88.

Tribe, Keith, 'Cameralism and the Science of Government', *Journal of Modern History*, 56:2 (1984), 263–84.

——, 'Cameralism and the Sciences of the State', in Mark Goldie and Robert Wokler (eds.), *The Cambridge History of Eighteenth-Century Political Thought* (Cambridge, 2006), 525–46.

——, *The Economy of the Word. Language, History, and Economics*, Oxford Studies in the History of Economics (Oxford, 2015).

Turner, Michael J., *The Age of Unease. Government and Reform in Britain, 1782–1832*, Sutton Modern British History, 7 (Stroud, 2000).

Urquhart, Robert, 'Steuarts Method. Aristotelian Political Economy', in Ramón Tortajada (ed.), *The Economics of James Steuart* (London et al., 1999), 121–36.

Wagoner, Philip B., 'Precolonial Intellectuals and the Production of Colonial Knowledge', *Comparative Studies in Society and History*, 45:4 (2003), 783–814.

Walter, Ryan, *Before Method and Models. The Political Economy of Malthus and Ricardo*, Oxford Studies in the History of Economics (Oxford, 2021).

Weber, Max, *Economy and Society. An Outline of Interpretive Sociology*, ed. by Guenther Roth and Claus Wittich (Berkeley, Los Angeles, London, 1968).

Whatmore, Richard, *Terrorists, Anarchists, and Republicans. The Genevans and the Irish in Time of Revolution* (Princeton, 2019).

Whiteley, Peter, *Lord North. The Prime Minister who Lost America* (London, 1996).

Wickwire, Franklin B. and Wickwire, Mary, *Cornwallis. The Imperial Years* (Chapel Hill, 1980).

Wilkinson, Clare, 'Abbot, Charles, first Baron Colchester (1757–1829)', *ODNB.*

Wilkinson, David, '"How Did They Pass the Union?" Secret Service Expenditure in Ireland, 1799–1804', *History,* 82:266 (1997), 233–51.

Wilson, Jon E., *The Domination of Strangers. Modern Governance in Eastern India, 1780–1835,* Cambridge Imperial and Post-colonial Studies Series (Basingstoke, 2008).

——, *India Conquered. Britain's Raj and the Chaos of Empire* (London et al., 2017).

——, 'The Silence of Empire. Imperialism and India', in David Craig and James Thompson (eds.), *Languages of Politics in Nineteenth-Century Britain* (London, 2013), 218–41.

Wilson, Kathleen, *The Sense of the People. Politics, Culture and Imperialism in England, 1715–1785* (Cambridge, 1995).

Wilson, Woodrow, 'The Study of Administration', *Political Science Quarterly,* 2:2 (1887), 197–222.

Winch, Donald, 'Scottish Political Economy', in Mark Goldie and Robert Wokler (eds.), *The Cambridge History of Eighteenth-Century Political Thought* (Cambridge, 2006), 443–64.

Wood, Paul (ed.), *The Scottish Enlightenment. Essays in Reinterpretation* (Rochester, 2000).

Wootton, David, 'Introduction. Understanding the Constitution', in David Wootton (ed.), *The Essential Federalist and Anti-Federalist Papers* (Indianapolis, 2003).

——, 'Liberty, Metaphor, and Mechanism. "Checks and Balances" and the Origins of Modern Constitutionalism', in David Womersley (ed.), *Liberty and American Experience in the Eighteenth Century* (Indianapolis, 2006), 209–74.

Wright, C. J., 'Musgrave, Sir William, sixth baronet (1735–1800)', *ODNB.*

Yamey, Basil S., *Essays on the History of Accounting* (New York, 1978).

Zembrowski, Martha, 'The Corruption of Politics and the Dignity of Human Nature. The Critical and Constructive Radicalism of James Burgh', *Enlightenment and Dissent,* 10 (1991), 78–103.

Ziegler, Philip, *Addington. A Life of Henry Addington, First Viscount Sidmouth* (London, 1965).

Unpublished Theses

Baumstark, Moritz, 'David Hume. The Making of a Philosophical Historian. A Reconsideration', PhD thesis (Edinburgh, 2007).

Breihan, John R., 'Economical Reform, 1785–1810', PhD thesis (Cambridge, 1977).

Index

Printed and bound by CPI Group (UK) Ltd, Croydon, CR0 4YY

24/06/2025

14694076-0001